Business
Plans
Handbook

Business Plans

A COMPILATION
OF BUSINESS
PLANS DEVELOPED
BY INDIVIDUALS
THROUGHOUT
NORTH AMERICA

Plans

Handbook

VOLUME

25

Michelle Lee,
Project Editor

GALE
CENGAGE Learning®

Detroit • New York • San Francisco • New Haven, Conn • Waterville, Maine • London

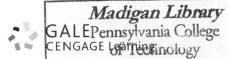

Business Plans Handbook, Volume 25

Project Editor: Michelle Lee

Product Manager: Jenai Drouillard

Product Design: Jennifer Wahi

Composition and Electronic Prepress: Evi Seoud

Manufacturing: Rita Wimberley

Gale, a part of Cengage Learning
27500 Drake Rd.
Farmington Hills, MI 48331-3535

ISBN-13: 978-1-4144-6837-2
ISBN-10: 1-4144-6837-7
1084-4473

Printed in Mexico
1 2 3 4 5 6 7 16 15 14 13 12

Contents

CONTENTS

Highlights

Business Plans Handbook, Volume 25 (BPH-25) is a collection of business plans compiled by entrepreneurs seeking funding for small businesses throughout North America. For those looking for examples of how to approach, structure, and compose their own business plans, *BPH-25* presents 20 sample plans, including plans for the following businesses:

- Arts and Crafts Company
- Child Transportation Service
- Computer Reseller
- Concierge Service
- Dance Studio
- Digital Assets Management Consultant
- Event Planning Company
- General Contracting Company
- Golf-Themed Restaurant and Conference Center
- Health Communications Consultant
- Home Brewing Supplies Company
- Landscaping Service
- Marketing Communications Firm
- Massage Therapist
- Messenger Service
- Produce and Flower Market
- Retail Popcorn Stand
- Retro Gaming Systems
- School Store
- Student Advocate

FEATURES AND BENEFITS

BPH-25 offers many features not provided by other business planning references including:

- Twenty business plans, each of which represent an attempt at clarifying (for themselves and others) the reasons that the business should exist or expand and why a lender should fund the enterprise.
- Two fictional plans that are used by business counselors at a prominent small business development organization as examples for their clients. (You will find these in the Business Plan Template Appendix.)

- A directory section that includes listings for venture capital and finance companies, which specialize in funding start-up and second-stage small business ventures, and a comprehensive listing of Service Corps of Retired Executives (SCORE) offices. In addition, the Appendix also contains updated listings of all Small Business Development Centers (SBDCs); associations of interest to entrepreneurs; Small Business Administration (SBA) Regional Offices; and consultants specializing in small business planning and advice. It is strongly advised that you consult supporting organizations while planning your business, as they can provide a wealth of useful information.

- A Small Business Term Glossary to help you decipher the sometimes confusing terminology used by lenders and others in the financial and small business communities.

- A cumulative index, outlining each plan profiled in the complete *Business Plans Handbook* series.

- A Business Plan Template which serves as a model to help you construct your own business plan. This generic outline lists all the essential elements of a complete business plan and their components, including the Summary, Business History and Industry Outlook, Market Examination, Competition, Marketing, Administration and Management, Financial Information, and other key sections. Use this guide as a starting point for compiling your plan.

- Extensive financial documentation required to solicit funding from small business lenders. You will find examples of Cash Flows, Balance Sheets, Income Projections, and other financial information included with the textual portions of the plan.

Introduction

Perhaps the most important aspect of business planning is simply doing it. More and more business owners are beginning to compile business plans even if they don't need a bank loan. Others discover the value of planning when they must provide a business plan for the bank. The sheer act of putting thoughts on paper seems to clarify priorities and provide focus. Sometimes business owners completely change strategies when compiling their plan, deciding on a different product mix or advertising scheme after finding that their assumptions were incorrect. This kind of healthy thinking and re-thinking via business planning is becoming the norm. The editors of *Business Plans Handbook, Volume 25 (BPH-25)* sincerely hope that this latest addition to the series is a helpful tool in the successful completion of your business plan, no matter what the reason for creating it.

This twenty-fifth volume, like each volume in the series, offers business plans used and created by real people. *BPH-25* provides 20 business plans. The business and personal names and addresses and general locations have been changed to protect the privacy of the plan authors.

NEW BUSINESS OPPORTUNITIES

As in other volumes in the series, *BPH-25* finds entrepreneurs engaged in a wide variety of creative endeavors. Examples include a proposal for a Dance Studio, a Landscaping Business, and Concierge Service. In addition, several other plans are provided, including a Produce and Flower Market, a Digital Asset Management Consultant, and a Massage Therapist, among others.

Comprehensive financial documentation has become increasingly important as today's entrepreneurs compete for the finite resources of business lenders. Our plans illustrate the financial data generally required of loan applicants, including Income Statements, Financial Projections, Cash Flows, and Balance Sheets.

ENHANCED APPENDIXES

In an effort to provide the most relevant and valuable information for our readers, we have updated the coverage of small business resources. For instance, you will find a directory section, which includes listings of all of the Service Corps of Retired Executives (SCORE) offices; an informative glossary, which includes small business terms; and a cumulative index, outlining each plan profiled in the complete *Business Plans Handbook* series. In addition we have updated the list of Small Business Development Centers (SBDCs); Small Business Administration Regional Offices; venture capital and finance companies, which specialize in funding start-up and second-stage small business enterprises; associations of interest to entrepreneurs; and consultants, specializing in small business advice and planning. For your reference, we have also reprinted the business plan template, which provides a comprehensive overview of the essential components of a business plan and two fictional plans used by small business counselors.

SERIES INFORMATION

If you already have the first twenty-four volumes of *BPH*, with this twenty-fifth volume, you will now have a collection of over 506 business plans (not including the updated plans); contact information for hundreds of organizations and agencies offering business expertise; a helpful business plan template; more than 1,500 citations to valuable small business development material; and a comprehensive glossary of terms to help the business planner navigate the sometimes confusing language of entrepreneurship.

ACKNOWLEDGEMENTS

The Editors wish to sincerely thank the contributors to *BPH-25*, including:

- Heidi Denler
- Paul Greenland
- Zu Zu Enterprises

COMMENTS WELCOME

Your comments on *Business Plans Handbook* are appreciated. Please direct all correspondence, suggestions for future volumes of *BPH*, and other recommendations to the following:

Managing Editor, Business Product
Business Plans Handbook
Gale, a part of Cengage Learning
27500 Drake Rd.
Farmington Hills, MI 48331-3535
Phone: (248)699-4253
Fax: (248)699-8052
Toll-Free: 800-347-GALE
E-mail: BusinessProducts@gale.com

Arts & Crafts Company

3 Sister Crafts

127 W. Elm St.
Sault Ste. Marie, MI 49783

Zuzu Enterprises

3 Sister Crafts offers a variety of distinctive, colorful children's clothes, including customized onesies, tees, tanks, dresses, hair bows, bags, totes, and aprons. It also offers unique jewelry such as stamped metal necklaces, bracelets, and rings; bottlecap jewelry; paper bead jewelry; clay and stone jewelry; and barrettes. Both premade pieces and custom pieces are available.

EXECUTIVE SUMMARY

3 Sister Crafts offers a variety of distinctive, colorful children's clothes, including customized onesies, tees, tanks, dresses, hair bows, bags, totes, and aprons. It also offers unique jewelry such as stamped metal necklaces, bracelets, and rings; bottlecap jewelry; paper bead jewelry; clay and stone jewelry; and barrettes. Both premade pieces and custom pieces are available.

SALES OPPORTUNITIES

Several sales avenues will be pursued simultaneously to ensure maximum exposure and potential market. Online sales will comprise approximately 55% of all sales and will be done through several venues. Arts and crafts shows will comprise another 20% of sales, and the final 25% of sales will be made through small retail boutiques.

Online Sales

Online sales are anticipated to bring in approximately 55% of all sales. Sales will be conducted through the following online retail sites:

- Company website (www.3sistercrafts.com)

- Etsy (www.etsy.com)

- eBay (www.ebay.com)

- Hand Made in Michigan (www.mi-made.com)

Accounts on Etsy and eBay have been in place for over one year with moderate success. Customers who have purchased an item from us have given us 100% satisfaction ratings on both sites, and approximately 75% have become repeat customers. Our projects have been featured on the main search page and have been "pinned" on the growing Pinterest website. Since we were first "pinned," new customers have reported hearing about us from Pinterest at a rate of 25%.

This growing sales record has led us to expand into other online opportunities as well as the craft show and boutique retail outlets.

Sales via Arts & Crafts Shows

Sales via craft shows are new to us, but are expected to bring in 20% of sales. We have chosen a number of different shows to attend throughout the summer, most of which are fairly large (more than 100 exhibitors). These large shows are established and draw thousands of visitors each weekend. The shows are spread throughout the state so we are likely to hit a wider audience than if we concentrated our efforts in one area.

Show Dates and Locations

Below is a list of the shows we have committed to, including show, date, city, times, and total number of exhibitors.

Date	City	Show	Times	No. of exhibitors
June 2–3	Farmington Hills	Art on the Grand	Saturday, 10 am to 8 pm Sunday, 11 am to 6 pm	100 exhibitors
June 9	Berkley	Berkley Art Bash	Saturday, 10 am to 6 pm	100 exhibitors
June 16–17	Lathrup Village	9th Annual Michigan First Summer in the Village	Saturday, 11 am to 7 pm Sunday, 11 am to 5 pm	50 exhibitors
June 23–24	St. Clair	40th Annual St. Clair Art Fair	Saturday, 10 am to 7 pm Sunday, 10 am to 5 pm	134 exhibitors
June 30	Saugatuck	Waterfront Invitational Art Fair	Saturday, 10 am to 5 pm	80 exhibitors
July 11–14	Wyandotte	Wyandotte Street Art Fair	Thursday, 10 am to 9 pm Friday, 10 am to 9 pm Saturday, 10 am to 9 pm	300 exhibitors
July 21	Petoskey	Art in the Park	Saturday, 10 am to 6 pm	130 exhibitors
July 27–29	West Bloomfield	10th Annual Orchard Lake Fine Art Show	Friday, 5 pm to 9 pm Saturday, 10 am to 9 pm Sunday, 10 am to 5 pm	150 exhibitors
August 4–5	Rochester Hills	Summer Fine Art at the Village	Saturday, 10 am to 8 pm Sunday, noon to 6 pm	100 exhibitors
August 10–12	Milford	Milford Memories Art in the Village	Friday, 10 am to 8 pm Saturday, 10 am to 7 pm Sunday, 10 am to 5 pm	250 exhibitors
August 31–September 3	Royal Oak	15th Annual Ford Arts, Beats & Eats	Friday, 11 am to 9 pm Saturday, 11 am to 9 pm Sunday, 11 am to 9 pm Monday, 11 am to 5 pm	155 exhibitors

Retail Sales

Sales will also be made in retail stores in one of two ways, including the following:

- Consignment in small, local retail boutiques

- Custom orders for sale in small retail boutiques, both locally and throughout the United States

This sales outlet is expected to bring 25% of all sales.

Several stores have already placed preliminary orders, with plans to order more pending successful sales of the introductory order. These retail outlets include the following:

- Carol Roeda Studio, Ann Arbor, MI

- Catching Fireflies, Berkley MI

- Toni's Boutique, Richmond, MI

- Jazzie's Boutique, Saugatuk, MI

STAFF

Colleen (Ferkowicz) Marasco is the oldest of the three sisters. Colleen is an expert seamstress and began sewing custom outfits when her daughters, now 14 and 16, were babies. She has worked for a dry cleaner as a tailor and has made custom quilts for people throughout the years. Her quilting work is on display at the local sewing store, Sew Together. She enjoys sewing, quilting, appliqué, knitting, and crochet.

Colleen will design and produce all of the sewing projects for sale as part of 3 Sister Crafts as well as some knitted and crocheted items. Colleen will also write weekly blog entries for the 3 Sister blog and be the main contact for all boutique sales.

Mary (Ferkowicz) Kaltz is the middle sister. She formerly had a budding career as a computer technician but gave that up when she had three young girls of her own, ages 8, 6, and 4. She enjoys sewing, jewelry making, and knitting/crochet.

Mary will set up and maintain the website, blog, and Twitter and Facebook accounts. In addition, she will maintain the 3 Sister accounts on Etsy, eBay, and Hand Made in Michigan online retail accounts. She will also contribute knitted and crocheted items for sale as part of 3 Sister Crafts as well as hair accessories such as beaded barrettes, fabric headbands, crocheted flower hats, and decorated bobby pins.

Shannon Ferkowicz is the baby of the family. She is outgoing and friendly and has the talent of being able to talk to anyone and put everyone at ease. She graduated with an Associate of Fine Arts degree, specializing in graphic arts. She is a talented graphic designer and has her own independent contractor business in graphic design, computer graphics, and typography. She specializes in jewelry making and has lately branched out to include stamped metal jewelry pieces.

Shannon will design the 3 Sister logo and branding materials as well as the look of the company website and blog. She will also design and create all of the jewelry projects for sale as part of 3 Sister Crafts. Initially, Shannon will also be the point person in charge of manning all of the arts and crafts shows, with either Colleen or Mary helping her as needed on a rotating basis.

START-UP REQUIREMENTS

3 Sister Crafts will need a variety of furniture, supplies, and other items to ramp up operations. All requirements are listed below according to category. A financial breakdown follows.

Show Supplies
- Display tables
- Clothes racks
- Tent
- Jewelry display stands (necklace, bracelet bars, etc.)
- Tiered shelving
- Signage
- Cash box
- Bags
- Tissue paper
- Trolley
- Large vehicle

Materials & Supplies (Consumable)

- Fabric
- Yarn
- Ribbon
- Generic cotton onesies, tees, tanks, etc.
- Thread, fasteners, etc.
- Beads, charms, and crystals
- Wire
- Findings (clasps, crimps, bails, etc.)
- Barrettes, bobby pins, etc.
- Stamping blanks
- Bottle caps
- Scrabble tiles
- Specialty papers
- Various chains, jump rings, etc.
- Adhesives
- Silver black
- Polishing pads
- Jewelry bags and boxes
- Tissue paper
- Mailing envelopes, boxes, and labels
- Bubble wrap

Equipment (Reusable)

Most needed equipment is already owned and in use by the sisters of 3 Sister Crafts. Future purchases will be tracked and paid for with company funds. Equipment needed by the sisters to produce their wares include the following:

- Work tables and chairs
- Sewing machines
- Storage and organization systems
- Assortment of pliers, scissors, rotary cutters, and other implements
- Pins, pin cushion, thimble, needles, bobbins, etc.
- Self-healing mats
- Knitting needles
- Crochet hooks
- Metal stamps (letter and number sets in various fonts and sizes; numerous design stamps)
- Hammers (1lb and 2lb)
- Bench blocks

- Measuring tools

- Camera

- Computer and software

- Display space for photographing pieces

- Postal scale

Start Up Costs

Item	Cost
Display tables	$1,500
Clothes racks	$ 200
Tent	$ 350
Jewelry display stands (necklace, bracelet bars, etc.)	$ 200
Tiered shelving	$ 500
Signage	$1,000
Cash box/credit card machine	$ 300
Bags	$ 200
Tissue paper	$ 50
Trolleys-2	$ 500
Fabric, yarn, ribbon, thread, fasteners, etc.	$1,000
Generic cotton onesies, t-s, tanks, etc.	$ 500
Jewelry supplies	$1,000
• Beads, charms, and crystals	
• Wire	
• Findings (clasps, crimps, bails, etc.)	
• Barrettes, bobby pins, etc.	
• Stamping blanks	
• Bottle caps	
• Scrabble tiles	
• Specialty papers	
• Various chains, jump rings, etc.	
• Adhesives	
• Silver black	
• Polishing pads	
Jewelry bags and boxes	$ 500
Mailing envelopes, boxes, labels, and bubble wrap	$ 500
Total	**$8,300**

MARKETING & ADVERTISING

Marketing and advertising will be done through a number of different channels, including the following:

- Website (www.3sistercrafts.com) with email list. This will contain photos of all of our different creations along with their coordinating items.

- Blog (www.3sistercrafts.blogspot.com) with subscriptions. The blog will have information about our travels for the arts and crafts shows, inspirations for new ideas, notifications of new products, and the like.

- Pinterest (www.pinterest.com). We will start our own Pinterest board where we will "pin" photos of our merchandise with links to purchase them.

- Twitter (www.twitter.com; @3sistercrafts). Our twitter account will notify followers of new products, sales, and show dates and times.

- Facebook (www.facebook.com). Our Facebook page will contain basic information about our business, photos, and links to our website. We will periodically post status updates announcing new products, sales, and appearances at arts and crafts shows.

- Unique colors and logo for branding purposes. A logo for 3 Sister will be created for the business using the colors lime green and blue combined with and zebra print. This brand and will be used on the website, packaging materials, business cards, bags, etc.

- Business cards. General business cards will be made with our website and other contact information. It will be included with all purchases and available for browsers at the arts and crafts shows.

- Custom labels. Custom labels featuring our logo and colors will be created to be used on jewelry boxes, mailing boxes, and clothes labels.

PREFERRED SUPPLIERS

3 Sister Crafts has several preferred suppliers that have the most unique and colorful fabrics and supplies. These are suppliers we have worked with in the past and have proven to be reliable and sell quality merchandise. The suppliers are listed below according to type of materials sold.

Fabric, Yarn, and Ribbon:

- Marimekko Concept Store, www.kiitosmarimekko.com. Although the fabrics are pricey, we love the bright colors and distinctive patterns of the Marimekko fabric.

- Sew, Mama, Sew!, sewmamasew.com. Sew, Mama, Sew! has a wide variety of colorful fabrics at reasonable prices.

- Purl Soho, www.purlsoho.com. Purl Soho offers a wide variety of yarns and fabrics.

- Hawthorne Threads, www.hawthornethreads.com.

- Joann's. Offers a wide variety of fabrics, ribbon, yarn and jewelry components with weekly sales and coupons.

- Hobby Lobby. Offers a wide variety of fabrics, ribbon, yarn and jewelry components with weekly sales and coupons.

- Michaels. Offers a wide variety of ribbon, yarn and jewelry components with weekly sales and coupons.

- Hancock Fabrics—Offers a wide variety of fabrics and ribbon.

- The Ribbon Retreat, www.theribbonretreat.com. The Ribbon Retreat has a wide variety of ribbons, fabric, and trims.

Metal Stamping

Our primary supplier of metal stamping tools is Beaducation (beaducation.com). They sell all tools and materials needed to create stamped metal jewelry.

Jewelry

Several online retailers sell the components needed to make our jewelry, barrettes and other accessories.

- Artbeads, www.artbeads.com. Artbeads has a wide variety of crystals, charms, clasps, findings at reasonable prices.

- Bottle Cap Art Supplies, www.etsy.com/shop/BottlecapArtSupplies. Bottle Cap Art Supplies sells a variety of bottle cap supplies, bails, and chains.

- Annie Howes, www.etsy.com/shop/AnnieHowes. Annie Howes offers glass shapes of various shapes and sizes, bezels, blanks, and chains.

- Sun and Moon Craft Kits, www.etsy.com/shop/SunAndMoonCraftKits. Sun and Moon Craft Kits provide glass shapes, chains, bottle caps, and trays.

Child Transportation Service

Trusted Transport Inc.

570 Main St.
Apple Grove, WI 54667

Paul Greenland

Trusted Transport Inc. is a transportation service for school-aged children.

EXECUTIVE SUMMARY

Business Overview

Established by Natalie Robertson, Trusted Transport Inc. is a transportation service for school-aged children.

Natalie Robertson is a mother of four children, two of whom are still in college. When her children were younger, Robertson was very engaged in their school and extracurricular activities, serving as a Cub Scout den mother, classroom aide, soccer coach, and president of the PTA. She spent many years transporting her children (and their teammates and friends) safely to and from various locations. In the midst of juggling so many schedules, she often experienced the frustration of trying to make it all work. "If only I could clone myself," she would sometimes joke to fellow parents.

Now that her children have left home, Robertson misses the daily interaction she once enjoyed with them. Desiring to establish her own small business, Robertson has decided to combine her love of children with her parent's perspective and a natural entrepreneurial flair that others appreciated when she served on the PTA. As a transportation service for school-aged children, Trusted Transport Inc. will offer busy parents in Apple Grove a cost-effective solution for safely getting their kids where they need to be when extra help is needed.

MARKET ANALYSIS

Apple Grove, Wisconsin, was home to 35,681 people in 2011. The population base is expected to grow at a modest pace through 2016, at which time the community will include about 37,654 people, according to projections from DAX Research LLC.

Because the bulk of Trusted Transport's business initially will come from elementary school-aged children, the community's elementary schools are of central importance. The community is home to six elementary schools with a combined population of 3,278 students:

- Barton
- Thompson

- Green
- Ferris
- Lane
- McKenna

In addition, Apple Grove is served by two middle schools (a potential future market), with a combined population of 1,692 students:

- George Washington
- Fullbrook

Daycare centers represent another potential future market for Trusted Transport. In 2012, Apple Grove was home to 15 daycare centers. Another 12 centers were located in neighboring communities. Of these 27 centers, seven offer all-day kindergarten programs.

Market Potential

Natalie Robertson worked in partnership with Stephen Hillman, PhD, a marketing professor at Apple Grove College, to conduct a market analysis and determine potential demand for Trusted Transport's services. Complete details of this research (sample size, margin of error, response rates, etc.) are available upon request. However, the analysis indicated that among our target market (e.g., parents of elementary school-aged children), 65 percent of those in need of transportation assistance would consider using Trusted Transport immediately. Twenty percent indicated that they prefer to rely upon family and friends, while the remaining 15 percent were unsure.

Competitive Analysis

There currently is no competing child transportation service in Apple Grove or the surrounding region.

INDUSTRY ANALYSIS

Taxi and shuttle services are part of the larger contracted transportation industry. Services such as these employ taxi drivers, chauffeurs, para-transit drivers, and bus drivers. Non-bus transportation services specific to children are becoming more commonplace in many markets as a result of households in which both parents work outside of the home or care for their own aging parents. Although no specific data is available for children's transportation services, the U.S. Bureau of Labor and Statistics projects that the number of taxi driver and chauffeur jobs will increase 20 percent between 2010 and 2020, resulting in the creation of 47,000 new jobs.

PERSONNEL

Natalie Robertson (Owner)

Trusted Transport Inc. is owned and operated by Natalie Robertson, who will have overall responsibility for daily operations. She is a mother of four children, two of whom are still in college. Now that her children have left home, Robertson misses the daily interaction she once enjoyed with them. Desiring to establish her own small business, Robertson has decided to combine her love of children with her parent's perspective and natural entrepreneurial skills.

Although she was a full-time stay-at-home mom for 10 years, Robertson has spent the last five years working as a part-time bookkeeper for Allied Associates LLC, a manufacturing firm owned by her husband, Rick. She holds a Bachelor's degree in business administration from the University of Wisconsin-Whitewater. Recently, Robertson completed refresher training in human resources management from a local community college. In addition, she has completed several specialized courses to familiarize herself with transportation safety.

Staff

Trusted Transport will begin operations with the following positions:

- 3 Full-Time Drivers
- 3 Part-Time Drivers
- 1 Full-Time Dispatch Coordinator
- 1 Full-Time Administrative Assistant/Backup Dispatch Coordinator

Job descriptions for each position are available upon request.

Professional & Advisory Support

Trusted Transport has established a business banking account with Apple Grove Community Bank, including a merchant account for accepting credit card payments. Tax advisement is provided by Lewis Tax Advisors LLC. In addition, legal services are provided by Fairway Legal. The company has retained consultant Martin Frenzing to provide as-needed transportation safety advice and perform an annual audit.

GROWTH STRATEGY

Natalie Robertson spent six months during the 2011-2012 school year marketing to area elementary school parents and schools. Contracts for the summer of 2012, and the 2012-2013 school year have been signed, and all available slots are now full. The business has developed the following growth strategy pertaining to the first five years of its operations:

Year One: Focus on maintaining core elementary school-age customer base. Commence operations with three 16-passenger vans. Each van will be assigned to two dedicated elementary schools. Begin pursuing contracts for middle school student service during the 2013-14 school year.

Years Two-Three: Add two to three additional 16-passenger vans in order to provide service to middle school-age students. Hire two additional full-time drivers and one additional part-time driver.

Year Four: Conduct initial research regarding opportunities within the preschool-age transportation market. Meet with the directors/owners of all preschools within Apple Grove and conduct a market survey of area parents to determine demand. Add an additional van equipped with a wheelchair lift to meet the needs of students with disabilities. Hire one additional part-time driver.

Year Five: Based on the results of research during year four, potentially expand into the pre-school transportation market (number of vans and additional staff to be determined).

SERVICES

School-based Transportation

During the school year (September-May) Trusted Transport initially will concentrate on the provision of before- and after-school transportation services for elementary school students (grades K-6). The business will provide transport for students engaged in activities that prevent them from taking advantage of regular school bus or parental transportation. Examples include the following:

- Aftercare Programs

- Sports

- Special Interest Clubs

- Creative & Performing Arts

During the first year of operations, the business will operate three 16-passenger vans. Each van will serve two elementary schools:

Van #1

    Barton

    Green

Van #2

    Thompson

    Ferris

Van #3

    McKenna

    Lane

During the summer (June-August), services will focus on Barton and Lane Elementary Schools, which offer summer school programs, as well as transportation to and from the Boys Club, YMCA, and Apple Grove Sports Center, which offer various summer programs.

Special Contracts

In addition to regularly scheduled school-based transportation services, Trusted Transport will provide services on an as-needed basis outside of school hours to special interest groups and private sports club teams.

MARKETING & SALES

Trusted Transport has developed a marketing plan that includes the following primary tactics:

1. Sponsorship of at least one event or function at all six of the elementary schools that we serve, in order to generate/maintain awareness of our services.

2. Bi-annual direct mailings to households in our primary service area with elementary school-age children in the home.

3. A color flier describing our business.

4. Quarterly lunch meetings (focus on relationship building) with all elementary school principals.

5. A Web site with complete details about our business and the services we offer.

6. A presence on Facebook, in order to connect with prospective parents through social media.

7. Monthly direct mailings to area private sports and special interest clubs (list available upon request) that would potentially utilize our services for transportation to sports meets, field trips, etc.

*This marketing plan will be adjusted/expanded annually as the business expands into new markets (e.g., middle school, pre-school, etc.)

OPERATIONS

Facility & Location

Trusted Transport has agreed to lease a heated warehouse facility at 570 Main St. in central Apple Grove with capacity for 15 vehicles. The building includes overhead door access at two different points. It also includes a small office space that will accommodate the owner, administrative assistant, and dispatch coordinator. The larger vehicle area includes locker space for both full- and part-time drivers.

Vehicles

Our business will lease three 2010 Ford E-Series 16-passenger vans, at a cost of $10,800 annually. By leasing, Trusted Transport will be able to effectively manage its maintenance and repair costs.

Equipment

Trusted Transport will need to purchase several items prior to start-up:

- Office Furniture ($2,500)
- Personal Computers ($1,600)
- GPS Navigation Systems (3) ($500)
- Used VoIP 18-Channel Radio Dispatch Counsel with Five Radios ($750)
- First Aid Kits ($350)

Hours of Operation

Trusted Transport will provide school-based transportation services between the hours of 7 AM and 9 AM, and 2 PM and 6 PM Monday through Friday. Contract transportation will be negotiated separately on an as-needed basis. Customers may leave voicemail messages for staff 24-7. Administrative staff (e.g., dispatch coordinator and administrative assistant) will promptly return and accept phone calls from 6:30 AM to 6:30 PM on regular business days (shared call coverage).

Our business will be closed on major holidays:

- Christmas Day
- Christmas Eve
- July 4
- Labor Day
- Memorial Day
- New Year's Day
- Thanksgiving Day

Pricing

Trusted Transport will provide school-based transportation services based on the following fee structure:

Miles	Single trip	Daily round-trip	One way weekly	Round-trip weekly
0–1	$ 9.78	$18.40	$48.88	$ 86.25
2–5	$11.50	$20.70	$57.50	$ 97.75
6–8	$13.80	$23.00	$69.00	$103.50
9–10	$17.25	$28.75	$86.25	$138.00

Customers will be required to contract and pre-pay for services on a monthly basis.

Fees for contract transportation services will vary, depending on the needs of the customer (e.g., mileage, time, etc.).

LEGAL

Trusted Transport will adhere to all local, state, and federal transportation and vehicle safety regulations. The Wisconsin Department of Transportation's requirements pertaining to the operation of a school shuttle van are available at the following website:

http://www.dmv.org/wi-wisconsin/special-licenses.php

In accordance with Chapter XII, Section 17.02 of the Code of General Ordinances of the City of Apple Grove, Trusted Transport will pay annual taxi driver license fees of $30 for all of its drivers, which will be renewed annually in June.

The business will maintain appropriate liability and automotive insurance policies (available upon request). In addition, criminal background checks, drug & alcohol testing, and CPR/first aid certification will be required for all part- and full-time drivers.

FINANCIAL ANALYSIS

During its first year of operations, Trusted Transport anticipates revenues of $314,174. The business is expected to generate a net profit of $16,570. The majority (95%) of revenues will be attributed to school-based transportation services, while special/contract transportation services are expected to generate revenues of $15,000. Based on our growth projections, expansion into the middle school market will result in at least $199,450 in additional gross revenues during our second and third years of operation.

Natalie Robertson will cover the nominal startup costs referenced in the Operations section of this plan, which total $5,700. In addition, she will invest $25,000 of her own funds to cover initial operations. A $25,000 commitment from a private investor in Apple Grove also has been secured should additional funding be needed.

Trusted Transport has prepared a complete set of pro forma financial statements in partnership with our accountants, which are available upon request. The following tables provide an overview of key projections during the first year of operations:

2012–13 pro forma profit and loss statement

Sales	$314,174
Expenses	
Payroll	$201,580
Facility lease	$ 13,200
Vehicle leases	$ 10,800
Marketing	$ 15,500
Licenses & fees	$ 1,750
Consulting & legal	$ 5,500
Training	$ 2,500
Insurance	$ 3,600
Fuel	$ 5,737
Software	$ 1,200
Telecommunications	$ 3,500
Utilities	$ 1,500
Payroll taxes	$ 30,237
Miscellaneous	$ 1,000
Total operating costs	**$297,604**
Net profit	**$ 16,570**

Average Weekly Transportation Projections 2012-13

The following table provides a detailed breakdown of projected school-based transportation services for the months of September through May, when school is in session:

School year transportation projections (weekly by school—September–May)

Miles	Single trip	Green park	Ferris	Barton	Lane	McKenna	Thomson	Trip totals	Weekly revenue	Miles
0–1	$ 9.78	1	0	0	1	3	0	5	$ 49	5
2–5	$11.50	2	0	0	0	0	0	2	$ 23	8
6–8	$13.80	0	2	1	1	1	2	7	$ 97	49
9–10	$17.25	0	1	1	2	1	1	6	$104	54

Miles	Daily round-trip	Green park	Ferris	Barton	Lane	McKenna	Thomson	Trip totals	Weekly revenue	Miles
0–1	$18.40	0	2	0	1	0	2	5	$ 92	5
2–5	$20.70	3	0	1	1	1	1	7	$145	21
6–8	$23.00	1	0	2	0	2	1	6	$138	42
9–10	$28.75	2	0	1	2	3	2	10	$288	90

Miles	One way weekly	Green park	Ferris	Barton	Lane	McKenna	Thomson	Trip totals	Weekly revenue	Miles
0–1	$48.88	2	1	2	1	3	1	10	$489	10
2–5	$57.50	1	2	1	3	1	0	8	$460	24
6–8	$69.00	0	0	2	0	0	1	3	$207	21
9–10	$86.25	0	0	1	1	0	3	5	$431	45

Miles	Round-trip weekly	Green park	Ferris	Barton	Lane	McKenna	Thomson	Trip totals	Weekly revenue	Miles
0–1	$ 86.25	2	3	2	1	1	2	11	$ 949	11
2–5	$ 97.75	3	3	1	3	2	2	14	$1,369	42
6–8	$103.50	1	1	1	0	3	0	6	$ 621	42
9–10	$138.00	1	0	2	1	2	1	7	$ 966	63
								112	$6,426	532

The following table provides a detailed breakdown of projected school/facility-based transportation services for the months of June through August, when school is not in session:

Summer transportation projections (weekly by school/facility—June–August)

Miles	Single trip	Barton	Lane	Boys club	YMCA	Sports ctr	Trip totals	Weekly revenue	Miles
0–1	$ 9.78	1	0	3	0	1	5	$ 49	5
2–5	$11.50	2	0	0	0	2	4	$ 46	16
6–8	$13.80	0	2	1	2	0	5	$ 69	35
9–10	$17.25	0	1	1	1	0	3	$ 52	27

Miles	Daily round-trip	Barton	Lane	Boys club	YMCA	Sports ctr	Trip totals	Weekly revenue	Miles
0–1	$18.40	0	1	0	2	0	3	$ 55	3
2–5	$20.70	1	0	1	0	3	5	$ 104	25
6–8	$23.00	1	0	2	0	1	4	$ 92	28
9–10	$28.75	2	0	3	0	2	7	$ 201	63

Miles	One way weekly	Barton	Lane	Boys club	YMCA	Sports ctr	Trip totals	Weekly revenue	Miles
0–1	$48.88	0	1	3	1	2	7	$ 342	7
2–5	$57.50	1	1	1	2	1	6	$ 345	18
6–8	$69.00	0	0	0	0	0	0	$ 0	0
9–10	$86.25	0	0	0	0	0	0	$ 0	0

Miles	Round-trip weekly	Barton	Lane	Boys club	YMCA	Sports ctr	Trip totals	Weekly revenue	Miles
0–1	$ 86.25	1	0	1	3	2	7	$ 604	7
2–5	$ 97.75	0	0	2	3	3	8	$ 782	32
6–8	$103.50	1	1	3	1	1	7	$ 725	49
9–10	$138.00	1	0	2	0	1	4	$ 552	36
							75	$4,018	351

*Summer school offered at Barton & Lane Elementary Schools

Computer Reseller

Computech Management

14853 Holyfield Ave.
Denver, CO 96774

This plan for revamping an aging technology reseller reflects the changes that any mature company needs to make to compete in a changing business climate. Capital infusion will allow the company to expand its service capacity and carve out a more secure place for itself in a highly competitive field. Note the increased emphasis on promotional efforts to help the company re-launch itself.

This business plan appeared in Business Plans Handbook, Volume 5. It has been updated for this edition.

EXECUTIVE SUMMARY

By focusing on its strengths, its key customers, and the underlying values they need, CompuTech Management (CTM) will increase sales to more than $14 million in three years, while also improving the gross margin on sales and cash management and working capital.

This business plan leads the way. It renews our vision and strategic focus by adding value to our target market segments, the small business and high-end home office users, and in our local market. It also provides the step-by-step plan for improving our sales, gross margin, and profitability.

In addition to this summary, this plan includes sections on the company's products and services, market focus, action plans and forecasts, management team, and financial plan.

Objectives
1. Increase sales to more than $10 million by the third year.
2. Bring gross margin back up to above 25% and maintain that level.
3. Sell $2.8 million of service, support, and training by 2013.

Mission
CTM is built on the assumption that the management of information technology for business is like legal advice, accounting, graphic design, and other bodies of knowledge, in that it is not inherently a do-it-yourself prospect. Smart business people need to find quality vendors of reliable hardware, software, service, and support. They need to use these quality vendors as they use their other professional service suppliers, as trusted allies.

CTM is such a vendor. It serves its clients as a trusted ally, providing them with the loyalty of a business partner and the economics of an outside vendor. We make sure that our clients have what they need to run their businesses as well as possible, with maximum efficiency and reliability. Many of our information applications are mission critical, so we give our clients the assurance that we will be there when they need us.

Keys to Success

1. Differentiate from box-pushing, price-oriented businesses by offering and delivering service and support—and charging for it.

2. Increase gross margin to more than 25%.

3. Increase our non-hardware sales to 20% of the total sales by the third year.

COMPANY SUMMARY

CTM is a 10-year-old technology reseller with sales of $10 million per year, declining margins, and market pressure. It has a good reputation, excellent people, and a steady position in the local market, but has been having trouble maintaining healthy financials.

Company Ownership

CTM is a privately held C corporation owned in majority by its founder and president, Eugene Foley. There are six part-owners, including four investors and two past employees. The largest of these (in percent of ownership) are Dean Radcliff, our attorney, and Steve Holcomb, our public relations consultant. Neither owns more than 15%, but both are active participants in management decisions.

Company History

CTM has been caught in the vice grip of margin squeezes that have affected technology resellers worldwide. This has resulted in the following:

- A gross margin percentage that has been declining steadily.
- Inventory turnover that is getting steadily worse.

These concerns are part of the general trend affecting technology resellers. The margin squeeze is happening throughout the computer industry worldwide.

Company Locations and Facilities

We have one location, a 7,000-square-foot site located conveniently close to the downtown area. It includes a training area, service department, offices, and showroom area.

PRODUCTS

Competitive Comparison

The only way we can hope to differentiate well is to define the vision of the company to be an information technology ally to our clients. We will not be able to compete in any effective way with the chains using boxes or products as appliances. We need to offer a real alliance.

The benefits we sell include many intangibles, including confidence, reliability, and the knowledge that somebody will be there to answer questions and help at the important times.

Many of the products we sell are complex, requiring serious knowledge and experience to use, and our competitors sell only the products themselves.

Unfortunately, we cannot sell the products at a higher price just because we offer services; the market has shown that it will not support that concept. We have to also sell the service and charge for it separately.

Promotion

Our Web site is available for review and copies of our brochure and advertisements are available upon request. Of course, one of our first tasks will be to change our promotional messaging to make sure we are selling the company, rather than focusing too heavily on products.

Sourcing

Our costs are part of the margin squeeze. As competition on price increases, the squeeze between manufacturer's price into channels and end-users ultimate buying price continues.

With the hardware lines, our margins are declining steadily. We are also starting to see that same trend with software. In accessories and add-ons we can still get decent margins of 25% to 40%.

In order to hold costs down as much as possible, we concentrate our purchasing with Martinson, which offers 30-day net terms and overnight shipping from the warehouse in Denver. We need to concentrate on making sure our volume gives us negotiating strength.

Technology

In addition to selling computer hardware (Microsoft and Macintosh), our business also markets Voice Over Internet Protocol (VOIP)-based telephone systems, computer networking hardware, and video surveillance systems. We offer the technical expertise to accompany the products we sell. Our company has achieved Microsoft Gold, Hewlett-Packard Gold, and Cisco Premier status, providing our customers and partners with peace of mind.

MARKET ANALYSIS SUMMARY

CTM focuses on local markets, small business and home offices, with special focus on the high-end home office and the 5-20 unit small business office. The home offices in Denver are part of an important growing market segment. According to the research firm IDC, more than 85 percent of businesses in the United States offered some form of flexible scheduling, including home or virtual offices, for their employees, as of 2011.

Home offices include several types. The most important, for our plan's focus, are the home offices that are the only offices of real businesses, from which people make their primary living. These are likely to be professional services such as graphic designers, writers, and consultants, some accountants and the occasional lawyer, doctor, or dentist. There are also part-time home offices with people who are employed during the day but work at home at night, people who work at home to provide themselves with a part-time income, or people who maintain home offices relating to their hobbies; we will not be focusing on this segment.

Small business within our market includes virtually any business with a retail, office, professional, or industrial location outside of someone's home, and fewer than 30 employees. We estimate 45,000 such businesses in our market area.

The 30-employee cutoff is arbitrary. We find that the larger companies turn to other vendors, but we can sell to departments of larger companies, and we shouldn't be giving up leads when we get them.

Market Analysis

Potential customers	Total customers	Growth rate
Consumer	12,000	2.00%
Small business	15,000	5.00%
Large business	33,000	8.00%
Government	36,000	−2.00%
Other	19,000	0.00%
Total	**115,000**	2.78%

Market Segmentation

The segmentation allows some room for estimates and nonspecific definitions. We focus on a small-medium level of small business, and it is hard to find information to make an exact classification. Our target companies are large enough to need the high-quality information technology management we offer, but too small to have a dedicated computer management staff such as an IT department. We say that our target market has 10-50 employees and needs 5-20 workstations tied together in a local area network; the definition is flexible.

Defining the high-end home office is even more difficult. We generally know the characteristics of our target market, but we can't find easy classifications that fit into available demographics. The high-end home office business is a business, not a hobby. It generates enough money to merit the owner's paying real attention to the quality of information technology management, meaning that there is both budget and concerns that warrant working with our level of quality service and support. We can assume that we aren't talking about home offices used only part-time by people who work elsewhere during the day, and that our target market home office wants to have powerful technology integration involving computing, telecommunications, and video.

Industry Analysis

We are part of the technology reselling business, which includes several kinds of businesses:

1. Technology resellers: These are businesses similar to our own.

2. Chain stores and computer superstores: These include major chains such as CompUSA, Best Buy, etc. They are almost always more than 10,000 square feet of space, usually offer decent walk-in service, and are often warehouse-like locations where people go to find products in boxes with very aggressive pricing, and little support.

3. Online: The market is dominated by e-commerce players like CDW, New Egg, Tiger Direct, Dell, and HP, which offer aggressive pricing of boxed product. For the purely price-driven buyer, who buys boxes and expects no service, these are very good options.

4. Others: there are many other channels through which people buy technology products, usually variations of the main three types above.

Industry Participants

National retailers (virtual and physical) are a dominant presence. These include CompUSA, Best Buy, and others. They benefit from national advertising, economies of scale, volume buying, and a general trend toward name-brand loyalty for buying in the channels, as well as for products.

Distribution Patterns

Small business buyers are accustomed to buying from vendors who visit their offices. They expect the copy machine vendors, office products vendors, and office furniture vendors, as well as the local graphic designers, freelance writers, or whomever, to visit their office to make their sales.

There usually is a lot of leakage in ad-hoc purchasing through local chain stores and online retailers.

Unfortunately, our home office target buyers may not expect to buy from us. Many of them turn immediately to the superstores (office equipment, office supplies, and electronics) and online retailers to look for the best price, without realizing that there is a better option for them at only a little bit more.

Competition and Buying Patterns

The small business buyers understand the concept of service and support, and are much more likely to pay for it when the offering is clearly stated.

There is no doubt that we compete much more against all the box pushers than against other service providers. We need to effectively compete against the idea that businesses should buy technology without ongoing service, support, and training.

Our focus group sessions indicated that our target home offices think about price but would buy based on quality service if the offering is properly presented. They think about price because that's all they ever see. We have very good indications that many would rather pay 10-20% more for a relationship with a long-term vendor providing back-up and quality service and support; they end up in the box-pusher channels because they aren't aware of the alternatives.

Availability is also very important. The home office buyers tend to want immediate, local solutions to problems.

Main Competitors

Chain stores

We have Store 1 and Store 2 already within the valley, and Store 3 is expected by the end of next year. If our strategy works, we will have differentiated ourselves sufficiently to not have to compete against these stores.

Strengths: national image, high volume, aggressive pricing, economies of scale.

Weaknesses: lack of product, service and support knowledge, lack of personal attention.

Local technology resellers

RAM Electronics and CT Computer Solutions are local technology resellers like us. RAM has pursued a product-focused strategy and is in poor financial health. CT has done an excellent job selling its technology services. Although our markets overlap somewhat, CT tends to focus more on custom programming solutions, POS systems, and inventory software, which we do not offer.

STRATEGY AND IMPLEMENTATION SUMMARY

1. Emphasize service and support. We must differentiate ourselves from the box pushers. We need to establish our business offering as a clear and viable alternative for our target market, to the price-only kind of buying.

2. Build a relationship-oriented business. Build long-term relationships with clients, not single-transaction deals with customers. Become their technology department, not just a vendor. Make them understand the value of the relationship.

3. Focus on target markets. We need to focus our offerings on small business as the key market segment we should own. For example, in the case of desktop computers, this means the 5-20 unit system, tied together in a local area network, in a company with 5-50 employees. Our values

(training, installation, service, support, knowledge) are more cleanly differentiated in this segment. As a corollary, the high end of the home office market is also appropriate. We do not want to compete for the buyers who go exclusively to the chain stores or online retailers, but we definitely want to be able to sell individual systems to the smart home office buyers who want a reliable, full-service vendor.

4. Differentiate and fulfill the promise. We can't just market and sell service and support, we must actually deliver as well. We need to make sure we have the knowledge-intensive business and service-intensive business we claim to have.

Marketing Strategy

The marketing strategy is the core of the main strategy:

1. Emphasize service and support

2. Build a relationship business

3. Focus on small business and high-end home offices as key target markets

Pricing Strategy

We must charge appropriately for the high-end, high-quality service and support we offer. Our revenue structure has to match our cost structure, so the salaries we pay to assure good service and support must be balanced by the revenue we charge.

We cannot build the service and support revenue into the price of products. The market can't bear the higher prices and buyers feel disappointed when they see the same product priced lower at the chains. Despite the logic behind this, the market doesn't support this concept.

Therefore, we must make sure that we deliver and charge for service and support. Training, service, installation, networking support—all of this must be readily available and priced to sell and deliver revenue.

Promotion Strategy

We depend on direct marketing and interactive advertising as our main ways to reach new buyers. As we change strategies, however, we need to change the way we promote ourselves:

1. Advertising. We'll be developing our core positioning message: "24 Hour On-Site Service - 365 Days a Year With No Extra Charges" to differentiate our service from the competition. We will be using print mailings, e-mail, online advertising, and some print advertising to launch the initial campaign.

2. Interactive Marketing. We will take advantage of online advertising and social media channels such as Twitter, Facebook, and LinkedIn to sell our products and services.

3. Media Relations. It's time to work more closely with the local media. We could offer the local radio a regular talk show on technology for small business, as one example.

Sales Strategy

1. We need to sell the company, not the product. We sell CTM, not Microsoft, Cisco, or any of our software brand names.

2. We have to sell our service and support. The hardware is like the razor, and the support, service, software services, training, and seminars are the razor blades. We need to serve our customers with what they really need.

Sales Forecast

	2012	2013	2014
Unit sales			
Hardware	1,666	1,750	1,850
Service	4,975	6,000	7,500
Software	3,725	5,000	6,500
Training	2,230	4,000	8,000
Other	4,575	5,000	5,500
Total unit sales	**17,171**	**21,750**	**29,350**
Unit prices			
Hardware	$ 2,847	$ 2,857	$ 2,847
Service	$ 105	$ 121	$ 125
Software	$ 310	$ 281	$ 259
Training	$ 68	$ 104	$ 114
Other	$ 432	$ 432	$ 432
Total sales			
Hardware	$ 4,742,640	$ 5,000,930	$ 5,266,437
Service	$ 525,600	$ 725,760	$ 939,600
Software	$ 1,150,920	$ 1,404,000	$ 1,684,800
Training	$ 149,566	$ 414,720	$ 910,080
Other	$ 1,976,400	$ 2,160,000	$ 2,376,000
Total sales	**$8,545,126**	**$9,705,410**	**$11,176,917**
Unit direct costs			
Hardware	$ 1,440	$ 1,428	$ 1,423
Service	$ 86	$ 96	$ 101
Software	$ 144	$ 141	$ 130
Training	$ 32	$ 62	$ 68
Other	$ 216	$ 216	$ 216
Direct costs			
Hardware	$ 2,399,040	$ 2,500,465	$ 2,633,219
Service	$ 429,840	$ 580,608	$ 751,680
Software	$ 536,400	$ 702,000	$ 842,400
Training	$ 71,289	$ 248,832	$ 546,048
Other	$ 988,200	$ 1,080,000	$ 1,188,000
Subtotal direct costs	**$4,424,769**	**$5,111,905**	**$ 5,961,347**

Service and Support

Our strategy hinges on providing excellent service and support. This is critical. We need to differentiate on service and support, and to therefore deliver as well.

- Training

- Upgrade offers

- Our own internal training

- Installation services

- Custom software services

- Network configuration services

Milestones

Our important milestones are shown on the table below.

Business Plan Milestones

Milestone	Mngr	Date	Dept.	Budget	Act date
Corporate identity	TJ	12/17/2010	Marketing	$ 14,400	01/15/2011
Seminar implementation	IR	01/10/2011	Sales	$ 1,440	12/27/2010
Business plan review	RJ	01/10/2011	GM	$ 0	01/23/2011
Upgrade mailer	IR	01/16/2011	Sales	$ 7,200	02/12/2011
New corporate brochure	TJ	01/16/2011	Marketing	$ 7,200	01/15/2011
Delivery vans	SD	01/25/2011	Service	$ 18,000	02/26/2011
Direct mail	IR	02/16/2011	Marketing	$ 5,040	02/25/2011
Advertising	RJ	02/16/2011	GM	$165,600	03/06/2011
X4 Prototype	SG	02/25/2011	Product	$ 3,600	02/25/2011
Service revamp	SD	02/25/2011	Product	$ 3,600	02/25/2011
6 Presentations	IR	02/25/2011	Sales	$ 0	01/10/2011
X4 Testing	SG	03/06/2011	Product	$ 1,440	01/16/2011
3 Accounts	SD	03/17/2011	Sales	$ 0	03/17/2011
L30 Prototype	PR	03/26/2011	Product	$ 3,600	04/11/2011
Tech expo	TB	04/12/2011	Marketing	$ 21,600	01/25/2011
VP S&M hired	JK	06/11/2011	Sales	$ 1,440	07/25/2011
Mailing system	SD	07/25/2011	Service	$ 7,200	07/14/2011
Totals				**$261,360**	

MANAGEMENT SUMMARY

Our management philosophy is based on responsibility and mutual respect. People who work at CTM want to work at CTM because we have an environment that encourages creativity and achievement.

Organizational Structure

The team includes 22 employees, under a president and four managers.

Our main management divisions are sales, marketing, service, and administration. Service handles service, support, training, and development.

Management Team

Eugene Foley, President: 46 years old, founded CTM in 2000 to focus on reselling personal computers to small business. Degree in computer science, 15 years with Large Computers, Inc. in positions ending with project manager. Eugene has been attending courses at the local Small Business Development Center for more than six years now, steadily adding business skills and business training to his technical background.

Janice Carly, VP Marketing: 36 years old, joined us last year following a very successful career with Continental Computers. Her hiring was the culmination of a long recruiting search. With Continental she managed the VAR marketing division. She is committed to re-engineering CTM to be a service and support business. MBA, undergraduate degree in history.

Max Webber, VP Service and Support: 48 years old, 18 years with Large Computers, Inc. in programming and service-related positions, 7 years with CTM. MS in computer science and BS in electrical engineering.

Annette Yezbick, VP Sales: 32, former teacher, joined CTM part-time in 2005 and went full-time in 2006. Exceptional people skills, BA in elementary education. She has taken several sales management courses at the local SBDC.

Mark Saul, Director of Administration: 43, started with CTM as a part-time bookkeeper in 2001, and has become full-time administrative and financial backbone of the company.

Management Team Gaps

At present we believe we have a good team for covering the main points of the business plan. The addition of Janice Carly was important as a way to cement our fundamental re-positioning and re-engineering.

At present, we are weakest in the area of technical capabilities to manage the database marketing programs and upgraded service and support, particularly with cross-platform networks. We also need to find a training manager.

Personnel Plan

The Personnel Plan reflects the need to bolster our capabilities to match our positioning. Our total headcount should increase to 22 this first year, and to 30 by the third year. Detailed monthly projections are available upon request.

	2012	2013	2014
Production			
Manager	$ 17,280	$ 18,720	$ 20,160
Assistant	$ 51,840	$ 57,600	$ 57,600
Technical	$ 18,000	$ 50,400	$ 50,400
Technical	$ 18,000	$ 50,400	$ 50,400
Technical	$ 34,560	$ 39,600	$ 39,600
Fulfillment	$ 34,560	$ 43,200	$ 86,400
Fulfillment	$ 25,920	$ 31,680	$ 72,000
Other		$ 0	$ 0
Subtotal	**$ 200,160**	**$ 291,600**	**$ 376,560**
Sales and marketing			
Manager	$ 103,680	$ 109,440	$ 115,200
Technical sales	$ 86,400	$ 90,720	$ 122,400
Technical sales	$ 65,520	$ 66,240	$ 66,240
Salesperson	$ 58,320	$ 79,200	$ 92,160
Salesperson	$ 58,320	$ 72,000	$ 79,200
Salesperson	$ 48,240	$ 48,960	$ 64,800
Salesperson	$ 44,640	$ 54,720	$ 64,800
Salesperson	$ 30,240	$ 43,200	$ 47,520
Salesperson	$ 0	$ 43,200	$ 47,520
Other	$ 0		$ 0
Subtotal	**$ 495,360**	**$ 607,680**	**$ 699,840**
Administration			
President	$ 95,040	$ 99,360	$ 136,800
Finance	$ 40,320	$ 41,760	$ 43,200
Admin assistant	$ 34,560	$ 37,440	$ 40,320
Bookkeeping	$ 25,920	$ 36,000	$ 43,200
Clerical	$ 17,280	$ 21,600	$ 25,920
Clerical	$ 10,080	$ 21,600	$ 25,920
Clerical	$ 0	$ 0	$ 21,600
Other	$ 0	$ 0	$ 0
Subtotal	**$ 223,200**	**$ 257,760**	**$ 336,960**
Other			
Programming	$ 51,840	$ 57,600	$ 63,360
Other technical	$ 0	$ 43,200	$ 47,520
Other	$ 0	$ 0	$ 0
Subtotal	**$ 51,840**	**$ 100,800**	**$ 110,880**
Total headcount	**22**	**25**	**30**
Total payroll	$ 970,560	$1,257,840	$1,524,240
Payroll burden	$ 155,290	$ 201,254	$ 243,878
Total payroll expenditures	**$1,125,850**	**$1,459,094**	**$1,768,118**

Other Management Considerations

Our attorney, Dean Radcliff, is also a co-founder. He invested significantly in the company over a period of time during the early 2000s. He remains a good friend of Eugene and has been a steady source of excellent legal and business advice.

Steve Holcomb, public relations consultant, is also a co-founder and co-owner. Like Radcliff, he invested in the early stages and remains a trusted confidant and vendor of public relations and advertising services.

FINANCIAL PLAN

The most important element in the financial plan is the critical need for improving several of the key factors that impact cash flow:

- We must at any cost stop the slide in inventory turnover and develop better inventory management to bring the turnover back up to 8 turns by the third year. This should also be a function of the shift in focus toward service revenues.

- We must also bring the gross margin back up to 25%. This too is related to improving the mix between hardware and service revenues, because the service revenues offer much better margins.

- We plan to borrow another $216,000 long-term this year. The amount seems in line with the balance sheet capabilities.

A projected Profit and Loss Statement and Balance Sheet follow. Additional financial statements, including projected cash flow, are available upon request.

Projected Profit and Loss

The most important assumption in the Projected Profit and Loss statement is the gross margin, which is supposed to increase to 25% in 2011 and exceed 45 percent in 2012. This is up from barely 21% in 2010. The increase in gross margin is based on changing our sales mix, and it is critical.

Month-by-month assumptions for profit and loss are available upon request.

	2012	2013	2014
Sales	$8,545,126	$9,705,410	$11,176,917
Direct cost of sales	$4,424,769	$5,111,905	$ 5,961,347
Production payroll	$ 200,160	$ 291,600	$ 376,560
Other	$ 8,640	$ 9,504	$ 10,454
Total cost of sales	**$4,633,569**	**$5,413,009**	**$ 6,348,361**
Gross margin	$3,911,557	$4,292,401	$ 4,828,556
Gross margin percent	45.78%	44.23%	43.20%
Operating expenses:			
Sales and marketing expenses			
Sales/marketing salaries	$ 495,360	$ 607,680	$ 699,840
Ads	$ 216,000	$ 456,096	$ 478,901
Catalog	$ 36,000	$ 27,416	$ 28,787
Mailing	$ 163,152	$ 0	$ 0
Promo	$ 23,040	$ 0	$ 0
Shows	$ 29,088	$ 0	$ 0
Literature	$ 10,080	$ 0	$ 0
PR	$ 1,440	$ 0	$ 0
Seminar	$ 44,640	$ 0	$ 0
Service	$ 14,760	$ 0	$ 0
Training	$ 86,400	$ 0	$ 0
Total sales and marketing expense	**$1,119,960**	**$1,091,192**	**$ 1,207,528**
Sales and marketing percent	13.11%	11.24%	10.80%
General & administrative expenses			
G&A salaries	$ 223,200	$ 257,760	$ 336,960
Leased equipment	$ 43,200	$ 45,360	$ 47,628
Utilities	$ 12,960	$ 13,608	$ 14,289
Insurance	$ 8,640	$ 9,072	$ 9,526
Rent	$ 120,960	$ 127,008	$ 133,358
Depreciation	$ 18,261	$ 19,174	$ 20,133
Payroll burden	$ 155,290	$ 201,254	$ 243,878
Other	$ 9,117	$ 9,573	$ 10,051
Total general and administrative expense	**$ 591,627**	**$ 682,809**	**$ 815,823**
General and administrative percent	6.92%	7.04%	7.30%
Other operating expenses			
Other salaries	$ 51,840	$ 100,800	$ 110,880
Contract/consultants	$ 17,280	$ 43,200	$ 43,200
Other	$ 4,320	$ 4,536	$ 4,764
Total other operating expenses	**$ 73,440**	**$ 148,536**	**$ 158,844**
Percent of sales	0.86%	1.53%	1.42%
Total operating expenses	**$1,785,027**	**$1,922,537**	**$ 2,182,195**
Profit before			
Interest and taxes	$2,126,530	$2,369,864	$ 2,646,361
Interest expense ST	$ 11,712	$ 8,640	$ 8,640
Interest expense IT	$ 32,465	$ 27,929	$ 22,823
Taxes incurred	$ 416,471	$ 466,659	$ 522,979
Net profit	**$1,665,883**	**$1,866,636**	**$ 2,091,920**
Net profit/sales	**19.50%**	**19.23%**	**18.72%**

Projected Balance Sheet

The Projected Balance Sheet is quite solid. We do not project any real trouble meeting our debt obligations—as long as we can achieve our specific objectives.

Short-term assets	Starting balances	2012	2013	2014
Cash	$ 79,822	$ 979,131	$1,983,573	$3,031,380
Accounts receivable	$ 568,954	$1,007,748	$1,226,339	$1,506,424
Inventory	$ 937,457	$ 960,307	$1,346,216	$1,578,838
Other short-term assets	$ 36,000	$ 36,000	$ 36,000	$ 36,000
Total short-term assets	**$1,622,233**	**$2,983,186**	**$4,592,128**	**$6,152,642**
Long-term assets				
Capital assets	$ 504,000	$ 936,000	$1,224,000	$1,800,000
Accumulated depreciation	$ 72,000	$ 90,261	$ 109,434	$ 129,567
Total long-term assets	**$ 432,000**	**$ 845,739**	**$1,114,566**	**$1,670,433**
Total assets	**$2,054,233**	**$3,828,925**	**$5,706,694**	**$7,823,075**
Debt and equity				
Accounts payable	$ 322,412	$ 505,682	$ 574,344	$ 661,425
Short-term notes	$ 129,600	$ 108,000	$ 108,000	$ 108,000
Other ST liabilities	$ 21,600	$ 21,600	$ 21,600	$ 21,600
Subtotal				
Short-term liabilities	$ 473,612	$ 635,282	$ 703,944	$ 791,025
Long-term liabilities	$ 410,201	$ 357,342	$ 299,809	$ 237,192
Total liabilities	**$ 883,813**	**$ 992,624**	**$1,003,753**	**$1,028,218**
Paid in capital	$ 720,000	$ 720,000	$ 720,000	$ 720,000
Retained earnings	$ 342,922	$ 450,420	$2,116,303	$3,982,939
Earnings	$ 107,499	$1,665,883	$1,866,636	$2,091,920
Total equity	**$1,170,420**	**$2,836,303**	**$4,702,939**	**$6,794,859**
Total debt and equity	**$2,054,233**	**$3,828,925**	**$5,706,694**	**$7,823,075**
Net worth	**$1,170,420**	**$2,836,303**	**$4,702,939**	**$6,794,859**

Concierge Service
Business Errands

12390 E. Big Beaver Rd.
Troy, MI 48084

Heidi Denler

Business Errands is a full-service concierge that will serve the corporate market in Troy, Michigan, by running errands that will allow clients to take care of business. Major objectives include at least 25 clients within the first year, which will increase 20 percent annually based on efficient, friendly, competent service; referrals; an Internet presence; and personal contact with prospective clients.

COMPANY SUMMARY

Business Errands is located in Troy, Michigan, a suburb of Detroit that has a proliferation of all size offices comprising a wide variety of local and national corporations and businesses. The intent of Business Errands is to offer a service to business owners and office managers that will allow them to run their business rather than run errands. Services will include all types of errands, including airport pickup/drop off, event planning, making copies, and grocery shopping. The sky is the limit for the services provided, depending on the customer's imagination and the lawfulness of the request.

Profitability should be achieved within the first month and show steady growth in the months to come. Company owner, Yvonne Smith, plans to hired three (3) employees for the opening of the business, followed by hiring of qualified, high quality employees as required by growth of the business. Employees will receive intensive training that will continue as the business grows.

MANAGEMENT SUMMARY

The owner of Business Errands is expanding her current company, Mommy's Little Helper (MLH), which provides an errand service for harried parents and caregivers. Yvonne Smith decided to branch out and leave her other company in the hands of an extremely able manager as she devotes her time and energy to the corporate world, which will offer better working hours and free time to spend with her own family. Smith has a track record of hiring efficient, hard-working, dependable employees, and she is confident that she will add suitable staff for Business Errands while maintaining MLH. Her MBA will stand her in good stead as she gets Business Errands up and running and continuing to oversee MLH. Her experience with MLH has given Smith the practical knowledge required to expand and develop a high-quality concierge service for the corporate world, particularly the understanding that employees are a key component to the development of a successful business.

Legal matters will be handled by the attorney who has been working with Smith at MLH. She is a general practice attorney who is familiar with legal affairs related to small businesses. Smith will continue to work with the same CPA who keeps MLH's books.

MISSION STATEMENT

The mission of Business Errands is to serve the local corporate world by taking care of the business of providing legitimate services that keep the business running.

VISION STATEMENT

Business Errands will build a local corporate base that is served cheerfully and efficiently by a team of employees running the errands that are necessary to keep businesses running smoothly.

VALUES STATEMENT

Customer service is the number one priority of Business Errands. To that end, Yvonne Smith and her employees are dedicated to serving local corporate owners and managers efficiently and cheerfully. Employees will be highly trained to not only meet, but also exceed client expectations. Employees will be empowered to take pride in their service to the clients.

BUSINESS PHILOSOPHY

Business Errands will provide friendly, efficient service to enhance customer reaction and satisfaction.

GOALS AND OBJECTIVES

Objectives will include exceeding client expectations, building a customer base through efficient, high-quality service, and profitability within the first month of operations. Growth at a rate of at least 20 percent per year is anticipated.

Yvonne plans to build her customer base through efficient, high-quality service. Promotion and advertising will be through a company website, letters to prospective clients explaining Business Errands' services, and personal calls and visits to follow up with corporate owners and managers. The first local efforts will be concentrated in the Troy, Michigan, suburb of Detroit, followed by expansion in neighboring suburbs that have high concentrations of offices.

ORGANIZATION STRUCTURE

Yvonne Smith will remain sole proprietor of Business Errands. She acknowledges that because some expenses will be shared with MLH, minimal start-up expenses will be incurred. Hiring will follow the same procedures Smith uses for MLH, with similar qualifications required for employees, including being cheerful, having a positive outlook, having the ability to adjust to adverse requests and changes, and providing high-quality, efficient service to all legitimate requests made by clients.

Smith will have full control and final say over decisions that have to be made for Business Errands. She will seek the input of the managers she has hand selected for both MLH and Business Errands as part of their training for further expansion of the companies.

ADVERTISING AND PROMOTION

Promotion and advertising will be through a company website, letters to prospective clients explaining Business Errands' services, and personal calls and visits to follow up with corporate owners and managers. Initially, efforts will be concentrated in the Troy, Michigan, suburb of Detroit, which will be followed by contact with prospective clients in neighboring communities with high concentrations of offices and businesses. In addition, advertisements will be placed in local newspapers and magazines directed at business owners and office managers.

Press releases announcing Business Errands' services will be sent to all local print, radio, and television in the Metropolitan Detroit area, particularly those that serve Troy. Personal phone and e-mail follow-up will be made to build a relationship with area media personalities, who have the potential to result in free marketing and promotion.

CUSTOMER BASE

The primary customer base for Business Errands will be small corporate and business owners and office managers for large corporations. There are nearly 15,000 companies in Troy, Michigan, according to Manta. These range from Tae Kwon Do dojos to home health care to IT to individual storefronts, as well as insurance and financial institutions. Yvonne Smith plans to expand her customer base with personal contact and follow-up on references from existing customers. In addition, she will attend local business organization meetings to introduce her services to business owners.

Corporate clients will be encouraged to use Business Errands' services for not only office needs, but also for individual employee needs as an employment perk that will allow them more free time after business hours, and will eliminate the need for employees to take longer lunch hours or leave work early to run personal errands. It provides a win-win situation for the business owner or manager, who will benefit from less employee down time, and for the employee, who will benefit with more free time.

There is currently one other corporate concierge service in Southfield, Michigan, which will not impact Business Errands' target market.

PRODUCTS AND SERVICES

The range of services provided by Business Errands will be limited only by the legality of the request. The basic assumption is that the fundamental needs of clients will be met during normal business hours when the business owner or office manager need typical office errands run and would prefer employees to be working instead of running errands. Companies recognize that as more demands are placed on individuals outside the office, those employees have become creative in the ways they accomplish errands on company time. Therefore, providing employees with the perk of concierge service, companies regain productive work time.

LOCATION

Owner Yvonne Smith conducted simple market research in the fall of 2011 that found the Troy, Michigan, suburb of Detroit, to have the potential for initial success as well as growth. In addition, Yvonne has many clients for MLH in the Troy area, some of whom own small businesses and have already begun to use Business Errands' services for those businesses.

OFFICE DESIGN AND EQUIPMENT

Smith will continue to use her storefront office that serves as the base for MLH as she develops Business Errands. The office computer will require updated software to maintain records for both companies. These records will include client data, a client request database, payroll, employee benefits, taxes, and business expenses, including utilities, mortgage, banking, and insurance.

Equipment required will be additional vans and cars for the fleet already leased for MLH. Yvonne Smith has a working relationship with Will McCartney at the local Ford dealership for this fleet lease and maintenance of company cars. Each car will have the company logo, phone number, and web site URL on the side doors and back as additional advertising.

FINANCIAL

Business Errands' minimal start up costs will include adding two to four cars/vans to the fleet currently used by MLH, legal fees, web site creation, advertising, and stationary (letterhead, envelopes, business cards), taxes, payroll, payroll taxes, advertising, and liability insurance. Other start up costs will include fees to register the Business Errands name with government authorities. In addition, Business Errands will share overhead costs of rent/mortgage payments, property insurance, telephone and utilities, and an alarm system with MLH.

At the current time, Yvonne Smith does not plan to incorporate Business Errands or MLH, but will review that decision every quarter. The primary advantage to incorporating is to control the liability factor, which will be considered regularly in comparison to the costs involved. The insurance policy Smith has for MLH will be supplemented to cover Business Errands and she has been assured that this will be enough to cover any liability.

Clients will be billed an hourly rate and sent an invoice once a month.

PROFESSIONAL AND ADVISORY SUPPORT

Yvonne Smith has an established relationship with a corporate attorney who is well-versed in small business practices and law in the state of Michigan. He bills on a sliding scale basis, charging minimal fees.

Smith will continue to work with Jay Danlon and the Gill Agency to provide optimal coverage for life, health, and dental insurance and retirement savings. Mr. Danlon will work with a local property-casualty agency to cover other insurance, including liability and auto for the fleet. All employees will be offered low cost benefits at their own expense.

Smith has an established relationship with Flagstar Bank and has secured a line of credit to cover start-up costs.

BUSINESS AND GROWTH STRATEGY

Yvonne Smith will aggressively seek contracts with corporate office managers as well as business owners through the company web site, personal follow up and contact, and high-quality service. The target market will include companies that need Business Errands' service during business hours to perform errands and tasks that will allow employees to attend to business rather than extend lunch hours or leave early to attend to those errands themselves. Clients will be billed monthly.

Human capital in the form of high-quality employees is a key component for the success of Business Errands. Employees will be trained and mentored to serve clients. Initially, clients will be served by Yvonne Smith and employees of MLH as their schedules allow. Hiring will take place slowly and carefully, with new employees being hired on a probationary basis for one month to assess the quality and efficiency of their service to clients and to allow for a training period with a mentor (either Yvonne Smith or a current MLH employee).

The employee manual from MLH will be adapted for Business Errands. It covers such topics as employee benefits, ways to handle clients of all kinds, ways to promote the company, and contact information for the main office and mentors.

COMPETITION

The concierge business for corporate offices and small businesses in Troy, Michigan, and the surrounding suburbs of Detroit is minimal. Only one other such business is in operation in Southfield, several miles away, and that service is not expected to compete for clients in Troy. Some large companies have their own in-house concierge service for their employees, but economies of scale and efficiencies of high-quality employees of Business Errands will allow those companies to save money by using Business Errands.

Business Errands will discern and provide the shared and individual needs of companies in Troy, Michigan. The company will set itself apart from any future competition with high-quality employees and service, flexibility, monthly billing, efficiency, and economies of scale.

WEBSITE

A significant portion of promotion and advertising will be developed via Business Errands' website, which will describe the variety of services available to clients, as well as contact information. A form will be available for requests for estimates and additional information. One page of the website will feature references and reviews.

CONCLUSION

Business Errands will provide services to corporate office managers and business owners who understand that an outside party performing tasks for employees and running office errands is a cost saving measure. It is also a perk for employees who will be able to spend more time working for the company, which benefits the company itself.

Dance Studio

New Baltimore Dance Academy

12345 Washington Street
New Baltimore, MI 48047

Zuzu Enterprises

Elizabeth Nowak is opening a dance studio in her hometown of New Baltimore, Michigan. The city has grown significantly in recent years, and the population growth among college-educated parents with young children will provide a more than adequate market to support the new venture.

EXECUTIVE SUMMARY

Elizabeth Nowak is opening a dance studio in her hometown of New Baltimore, Michigan. The city has grown significantly in recent years, and the population growth among college-educated parents with young children will provide a more than adequate market to support the new venture.

FACILITY

The studio is located at 12345 Washington Street in New Baltimore, Michigan. The facility has 2,300 square feet divided among two separate studios, small office, unisex bathroom, locker room, storage space, and a waiting room for parents. The waiting room features comfortable seating, flat-screen television, and free Wi-Fi along with a snack machine, beverage machine, and water cooler.

All rooms have been freshly painted and decorated. The dance studios feature a professional-grade floating dance floor, two mirrored walls, a ballet barre, and a corner cabinet that houses a state-of-the-art sound system and other supplies.

A 3-year rental agreement has been signed for the facility. Committing to a multi-year lease enabled us to negotiate and lock in a very reasonable monthly rental rate of $5 per square foot, or $958/month. Other comparable spaces ranged from $6-$12 per square foot.

STAFF

Owner/Instructor

Elizabeth Nowak began her dance career at age 2. She quickly determined that she loved dancing above all other activities and devoted much of her childhood to taking every dance class available and learning all the various dancing styles and techniques. She danced competitively and studied dance at Eastern

Michigan University. She decided to open her own studio in her hometown so that she could pass along her love and passion for dance to the children of her beloved community.

Instructors

Katie Reid

Katie Reid has 25 years of dance experience. She started dancing when she was only 3 years old at her aunt's dance studio in Emmett, Michigan. She participated in competitive dance and won countless first place and platinum awards. She attended Macomb County Community College, earning a degree in early childhood education. She would like to combine her love of children and her love of dance to instruct our youngest dancers.

Becky Bergeon

Becky Bergeon has nearly 15 years dance experience, focusing mainly on ballet and pointe. She attended the Geiger Ballet Academy and has performed with the Michigan Classic Ballet Company. She is currently attending Oakland University and is available to teach classes in the evenings and weekends.

Office Staff

Genevieve Simmons is a childhood friend of Elizabeth. She was formerly an office manager for a local women's health clinic but became a stay-at-home mom with the birth of her daughter 4 years ago. She has agreed to staff the office, process registrations and payments, etc., in exchange for free unlimited classes for her daughter. She will also receive photo packages and costumes at cost.

CLASS DESCRIPTIONS

The instructors have a wide variety of dance experience and expertise, so they are able to provide instruction on all dance styles. Specifically, the following classes will be offered:

- Ballet
- Tap
- Jazz
- Hip Hop
- Lyrical
- Poms/Acro
- Musical theater
- Pointe
- Clogging

Other classes may be offered in the future as demand warrants, including Ballroom, Modern, Hawaiian, Salsa, and Production.

Class Levels

Each class will be offered several times a week for each of these different age categories:

- Tot: ages 2-4
- Junior: ages 5-7
- Beginning: ages 7-9
- Intermediate: ages 10-14

- Advanced: ages 12 and up

- Adult

Students with advanced skills may be placed into a class one level higher than their appropriate age category.

SCHEDULE—FALL

	Monday		Tuesday		Wednesday		Thursday		Friday		Saturday	
	Studio A	Studio B	Studio A	Studio B	Studio A	Studio B	Studio A	Studio B	Studio A	Studio B	Studio A	Studio B
09:00											Tot Jazz	Jr. Tap
10:00							Tot Ballet				Tot Poms	Jr. Jazz
10:30							Tot Tap				Tot Tap	Jr. Ballet
11:00							Tot Jazz				Tot Ballet	Beg. Tap
11:30							Tot Poms				Beg. Ballet	Beg. Jazz
03:00	Jr. Jazz	Beginning Tap	Pointe	Int. Lyrical	Beg. Hip Hop	Adv. Jazz	Jr. Lyrical	Int. Hip Hop				
04:00	Jr. Poms	Beginning Ballet	Solo	Int. Jazz	Adv. Tap	Adv. Poms	Jr. Tap	Int. Ballet				
05:00	Jr. Ballet	Beginning Jazz	Pointe	Int. Poms	Adv. Hip Hop	Adv. Ballet	Beginning Hip Hop	Adv. Hip Hop				
06:00	Jr. Theater	Beginning Lyrical	Duo/Trio	Int. Theater	Adv. Lyrical	Adv. Theater	Beginning Theater	Adv. Tap				
07:00	Jr. Hip Hop	Beginning Poms	Solo	Int. Tap	Solo	Clogging	Duo/Trio	Adv. Lyrical				
08:00	Adult Jazz	Adult Tap	Duo/Trio	Solo	Adult Hip Hop	Adult Ballet	Solo	Duo/Trio				
09:00												

SCHEDULE—SUMMER

	Monday		Tuesday		Wednesday		Thursday		Friday		Saturday	
	Studio A	Studio B	Studio A	Studio B	Studio A	Studio B	Studio A	Studio B	Studio A	Studio B	Studio A	Studio B
09:00							Tot Ballet	Beginning Tap	Beginning Jazz	Tot Jazz		
10:00							Tot Tap	Beginning Ballet	Beg. Hip Hop	Tot Poms		
11:00							Int. Lyrical	Jr. Jazz	Beginning Poms	Int. Poms		
12:00							Int. Jazz	Jr. Poms	Jr. Tap	Int. Hip Hop		
01:00							Int. Ballet	Jr. Ballet	Jr. Hip Hop	Adv. Lyrical		
02:00							Int. Tap	Adv. Ballet	Jr. Lyrical	Adv. Tap		
03:00							Adv. Hip Hop	Adv. Jazz	Adv. Jazz			
04:00												
05:00												
06:00												
07:00												
08:00												
09:00												

TARGET MARKET

The population of New Baltimore has increased by more than 60% since 2000; the number of households with children has risen nearly 80% during this same time period. A majority of residents (67%) have some college or hold college degrees and the median household income is nearly $84,000 a year.

COMPETITION

There is only one other dance studio in the city of New Baltimore. There are at least 4 other studios within a 25 mile radius, but these are not direct competitors because of the distance. Parents of young children are interested in the social aspects of class, i.e. meeting other children and parents, making friends, etc., in addition to the actual instruction. Parents of school-age children are often shuffling many kids between several different activities; having the activities close to home eases the commuting time and kids are more likely to be in classes with their friends and thus more likely to be able to share rides when necessary.

Strengths:

- Experienced and approachable staff
- Renovated facility
- Local, convenient location
- 2,300 square feet of professional-grade floating dance floor
- Competitive prices
- Family and multiple class discounts
- Smaller class sizes
- Family atmosphere
- Age appropriate and affordable costumes
- Age appropriate music and movements
- Holiday program
- End-of-year recital

Weaknesses:

- New business—we have to prove ourselves

MARKETING AND ADVERTISING

Website/Social Media

A website will be created and advertised to do the following: profile the business, provide contact information, post schedules, calendars, and registration forms, and add customer notifications of upcoming events, deadlines, unexpected closures, and the like. We will also utilize social media including Facebook, Twitter, and Foursquare.

Flyers

Flyers advertising our classes, schedule, and instructors will be created using Microsoft Publisher and printed on glossy paper. Approximately 1,000 flyers will be printed and distributed to the following locations:

- Daycare center
- Library
- Schools and preschools
- City recreation department

Sign

A portable sign will be placed in front of the building publicizing registration and featured classes. A significant amount of traffic passes by the building on a daily basis, making this type of advertising extremely effective.

Word-of-Mouth

Word-of-mouth advertising will be a very important to our business. In a small community, word travels fast among residents about both positive and negative experiences. It is essential that all customers be treated respectfully and great pains are made to insure all customers are completely satisfied with their experience. Children, especially, should be cared for; if they have a fun, rewarding learning experience, they will likely have a lifelong love of dance. Bad experiences may damage their self-esteem and turn them off dance for good.

FINANCIAL INFORMATION

Registration Fees

Each student will be charged a registration fee in the amount of $10 per session (Fall, Winter, and Summer), regardless of the number of classes for which they sign up.

Class Fees

		Each additional class	Student max (6 classes)	Family max (10 classes)
30-minute class	$33/month	$28	$150/month	$250/month
45-minute class	$40/month	$30	$175/month	$275/month
60-minute class	$43/month	$33	$200/month	$300/month
Solo lesson	$65/month			
Duo/Trio lesson	$35/month			

Other Sources of Income

Apparel/Shoes

The studio's official colors are electric blue and lime green. Studio sweatshirts, warm-up jackets, t-shirts, drawstring bags, bottle cap necklaces, and automobile decals will be sold to all dancers and their families. This merchandise will be marked up 20% from the actual cost (rather than the standard 50-100%) to keep items reasonable and encourage families to purchase them. All of these items serve as walking advertisements for the business.

An order form will be sent home in late September/early October with delivery of items in late October/ early November, perfect for holiday gift-giving. A small assortment of items in various sizes will be ordered at this time and kept on hand for future sales.

Appropriate dance apparel and shoes will also be available for purchase. Again, a large order will be placed at the start of classes in September, and a small assortment of items will be kept on hand for customers to purchase as the session continues.

Photos

Class and individual photos will be done in April. A local studio has agreed to come in to the studio on a predetermined Saturday and Sunday to photograph every class and those individuals/family members who would like to have custom photos taken.

Picture delivery will be the weekend before Mother's Day, perfect for gift-giving to Mothers and Grandmothers.

A percentage of all photo sales will be earned by the studio, with a percentage increasing at specific sales targets; the minimum guaranteed is $500.

Costumes

All students participating in the holiday show and spring recital will be required to purchase costumes. Costumes will be chosen to coordinate with the theme of the song and choreography. They will be purchased through various online dance retailers and costume prices will be marked up an average of 50% above the wholesale or bulk prices.

Makeup and hair accessories will also be purchased and marked up an average of 50%.

Holiday Show
The holiday show will take place in mid-December. This show is smaller than the spring recital and is meant to celebrate the season. Tickets will cost $5 apiece and many tickets will be given away free of charge to local retirement communities and other charitable causes.

Spring Recital
The spring recital will take place in late May or early June. Tickets will be sold for $10 apiece, with approximately 450 available seats. Other sources of income at the spring recital include the following:

- Program Ads and Family Messages

- Flowers

- Snacks

Practice CDs
Students wishing to purchase practice CDs will be able to do so. A licensing fee of $1.29 per song is included in this cost, as well as the physical CD itself. The song will be the same version as the dance routine and will be cut as needed. The cost to students is $5.00 per CD.

Locker Rentals
The locker room features 200 lockers and bench seating. This space is especially useful for students who take multiple classes and those who require a place to change into their dance apparel before class. Students may rent lockers on a monthly basis and include the cost in their monthly class fees payment.

YEAR-ONE PROJECTED INCOME

Item	Cost
Registration fees	$ 1,150
Class fees	$64,900
Studio apparel	$ 1,500
Dance apparel/shoes	$ 500
Photos	$ 500
Costumes	$ 2,250
Holiday show tickets	$ 1,500
Spring recital tickets	$ 4,500
Program ads and family messages	$ 2,000
Flowers	$ 300
Snacks (recitals and machines)	$ 1,000
Practice CDs	$ 100
Locker rentals	$ 1,000
Total Y1 income	**$81,200**

YEAR-ONE INCOME STATEMENT

Total Y1 income	**$81,200**
Start up costs	($ 8,616)
Yearly costs	($72,580)
Income	**$ 4**

COSTS

Start-up Costs

Item	Cost
Legal fees	$ 500
Rental deposit	$1,916
Utility activation	$ 200
Advertising	$1,000
Building improvements	$5,000
Total start up costs	**$8,616**

Monthly Costs

Item	Cost
Rent	$ 958
Utilities	$ 400
Salaries	$ 5,700
Advertising	$ 100
Phone service	$ 100
Total monthly costs	**$ 7,258**
Total yearly costs	**$72,580**

GROWTH PLAN

Year One: 40 summer students, 75 fall students

Year Two: 60 summer students; 150 fall students

Year Three: 80 summer students; 225 fall students. Begin competitive dance classes and enter at least 3 competitions in the spring.

Year Four: 100 summer students; 300 fall students. Expand competitive dance options.

Appendix A–Registration Form

Dancer's Name: _____

Parent Name: _____ Phone # _____

Dancer's D.O.B.____-____-_____ Age _____ Last Grade Completed_____

Address _____ City _____ Zip _____

Name of Class _____ Day/Time _____ Price _____

_____

_____

_____

_____

Non-Refundable Registration Fee	$10.00
Total Amount Due	$_____
Total monthly amount for dance year	$_____

I agree to pay all incidental expenses as incurred by this student which include, but are not limited to, tuition for all related classes, costumes, dancewear, tickets, optional dance conventions, competitions and special events, etc. Please note that any late payment of tuition, fees and any other expenses are subject to a finance charge. The undersigned recognizes that injuries sometimes occur in connection with this activity and hereby exonerates JLP's Leap of Faith Dance Studio, L.L.C., for any liabilities in connection therewith.

Signature:_____ Date:____-____-_____

Comments:_____

_____

_____

- -

Payment Method
( ) Cash ( ) Check—Check # _____   Total Amount Paid $_____

Digital Asset Management Consultant

Stephen Jacobson LLC

7829 Clybourn Ave.
Elgin, IL 60123

Paul Greenland

Stephen Jacobson LLC is an independent digital asset management consulting practice specializing in smaller and medium-sized businesses.

EXECUTIVE SUMMARY

Business Overview

In stark contrast to past decades, when individuals and businesses mainly relied on paper documents, videotapes, and photographic film for communications and correspondence, by 2012 the advent of digital technology had resulted in massive collections of "digital goods," or digital assets. Examples include electronic documents, as well as digital photographs and video files. As these types of media have become more commonplace, it has become necessary to develop effective organization, storage, search, and retrieval strategies. Generally, this process is known as digital asset management.

Stephen Jacobson has nearly a decade of experience in the area of digital asset management. After earning an undergraduate computer science degree from Brookstone College, he earned a Master's in Library and Information Science from Central Colorado University. He began his career as an assistant archivist at the Institute for International Studies in San Francisco and later became director of digital asset management for Alexandria Worldwide Publishing. Jacobson then joined Orange Hill Technologies, a leading digital asset management vendor, where he applied his knowledge to help the company interface with customers and end-users and develop new iterations of its products.

Jacobson established a part-time consulting practice in 2011. Initial success has resulted in the decision to operate the consulting practice on a full-time basis beginning in 2013. Utilizing his knowledge and experience, Jacobson will assist small- and medium-sized organizations to develop an effective digital asset management strategy. This process will involve guiding clients through a discovery and planning process. Jacobson will then help clients execute their strategy, which may involve implementing a related technology solution from one of the many vendors that offer digital asset management systems.

MARKET ANALYSIS

In situations where a limited number of digital assets must be managed, or the organization scheme is relatively straightforward, it is possible to develop a custom solution or implement a third-party solution in-house. This especially is true in the case of larger organizations with a robust information technology staff. Alternatively, smaller and medium-sized organizations may require the guidance and expertise of an experienced consultant, such as Stephen Jacobson.

With this in mind, Jacobson will concentrate his efforts on organizations with between 250 and 500 employees. Because certain types of organizations are more likely to utilize digital asset management systems than others, Jacobson has defined his primary market as advertising agencies, colleges/universities, and computer services providers. Utilizing market data from Greenlight Research Associates, Jacobson's primary market breaks down as follows:

- Advertising Agencies (646 prospects)

- Colleges & Universities (205 prospects)

- Computer Services Providers (757 prospects)

In addition, Jacobson has defined a secondary market that includes the following:

- Entertainment & Recreation Services Providers (1,253 prospects)

- Professional Services Providers (3,765 prospects)

When marketing services to prospects, Jacobson will target his approach to individuals in the following professional positions:

- Brand Managers

- Graphic Designers

- Instructors/Professors

- IT Professionals

- Librarians

- Marketing Specialists

- Photographers

- Research Specialists

- Salespeople

- Videographers

INDUSTRY ANALYSIS

According to a report from Proxvision Media LLC, digital asset management industry revenues exceeded $300 million in 2007 and were expected to surpass $1 billion by 2011. The report indicated that, on an annual basis, organizations spend about $8,200 per employee on file management activities. Within the creative industry specifically, the implementation of digital asset management solutions was able to decrease unsuccessful searches from 35 percent to less than 5 percent. During the late 2000s, North America accounted for more than 70 percent of industry revenues. Western Europe represented around 17 percent, followed by the Asia Pacific region at 7.5 percent.

According to the U.S. Department of Labor's *Occupational Outlook Handbook,* nearly 719,000 management consultants were employed in 2010. Employment was expected to increase at an above average pace through 2020. Specifically, this profession was forecast to grow at a rate of 22 percent, resulting in the addition of more than 157,000 additional management consultants. Driving growth was the need for organizations to control costs and improve efficiency, which are among the main benefits of digital asset management technology.

There are a number of professional organizations that pertain to digital asset management consulting. Generally, consultants in this field may find membership in the American Society for Training and Development and the Association of Management Consulting Firms to be especially useful. In addition, the American Society for Indexing (ASI) is useful for those involved in taxonomy and indexing. ASI helps to connect its members with potential clients, and provides benefits such as a quarterly newsletter.

PERSONNEL

Stephen Jacobson

A native of Chicago, Stephen Jacobson earned an undergraduate computer science degree from Brookstone College, followed by a Master's in Library and Information Science from Central Colorado University. He began his career as an assistant archivist at the Institute for International Studies in San Francisco. There, he gained significant practical knowledge regarding digital asset management and taxonomy. In addition, he was part of the team that oversaw the implementation of a new digital asset management system.

After working at the institute for seven years, Jacobson then transitioned to the electronic publishing field when he became director of digital asset management for Alexandria Worldwide Publishing. There, he was given responsibility for choosing a new digital asset management vendor and overseeing the implementation of a new technology platform. Ultimately, Jacobson's next career move took him to Orange Hill Technologies, a leading digital asset management vendor, where he applied his knowledge to help the company interface with customers and end-users and develop new iterations of its products.

In addition to his formal library science education, Jacobson will assist his consulting clients by sharing the knowledge he has gained as a digital asset management system user and developer.

Professional & Advisory Support

Jacobson has established a business banking account with North Shore Financial, as well as a merchant account for accepting credit card payments. Accounting and tax advisory services will be provided by Larson & Brooks LLC. In the event that legal counsel is needed, Schelling Legal Partners LLP, which specializes in business law, has been identified as an appropriate resource.

GROWTH STRATEGY

Although the economic climate was improving in 2012, market conditions remained challenging. With this in mind, Stephen Jacobson has committed to a conservative growth strategy when he launches his new consulting practice in 2013.

During his first year of business, Jacobson's goal is to average 25 hours of billable consulting time per week. He expects to increase this target to 30 weekly hours of billable consulting time during year two, and 35 hours during year three. Jacobson recognizes that he will need to devote additional (non-billable) administrative time to the consulting practice. This will be necessary for aspects such as project estimating, recordkeeping, invoicing, prospecting, etc.

SERVICES

Because digital asset management is highly specialized, implementing strategies and solutions can be very difficult for organizations with no experience.

Successful implementations require success on a number of fronts, including involving the right people, establishing effective processes, and finally, choosing a technology solution that meets the unique needs of an organization and its staff. A failure in any one of these areas will result in wasted time and financial resources, leaving the organization with a system that is not used.

By sharing his knowledge and expertise, Stephen Jacobson will help organizations ensure that all of the appropriate bases are covered. Better still, because he has been through the implementation process many times, he will help his clients avoid costly and time-consuming mistakes, thereby enabling them to implement the very best solution as quickly as possible.

Generally speaking, Jacobson will divide his consulting services into one of several categories:

Discovery: This phase will include a detailed study of a customer's situation and operations. Specific types of digital assets will be identified, along with the customer's existing method of organization and utilization. Examples of specific digital assets that customers need to manage include:

- Audio Files
- Product Images
- Illustrations
- Presentations
- Word Processing Documents
- CAD Drawings
- Database Files
- Logos
- Digital Signatures
- Spreadsheets

Strategic Planning: Using information gathered during the discovery phase, Jacobson will work with his client to establish a strategic plan that includes budgetary information, specific objectives, recommended tactics, and project milestones that name responsible individuals and include completion dates. When appropriate, this phase also will involve the selection of a digital asset management vendor.

During this phase, Jacobson also will advise clients on the development of specific taxonomies or organization/classification schemes for their specific assets. In addition, consultations will focus on the information associated with specific assets. This type of information is technically known as metadata. Examples of searchable attributes include everything from file names and keywords to specific descriptive "tags" that a user assigns to particular assets, thereby making them easy to search for.

Implementation: This phase will involve implementation of the digital asset management solution of choice. Jacobson will serve as the liaison between a customer's end-users and the solution developer or vendor. In addition, he will provide customer training sessions and tutorials to help clients configure and optimize solutions.

MARKETING & SALES

In order to promote his consulting services, Stephen Jacobson has developed a marketing plan that involves the following primary tactics:

- Business cards that include contact information, including Jacobson's Twitter handle, LinkedIn address, Web site, and e-mail address.
- Printed collateral describing Jacobson's consulting philosophy, as well as the services he offers. This will be used as a leave-behind following sales calls, and also for direct mail purposes.

- A Web site with complete details about Stephen Jacobson's practice and services offered.

- A social media strategy involving Twitter and LinkedIn, in order to position Jacobson as a thought leader within the digital asset management industry.

- A blog, through which Jacobson will provide observations regarding various business issues and industry trends.

- A monthly e-mail newsletter for target prospects that provides case studies, tips, and insight from experiences with past digital asset management projects.

- Direct mailings to key prospects referenced in the Marketing section of this plan (detailed list available upon request).

- A media relations strategy that involves the submission of case studies/success stories to appropriate business and trade magazines.

- Presentations and networking at industry conferences. One example is Welcome to The Art and Practice of Managing Digital Media—2012, a digital asset management conference hosted by Henry Stewart Events that is attended by many leading industry players.

OPERATIONS

Stephen Jacobson will operate his consulting practice from an existing home office in suburban Chicago. This will enable him to keep overhead low. He already is equipped with a laptop computer, as well as a smartphone, giving him the ability to remain in contact with prospects and customers from any location at any time. When long-distance business travel is required, Johnson's home is located near O'Hare Airport in Chicago.

Jacobson will need to make several capital purchases in order to operate his consulting practice, including a portable projector for presentations, as well as a tablet computer and a digital audio recorder.

Fees

New independent consultants sometimes enter their practice with an inadequate fee structure. By not charging enough (in an effort to out-price gain new clients quickly), problems can occur down the road when fee increases become necessary with existing customers. Because many clients are more comfortable working with new consultants on an hourly basis, Jacobson has established an hourly rate structure. He will, however, handle jobs on a project-based rate when necessary.

According to data from Sharp Point Research, entry-level management consultants often charge as much as $175 per hour for their services. Fees generally are higher in coastal regions, and lower in the central states. With this in mind, Jacobson will set his hourly consulting rate at $145. He will require clients to pay for a minimum, pre-determined/agreed-upon number of service hours.

FINANCIAL ANALYSIS

Following is Stephen Jacobson's projected balance sheet for 2013. Revenue calculations are conservative, and are based upon 25 hours of billable consulting time per week for the first year. Jacobson anticipates that his net income will increase significantly in 2014 and 2015 as he increases his average weekly billable consulting hours to 30 and 35 hours, respectively. In addition, additional income will result from speaking engagements.

2013 balance sheet

Revenue

Consulting	$142,000
Public speaking	$ 12,000
Total revenue	**$154,000**

Expenses

Salary	$104,500
Home office	$ 963
Insurance	$ 3,500
Office supplies	$ 627
Equipment	$ 6,850
Marketing & advertising	$ 7,500
Telecommunications & internet	$ 1,650
Professional development	$ 3,750
Travel & entertainment	$ 16,803
Subscriptions & dues	$ 1,500
Miscellaneous	$ 550
Total expenses	**$148,192**
Net income	**$ 5,808**

Event Planning Company
Unforgettable Event Partners LLC

25 Brick St.
Stonebridge, KY 40555

Paul Greenland

Unforgettable Event Partners LLC is an event planning business.

EXECUTIVE SUMMARY

Business Overview

Unforgettable Event Partners LLC is an event planning business. Relying upon its partners' decades of collective experience, the business is capable of managing a wide range of events. Generally speaking, Unforgettable Event Partners tends to handle events in three broad categories. These include life celebrations such as weddings, anniversary celebrations, reunions, and graduation parties; group events, such as charity balls, fundraisers, and holiday parties; and business/corporate events, such as seminars, trade shows, and conferences. The latter category is a strategic priority for the business.

Unforgettable Event Partners has three owners, each of whom brings different strengths and skill sets to the business. Christine Carlson is a seasoned hospitality management professional whose focus is on developing creative and unforgettable event experiences for the business's customers. Janice Mark has extensive experience with event operations, and will focus on front-line management of independent contractors and freelance event staff. Finally, Mary Longfield will oversee the administrative and financial aspects of the business.

Carlson, Mark, and Longfield have known one another on a professional basis for five years. Their association began at a local business networking event in Lexington. Since that time, they remained in contact in order to share professional experiences. In 2011, Carlson and Mark began providing event planning services on a part-time, freelance basis. After realizing that significant opportunities existed to develop a full-time practice, they contacted Longfield and began making preparations to establish their own business.

Mission Statement

Our promise is in our name: to deliver unforgettable events for our customers.

INDUSTRY ANALYSIS

The event planning industry includes a large number of independent practitioners. In addition, hotels, conference centers, and other vendors also employ professionals who provide event management services like those offered by Unforgettable Event Partners. The industry includes several trade and professional organizations. Established in 1972, MPI exists to "build a rich global meeting industry community." The association provides its members with a number of different business and professional development opportunities. In addition to event planners, the association includes suppliers, faculty, and students among its membership base.

Another leading organization is the International Special Events Society, which was formed in 1987. In 2012 the organization included more than 7,000 members from 38 different countries. Its broad membership base is broader than event planners, and includes the likes of audio-visual technicians, balloon artists, journalists, convention center managers, florists, caterers, and decorators. According to ISES, its mission is "to educate, advance and promote the special events industry and its network of professionals along with related industries."

A newer industry organization is the Event Planners Association, which was formed in 2004. It also includes a broad and diverse membership base, including professionals from areas such as game rental, catering, inflatables, and wedding planning. The EPA's mission is to "provide the foundational elements of a successful business and facilitate the highest standards of excellence and professionalism." Member benefits include continuing education, networking, and access to an in-house insurance agency and law business.

MARKET ANALYSIS

Unforgettable Event Partners is located in Stonebridge, Kentucky. This strategic location is positioned immediately between two major markets: Lexington and Louisville. These communities will constitute our business's primary market area.

Known as the Horse Capital of the World, Lexington is located in Fayette County, and is within a one-day drive of about 66 percent of the nation's population. The Blue Grass Airport (LEX) provides easy access to the region from all points. In 2010 the Lexington-Fayette County area had a population of 295,800 people. This figure increases to 555,000 when the larger metropolitan statistical area of Bourbon, Clark, Fayette, Jessamine, Madison, Scott, and Woodford counties is factored in.

Known as the City of Parks, Louisville had a population of 741,096 in 2010. The city offers multiple options for special events, including the downtown entertainment complex, 4th Street Live! Other advantages include a wide selection of sports and athletic options for themed events. These include numerous golf courses and Churchill Downs, for example. Other options include a number of museums, such as the Louisville Slugger Museum and the Kentucky Derby Museum.

Primary Markets

Generally speaking, Unforgettable Event Partners tends to handle events in three broad categories. These include life celebrations such as weddings, anniversary celebrations, reunions, and graduation parties; group events, such as charity balls, fundraisers, and holiday parties; and business/corporate events, such as seminars, trade shows, and conferences. The latter category is a strategic priority for the business.

Business/Corporate Events:

- Business Dinners
- Business Meetings
- Conferences
- Conventions & Expos
- Networking Events
- Product Launches
- Receptions

- Seminars

- Team-building Exercises

- Trade Shows

Group Events:
- Award Ceremonies

- Bar-B-Que

- Bowling Banquets

- Charity Balls

- Concerts

- Fairs & Festivals

- Fundraisers

- Golf Groups

- Holiday Parties

- Ladies Luncheons

- Murder Mysteries

- Political Rallies

- Professional and Amateur Sporting Events

- Theme Parties—Hawaiian Luau/Mexican Fiesta/Mardi Gras

Life Celebrations:
- Anniversary Party

- Baby Shower

- Baptism

- Bar/Bat Mitzvah

- Birthday Party

- Engage in Parties

- Graduation Parties

- Holiday Celebrations

- House Warming

- Memorial Service

- Retirement

- Reunions

- Special Achievement Reception

- Weddings & Rehearsal Dinners

Relying upon data from Hamilton-Field & Associates LLC, the corporate event prospects in the Lexington-Fayette, Louisville market can be broken down as follows:

- Colleges & Universities (60 establishments)

- Large Companies (26 establishments)

- Mid-sized Companies (143 establishments)

- Hospitals (42 establishments)

- Health & Medical Services (2,735 establishments)

- Membership Organizations (1,427 establishments)

- Museums & Zoos (42 establishments)

- Churches & Religious Organizations (1,997 establishments)

In particular, we have identified the following organizations as top prospects, and will make them a special focus of our sales and direct marketing efforts:

- United Parcel Service

- Toyota Motor Manufacturing, U.S.A., Inc.

- The Valvoline Company

- The Trane Company

- Square D Company

- Long John Silver's

- Lexmark International

- Johnson Controls

- J M Smuckers

- GTE Products Corporation

- General Electric Company

- Ashland Inc.

Competition

Competition will be very strong in our market. There are many individuals who market themselves as "event planners," but few offer the depth of experience provided by Unforgettable Event Partners. After considerable research, we have identified who we consider to be our most substantial competition:

- Jennifer Lancaster Inc.

- Robinson Event Source

- Stonebridge Events

- Sheila Hamilton & Associates

Like our business, these event planners have considerable knowledge and experience. Because they all have been in operation for more than five years, they will have an advantage in the area of brand recognition. However, based on conversations with employees at Stonebridge Events and Robinson Event Source, there is considerable opportunity within the local market for firms capable of offering comprehensive services (especially within the market for business/corporate events).

PERSONNEL

Owners

Christine Carlson—While pursuing an undergraduate hospitality management degree, Christine Carlson worked for a leading catering company in Flagstaff, Arizona, gaining practical hands-on experience. After demonstrating a knack for "sweating the small stuff," she was given additional responsibilities in the area of event planning. Next, her career took her to the 500,000-square-foot Marble Ridge Exposition Center in Centerville, Kentucky, where she served as a conference coordinator. In that role, Carlson served as the interface between customers and the various services offered by the exposition center, including audio-visual and catering. After four years, she was promoted to the role of program coordinator, where her responsibilities involved event programming. Christine will mainly focus on developing creative and unforgettable event experiences for the business's customers.

Janice Mark—Janice Mark's career began in the media services department of St. Bridget's Hospital in Bridgestone, Kentucky. After working for three years as a conference center technician, where her responsibilities involved overseeing conference room and audio-visual equipment setups, Janice was elevated to the role of conference center supervisor. This involved overseeing all of the hospital's conference center operations, including the planning and coordination of internal and external events. She gained experience working with a wide range of hospital staff members, including physicians, as well as individuals from the public. She developed a reputation for making meetings more enjoyable and memorable for guests by ensuring excellent customer service. Front-line management of independent contractors and freelance event staff will be Janice's key responsibilities.

Mary Longfield—After earning an undergraduate degree in business, Mary Longfield began her career with Richardson Entertainment LP. There, she was responsible for handling the administrative and financial aspects of a mid-sized talent management firm, leveraging her exceptional communication, problem-solving, and financial skills. At Richardson, Mary was responsible for managing a wide range of reports and financial records. In addition, her duties also included negotiating contracts with entertainment venues on behalf of performing artists. Mary's strengths in the area of business administration will be a strong complement to the event planning expertise of Christine and Janice.

Freelance Support Staff

Unforgettable Event Partners will rely upon a network of reliable independent contractors to provide its customers with desired services. Examples include audio-visual equipment rental and operation, DJ services, bartending, catering, tent and venue rental, and security. When needed, the business will hire freelance staff to provide additional event management supervision and support. This will allow Unforgettable Event Partners to keep its personnel expenses to a minimum.

Professional and Advisory Support

Unforgettable Event Partners will rely upon Shelby Rockman Tax Advisors, an accounting firm in Lexington, for tax preparation and accounting assistance. Commercial checking accounts have been established with the Greater Bank of Lexington, along with merchant accounts for accepting credit card and debit card payments. Legal services will be provided by attorney Robert Bookbinder.

GROWTH STRATEGY

Year One: During its first year of operations, Unforgettable Event Partners will concentrate on establishing its brand in the Lexington-Fayette, Louisville market. Because the owners already are well-known within the business community, the partners will put an emphasis on leveraging their respective reputations in order to generate new event contracts within the corporate sector, which offers excellent growth prospects. With all other categories of events, the business will concentrate on delivering excellent customer service and achieving steady, measured growth through positive word-of-mouth and marketing.

Year Two: During the second year of operations, the owners anticipate a 15 percent increase in sales as momentum continues to build and Unforgettable Event Partners' reputation begins to grow.

Year Three: The owners are confident that Unforgettable Event Partners can achieve 25 percent sales growth during year three, by which time the business will have planned many successful events and established a strong referral base.

MARKETING & SALES

A marketing plan has been developed for Unforgettable Event Partners that includes these main tactics:

Public/Media Relations:

A major emphasis will be placed upon securing free publicity from the news media. When clients are agreeable, we will submit interesting photographs/captions to the newspapers in our primary market area, including:

- *Business First*
- *The Courier-Journal Newspaper*
- *HelloLouisville.com*
- *The Kentucky Press Association*
- *LEO Weekly*
- *The Lexington Herald-Leader*
- *Louisville.com*

We also will target the same media outlets with guest columns on topics such as "How to Plan the Perfect Wedding Reception." In addition, we will take the same approach by offering to make appearances on the morning and/or noon shows of leading network affiliates, including the following:

Lexington
- WLEX-TV
- WKYT-TV
- WTVQ-TV
- WDKY-TV

Louisville
- MetroTV
- WAVE TV
- WBKI TV
- WDRB TV
- WHAS TV
- WLKY TV

We also will coordinate with our business/organizational clients to ensure media coverage (when appropriate/agreeable) at their events, providing us with additional exposure and interview opportunities.

Web Site:

Unforgettable Event Partners will develop a website that lists information about our business, including customer testimonials and a substantial photo/video gallery, in order to give prospective customers a flavor for our capabilities. The site also will include contact information and a list of services that we offer.

Brochure:

A four-color brochure, featuring some of the most popular and profitable types of events, will be developed.

Advertising:

Unforgettable Event Partners will pursue an advertising strategy that is highly targeted. Initially, we will concentrate our resources by advertising in area bridal guides in order to target the wedding market, as well as Business First, in order to generate awareness within the business/corporate sector.

Sales Promotion:

Each month, our partners will make at least eight lunch presentations to local organizations promoting Unforgettable Event Partners, in an effort to secure corporate event planning contracts.

Bridal Expos:

Unforgettable Event Partners will have a regular presence at local and regional bridal expositions, in order to maintain visibility among those who are planning their wedding.

Social Media:

Our business will have a presence on LinkedIn, Facebook, and Twitter, in order to maintain multiple channels of communications with prospective customers.

Direct Marketing:

A quarterly direct-marketing campaign will concentrate on the corporate event market. A mailing list broker has been identified, and arrangements have been made with a local mail house to handle mailings.

During our first year of operation, we will evaluate our marketing plan on a quarterly basis. Adjustments will be made as necessary.

SERVICES

In order to create a comprehensive and unique event experience for customers, Unforgettable Event Partners has established relationships with an extensive listing of different vendors. Our business will serve as the liaison between the vendor and our customer, with the goal of ensuring total satisfaction. In addition, special arrangements have been made so that our customers can make one payment (to our business), instead of to multiple parties. A detailed listing of these vendors is available upon request. Examples of different service providers include:

- Audio-visual (lighting, sound, video)
- Business/Corporate Event Insurance
- Catering
- Decorations (balloons, table decorations, plants)
- Entertainment (musicians and performers, comedians, guest speakers)
- Equipment Rental (tents, chairs, podiums, staging)
- Marketing (print advertising, Web promotion, social media)
- Media Relations (news releases, interview coordination)
- Premiums (T-shirts, pens, and other promotional items)

- Registration

- Security (loss prevention, traffic/parking control, guest safety)

When working with our customers, we typically will follow the following process:

1. Meet with customers to determine expectations (e.g., menu & beverage selection, etc.).

2. Identify appropriate resources/vendors, develop creative themes, and secure initial client feedback.

3. Obtain all necessary estimates.

4. Develop room/location diagrams and maps.

5. Create a detailed planning timeline with specific milestones.

6. Share proposal with client.

7. Make necessary modifications to event proposal, based on client feedback.

8. Secure final client approval and secure deposit as negotiated.

9. Make necessary vendor/event arrangements.

10. Oversee event planning, coordination & set-up.

11. Provide on-site supervision of events to ensure customer satisfaction.

12. Final customer invoicing.

13. Settle all vendor accounts.

OPERATIONS

Location

Unforgettable Event Partners has negotiated a three-year lease for office space in the Landmark Center, located within a historic building in downtown Stonebridge that was recently renovated. The facility includes a 10 x 10 waiting area, three 15 x 15 offices, a 20 x 20 conference room, and a small kitchenette. The offices are wired for high-speed Internet service. Furnishings will be purchased at a cost of $10,000. An additional $10,000 will be needed to purchase a flat-panel monitor for the conference room, three PCs, and three tablet computers. The owners have agreed to split these start-up costs amongst themselves, so no financing will be needed.

Fees

Although our rental fees are negotiable to a certain extent, the owners of Unforgettable Event Partners have established a fee structure based on an hourly rate of $80. Based on a client's desire, this metric will be used to estimate projects on an hourly basis, flat fee/per-project basis, percentage-of-expense basis, or some combination of the three.

Legal

Unforgettable Event Partners will require customers to sign a service contract, specifying major aspects of our business arrangement, including specific information regarding rentals, deposits, liability & indemnification, cancellation, event insurance, and more. A detailed copy of this agreement, which has been prepared by our attorney, is available upon request.

FINANCIAL ANALYSIS

Following is a three-year pro forma profit and loss statement for Unforgettable Event Partners. Additional financial projections have been prepared in conjunction with our accounting firm and are available upon request. The business essentially is projected to break even in years one and two, and began achieving a modest profit in year three.

The owners believe that their financial projections are conservative. However, in the event that they prove to be too ambitious, each partner is prepared to reduce their respective salary to ensure the financial stability of Unforgettable Event Partners.

*The owners will bring a total of $50,000 in financial capital to the new business, $20,000 of which will be used to cover start-up costs (e.g., furnishings, computers, etc.).

Pro Forma Profit and Loss Statement

	Year 1	Year 2	Year 3
Sales	$175,000	$201,250	$241,500
Expenses			
Payroll	$110,000	$130,000	$160,000
Lease	$ 10,000	$ 10,000	$ 10,000
Marketing	$ 15,000	$ 16,000	$ 17,000
Licenses & fees	$ 2,500	$ 2,500	$ 2,500
Insurance	$ 7,550	$ 8,250	$ 9,500
Travel & transportation	$ 5,500	$ 6,000	$ 6,500
Telecommunications	$ 5,000	$ 5,000	$ 5,000
Utilities	$ 1,500	$ 1,750	$ 2,000
Payroll taxes	$ 16,500	$ 19,500	$ 24,000
Miscellaneous	$ 1,000	$ 1,500	$ 2,000
Total operating costs	**$174,550**	**$200,500**	**$238,500**
Net profit	**$ 450**	**$ 750**	**$ 3,000**

General Contracting Company

HandyWoman Services

67899 Pine Grove Ave.
Port Huron, MI 48062

Zuzu Enterprises

HandyWoman Services (HWS) is a unique contractor that offers traditional "handyman" services performed by a knowledgeable and experienced woman. With an eye for detail and a friendly disposition, the owner-operator of HWS appeals to clients not only because of the quality of the work she can do, but also because she quickly puts homeowners at ease.

EXECUTIVE SUMMARY

HandyWoman Services (HWS) is a unique contractor that offers traditional "handyman" services performed by a knowledgeable and experienced woman. With an eye for detail and a friendly disposition, the owner-operator of HWS appeals to clients not only because of the quality of the work she can do, but also because she quickly puts homeowners at ease. They feel comfortable having her in their homes and around their children and she quickly becomes a welcome ally and a "part of the family."

SERVICES

HandyWoman Services (HWS) is a unique contractor that offers traditional "handyman" services performed by a knowledgeable and experienced woman. In the fast pace of modern-day life, home maintenance and renovation projects often are overlooked and ignored, often until they become a more serious, and more costly, problem. People simply don't have the time or knowledge to take care of all home projects themselves in a timely manner.

HWS offers homeowners an affordable solution to this problem. The experience and attention to detail allows HWS to tackle almost any issue and get home affairs under control. All work is guaranteed and indemnified, and quotes, pricing, and invoices are straightforward and fair. After the work is done to the client's satisfaction, HWS leaves the home clean and tidy, making the entire experience positive and satisfying for everyone.

Below is a description of the types of services HWS offers.

Preventative Maintenance and Cleaning

All aspects of basic home maintenance will be offered, including such things as changing furnace filters, cleaning air conditioner compressors, and cleaning and repairing gutters. Specifically, HWS will perform preventative maintenance on the following:

- Air conditioners
- Dishwashers
- Dryers and dryer vents
- Fireplaces
- Furnaces
- Gutters
- Hot water heaters
- Lawn mowers
- Refrigerators
- Stoves/ovens
- Sump pumps and alarms
- Washing machines
- Water softeners

Installation and Repair

When problems do arise, HWS is available to help solve them. A thorough examination of the issue will be done and an appropriate solution will be identified and implemented. Installation and repair services include such things as the following:

- Basic plumbing, including changing taps/washers and fixing basic leaks
- Carbon monoxide detectors
- Caulking
- Ceiling fans
- Door bells
- Door locks
- Drywall—small areas, holes, etc.
- Faucets
- Garbage disposals
- Gutters
- Light dimmers
- Mailboxes
- Microwave ovens
- Pet doors
- Smoke detectors
- Wall plates
- Window and door screens

Referral and Project Management

In the event that extensive repairs are needed to appliances or the structure of the home, HWS is available to find the right contractor and ensure they do the work as promised, both on time and on budget. We will interview potential contractors and provide feedback on each so that the client can choose the best fit for their needs. Once the contractor has been decided and has begun work, HWS can act as site manager to oversee the work and make sure it is being done both correctly and safely, while, at the same time, the home is being treated with respect.

Extensive projects of this type include the following:

- Asbestos removal
- Building additions
- Carpet and flooring installation
- Concrete work
- Construction of decks and/or patios
- Electrical work (licensed electricians)
- Exterior paint
- Fence erection
- HVAC repairs (licensed mechanics)
- Lead paint removal
- Major appliance repairs
- Masonry/brickwork
- Mold removal
- Plumbing (licensed plumbers)
- Pool installation
- Roof repairs/rebuilds
- Structural room renovations, including finishing basements
- Skylights
- Tree/stump removal
- Wall erection/demolition
- Window replacement

Decor

In addition to maintenance, repair, and installation services, HWS is also available for home decorating projects, including finding and/or installing such things as the following:

- Blinds
- Closet systems
- Curtain rods
- Drawer pulls/knobs
- Faucets
- Light fixtures
- Shelves
- Toilet seats

- Towel bars

- Wainscoting and chair rail

- Wallpaper

Other decor work that can be done includes the following:

- Furniture assembly

- Painting

- Tile work

Landscaping

Work is not restricted to the home's interior. HWS is also available for basic landscaping services, such as the following:

- Aerating

- Edging

- Lawn mowing

- Raking

- Tree/shrub trimming

Teaching

A unique revenue stream to HWS is teaching homeowners to perform these tasks themselves. Some homeowners may have the time, but lack the expertise to know how to maintain or repair their home, or may lack the self-confidence to attempt to tackle issues on their own.

In this case, HWS is willing and able to come in and teach homeowners the skills they need to take care of their homes. HWS will make a preliminary examination of the home and meet with the homeowner to gather all of the information and paperwork necessary to begin, including age of the home and various appliances, any manuals and receipts, as well as a wish list of things to be done. Photos will be taken for reference.

After the initial meeting, HWS will prepare a Home Maintenance Binder for the homeowner. The binder will organize all of the manuals, warranties, and receipts as well as contact information for repair and maintenance contractors; a schedule for basic maintenance, upkeep, and cleaning; a calendar to record when tasks are completed; various how-to guides, including such things as painting; and seasonal home maintenance checklists. (See Appendices for examples.) Photos of the appliances, including switches, filters, and other pertinent information will be included for reference.

Once the Home Maintenance Binder is complete, the first "training" session will be planned, with subsequent meetings scheduled as needed. HWS will start the meeting by providing the homeowner with their customized binder as well as their own basic tool set. After going over the binder and giving an introduction to the various tools, the real work will begin. HWS staff will perform the maintenance/repair tasks on the wish list, teaching the homeowner throughout the process and encouraging them to do as much as possible.

Basic Tool Set

Each client will be presented with a small, basic tool set including the following:

- Adjustable wrenches

- Assortment of nails and screws

- Cordless drill with bits

- Electronic stud finder

- Hammer

- Level

- Locking tape measure

- Paint can key

- Pliers

- Screwdrivers (Phillips and flat of various sizes)

- Spackle and putty knife

- Utility knife

- Wire cutters

PERSONNEL

HWS is owned and operated by Anna George. Ms. George has 25+ years' experience with home maintenance and repair, having learned many skills from her own father and grandfather when she was growing up. She has earned her Residential Building licensure from the State of Michigan and has worked for a construction company for 21 years before being laid off due to a downturn in the economy and the resultant decline in business.

This situation led Ms. George to evaluate what she loved about her work and how she wanted to proceed. She realized that she loved making a difference in the day-to-day lives of clients, and she loved getting to know them and interact with them on a more personal basis. With this knowledge, it was an easy and natural decision for Ms. Green to venture out on her own and start a handywoman business.

To begin, Ms. George will be the only employee. If the business picks up to the point where she has to turn down work, she will consider adding additional staff.

FINANCIAL

Start Up Costs

Financial costs of starting a new handywoman business are fairly low because Ms. Green already owns her own tools and is already licensed. Costs only include those of setting up and advertising the business, including legal fees, advertising, insurance, and technology. A complete breakdown follows.

	Costs
Advertising/marketing	$1,000
Legal	$ 800
Office supplies	$ 300
Binders/tool sets (10 of each)	$2,500
Insurance	$1,200
Technology (computer, printer, software, etc.)	$1,500
Total	**$7,300**

Hourly Rate

The basic hourly rate for all services is $50 per hour. Each job is started with an assessment of the work involved and an estimate of the time and costs associated with successfully completing the work; work will only proceed only after approval of the estimate and charges.

Teaching homeowners to care for their homes starts at $350 for three sessions (or 6 hours), with additional sessions billed at the $50 hourly rate.

This rate will be lowered when services are offered for nonprofit organizations. Many such organizations are interested in providing teaching services, tools, and binders for new homeowners that receive services to help ensure their successful transition to homeownership. Organizations that have expressed interest in providing this type of service for their clients include the following:

- Blue Water Habitat for Humanity

- Community Foundation of St. Clair County

- Michigan Community Action Association

- United Way of St. Clair County

- Various domestic violence organizations

Any services offered in conjunction with these organizations will be highly discounted, if not pro bono.

MARKETING & ADVERTISING

Several avenues will be taken to reach the target market of new and current homeowners.

1. Targeted, direct mailings to current homeowners.

2. Meeting with local real estate agents and providing them with brochures and advertisements.

3. Establishing communication with local nonprofit organizations dedicated to assisting individuals with home ownership.

4. Working with contacts in the industry to spread the word about the company and promote its services whenever possible.

5. Create an online presence including website, LinkedIn profile, Facebook account, Google ads, and the like.

6. Small ads in the local newspaper and on local restaurant placemats.

Other advertising and marketing campaigns will be considered on a case-by-case basis.

APPENDIX A

Fall Home Maintenance Checklist

- Check for Drafts—Move a lighted candle along the edges of windows, doors, and moldings; if the flame flickers, there's probably a draft. Mark the areas with painters' tape and return to replace seals as needed. On the outside of your home, inspect the siding and shingles for cracks and holes and repair as necessary.

- Check Home Safety Devices—Replace batteries in smoke and carbon monoxide detectors, recharge fire extinguishers, and test for radon.

- Clean and Install Storm Windows and Doors

- Clean Gutters

- Clean Humidifiers—Replace old filters. Soak interiors with undistilled white vinegar and scrub with a soft-bristle brush.

- Compost Autumn Leaves—Start your own compost pile with fall leaves and other garden debris. The best compost contains two or three parts "brown," or carbon-rich matter (leaves, pine needles, sawdust, shredded newspaper), to one part "green," or nitrogen-rich matter (grass clippings, vegetable and fruit scraps, coffee grounds, eggshells). You can also contact your town hall to find out if your area's sanitation department collects leaves to compost.

- Disinfect Flowerpots—Soak in a solution of one part bleach to 10 parts water, scrub with a stiff brush, and dry thoroughly before storing.

- Have Your Chimney Inspected and Cleaned—Hire a chimney sweep.

- Have Your Furnace Inspected—Hire a professional to check for leaks, replace filters, and condition the system.

- Inspect Trees—Now that the branches are bare, check for limbs that interfere with power lines or come too close to the roof.

- Order Firewood

- Organize the Shed—Remove any liquids that will freeze in the winter, transfer fertilizer boxed in cardboard to metal or plastic containers, and move snow- and ice-removal equipment to the front for easy access.

- Prepare Flowers—Deadhead annuals and perennials regularly to groom and promote blooming. Wrap roses and other fragile shrubs with burlap; after the soil freezes, mulch garden beds to prevent the soil from heaving.

- Remove Window Air-Conditioning Units—Clean filters, and drain the units of water before storing them.

- Service Snow Blower; Purchase Gasoline

- Service Sprinklers—Have your system drained and serviced by a professional, and flag any heads near driveways or walkways to prevent damage during snow removal.

- Take Down Outdoor Clothesline

- Turn Off Faucets and Roll Hoses; Store for the Season

APPENDIX B

Spring Home Maintenance Checklist

Inside:

- Check Home-Safety Devices—Replace batteries in smoke and carbon monoxide detectors, recharge fire extinguishers, and test for radon.

- Clean Ceiling Fans

- Clean Out the Refrigerator and Freezer

- Clean, Pack, and Store Humidifiers

- Deep-Clean Carpets—Vacuum thoroughly, then shampoo.

- Dust Light bulbs

- Guard Against Pests—Store dry goods in airtight containers or in the refrigerator; wash pet dishes immediately after use; place trash in tightly sealed receptacles.

- Maintain Air Conditioners—Remove and clean filters and have central-air units serviced professionally.

- Refresh Bedding—Replace heavy winter bedding with lighter fabrics; vacuum and rotate mattresses. Air out down comforters before storing for the season.

- Replace Storm Windows with Screens—Clean screens by vacuuming them with the dust-brush attachment; if they're very soiled, wet them with a hose and scrub with a soft-bristle brush and an all-purpose cleaner that doesn't contain ammonia, which can discolor aluminum. Rinse screens well, and let dry in the sun before installing.

- Turn Off Heating System; Have It Cleaned

- Wash Glassware that Has Been Stored on Open Shelves

Outside:
- Bring Patio Furniture out of Storage—Wipe off dirt and inspect pieces for damage.

- Bring Window Boxes, Planters, and Hanging Baskets Out of Storage

- Clean and Condition Your Grill

- Clean, Sharpen, and Oil Garden Tools

- Clean Winter Debris from Gutters

- Have Your Sprinkler System Serviced

- Organize the Garage and Shed—Move winter equipment to the back and bring the lawn mower and garden tools to the front.

- Prepare Garden Beds for Planting—Cover soil with a layer of well-aged compost, and mix with a garden fork.

- Prepare the Lawn—Check for any dead or damaged areas, cultivate and reseed; aerate if necessary.

- Reactivate Outdoor Faucets—Remove any insulation around them, and turn on the water supply. Hook up hoses and test them; patch any holes or replace hose if necessary.

- Reacquaint Houseplants with the Outdoors—If you brought plants inside for the winter, put them in a sheltered place, such as a porch, for an hour, and increase exposure gradually until the weather warms enough for full-time exposure.

- Remove Protective Winter Mulch from Garden Beds

- Service the Lawn Mower; Fill Gas Tank

- Shake Out or Replace Doormats

- String Up the Outdoor Clothesline

- Wash Porch and Patio Floors—Thoroughly sweep, and then scrub floors with a long-handled brush and mixture of all-purpose cleaner and hot water.

APPENDIX C

Painting Checklist

Before You Start:
- Buy the Right Paint—Choose the highest-quality paint that your budget allows. If you buy the finest-quality paint and apply it properly, you won't have to paint again for six or seven years. Many experts prefer oil-based paint for trim and floors, and water-soluble latex for walls and

ceilings. If you're in doubt about which kind of paint to use, consult the paint store or home center where you plan to buy your paint.

- Determine the Correct Amount of Paint—Given your room dimensions, most paint stores will help estimate how many gallons of paint and primer you'll need. In general, you'll need enough for one coat of primer and two coats of paint. The primer should be tinted to match the paint if the room is going from a light color to a dark one.

One Day to One Week Before You Start:
Plan to devote a full day to the four P's: protecting floors and furnishings, patching holes, prepping walls, and priming.

- Setup—Assemble all of the tools and materials you will need for the job on a table before you begin working.

- Safeguard Belongings—Remove small objects from the room; gather large ones in the center and cover with a plastic drop cloth. Unscrew switch and outlet face plates. Lay masking paper over wood floors and tape it down at the edges. Protect carpeting with canvas drop cloths.

- Fill Holes—With a flexible putty knife, apply spackling paste to nail holes in the wall and wood filler to small cavities in trim (overfill slightly, as compounds will shrink). Let dry completely, and then sand using a medium-grit paper on walls and a coarse-grit one on wood.

- Repair Wall Crevices—Cover crevices in the wall with self-adhesive fiberglass-mesh joint tape. Apply a thin layer of joint compound over the tape with a flexible taping or joint knife; work quickly to smooth before the paste dries. Lightly sand with a fine-grit paper.

- Fill Cracks Between Trim and Walls—To fill cracks between the baseboard—or any trim—and the wall, apply latex caulk (which can be painted over) with a caulking gun, following the manufacturer's instructions. Immediately after applying caulk, use a damp sponge to even it out and wipe off excess. (It is impossible to do this after caulk dries.)

- Clean and Prime—Peel back drop cloth and vacuum the room and wash walls with a sponge and warm water. Tape off the ceiling, then apply a coat of primer. Priming ensures better adhesion of the paint to the walls, and increases its durability.

Painting Day:
- Decant Paint—Flatten a cardboard box and place it under paint containers to give floors an extra layer of protection. Mix paint with a wooden stir stick, and then pour some into a smaller plastic vessel, filling about halfway.

- Dip Your Brush—Insert the bristles about 2 inches into the paint, and then tap them against the sides of the container to remove excess. This minimizes the risk of drips.

- Cut In—Paint part of a corner or around the trim (don't worry about taping yet) with a 2-inch angled brush. This is called "cutting in." To avoid the marks that appear when paint starts to dry, do only 4-foot sections at a time before continuing on to the next section.

- Roll on Paint—Pour paint into the reservoir of your roller tray. Dip in one edge of the roller, then move it back and forth on the tray bed until it's saturated but not dripping. Paint a 2-foot-wide V on the wall, and, without lifting the roller, fill it in with tight vertical strokes—this will ensure even coverage. Repeat, working top to bottom, until you've completed the wall. We recommend painting your walls before taping off the trim, since you'll be painting this later. Apply at least two coats to both, allowing four hours of drying time in between.

- Finish Trim and Baseboards—Let wall paint dry overnight, then tape off the trim (all window edges, doorways, ceilings, molding) with painters' masking tape. (For proper adhesion, burnish tape with your fingertips as you go.) Apply paint with an angled 2-inch brush.

- Paint Doors—Remove all hardware, then sand and prime the surface. With a 3-inch roller, paint one area of the door, such as an inset panel, then immediately brush over it with a 3-inch brush. Continue working in sections until you've finished the body of the door, then do the stiles and rails (the vertical and horizontal framing, respectively).

Paint Window Frames and Trim:

Once your last coat of paint has dried (see the instructions on your paint can for guidelines) you can paint the window frames and trim. This task requires a lot of detail work, so set aside a day to complete it. (Aluminum and plastic window frames don't need to be painted.)

- Prepare Windows—Line the perimeter of each pane with painters' tape, leaving 1/16 inch between the edge of the tape and the muntins (the strips of wood or metal that separates and holds panes of glass in a window). (When painted, this will create a seal that prevents moisture from getting in and rotting the wood.) Remove locks and other hardware, and clean wood with a tack cloth.

- Tape Off Trim—Apply painters' tape flush against the trim, protecting the painted wall.

- Paint the Window Frames and Trim—Use a 1-inch angled brush to paint the muntins and an angled 2-inch brush to do the frame and trim, taking care to fill in your seal.

- Remove Excess Paint from Windows—To clean off paint that has seeped underneath the tape, spray a single-edge razor blade with glass cleaner—this will prevent scratches—and gently scrape the panes. (Using a razor blade on some new windows will void the warranty; double-check yours to be sure.)

Cleanup:

- Assemble Supplies—Keep these items in your cleaning arsenal: liquid dish soap for washing brushes, a brush comb for removing persistent particles, sponges and rags for wiping surfaces, glass cleaner, and a razor blade for scraping windows.

- Storing Extra Paint—Transfer leftover paint to smaller airtight plastic containers. (Paint kept in opened cans is prone to drying out.) Make labels with the name of the room the color was used in, and keep the paint on hand for touch-ups.

- Washing Brushes—Run each brush under lukewarm water, then add a few drops of liquid dish soap and continue rinsing. Dislodge dried bits with a metal brush comb. Wrap bristles in paper towels (to maintain their shape), and lay flat to dry.

Golf-Themed Restaurant and Conference Facility

The Golf Garden at Sandy Rock Inc.

27 Bayview Dr.
Sandy Rock, AZ 86031

Paul Greenland

The Golf Garden at Sandy Rock is a golf-themed restaurant and conference facility.

EXECUTIVE SUMMARY

Business Overview

Located in Sandy Rock, Arizona, The Golf Garden at Sandy Rock is a golf-themed restaurant and conference facility.

Real estate developer Peter Franklin, contractor Larry Hagman, and entrepreneur Craig Simmons plan to transform Puttin' Around, Simmons' former mini golf and driving range facility, into a unique golf-themed destination focused on the business community.

Features of The Golf Garden at Sandy Rock include the following:

- A 250-yard driving range (15 hard stations/15 grass tee stations)

- A 1,500-square-foot indoor dining room

- Four 350-square-foot meeting rooms (these can be combined into two, 700-square-foot meeting rooms), providing ideal meeting space for business/group meetings of 15-30 people

- A 750-square-foot bar area with an indoor golf simulator

- 18 outdoor seating areas, each surrounded by beautiful gardens and putting greens

Business Philosophy

The Golf Garden at Sandy Rock is the premier destination for business lunches, dinners, and networking.

MARKET ANALYSIS

Sandy Rock is located halfway between Phoenix and Tucson, providing an ideal meeting location for businesspeople in either city, as well as access to two large metropolitan areas. The Arizona Department of Transportation is currently engaged in a number of projects to improve transportation between Phoenix and Tucson on Interstate 10, which will benefit The Golf Garden at Sandy Rock.

In total, Phoenix and Tucson are home to 68,267 business establishments. Specifically, the employee base at these establishments breaks down as follows:

Employees	Phoenix	Tucson
1–4	28,539	11,104
5–9	8,799	3,617
10–19	5,569	2,241
20–49	3,657	1,419
50–99	1,425	557
100–249	631	309
250–499	187	62
500–999	63	25
1,000+	48	15
Total	**48,918**	**19,349**

The Golf Garden at Sandy Rock will focus its marketing efforts on executive managers and administrators/sales professionals. Collectively, these categories represent 129,535 employees. In each market, these professions break down as follows:

Occupation	Phoenix	Tucson
Executive managers & administrators	77,860	28,198
Sales professionals	17,527	5,950
Total	**95,387**	**34,148**

Phoenix and Tucson each have very active business communities. Established in 1888, the Greater Phoenix Chamber of Commerce included 2,600 members in 2012. Likewise, The Tucson Metro Chamber included 1,350 members and has been active for more than 110 years.

Although we anticipate the majority of our business to occur during the workweek, The Golf Garden at Sandy Rock will be open on weekends as well, in order to serve general customers from both Phoenix and Tucson.

INDUSTRY ANALYSIS

The Golf Garden at Sandy Rock is part of the restaurant industry. According to the National Restaurant Association, industry revenues were projected to reach $632 billion in 2012 on the strength of 12.9 million employees. That year, the industry generated sales of $1.7 billion per day. Despite difficult economic conditions during the first decade of the 21st century, from 2000 to 2011 the restaurant industry experienced job growth at a greater rate than the national economy.

PERSONNEL

Ownership Summary

The Golf Garden at Sandy Rock's owners include real estate developer Peter Franklin, contractor Larry Hagman, and entrepreneur Craig Simmons. Franklin and Hagman are well-known members of the business community in Phoenix, while Simmons (a Tucson native) has an excellent reputation in the smaller Sandy Rock area, having been the owner and operator of the mini golf and driving range facility that the new owners have agreed to transform into The Golf Garden at Sandy Rock.

Craig Simmons will serve as president of The Golf Garden at Sandy Rock, overseeing operations on a full-time basis. Simmons has extensive experience as a business owner and operator. In addition to several apartment complexes, Simmons owns Chester's Tap and Awesome Arcade in Tucson. Valued at $1.2 million, his Puttin' Around driving range/mini golf facility has been a profitable venture for 10 years. However, he is convinced that the business will have much greater potential as The Golf Garden at Sandy Rock. Simmons holds an undergraduate business administration degree from Whitfield College.

Larry Hagman will serve as co-owner and vice president of The Golf Garden at Sandy Rock, with no daily involvement in the business's operations. He is the owner and CEO of Hagman Construction, a commercial design-build general contractor. A 1990 Arizona State University, Hagman holds an undergraduate degree graduate in civil and construction engineering. His company has overseen a wide range of construction projects, costing between $15 million and $150 million.

Peter Franklin will serve as co-owner and treasurer of The Golf Garden at Sandy Rock, with no daily involvement in the business's operations. He is president of Franklin-Hill, a real estate development firm based in Phoenix. He has served in that role since 1998. During the course of his career, Franklin has been involved in many well-known commercial real estate ventures in the Phoenix area, including development of the Golden Sands Technology Park. Franklin is a graduate of Central Colorado University, where he earned a master's degree in business administration.

Because Franklin and Hagman will not have day-to-day involvement with operations, they have agreed to forgo payment of an annual salary, and will instead share in the profits in accordance with their respective investments (see Financial Analysis section).

Staff Employees

Including the owners, The Golf Garden at Sandy Rock will employ a staff consisting of the following:

Title	Salary
Pres. & co-owner	$ 70,000
Treas. & co-owner	$ 0
VP & co-owner	$ 0
1 full-time cook	$ 40,000
3 part-time cooks	$ 45,000
2 full-time bus staff	$ 25,000
2 part-time bus staff	$ 20,000
1 full-time dishwasher	$ 20,000
1 full-time hostess	$ 25,000
2 part-time hosts/hostesses	$ 20,000
3 full-time wait staff	$ 45,000
5 part-time wait staff	$ 37,500
Total	**$347,500**

Professional and Advisory Support

The Golf Garden at Sandy Rock has retained Smith & Hampton, a Phoenix-based accounting firm, to provide tax advisory services. Commercial checking accounts have been established with Central Bank, which also will provide merchant accounts needed to accept credit card and debit card payments. Legal services will be provided by Lawrence Brick, a partner in the Tucson-based business law firm of Webster & Man, who has provided the business with human resources policies and procedures.

BUSINESS STRATEGY

The Golf Garden at Sandy Rock will commence operations in the spring of 2013.

The business will focus its first three years of operations on generating awareness and word-of-mouth referrals among the business communities of Phoenix and Tucson. During this timeframe, the primary objective will be to establish our facility as the premier choice for business lunches, dinners, and networking.

The owners have prepared conservative financial projections (see Financial Analysis section), and expect to generate nearly $1 million in gross sales during the first year, with projected compound annual increases of 10 percent during years two and three. Total net profits of $254,420 and are expected during the first three years, after which Franklin and Hagman will have recouped their investments.

SERVICES

The Golf Garden at Sandy Rock is a full-service restaurant. The business has contracted with the chef of a popular restaurant in Tucson, who has agreed to oversee the development of our initial menu. A detailed listing of food selections and corresponding prices is available upon request. However, the menu will offer a wide range of choices, from salads and sandwiches to steak and seafood, providing selections and price points that appeal to virtually everyone.

In addition to ordering off the menu, we will offer a special á la carte menu and appetizer selection for group lunch and dinner functions in one of our private meeting rooms. In addition to Arizona sales tax, a minimum gratuity of 18 percent will be applied for all group parties.

Beverages for group functions will be provided according to the following price structure:

Coffee Service
Less than 20 guests: $40

21 to 30 guests: $45

Soft Drink, Iced Tea, Water/Lemon
Less than 20 guests: $50

21 to 30 guests: $60

Alcoholic Beverages
House Wine: $6/glass

List Wine: $8-$12/glass

Draft Beer: $4-8/glass

Domestic Beer Bottles: $4/bottle

Spirits: Prices Start at $5/glass

Entertainment

Besides great food, The Golf Garden at Sandy Rock will offer entertainment options that will help customers to relax and engage in productive conversation. These include the following:

- A driving range with 30 stations (hard and grass tees)

- Complimentary putting greens for lunch/dinner guests adjacent to every outdoor table

- Live entertainment—The Golf Garden at Sandy Rock will occasionally treat guests to live music from Phoenix-and Tucson-area vocalists and jazz musicians, adding to the ambience of our facility. Ideal locations are available for bands to perform either indoors or outdoors.

- Golf Pros—Guests can request the presence of a golf pro (independent contractors) at the driving range or their outdoor table. Billed at $30 per half-hour or $50 per hour, this is an affordable/ attractive add-on for any lunch or dinner group.

- Indoor Golf Simulator—A lease has been negotiated with the developer of a leading golf simulator. At 22 feet wide, 20 feet deep, and 10 feet high, the simulator is pre-loaded with challenging holes from 75 of the world's top golf courses, providing guests with hours of entertainment, even during inclement weather ($15 per half-hour/$25 per hour).

MARKETING & SALES

A marketing plan has been developed for The Golf Garden at Sandy Rock that includes these main tactics:

1. Social Media: Guests will be able to follow our business on Facebook and Twitter, and take advantage of exclusive lunch and dinner specials.

2. Website: A site that lists information about our restaurant and meeting facilities will be developed. The site will include information about our menu selections, location, hours, and special discounts. It also will include video and still photography, in order to showcase the unique elements of The Golf Garden at Sandy Rock. Finally, an online reservation feature will be developed, allowing guests to reserve specific tables and meeting rooms online.

3. Mailer: A four-color, glossy direct-mail piece will be developed. This will be utilized for ongoing direct mailings to key business prospects in both Phoenix and Tucson. Mailing lists will be obtained from the chambers of commerce in both Phoenix and Tucson, and also from Langenfeld Associates, a mailing list broker concentrating on the business market.

4. Print & Online Advertising: In order to establish The Golf Garden at Sandy Rock as the premier choice for business lunches, dinners, and networking, the business will maintain a regular advertising presence. This will include advertisements in *The Chamber Edge,* a monthly publication of the Tucson Metro Chamber. The publication has an estimated readership of more than 5,000 people, and is distributed to top executives and business owners throughout Tucson. We also will place online advertisements on the Tucson Chamber's Web site. In addition, we also will advertise in *IMPACT Magazine,* a monthly publication of the Greater Phoenix Chamber of Commerce. Finally, each quarter The Golf Garden at Sandy Rock will sponsor one event hosted by each chamber of commerce. Finally, we will place regular advertisements in *Tucson Lifestyle Magazine.* A detailed advertising schedule is being developed for all of the aforementioned publications, and can be provided upon request.

5. Sales Promotion: Each month, Craig Simmons will make 4-8 presentations to corporate meeting/event planners at both large and medium-sized organizations in Phoenix and Tucson. Passes for complementary lunches, sessions with golf pros, or free buckets of balls on the driving range, will be distributed to decision-makers as an incentive for trying out The Golf Garden at Sandy Rock.

6. Outdoor Advertising: In order to generate awareness among businesspeople traveling between Phoenix and Tucson, The Golf Garden at Sandy Rock will take advantage of billboard advertisements on Interstate 10, which connects the two metropolitan areas.

The Golf Garden at Sandy Rock will evaluate its marketing plan on a quarterly basis during our first year of operations, and semi-annually thereafter.

OPERATIONS

Hours

Monday - Thursday: 11 AM to 11 PM*

Friday: 11 AM to 1 AM*

Saturday: 11 AM to 1 AM*

Sunday: 11 AM to 7 PM

*After 9 PM, bar only

Facility and Location

Features of The Golf Garden at Sandy Rock will include the following:

- A 250-yard driving range (15 hard stations/15 grass tee stations)

- A 1,500-square-foot indoor dining room

- Four 350-square-foot meeting rooms (these can be combined into two 700-square-foot meeting rooms), providing ideal meeting space for business/group meetings of 15-30 people

- A 750-square-foot bar area with an indoor golf simulator

- 18 outdoor seating areas, each surrounded by beautiful gardens and putting greens (greens have existing waterfalls/streams/ponds that will add aesthetic appeal)

- ADA compliant entrances and washrooms

- Free Wi-Fi service

- A 14-acre lot, providing opportunity for additional expansion

- Ample parking

- An overhang that provides protection from the elements for guests who are being dropped off at the main entrance

Our facility is easily accessible from Interstate 10, which connects the major metropolitan markets of Tucson and Phoenix.

LEGAL

Our business is in full compliance with all legal and regulatory requirements pertaining to the operation of our business in the state of Arizona. Specifically, we adhere to all food safety and environmental sanitation regulations set forth by the State of Arizona in accordance with Arizona Revised Statutes and the Arizona Administrative Code. We also meet requirements of the Americans with Disabilities Act. In addition, we have obtained appropriate business and liability insurance.

FINANCIAL ANALYSIS

Start-up Costs

The main startup costs for The Golf Garden at Sandy Rock are as follows:

- Exterior renovations (to transform mini golf area into attractive outdoor seating areas with corresponding putting greens): $75,000

- Interior renovations (to transform existing clubhouse, snack bar, and arcade area into a restaurant and bar): $175,000

- Total: $250,000

Detailed documentation and architectural renderings, along with a proposed construction timeframe, are available upon request.

Partners Franklin and Hagman have each agreed to contribute $125,000 in cash to the business, for a total investment of $250,000. This funding will be used to cover startup costs. Because they will not have day-to-day involvement with operations, they have agreed to forgo payment of an annual salary, and will instead share in the profits.

Simmons is contributing the actual facility and 14 acres of land to the business, and will have a 70 percent ownership stake. The owners have agreed that Franklin and Hagman (who will each have a 15% stake in the business) will be entitled to equally split all net profits during the first three years, or until they recoup their initial investments.

Following is a pro forma profit and loss statement for the first three years of operations. Additional financial statements have been prepared in conjunction with our accountants, and are available upon request.

Pro forma profit and loss statement

	Year 1	Year 2	Year 3
Sales	$956,787	$1,052,466	$1,157,712
Cost of goods sold	$430,554	$ 473,608	$ 520,970
Gross margin	45%	45%	45%
Operating income	$526,233	$ 578,858	$ 636,742
Expenses			
Payroll	$347,500	$ 357,925	$ 368,663
Administrative	$ 15,500	$ 16,000	$ 16,500
Marketing	$ 15,000	$ 15,500	$ 16,000
Licenses & fees	$ 3,500	$ 3,500	$ 3,500
Insurance	$ 6,578	$ 6,907	$ 7,252
Independent contractors	$ 25,000	$ 30,000	$ 35,000
Utilities	$ 3,850	$ 4,235	$ 4,658
Consultants	$ 12,000	$ 12,000	$ 12,000
Miscellaneous	$ 3,500	$ 4,500	$ 5,500
Total operating costs	$432,428	$ 450,567	$ 469,073
EBITDA	$ 93,805	$ 128,291	$ 167,669
Federal income tax	$ 26,584	$ 27,381	$ 28,203
State income tax	$ 6,950	$ 7,186	$ 7,373
Depreciation	$ 9,567	$ 10,524	$ 11,577
Net profit	$ 50,704	$ 83,200	$ 120,516

Health Communications Consultant

Stanton Health Communications LLC

4789 W. Main St.
Washington, DC 20009

Paul Greenland

With more than a decade of professional experience, Molly Stanton has now decided to establish her own health communications consulting firm. In this role, she will be positioned to assist national non-profit organizations with issue-related health campaigns, and to work with smaller organizations on health-related communications projects.

EXECUTIVE SUMMARY

Health education is Molly Stanton's passion. After earning an undergraduate degree in health education, she attended Central College in Waynesville, Ohio, and earned a master's degree in health communications. While completing her studies, she was fortunate to have internship experiences at the National Institutes of Health, as well as several public health departments.

With more than a decade of professional experience, Stanton has now decided to establish her own health communications consulting firm. In this role, she will be positioned to assist national non-profit organizations with issue-related health campaigns, and to work with smaller organizations (e.g., public health departments and community hospitals) on health-related communications projects.

INDUSTRY ANALYSIS

According to the U.S. Department of Labor, above-average growth is expected within the health education sector. Specifically, the employment of health educators is projected to increase 18 percent from 2008 to 2018. During that time, the number of employed health educators is expected to increase from 66,200 to 78,200. Professionals within the industry are served by the Society for Public Health Education, as well as the American Association for Health Education.

Conditions within the overall healthcare industry support the need for health educators and related consultants. This is because the industry is moving away from payment models that focus on volume, and toward ones centered on quality and value. In this scenario, organizations may be penalized (or not compensated for) for patients who are readmitted to hospitals following treatment. There are financial incentives for keeping patients healthy, and out of the hospital.

Another favorable industry condition involves the need for non-profit hospitals to defend their non-profit status. Financially strained state governments, in search of additional revenue streams, are a key driver of this trend. Public health educators and consultants are resources that can assist organizations demonstrate their focus on improving community health.

Finally, the increasing complexity of the healthcare field is another key consideration. Compared to simpler communication patterns many years ago, healthcare industry employees have become responsible for communicating with a growing number of different audiences. Examples include not only patients and providers, but government officials, community organizations, and patient advocates. Skilled public health communicators can provide valuable insight to all of these key publics.

MARKET ANALYSIS

Primary Target Markets

Molly Stanton will focus her consulting practice on the following key markets:

Hospitals & Healthcare Systems: Nationwide, there are nearly 3,000 non-government, non-profit community hospitals, and more than 1,000 investor-owned/for-profit community hospitals. Stanton will concentrate her initial marketing efforts on the top 50 organizations in each of these categories (specific list available upon request).

State Public Health Departments: (50)

Non-Profit Organizations: After careful consideration, the following national organizations have been identified as potential customers. These organizations all manage campaigns to promote various causes and national health observances (e.g., awareness weeks, months, etc.).

1. African American Blood Drive and Bone Marrow Registry for Sickle Cell Disease Awareness

2. Alzheimer's Disease International

3. American Academy of Ophthalmology (injury prevention)

4. American College of Sports Medicine (childhood obesity awareness)

5. American Foundation for Suicide Prevention

6. American Foundation for Women's Health

7. American Heart Association

8. American Lung Association

9. American Public Health Association

10. American Society of Safety Engineers (occupational safety and health)

11. Arthritis Foundation

12. Asthma and Allergy Foundation of America

13. Break the Cycle (Teen Dating Violence)

14. Congenital Heart Information Network

15. First Candle/SIDS Alliance

16. Global Alliance for Rabies Control

17. Health Information Resource Center (family health & fitness)

18. Hepatitis Foundation International

19. International Foundation for Functional Gastrointestinal Disorders

20. Leukemia & Lymphoma Society

21. Men's Health Network

22. Mental Health America

23. National Alliance on Mental Illness

24. National Association for Health and Fitness

25. National Birth Defects Prevention Network

26. National Cancer Survivors Day Foundation

27. National Center for Immunization and Respiratory Diseases

28. National Center for Safe Routes to School

29. National Center for Victims of Crime

30. National Cervical Cancer Coalition

31. National Council on Alcoholism and Drug Dependence

32. National Down Syndrome Society

33. National Education Center for Agricultural Safety

34. National Family Caregivers Association

35. National Family Partnership

36. National Federation of Families for Children's Mental Health

37. National Hospice and Palliative Care Organization

38. National Institute of Allergy and Infectious Diseases

39. National Native American AIDS Prevention Center

40. National Osteoporosis Foundation

41. National Rehabilitation Awareness Foundation

42. National Sleep Foundation

43. National Viral Hepatitis Roundtable

44. Network of Employers for Traffic Safety

45. No Stomach for Cancer

46. Platelet Disorder Support Association

47. Poison Prevention Week Counsel

48. Prevent Blindness America

49. Prevent Cancer Foundation

50. Produce for Better Health Foundation

51. Rape, Abuse & Incest National Network

52. RESOLVE: The National Infertility Association

53. Save Babies Through Screening Foundation

54. School Nutrition Association

55. Stop TB Partnership (World Health Organization)

56. Stuttering Foundation of America

57. The Autism Society

58. World Alliance for Breast-Feeding Action

59. Yoga Health Foundation

60. ZERO-The Project to End Prostate Cancer

Secondary Target Markets

Although the education market will not be a primary focus during the early years of her consulting practice, Molly Stanton will accept assignments from schools and colleges, including the following:

- Private Schools

- Public School Districts

- Community Colleges

- Universities

PERSONNEL

Molly Stanton, MS, CHES

Health education is Molly Stanton's passion. After earning an undergraduate degree in health education, she attended Central College in Waynesville, Ohio, and earned a master's degree in health communications. While completing her studies, she was fortunate to have internship experiences at the National Institutes of Health, as well as several public health departments.

Molly began her career with the Waynesville Public Health Department in Ohio, where she was employed for five years. She then found employment with The Richardson Foundation, a private, non-profit foundation dedicated to improving the health of children and young adults. There, she was responsible for designing, implementing, overseeing, and measuring several highly successful public health campaigns, including ones focused on abstinence and childhood obesity. She also established partnerships with several leading children's hospitals throughout the United States, and was responsible for working with them to develop and execute other issue-related campaigns, including a "Don't Text and Drive" campaign that received a Gold Communications Award at the national level.

Stanton is a Certified Health Education Specialist (CHES). This special certification is awarded by the National Commission on Health Education Credentialing Inc. In order to receive it, Stanton was required to pass a special examination. In addition, she must complete 75 hours of continuing education over the course of five years to maintain her certification.

With more than a decade of professional experience, Stanton has decided to establish her own consulting firm. Stanton Health Communications LLC will assist national, non-profit organizations with issue-related health campaigns, and work with smaller organizations (e.g., public health departments and community hospitals) on health-related communications projects.

Professional & Advisory Support

Stanton Health Communications has established a business banking account with Central State Bank, including a merchant account for accepting credit card payments. Legal representation is provided by Diamond & Will, and tax advisory services are provided by Bottom-Line Financial Advisors LLC. Molly Stanton relied upon her attorney, David Diamond, to prepare the documents needed to establish her limited liability company.

GROWTH STRATEGY

Molly Stanton is fortunate to establish a new consultancy with two clients, the Marysville Public Health Department (Marysville County, Maryland) and Willis Lexington Memorial Health System (Oak Ridge, Virginia). Together, these clients have contracted with her to provide an average of 25 hours of weekly billable consulting time through the end of 2012. While working on these projects, Stanton will initiate her marketing plan during the second quarter of 2012, with a goal of adding at least one additional client before the end of the year.

Stanton then plans to meet a weekly target of 30 billable hours during her second year of operation, followed by 40 hours during her third year. She realizes that additional non-billable hours will be required to manage administrative aspects of her business (e.g., billing, record keeping, project estimating, etc.), and will consider hiring an administrative assistant during year two, based on consulting volume.

During year three, Stanton will consider leasing dedicated office space and hiring an additional consultant, so that the practice can continue to grow in year four and beyond.

SERVICES

Stanton's consulting services typically will follow a pre-defined approach that involves some or all of the following steps (based upon client needs):

1. Needs Assessment (identify target audience, establish goals & objectives)

2. Tactical Development (formulate specific tactics to achieve defined objectives, such as lectures, printed educational material, health screenings, evidence, etc.)

3. Implementation (overseeing tactical execution)

4. Evaluation (performing measurements in order to gauge tactical success and determine whether or not objectives were met)

Stanton Health Communications will provide services that include, but are not limited to, the following:

-   Patient communication campaigns (e.g., developing strategies to improve patient-provider communications, planning engagement initiatives to encourage patients to be accountable for their own health and adopt lifestyle habits, etc.)

-   Public education planning (e.g., special events, marketing communications, media relations, etc.)

-   Staff training (e.g., educating healthcare providers on how to improve internal communications, patient-provider communications, etc., with a goal of increasing patient satisfaction)

-   Grant writing (e.g., helping hospitals and other non-profit organizations secure funding for health education initiatives).

-   Prevention campaigns (e.g., using social and traditional marketing to promote preventive practices that increase community health through health/behavioral change)

-   Issue-focused Campaigns (e.g., developing focused campaigns around issues such as drunk driving, healthy eating/childhood obesity, teen pregnancy, sexual abuse, drug addiction, etc.)

-   Non-Profit Status Consulting (e.g., assisting community hospitals and health systems develop programs focused on demonstrating and maintaining non-profit status (something that is being scrutinized more closely by many state governments)

MARKETING & SALES

Stanton Health Communications has developed a marketing plan that involves the following primary tactics:

1. The use of social media channels, including LinkedIn, to network with potential customers, as well as professional peers within the health education field.

2. Printed collateral describing the consultancy. A high-quality, four-color panel card will be developed. It will include Stanton's photo, a brief bio, a bulleted list of services offered, and testimonials from clients or former colleagues.

3. A website with complete details about the consultancy. This will include a customer inquiry form for prospective clients.

4. Semi-annual direct mailings, consisting of an introductory letter with a strong call to action and the panel card described above, to key prospects (e.g., the target markets detailed in the Marketing & Sales section of this plan). Stanton has secured a mailing list of the top 100 U.S. hospitals/healthcare systems, and also has manually compiled contact information for the non-profit organizations listed earlier in this plan. She will utilize the services of a letter shop to prepare and send the mailings.

5. Writing expert columns for health education publications, as well as the consumer trade press, in order to raise awareness of the services that Stanton provides in conjunction with timely public health or cause-related marketing issues.

6. Periodic presentations at industry conferences attended by healthcare professionals and health educators. When cost allows, advertisements will be placed in conference-related publications.

OPERATIONS

Molly Stanton will operate her consultancy from office space within her Washington, DC, home. This will enable her to keep expenses low during her practice's formative years. Stanton already is equipped with a tablet computer, laptop, and smartphone, allowing her to perform her work almost anywhere. Basing her operations in the Washington, DC, area is ideal because it provides easy access to many of the foundations, associations, and health councils located in Washington; Arlington, Virginia; Alexandria, Virginia; Bethesda, Maryland; Rockville, Maryland, etc. When travel is needed, she is located within close proximity to the Ronald Reagan Washington National Airport.

Fees

When establishing a new consulting practice, fees must be set appropriately. Setting fees too low to undercut the competition and quickly secure new business can be problematic down the road when it becomes necessary to raise fees with existing clients. According to data from Peterson & Meadows, entry-level management consultants often charge as much as $175 per hour for their services. Fees generally are highest in coastal regions, and lower in the central states. Stanton feels that, because many of her top prospects are located in the Washington, DC, area, or in the East Coast and West Coast markets, she will be able to charge a rate of $160 per hour for her services. With all projects, clients will be asked to contract for/agree upon a set number of service hours.

FINANCIAL ANALYSIS

The following statement shows Stanton Health Communications' projected revenue and net income for the years 2012, 2013, and 2014. Additional financial statements, prepared by our accountant, are available upon request.

Revenue	2012	2013	2014
Consulting	$100,800	$144,000	$192,000
Project management	$ 67,200	$ 96,000	$128,000
Total revenue	**$168,000**	**$240,000**	**$320,000**
Expenses			
Salary	$100,000	$150,000	$200,000
Insurance	$ 8,500	$ 8,500	$ 8,500
Accounting & legal	$ 2,500	$ 1,500	$ 1,500
Office supplies	$ 750	$ 750	$ 750
Equipment	$ 5,000	$ 2,500	$ 2,500
Marketing & advertising	$ 15,000	$ 10,000	$ 10,000
Telecommunications & Internet	$ 2,000	$ 2,250	$ 2,500
Professional development	$ 6,000	$ 7,000	$ 8,000
Unreimbursed travel	$ 10,000	$ 15,000	$ 20,000
Donations & contributions	$ 5,000	$ 10,000	$ 15,000
Subscriptions & dues	$ 565	$ 565	$ 565
Misc.	$ 500	$ 500	$ 500
Total expenses	**$155,815**	**$208,565**	**$269,815**
Net income	**$ 12,185**	**$ 31,435**	**$ 50,185**

Home Brewing Supplies Company

Peterson's Homebrew LLC

123 W. Division St.
Appleton, WI 54913

Paul Greenland

Peterson's Homebrew LLC is a direct seller of equipment kits and related supplies needed to brew beer in one's home.

EXECUTIVE SUMMARY

Peterson's Homebrew is a direct seller of equipment kits and related supplies needed to brew beer in one's home (e.g., for "homebrewing"). The business is being established as a part-time operation by Brian Peterson, a successful independent sales representative for several aftermarket automotive parts manufacturers.

When he's not selling auto parts, Peterson enjoys brewing his own beer. He has engaged in homebrewing for more than 10 years. His beer recipes have attracted the attention and admiration of others at parties and special events, and his nut brown ale has won awards at several Midwestern amateur brewing competitions.

Over the years, many of Peterson's automotive customers have expressed an interest in his hobby. Frequently, he is asked to provide information on how to get started with homebrewing. Sensing an opportunity, Peterson has decided to establish a part-time business focused on providing prospective homebrewers with the information and basic equipment and supplies that they will need.

Peterson's part-time operation is a perfect complement to his existing full-time sales career because, initially, it will involve selling to the same customer base. Better still, many of the customers who frequent his clients' automotive repair businesses also are prospective homebrewing customers.

A reputable wholesaler has agreed to provide Peterson with the pre-packaged equipment kits that will serve as the nucleus of his business. The wholesaler has agreed to drop-ship the kits to Peterson's customers for a nominal charge, allowing him to concentrate on sales, as opposed to inventory management and shipping.

Peterson's supplier also sells popular recipe kits (e.g. ingredients) for brewing many different types of beer. As with the homebrewing equipment kits, he will be able to purchase these ingredients at wholesale and have them dropped-shipped to customers. This will provide a steady stream of revenue from customers following the purchase of their initial homebrewing equipment. By employing a direct sales approach, Peterson will differentiate himself from competitors (mainly Internet- and catalog-based operations) by being available to answer homebrewing questions in person.

MARKET ANALYSIS

With the exception of the slightly larger markets of Appleton (78,000) and Green Bay (104,000), most of the automotive repair shops that Brian Peterson serves are located in communities with populations ranging between 40,000 and 60,000 people. Collectively, the communities of Eau Claire, Wausau, Oshkosh, Fond du Lac, Sheboygan, Appleton, and Green Bay are home to approximately 450,000 individuals, providing ample opportunity for growth and expansion.

Homebrewing appeals to both men and women. However, based on his knowledge of the hobby, Peterson is confident that men between the ages of 35 and 64, with household income of at least $50,000, represent the greatest opportunity. Therefore, he will target his sales and marketing efforts toward this specific demographic segment.

According to Royal & Associates Consulting LLC, in 2012 males represented more than 50 percent of the collective populations of Eau Claire, Wausau, Oshkosh, Fond du Lac, Sheboygan, Appleton, and Green Bay (229,500).

In terms of age, the population was further subdivided as follows in 2012:

- 35-44: 12.3%

- 45-54: 12.9%

- 55-64: 10.5%

Annual household income was categorized this way:

- $50,000-$74,999 (17.4%)

- $75,000-$99,999 (9.6%)

- $100,000-$149,999 (9.0%)

- $150,000+ (4.5%)

INDUSTRY ANALYSIS

Throughout the world, people have been brewing their own beer for thousands of years. However, the practice was not legal in the United States until 1978, when a related bill was signed by President Jimmy Carter. (The majority of states had legalized the practice by the early 21st century, with the exception of Mississippi and Alabama.) However, On December 7 of that year, Charlie Matzen and Charlie Papazian established the Boulder, Colorado-based American Home Brewers Association (AHA) and began publishing the magazine, Zymurgy. The following year, the AHA hosted its first National Homebrew Competition and National Homebrewers Conference.

National Homebrew Day was recognized by Congress on May 2, 1988, after being introduced by Colorado Rep. David Skaggs. The AHA achieved steady growth throughout the decades, and by 2011 counted approximately 28,000 people among its membership base. According to the association, by 2011 the United States was home to roughly 1 million homebrewers, 1,000 homebrewing clubs, and more than 300 homebrewing competitions.

Homebrewing appeared to be poised for continued success during the second decade of the 21st century. In 2011 the AHA reported that a record 1,650 homebrewers submitted an unprecedented 6,996 entries during its National Homebrew Competition, which was the largest international contest of its kind. Likewise, consumer interest in small and/or independent breweries (e.g., craft breweries) continued to rise. According to the Brewers Association, craft breweries achieved production increases totaling more than 1 million barrels from 2009 to 2010, as well as a 12 percent increase in sales. The number of U.S. breweries also increased 5 percent, reaching 1,759 and surpassing the previous high of 1,751 in 1900.

The direct selling model that Peterson's Homebrew will follow has been met with success in many industries. According to figures from the Direct Selling Association, direct sales totaled $28.56 billion in 2010, at which time the United States was home to more than 16 million direct salespeople. Face-to-face selling was responsible for more than 80 percent of the industry's revenue. More specifically, individual, or person-to-person sales, represented 63.5 percent of sales dollars, while group selling (e.g., "parties" or events) represented 27.9 percent.

PERSONNEL

Brian Peterson is a successful independent sales representative for several aftermarket automotive parts manufacturers. Working from a home office in his hometown of Appleton, Wisconsin (located about 75 miles north of Milwaukee), Peterson serves auto repair shops located in the Wisconsin markets of Eau Claire, Wausau, Oshkosh, Fond du Lac, Sheboygan, Appleton, and Green Bay.

Peterson began his career with Diamond Automotive Parts in 1995 and quickly rose through the ranks, becoming a senior sales associate in 2000 and regional sales manager (Midwest) in 2001. After developing relationships with his peers at other organizations, Peterson decided to satisfy his entrepreneurial spirit by going into business for himself as an independent sales representative for leading automotive parts manufacturers, including Heston Brothers, Smith & Granger, and the TRI Group.

Despite the difficult economic conditions that prevailed during the 21st century's last decade, Peterson continued to succeed, producing record earnings in both 2009 and 2010, as well as 2011. Peterson is now ready for a new challenge, and seeks to blend his passion for homebrewing with his natural sales and marketing skills. By employing a direct sales model on a part-time basis, Peterson feels that he will be able to pilot his new business with minimal risk, while formulating plans to transform the operation into a national business.

Professional & Advisory Support

Peterson's Homebrew has established a business banking account with Wisconsin State Bank, as well as a merchant account for accepting credit card payments. Accounting and tax advisory services will be provided by Appleton Accounting Services. Brian Peterson has utilized an online legal document service to incorporate his new business at a minimal cost.

GROWTH STRATEGY

Year One:
Focus on generating awareness of the business and establishing a base of core customers. Meet weekly sales targets of five basic kits, three intermediate kits, one advanced kit, and five ingredient packages. Achieve net sales of at least $25,000.

Year Two:
Continue to build awareness and a base of new customers. Meet weekly sales targets of seven basic kits, five intermediate kits, three advanced kits, and seven ingredient packages. Increase annual net sales by at least 75 percent.

Year Three:
Concentrate on aggressively expanding unit sales. Meet weekly sales targets of 10 basic kits, seven intermediate kits, five advanced kits, and 10 ingredient packages. Increase annual net sales 50 percent from the previous year.

Year Four:
Operate Peterson's Homebrew on a full-time basis. Continue focusing on the aggressive expansion of unit sales. Begin researching steps needed to transform Peterson's Homebrew into a regional business following a commission-based direct sales model.

Year Five:
Seek outside investment capital needed to become a regional operation.

PRODUCTS

Pederson's Homebrew will offer three different equipment kit packages (basic, intermediate, and advanced). This will allow individuals to begin homebrewing as their budget allows. The components needed for each kit will be supplied by our wholesaler, Whitman Emmett Enterprises, which has provided the commercial food and beverage industry with a wide range of supplies and equipment for more than 65 years.

Following are details regarding each type of kit:

Basic Homebrewing Kit ($85)
This kit includes all of the fundamental items one needs to begin brewing their own beer, except bottles and ingredients.

- Airlock
- Bottle Brush
- Bottle Capper
- Bottle Caps
- Bottle Filler
- Bottling Bucket
- Brew pot
- Carboy Brush
- Clamp
- Cleaner
- Glass Carboy
- How-to DVD
- Hydrometer
- Plastic Fermenter
- Thermometer
- Tubing
- Universal Carboy Bung

Intermediate Homebrewing Kit ($135)

Our intermediate kit includes all of the same items found in the basic kit, but features two carboys, thermometers, carboy bungs, and airlocks.

Advanced Homebrewing/Kegging Kit ($300)

Our advanced kit includes everything from the intermediate kit plus a kegging system and related equipment, such as a refrigerator thermostat control.

Beer Recipe Kits

Peterson's supplier also sells popular recipe kits for many different types of beer. As with the home-brewing equipment kits, the business will be able to purchase these ingredients at wholesale and have them dropped-shipped to customers. This will provide a steady stream of revenue from customers following the purchase of their initial homebrewing equipment kits. Recipes are available in a number of different categories, including:

- Amber Ales
- Amber Lagers
- Dark Ales
- Dark Lagers
- Light Ales
- Light Lagers
- Specialty Beers
- Wheat Beers

MARKETING & SALES

1. Brian Peterson's brother, a leading graphic designer in Milwaukee, has agreed to create the brand identity for Peterson's Homebrew (e.g., an attractive logo and color scheme).

2. Peterson has developed a flier template that includes basic information about Peterson's Homebrew. The flier has an area that he can update with information about special deals, as well as upcoming events. He will leave this printed item with the owners of the automotive repair shops that he serves, and encourage them to display or distribute it.

3. As a sales aid, Peterson has produced his own instructional video (which will be included with every homebrewing equipment kit) to demonstrate the homebrewing process and related concepts.

4. Peterson will utilize a direct sales approach by hosting after-hours homebrewing presentations or parties at his customers' homes or places of business. In addition to demonstrating the equipment included in each of level of homebrewing kit, Peterson will show his homebrewing DVD, and provide complementary samples of his own homebrews.

5. Peterson's Homebrew will develop a simple website, providing basic details about the business; an overview of homebrewing; an online store where customers can purchase kits and ingredient packages; and a calendar of events.

6. Peterson's Homebrew will use social media to promote the business, including a Facebook page and YouTube channel.

OPERATIONS

As an independent sales consultant, Brian Peterson already is equipped with a home office that he uses for his automotive supply work. Peterson will utilize this existing space for Peterson's Homebrew during the business' formative years. Because his wholesaler has agreed to drop-ship merchandise, no storage space or logistics will be required.

FINANCIAL ANALYSIS

Detailed financial projections (available upon request) have been prepared in partnership with Appleton Accounting Services. These are based on figures provided by our wholesaler/supplier, Whitman Emmett Enterprises, which were used to calculate cost of goods sold and produce estimated annual net revenues. Following is a projected income statement for Peterson's Homebrew's first three years of part-time operations:

	2013	2014	2015
Sales			
Gross sales	$45,512	$81,952	$123,552
Cost of goods sold	$17,692	$30,732	$ 46,332
Net sales	$27,820	$51,220	$ 77,220
Expenses			
Marketing & advertising	$ 5,000	$ 5,000	$ 5,000
General/administrative	$ 250	$ 250	$ 250
Accounting/legal	$ 1,500	$ 1,000	$ 1,000
Office supplies	$ 300	$ 350	$ 400
Insurance	$ 550	$ 550	$ 550
Salary	$15,000	$25,000	$ 45,000
Payroll taxes	$ 1,800	$ 3,000	$ 6,600
Postage	$ 150	$ 150	$ 150
Fuel	$ 1,438	$ 1,725	$ 2,875
Total expenses	**$25,988**	**$37,025**	**$ 61,825**
Net income	**$ 1,832**	**$14,195**	**$ 15,395**

Assuming these projections prove to be accurate, Brian Peterson is confident that net sales will exceed $100,000 during your four, when he takes the business full-time.

This plan will be evaluated on a semi-annual basis during the first three years of operations.

Landscaping Service
Greenscapes Lawn Care

34541 30 Mile Rd.
Lenox, MI 48050

Zuzu Enterprises

Greenscapes Lawn Care will offer exceptional landscaping and lawn care services to the residential, commercial, and municipality/school markets in the Northern Macomb and Southeaster St. Clair County area.

EXECUTIVE SUMMARY

Greenscapes Lawn Care will offer exceptional landscaping and lawn care services to the residential, commercial, and municipality/school markets in the Northern Macomb and Southeaster St. Clair County area.

SERVICES OFFERED

Greenscapes will offer a wide variety of services throughout the year to fit every need and every budget. A breakdown of our services, by season, is provided below:

Spring
- Lawn analysis—climate, soil condition, grass type, lawn usage
- Landscape design
- Planting/transplanting—trees, shrubs, annuals, perennials
- Mulch/decorative stone
- Trimming/shaping trees and shrubs
- Fertilization
- Aeration
- Weed prevention

Summer
- Fertilization
- Weed control
- Lawn care/mowing

- Edging

- Pest/disease control

- Trimming/shaping trees and shrubs

- Tree/stump removal

Fall

- Winterization of plants and lawn (tree wrapping, etc.)

- Sprinkler system

Winter

- Snow removal—plowing and shoveling

- Ice prevention/removal

- Holiday decorating

EQUIPMENT

To provide these services, Greenscapes Lawn Care will need to procure the following equipment:

- Trucks—2

- Plows—2

- Trailers—2

- Industrial riding mowers—2

- Sprayers—2

- Aerators—2

- Trimmers—2

- Shovels—4

- Rakes—4

- Blowers—2

- Hedge trimmers—2

- Dethatchers—2

- Edgers—2

- Pole saws—2

- Wheel barrels—2

The trucks will be leased at a competitive price and outfitted with trailer hitches and adhesive company logos. The trailers will be the same color as the trucks and feature the same company logo.

All equipment will be inspected weekly and repaired or replaced as necessary.

SERVICE AREA

Our primary service area is Northern Macomb and South Western St. Clair Counties, including Lenox, New Haven, Armada, Richmond, Richmond Township, Casco, Ray, Berlin, Riley, Ira, Memphis, and Columbus. This area features 400,000 homes, 85% of which are owner-occupied. The median home value is $175,000, and more than 90% have lived in the same house for the past 5 years.

Conversely, more than 50% of residents in this area commute at least 30 minutes or more to work each day. This dedicated travel time leave less time for homeowners to maintain their properties.

CUSTOMER BASE

Commercial

Commercial customers will comprise approximately 40% of our business. Commercial properties need to focus on their core business activities, not wasting their time and energies on landscape design and maintenance.

At the same time, commercial enterprises must present an eye-pleasing façade to their customers. The importance of curb appeal cannot be stressed enough; it can be a significant factor to potential customers in deciding whether or not to frequent a business—indicating if the business is successful, if it cares about details, and if it is likely to be in business for long.

Municipalities & Schools

Municipalities and schools comprise another 25% of our business. Typically these services have been provided by in-house departments, but our prices make us a more cost effective option. Consequently, many municipalities and school systems are looking to outsource this work to save money.

Residential

Residential customers will comprise the final 35% of our business. In the current fast pace of life where people are required to work longer hours and spend a significant amount of time commuting to and from work, people seem to have less and less time to devote to yard work. Add children and two-income families into the mix and it is a wonder anyone has adequate time to devote to the maintenance and beautification of their yard.

LEVELS OF SERVICE

Customers may pick and choose the specific services and frequency to meet their individual needs. Commercial and municipal/school properties tend to choose weekly maintenance, while residential customers may choose specific, periodic services or weekly, bi-weekly, or monthly packages.

Some clients may also elect to have services performed for certain time periods such as illness or extended vacations.

Greenscapes is proud to accommodate the specific schedule, budget, and need of each individual client.

SCHEDULING

When at all possible, we will schedule nearby locations on the same day to minimize travel time between job sites. This will allow us to complete as many jobs as possible on any given day.

If a client insists on service on a day that we are normally not in the area and thus requires a special trip, a travel fee may be added to the service cost.

PRICING

Job pricing varies from site to site depending on the specific services selected, the frequency of service, the travel time to the job site, and the overall square feet of the work area. A job quote will be prepared for each prospective client based on these factors, and a written assessment will be provided to the client for approval before work can begin.

Pricing for basic services on a half acre lot includes the following:

Service	Cost
Aeration	$ 75
Edging	$ 75
Fertilization	$ 100
Holiday decorating	$ 300
Ice prevention/removal	$ 75
Landscape design	$ 500
Lawn analysis—climate, soil condition, grass type, lawn usage	$ 200
Lawn care/mowing	$ 25–40
Mulch/decorative stone	$ 350
Pest/disease control	$ 200
Planting/transplanting—trees, shrubs, annuals, perennials	$75–150
Snow removal—plowing and shoveling	$ 150
Sprinkler system	$ 100
Tree/stump removal	$ 250
Trimming/shaping trees and shrubs	$ 75
Weed control/prevention	$ 30–50
Winterization of plants and lawn (tree wrapping, etc.)	$ 250

Customers who pre-pay for services or who opt for year-round coverage will receive a 10% discount. Those who purchase multiple services will also be provided with discounts on a sliding scale.

MARKETING & ADVERTISING

Initially, we will approach businesses, municipalities, and school systems with a synopsis of our services and competitive prices. Bids will be made when appropriate. Mailings will be sent to homeowners in our targeted market. When jobs are secured, we will promote ourselves to neighboring homes or businesses via signs, mailings, and door-to-door sales.

PERSONNEL

Owner/Operator

Jack Marshall is the owner/operator of Greenscapes Lawn Care. Jack earned a degree in horticultural services from Michigan State University where he minored in Business. He also has 12 years' experience in the landscape industry, including working for both a greenhouse and a landscaping service throughout high school and college. While at MSU, Jack was a member of the Horticulture Club and he won an internship as a horticulture assistant at the Country Club of Detroit in Grosse Pointe Farms, Michigan.

Jack's extensive hands-on experiences as well as his educational background make him uniquely positioned to open and operate a successful landscape business.

Jack will perform all site assessments and quotes as well as lawn analysis. He will draft a service plan for each property and discuss it with customers before service is agreed upon. The site plan will guide all workers on the service and specific needs of each individual property.

Staff

A staff of three employees will be employed on a regular basis to carry out the work of Greenscapes Lawn Care.

Seasonal Staff

Each spring and summer season, additional staff may be hired as needed. Ideally, college students home on break will be available to take on the additional summer business.

Uniforms

All employees will wear company uniforms at all times while on duty. This will make them easily recognizable to business and homeowners. Uniforms will consist of green pants or shorts, matching green t-shirt with company logo, and coordinating baseball hats. Each employee will receive 4 sets of uniforms, with the option to purchase additional items as necessary.

FINANCIALS

Accounting/Billing

All account billing will be handled by Jack's wife, Jane Marshall. Jane is employed as an accountant with a mid-size manufacturing plant in the area and will handle the businesses accounts in the evenings and weekends.

Start Up Costs

Equipment	Cost
Trucks—2	$ 5,000 (down payment)
Plows—2	$ 3,000
Trailers—2	$ 4,000
Industrial riding mowers—2	$22,000
Sprayers—2	$ 1,000
Aerators—2	$ 6,000
Trimmers—2	$ 800
Shovels—4	$ 300
Rakes—4	$ 200
Blowers—2	$ 450
Hedge trimmers—2	$ 1,000
Dethatchers—2	$ 3,000
Edgers—2	$ 1,100
Pole saws—2	$ 1,200
Wheel barrels—2	$ 600
Marketing & Advertising	$ 1,500
Website development	$ 500
Legal	$ 1,000
Office supplies, incl. computer	$ 1,500
Miscellaneous	$ 1,000
Total	**$55,150**

Marketing Communications Firm

Meridian Consulting

3439 San Jose Blvd.
Santa Monica, CA 60677

This plan describes an effort to launch a business on an international scale. Because of the nature of the business, the plan considers the business's positioning in the world marketplace and the heavy competition already in the arena.

This business plan appeared in Business Plans Handbook, Volume 5. It has been updated for this edition.

EXECUTIVE SUMMARY

Meridian Consulting will be formed as a consulting company specializing in marketing high-technology products in international markets. Its founders are former marketers of consulting services, technology products, and market research, all in international markets. They are founding Meridian to formalize the consulting services they offer.

Objectives

1. Sales of $507,500 in 2012 and $1 million by 2014.

2. Gross margin higher than 75%.

3. Net income more than 5% of sales by the third year.

Mission

Meridian Consulting offers high-tech manufacturers a reliable, high-quality alternative to in-house resources for business development, market development, and channel development on an international scale. A true alternative to in-house resources offers a very high level of practical experience, know-how, contacts, and confidentiality. Clients must know that working with Meridian is a more professional, less risky way to develop new business, even than working completely in-house with their own people. Meridian must also be able to maintain financial balance, charging a high value for its services and delivering an even higher value to its clients. Initial focus will be development in the European and Latin American markets, or for European clients in the United States market.

Keys to Success

- Excellence in fulfilling the promise—completely confidential, reliable, trustworthy expertise and information.

- Developing visibility to generate new business leads.

- Leveraging a single pool of expertise into multiple revenue generation opportunities: retainer consulting, project consulting, market research, and published market research reports.

COMPANY SUMMARY

Meridian Consulting is a new company providing high-level expertise in international high-tech business development, channel development, distribution strategies, and the marketing of high-tech products. It will focus initially on providing two kinds of international triangles:

- Providing United States clients with development for European and Latin American markets.

- Providing European clients with development for the United States and Latin American markets.

As the consultancy grows it will take on people and consulting work in related markets, such as the rest of Latin America and the Far East. The business will seek additional leverage by taking brokerage positions and representation positions to create percentage holdings in product results.

Company Ownership

Meridian Consulting will be created as a California C corporation based in Santa Marita County, owned by its principal investors and principal operators. As of this writing it has not been chartered yet and is still considering alternatives of legal formation.

Start-up Plan

Start-up expenses

Legal	$ 1,450
Stationery etc.	$ 4,350
Brochures	$ 7,250
Interactive marketing	$ 7,250
Insurance	$ 508
Expensed equipment	$ 4,350
Other	$ 1,450
Total start-up expense	**$26,608**

Start-up assets needed

Cash requirements	$36,250
Start-up inventory	$72,500
Other short-term assets	$10,150
Total short-term assets	**$46,400**

Long-term assets

Capital assets	$ 0
Total assets	**$46,400**
Total start-up requirements:	**$73,008**
Left to finance:	$ 0

Start-up funding plan

Investment

Investor 1	$29,000
Investor 2	$29,000
Other	$14,500
Total investment	**$72,500**

Short-term borrowing

Unpaid expenses	$ 7,250
Subtotal short-term borrowing	$ 7,250
Long-term borrowing	$ 0
Total borrowing	**$ 7,250**
Loss at start-up	($33,350)
Total equity	**$39,150**
Total debt and equity	**$46,400**
Checkline	$ 0

COMPANY SERVICES

Meridian offers expertise in channel distribution, channel development, and market development, sold and packaged in various ways that allow clients to choose their preferred relationship: these include retainer consulting relationships, project-based consulting, relationship and alliance brokering, sales representation and market representation, project-based market research, published market research, and information forum events.

Services

Meridian offers the expertise a high-technology company needs to develop new product distribution and new market segments in new markets. This can be taken as high-level retainer consulting, market research reports, or project-based consulting.

Service Description

1. Retainer consulting: we represent a client company as an extension of its business development and market development functions. This begins with complete understanding of the client company's situation, objectives, and constraints. We then represent the client company quietly and confidentially, sifting through new market developments and new opportunities as is appropriate to the client, representing the client in initial talks with possible allies, vendors, and channels.

2. Project consulting: Proposed and billed on a per-project and per-milestone basis, project consulting offers a client company a way to harness our specific qualities and use our expertise to solve specific problems, develop and/or implement plans and develop specific information.

3. Market research: group studies available to selected clients at $5,000 per unit. A group study is packaged and published, a complete study of a specific market, channel, or topic. Examples might be studies of developing consumer channels in Japan or Mexico, or implications of changing margins in software.

Competitive Comparison

The competition comes in several forms:

1. The most significant competition is no consulting at all or companies choosing to do business development and channel development and market research in-house. Their own managers do this on their own, as part of their regular business functions. Our key advantage in competition with in-house development is that managers are already overloaded with responsibilities; they don't have time for additional responsibilities in new market development or new channel development. Also, Meridian can approach alliances, vendors, and channels on a confidential basis, gathering information and making initial contacts in ways that the corporate managers can't.

2. The high-level prestige management consulting: McKinsey, Bain, Boston Consulting Group, etc. These are essentially generalists who take their name-brand management consulting into specialty areas. Their weakness is the management structure that has the partners selling new jobs and inexperienced associates delivering the work. We compete against them as experts in our specific fields, and with the guarantee that our clients will have the top-level people doing the actual work.

3. The third general kind of competitor is the international market research company: International Data Corporation (IDC), Dataquest, SRI International, etc. These companies are formidable competitors for published market research and market forums, but cannot provide the kind of high-level consulting that Meridian will provide.

4. The fourth kind of competition is the market-specific smaller house.

5. Sales representation, brokering, and deal catalysts are an ad-hoc business form that will be defined in detail by the specific nature of each individual case.

Sales Promotion

The business will begin with a corporate website, social media presence, and brochure establishing the positioning. This will be included as part of the start-up expenses.

Sourcing

1. The key fulfillment and delivery will be provided by the principals of the business. The real core value is professional expertise, provided by a combination of experience, hard work, and education (in that order).

2. We will turn to qualified professionals for freelance back-up in market research and presentation and report development, which are areas that we can afford to contract out without risking the core values provided to the clients.

Technology

Meridian Consulting will maintain latest Windows and Macintosh capabilities including:

1. Complete e-mail and FTP server connectivity for working and exchanging information with clients.

2. Complete presentation facilities for preparation and delivery of multimedia presentations on Macintosh or Windows machines in various formats (live and Web-based video presentations).

3. Complete desktop publishing facilities for delivery of regular retainer reports, project output reports, marketing materials, and market research reports.

Future Services

In the future, Meridian will expand by providing expanded coverage in additional markets (e.g., all of Latin America, Far East, Western Europe) and product areas (e.g., telecommunications and technology integration).

We also are studying the possibility of an e-newsletter, topical blogs, and a social media strategy involving Twitter and LinkedIn.

MARKET ANALYSIS SUMMARY

Meridian will be focusing on high-technology manufacturers of computer hardware and software, services, and networking, who want to sell into markets in the United States, Europe, and Latin America. These are mostly larger companies, and occasionally medium-sized companies.

Our most important group of potential customers is executives in larger corporations. These are marketing managers, general managers, and sales managers, sometimes charged with international focus and sometimes charged with market or even specific channel focus. They do not want to waste their time or risk their money looking for bargain information or questionable expertise. As they go into markets looking at new opportunities, they are very sensitive to risking their company's name and reputation.

Market Segmentation

1. Large manufacturer corporations: our most important market segment is the large manufacturer of high-technology products, such as Apple, IBM, Microsoft, or Siemens. These companies will be calling on Meridian for development functions that are better spun off rather than managed in-house, and for market research and market forums.

2. Medium-sized growth companies: particularly in software, multimedia, and some related high-growth fields, Meridian will be able to offer an attractive development alternative to the company

that is management constrained and unable to address opportunities in new markets and new market segments.

Industry Analysis

Consulting is a disorganized industry, with participants ranging from major international name-brand consultants to tens of thousands of individuals. One of Meridian's challenges will be establishing itself as a "real" consulting company, positioned as a relatively risk-free corporate purchase.

Industry Participants

The consulting "industry" is pulverized and disorganized, consisting of thousands of smaller consulting organizations and individual consultants for every one of the few dozen well-known companies.

At the highest level are the few well-established major names in management consulting. Most of these are organized as partnerships established in major markets around the world, linked together by interconnecting directors and sharing the name and corporate wisdom. Some evolved from accounting companies and some from management consulting. These companies charge very high rates for consulting, and maintain relatively high overhead structures and fulfillment structures based on partners selling and junior associates fulfilling.

At the intermediate level are some function-specific or market-specific consultants, including market research firms and channel development firms.

Some consulting work is little more than contract expertise provided by somebody looking for a job and offering consulting services as a stop-gap measure while looking.

Distribution Patterns

Consulting is sold and purchased mainly on a word-of-mouth basis, with relationships and previous experience being by far the most important factor.

The major name-brand houses have locations in major cities and major markets, and executive-level managers or partners develop new business through industry associations, business associations, and chambers of commerce and industry, etc., even in some cases social associations such as country clubs.

The medium-level houses are generally area-specific or function-specific, and are not easily able to leverage their business through distribution.

Competition and Buying Patterns

The key element in purchase decisions made at the Meridian client level is trust in the professional reputation and reliability of the consulting firm.

Main Competitors

1. High-level prestige management consulting

Strengths: International locations managed by owner-partners with a high level of presentation and understanding of general business. Enviable reputations that make purchase of consulting an easy decision for a manager, despite the very high prices.

Weaknesses: General business knowledge doesn't substitute for the specific market, channel, and distribution expertise of Meridian, focusing on high-technology markets and products only. Also, fees are extremely expensive, and work is generally done by very junior-level consultants, even though sold by high-level partners.

2. The international market research company

Strengths: International offices, specific market knowledge, permanent staff developing market research information on a consistent basis, good relationships with potential client companies.

Weaknesses: Market numbers are not marketing, not channel development or market development. Although these companies compete for some of the business Meridian is after, they cannot really offer the same level of business understanding at a high level.

3. Market-specific or function-specific experts

Strengths: Expertise in market or functional areas. Meridian should not try to compete with established players in their respective niches of market research or channel management.

Weaknesses: The inability to spread beyond a specific focus, or to rise above a specific focus, to provide actual management expertise, experience, and wisdom beyond the specifics.

4. In-house Expertise

The most significant competition is no consulting at all, or companies choosing to do business development and channel development and market research in-house.

Strengths: No incremental cost except travel; also, the general work is done by the people who are entirely responsible, the planning done by those who will implement.

Weaknesses: Most managers are terribly overburdened already, unable to find incremental resources in time and people to apply to incremental opportunities. Also, there is a lot of additional risk in market development and channel development done in-house from the ground up. Finally, retainer-based antenna consultants can greatly enhance a company's reach and extend its position into conversations that otherwise might never have taken place.

Market Analysis

As indicated in the following table, we must focus on a few thousand well-chosen potential customers in the United States, Europe, and Latin America. These few thousand high-tech manufacturing companies are the key customers for Meridian.

Market analysis

Potential customers	Customers	Growth rate
U.S. High Tech	5,000	10.00%
European High Tech	1,000	15.00%
Latin America	250	35.00%
Other	10,000	2.00%
Total	**16,250**	**6.27%**

STRATEGY SUMMARY

Meridian will focus on three geographical markets, the United States, Europe, and Latin America, and in limited product segments: personal computers (including tablets), software, networks, mobile telecommunications, handheld devices (non-telecommunication), and technology integration products.

The target customer is usually a manager in a larger corporation, and occasionally an owner or president of a medium-sized corporation in a high-growth period.

Pricing Strategy

Consulting will be based on $7,250 per day for project consulting, $2,900 per day for market research, and $14,500 per month and up for retainer consulting. Market research reports should be priced at $7,250 per report, which will of course require that reports be very well planned and focused on very important topics that are well presented.

Sales Forecast

Sales	2013	2014	2015
Retainer consulting	$290,000	$ 507,500	$ 616,250
Project consulting	$391,500	$ 471,250	$ 507,500
Market research	$176,900	$ 217,500	$ 290,000
Strategic reports	$ 0	$ 72,500	$ 181,250
Other	$ 0	$ 0	$ 0
Total sales	**$858,400**	**$1,268,750**	**$1,595,000**
Direct costs			
Retainer consulting	$ 43,500	$ 55,100	$ 69,600
Project consulting	$ 65,250	$ 81,200	$ 101,500
Market research	$121,800	$ 152,250	$ 189,950
Strategic reports	$ 0	$ 29,000	$ 58,000
Other	$ 0	$ 0	$ 0
Subtotal direct cost of sales	**$230,550**	**$ 317,550**	**$ 419,050**

Strategic Alliances

At this writing strategic alliances with Morgan and Daley are possibilities, given the content of existing discussions. Given the background of prospective partners, we might also be talking to European companies including Siemens and others, and to United States companies related to Apple Computer. In Latin America we would be looking at the key local high-technology vendors.

MANAGEMENT SUMMARY

The initial management team depends on the founders themselves, with little back-up. As we grow we will take on additional consulting help, plus graphic/editorial, sales, and marketing.

Organizational Structure

Meridian should be managed by working partners, in a structure taken mainly from Morgan Partners. In the beginning we assume 3-5 partners:

- Richard Wiley

- At least one, probably two partners from Morgan and Daley

- One strong European partner, based in Paris.

- The organization has to be very flat in the beginning, with each of the founders responsible for his or her own work and management.

- One other strong partner

Management Team

The Meridian business requires a very high level of international experience and expertise, which means that it will not be easy to leverage in the common consulting company mode—in which partners run the business and make sales, while associates fulfill. Partners will necessarily be involved in the fulfillment of the core business proposition, providing the expertise to the clients.

The initial personnel plan is still tentative. It should involve 3-5 partners, 1-3 consultants, 1 strong editorial/graphic person with good staff support, 1 strong marketing person, an office manager, and a secretary. Later we will add more partners, consultants and sales staff.

Personnel Plan

		2013	2014	2015
Partners	1.40	$208,800	$253,750	$290,000
Consultants	1.25	$ 0	$ 72,500	$ 91,350
Editorial/graphic	1.20	$ 26,100	$ 31,900	$ 37,700
VP marketing	1.10	$ 29,000	$ 72,500	$ 79,750
Sales people	1.10	$ 0	$ 43,500	$ 47,850
Office manager	1.10	$ 10,875	$ 43,500	$ 47,850
Secretarial	1.10	$ 7,613	$ 29,000	$ 31,900
Other	1.10	$ 0	$ 0	$ 0
Subtotal		**$282,388**	**$546,650**	**$626,400**

FINANCIAL PLAN

Projected Profit and Loss

A detailed monthly pro-forma income statement for the first year is available upon request. Annual estimates are included here.

	2013	2014	2015
Sales	$858,400	$1,268,750	$1,595,000
Cost of sales	$230,550	$ 317,550	$ 419,050
Gross margin	$627,850	$ 951,200	$1,175,950
Gross margin percent	73.14%	74.97%	73.73%
Operating expenses:			
Advertising/promotion	$ 52,200	$ 58,000	$ 63,800
Public relations	$ 43,500	$ 43,500	$ 47,850
Travel	$130,500	$ 87,000	$ 159,500
Miscellaneous	$ 8,700	$ 10,150	$ 11,600
Payroll expense	$282,388	$ 546,650	$ 626,400
Leased equipment	$ 8,700	$ 10,150	$ 10,150
Utilities	$ 17,400	$ 17,400	$ 17,400
Insurance	$ 5,220	$ 2,900	$ 2,900
Rent	$ 26,100	$ 0	$ 0
Depreciation	$ 290	$ 653	$ 870
Payroll burden	$ 39,534	$ 76,531	$ 87,696
Total operating expenses	**$614,532**	**$ 852,934**	**$1,028,166**
Profit before interest and taxes	$ 13,318	$ 98,266	$ 147,784
Interest expense ST	$ 5,220	$ 18,560	$ 18,560
Interest expense LT	$ 7,250	$ 7,250	$ 7,250
Taxes incurred	$ 212	$ 18,115	$ 30,494
Net profit	**$ 636**	**$ 54,341**	**$ 91,480**
Net profit/sales	**0.07%**	**4.28%**	**5.74%**

Projected Cash Flow

Cash flow projections are critical to our success. The annual cash flow figures are included here. Detailed monthly numbers are available upon request.

	2013	2014	2015
Net profit:	**$ 636**	**$ 54,341**	**$ 91,480**
Plus:			
Depreciation	$ 26,100	$ 0	$ 0
Change in accounts payable	$ 37,799	$ 2,079	$ 16,001
Current borrowing (repayment)	$ 87,000	$145,000	$ 0
Long-term borrowing (repayment)	$ 72,500	$ 0	$ 0
Subtotal	**$224,035**	**$201,420**	**$107,481**
Less:			
Change in accounts receivable	$145,000	$140,754	$ 73,480
Subtotal	**$145,000**	**$140,754**	**$ 73,480**
Net cash flow	**$ 79,035**	**$ 60,666**	**$ 34,001**
Cash balance	**$115,285**	**$175,951**	**$209,952**

Projected Balance Sheet

The balance sheet shows healthy growth of net worth, and strong financial position. The monthly estimates are available upon request.

	2013	2014	2015
Short-term assets starting balances			
Cash	$36,250	$115,285	$175,951	$209,952
Accounts receivable	$ 0	$145,000	$285,754	$359,235
Other short-term assets	$10,150	$ 10,150	$ 10,150	$ 10,150
Total short-term assets	**$46,400**	**$270,435**	**$471,856**	**$579,337**
Long-term assets			
Accumulated depreciation	$ 0	$ 26,100	$ 26,100	$ 26,100
Total long-term assets	**$ 0**	**($ 26,100)**	**($ 26,100)**	**($ 26,100)**
Total assets	**$46,400**	**$244,335**	**$445,756**	**$553,237**
Debt and equity			
Accounts payable	$ 7,250	$ 45,049	$ 47,128	$ 63,129
Short-term notes	$ 0	$ 87,000	$232,000	$232,000
Subtotal short-term liabilities	**$ 7,250**	**$132,049**	**$279,128**	**$295,129**
Long-term liabilities	$ 0	$ 72,500	$ 72,500	$ 72,500
Total liabilities	**$ 7,250**	**$204,549**	**$351,628**	**$367,629**
Paid in capital	$72,500	$ 72,500	$ 72,500	$ 72,500
Retained earnings	($33,350)	($ 33,350)	($ 32,713)	$ 21,628
Earnings	$ 0	$ 636	$ 54,341	$ 91,480
Total equity	**$39,150**	**$ 39,787**	**$ 94,128**	**$185,609**
Total debt and equity	**$46,400**	**$244,335**	**$445,756**	**$553,237**
Net worth	**$39,150**	**$ 39,787**	**$ 94,128**	**$185,609**

Massage Therapist

Healing Hands Massage Therapy LLC

25 Pine Ave.
Crater Ridge, AZ 59714

Paul Greenland

Healing Hands Massage Therapy is a newly established practice specializing in chair massage, and with a special focus on the corporate and healthcare markets.

EXECUTIVE SUMMARY

Healing Hands Massage Therapy is a newly established practice specializing in chair massage, and with a special focus on the corporate and healthcare markets. It consists of Lisa Robinson, a recent graduate of the Yuma, Arizona-based Hayden Locke School of Massage Therapy.

Robinson currently performs Swedish massages as an independent contractor at a local massage therapy clinic, where she has worked for six months. Recently, she was one of five Crater Ridge massage therapists to secure a contract to provide occasional massage therapy services (chair and bedside) to pre-surgical patients at Crater Ridge Memorial Hospital. Robinson desires to continue providing traditional massages at clinic, while expanding her business into the corporate and healthcare markets. The following business plan outlines her strategy for doing so.

Business Overview

Chair massage has become a popular option because it can provide immediate benefits during a short amount of time. The approach typically involves massages that are short in duration, spanning approximately 15 to 20 minutes. Utilizing a portable chair specially designed for massage, therapists provide upper-body massages that involve the head, neck, shoulders, back, arms, and hands. This style of massage can be delivered in different ways. For example, the objective may be relaxation for some individuals. In other situations, the focus may be on the alleviation of muscle tightness, tension, or pain in a specific area.

Healthcare can be a stressful experience, for both providers/caregivers and patients. Caregivers are faced with the challenge of caring for patients in environments that are increasingly complex, regulated, and fast-paced. In many cases, care must be delivered within the context of fewer resources. Because healthcare is often an "avoidance" issue, patients often enter the system with heightened levels of anxiety and stress. Certain situations, such as the moments before a surgical procedure, can greatly amplify anxiety and stress. For this reason, Lisa Robinson will make the healthcare industry a special focus for Healing Hands Massage Therapy. In addition, she will also concentrate on providing massages to employees in hectic corporate environments.

Organizational Structure

Lisa Robinson has chosen to establish Healing Hands Massage Therapy as a limited liability company. By choosing this structure, she will benefit from having limited personal liability for the debts and actions of the business. She has taken the necessary steps to establish an LLC in Arizona, including filing articles of organization with the Arizona Corporation Commission.

INDUSTRY ANALYSIS

According to Associated Bodywork & Massage Professionals, the United States was home to more than 1,500 state-approved massage therapy schools in 2009. In 2010 there were approximately 300,000 massage therapists in practice. Swedish massage and deep tissue/neuromuscular therapy were the two most widely used primary massage therapy techniques, and on-site massage was among the most popular secondary techniques. The vast majority of massage therapists are independent practitioners (77.9%). On average, independent practitioners see 10 clients per week (17.8 contact hours), generating annual income of $25,365.

MARKET ANALYSIS

Primary Market

Crater Ridge, Arizona, is located approximately 75 miles from Phoenix. The community has a strong service economy, as well as a sizable base of healthcare providers. According to recent population data, the city of Crater Ridge had an estimated 165,392 residents in 2011. This marked a 13 percent increase from 2005. Individuals over the age of 65 represent a significant (24.3%) percentage of the population, resulting in strong healthcare utilization levels.

The healthcare industry in Crater Ridge includes Crater Ridge Memorial Hospital, Greater Crater Ridge Medical Center, and Lewiston Hills Health System. Combined, these three hospitals discharged about 75,000 inpatients in 2011. That year, outpatient visits exceeded 1.3 million. Based on this information, annual patient growth rates are projected to be approximately 9 percent, according to figures from DT & Associates Research.

Crater Ridge Memorial Hospital and Greater Crater Ridge Medical Center have both received holistic health grants enabling them to provide massage therapy services. Crater Ridge Memorial Hospital's grant allows for the provision of massage therapy to both employees and patients, while Greater Crater Ridge Medical Center recently received a grant pertaining specifically to patients.

The Crater Ridge area also is home to other healthcare providers, including five outpatient surgery centers and a number of independent specialty groups (e.g., orthopedics, oncology, cardiology, etc.). These institutions also are considered to be prospects for Robinson's massage therapy practice.

Secondary Market

Healing Hands Massage Therapy also will market its services to larger organizations that have the resources to provide occasional chair massages to their employees as a workforce benefit. For the purposes of this plan, larger organizations will be defined as those with more than 100 employees. According to data obtained from the Crater Ridge Economic Development Council, organizations of this size account for about 16 percent of area employers:

- 50-99 Employees (13.3%)

- 100-249 Employees (3.1%)

PERSONNEL

Lisa Robinson

Lisa Robinson is a native of Phoenix, Arizona. Married with two children, she was inspired to enter the field of massage therapy after experiencing its benefits firsthand. In 2009 Robinson underwent a surgical procedure at a local hospital. The days leading up to her procedure were especially stressful. A complementary massage provided in the surgical holding area made all the difference in the world, allowing her to relax prior to the operation.

In 2010 Robinson graduated from the Yuma, Arizona-based Hayden Locke School of Massage Therapy. There, she completed a 32-week program consisting of more than 800 clock hours. Her studies included exposure to basic techniques and theories, as well as training and modalities such as acupressure and cranial sacral therapy. Upon graduation, she secured a professional liability policy and sat for the National Certification Examination for Therapeutic Massage and Bodywork. Certification requirements vary from state to state. She was certified in Arizona after meeting the specific requirements of the Arizona Board of Massage Therapy.

Robinson currently performs Swedish massages as an independent contractor at a local massage therapy clinic, where she has worked for six months. Recently, she was one of five Crater Ridge massage therapists to secure a contract to provide occasional massage therapy services to pre-surgical patients at Crater Ridge Memorial Hospital. Robinson plans to continue providing traditional massages at clinic in the short term, while expanding her new business into the corporate and healthcare markets.

Professional & Advisory Support

Healing Hands Massage Therapy has established a business banking account with Arizona State Bank, including a merchant account for accepting credit card payments. TaxMark, a local accounting firm, has been retained to provide tax advisory services. Lisa Robinson used an online legal forms service to prepare the documents needed to establish her limited liability company.

GROWTH STRATEGY

Many massage therapists are not marketing minded, choosing instead to concentrate on the non-business aspects of their profession. Realizing that her practice must meet defined business goals in order to be successful, Robinson has given a great deal of thought to how she will grow her practice during its formative years. She feels that, by focusing on chair massages, she will be able to better differentiate herself in the marketplace. By taking this approach, she will be able to charge a higher hourly rate for her services. While many massage therapists earn $25 per hour, she will charge between $40 and $60 per hour for her chair massage services, which will be billed in quarterly increments.

According to Associated Bodywork & Massage Professionals, most massage therapists have roughly 18 client contact hours per week, and about half of industry practitioners work at another job. Robinson's goal is to make Healing Hands Massage Therapy a full-time practice. In addition to the client contact hours listed below, Robinson understands that additional (e.g., non-compensated) hours will be needed to handle the administrative aspects of her business (e.g., invoicing, scheduling, ordering supplies, etc.).

- *Year One:* Concentrate on quality performance in her new role providing massages to pre-surgical patients at Crater Ridge Memorial Hospital. Execute marketing plan and secure at least one new major client by the year's end. Goal: 25 client contact hours per week.

- *Year Two:* Obtain at least two new major clients by the year's end. Goal: 30 client contact hours per week.

- *Year Three:* Consider expanding practice by adding an additional massage therapist (based on volume). Obtain three to five additional clients. Goal: 35 client contact hours per week.

SERVICES

1. *On-Site Patient Massage (healthcare):* services provided directly within the healthcare setting as appropriate (e.g., bedside, chair, etc.). Massages scheduled in 15-minute increments, billed to healthcare provider by the quarter-hour (two-hour minimum). Focus: reducing pain, discomfort, stress, and anxiety. Rate: $45/hour.

2. *Employee Chair Massages (healthcare & corporate):* services provided in a quiet, semi-private setting within the workplace. Focus: reducing pain, discomfort, stress and anxiety/increasing productivity, motivation, and morale. Massages scheduled in 15-minute increments, billed to client by the quarter-hour (two-hour minimum). Rate: $55/hour.

OPERATIONS

Lisa Robinson will need to purchase the following items to start her business, at a total cost of $485, which she will cover from her own savings:

- CD Player: $50
- CDs (selection of relaxing music): $30
- Disinfectant Wipes: $15
- Disposable Face Cradle Covers (500): $50
- Massage Table: $300
- Detergent (1 Gallon): $20
- Multi-purpose Massage Cream (32 Oz.): $20

Because she will provide services to clients on-site, there is no need to lease space to provide massage therapy services.

Robinson will handle client communications via her smartphone. She will use a popular online calendar service to provide prospective and existing customers with a real-time view of her schedule/availability.

MARKETING & SALES

Lisa Robinson has developed a marketing plan for her practice that includes several key tactics, including:

1. Printed collateral for prospective clients and referral sources that includes Robinson's photo, a brief bio, a bulleted list of services offered, and testimonials from former patients.

2. A website with complete details about the practice, including many of the same elements described in the printed collateral.

3. Targeted direct mail that promotes Healing Hands' capabilities to nursing administrators and holistic health managers at area hospitals and healthcare systems.

4. Targeted direct mail that promotes the practice's capabilities to human resources managers at large area corporations.

5. An incentive program that offers a free 15-minute massage to potential clients who request a meeting with Lisa Robinson.

6. Relationship building initiatives (e.g., coffee or business lunches) with individuals from the most promising client organizations.

7. An expanded Yellow Page advertisement with a short list of common services offered.

8. The use of social media channels, including LinkedIn, to network with potential clients, as well as other massage therapists.

9. Offer to write expert columns for the local newspaper and Chamber of Commerce publication, touting the patient and/or workforce benefits of massage therapy.

FINANCIAL ANALYSIS

The following income statement shows Healing Hands Massage Therapy's projected revenue and net income for the years 2012, 2013, and 2014. Additional financial statements, prepared by our accountant, are available upon request.

	2012	2013	2014
Revenues	**$61,250**	**$73,500**	**$85,750**
Expenses			
Salary	$45,000	$55,000	$65,000
Marketing & advertising	$ 3,000	$ 3,000	$ 2,500
Continuing education	$ 750	$ 750	$ 750
Accounting/legal	$ 1,000	$ 450	$ 450
Licenses & fees	$ 300	$ 300	$ 300
Supplies	$ 300	$ 300	$ 300
Equipment	$ 150	$ 150	$ 150
Insurance	$ 525	$ 550	$ 575
Payroll taxes	$ 4,200	$ 4,800	$ 5,400
Postage	$ 250	$ 250	$ 250
Transportation	$ 2,250	$ 2,587	$ 2,975
Telecommunications	$ 850	$ 850	$ 850
Total expenses	**$58,575**	**$68,987**	**$79,500**
Net income	**$ 2,675**	**$ 4,513**	**$ 6,250**

Messenger Service

Legal Deliveries

12 Woodward Ave.
Detroit, MI 48226

Heidi Denler

Legal Deliveries is a bicycle messenger/courier service in Detroit, Michigan, primarily to serve the legal market in the city. Documents and small packages will be delivered to clients and to the clerks of the courts. Law firms and attorneys will be able to expect reliable service, which is especially important because of court-imposed deadlines.

COMPANY SUMMARY

Legal Deliveries is a bicycle messenger/courier service in Detroit, Michigan, primarily to serve the legal market in the city. Documents and small packages will be delivered to clients and to the clerks of the courts. Law firms and attorneys will be able to expect reliable service, which is especially important because of court-imposed deadlines. While non-law clients will also be served, they will not be the primary market. Bicycle messengers are less expensive for clients due to lower overhead than car delivery services. In addition, they have the advantage of speed over cars because they can cut through traffic and don't need to spend time finding (and paying for) a parking place.

MISSION STATEMENT

Legal Deliveries will provide reliable, efficient delivery of small packages and documents from attorneys and law firms to court clerks as well as to other attorneys and law firms.

VISION STATEMENT

The owners of Legal Deliveries plan to exceed the expectations of clients and expand the service in other Southeast Michigan cities near courts and law offices. Employees will be carefully selected with good people skills and management skills in preparation for managing branches as they open.

BUSINESS PHILOSOPHY

In the first year of operation, marketing to law firms and attorneys will be a key component of Brad and Connie Deal's efforts. Legal Deliveries will offer the legal community a messenger service that is professional in looks, demeanor, and ethics, as well as reliable and efficient.

EXECUTIVE SUMMARY

The owners of Legal Deliveries, Brad and Connie Deal, have both worked for other delivery services in the region. After they were married, they decided to take the plunge one step further and start Legal Deliveries. Their experience at the other delivery services, along with Connie's BA in business, will serve them in good stead as they move forward with start up and planned expansion of the company.

Brad Deal's summer job during college was as a bike messenger, delivering small packages, messages, and even food. During that time he learned to repair bikes out of necessity and has all the equipment necessary for that purpose. Upon graduation with a BS in history, Brad took the LSAT and was admitted to law school. One semester was enough for him to recognize that he was not cut out to be an attorney, and he returned to his old summer employer, quickly moving into management/dispatch duties in addition to delivering.

Connie Deal took a more established route, graduating with a BS in economics and earning her MBA in two years. She minored in management, and will put the skills learned in college to use as the office manager/bookkeeper of Legal Deliveries.

ORGANIZATION STRUCTURE

Legal Deliveries will be run as a partnership of Brad and Connie Deal. The Deals plan to add messengers as needed, who will either have management skills or be trained in management so they can become managers of offices that open in other cities in Southeastern Michigan, such as Pontiac (Oakland County) and Mt. Clemens (Macomb County) with courts and high concentrations of law offices.

ADVERTISING AND PROMOTION

The Deals' marketing strategy will be to target attorneys and law firms via advertisements in the *Michigan Bar Journal*, which is sent to all accredited attorneys. In addition, ads will be bought in the Yellow Pages, *Hour Detroit*, and local papers, such as the *Monitor* to increase visibility. Brochures will be distributed among the legal community. Messengers will have t-shirts with the company name and logo, as well as an easy to remember web site URL. Ads will focus on reliability and an understanding of the needs of attorneys to have efficient, timely, professional results.

Networking is also important part of the plan to develop the business. The Deals will use their contacts in the legal community to advertise their messenger service by word of mouth. Many already know them from their prior employment in a similar service. Brad Deal's powerful persuasion tactics and people skills will be a primary part of his sales pitch to prospective customers.

In addition, a 20% discount will be offered for the first month of services upon a firm or attorney signing a year-long contract, with a long-term goal of gaining a long-term client.

Brochures will be produced by an outside print shop. The web site developer will update the site once a month, unless otherwise needed. Connie Deal will be responsible for checking the web site hourly to respond to requests from prospective clients. The computer will be set up to notify Connie of incoming e-mails immediately, by a noise sounding on the laptop. In addition, a notice will be sent to her cell phone to indicate a client e-mail.

As a sidebar to outstanding service, Legal Deliveries is an eco-friendly business, working to keep the environment safe in Detroit.

CUSTOMER BASE

Legal Deliveries will provide deliver of documents to the courts in Downtown Detroit, but the company's main focus will be deliveries made between attorneys and law firms. This strategy takes into account the shift in the legal community to settle law suits out of court, before trial.

The immediate area that will be served by Legal Deliveries is Downtown Detroit, within a 20 mile radius of Grand Circus Park and Woodward.

PRODUCTS AND SERVICES

Legal Deliveries will offer messenger/delivery services to law firms and attorneys in Downtown Detroit. Documents might include notice of subpoenas, filings with court clerks, or memos between opposing counsels. The service will be available during regular court hours. Delivery service will be available immediately upon a phone call or e-mail from a client (Connie Deal will receive notification electronically with a sound from her computer as well as a notice sent to her phone that an e-mail has arrived to provide instant responses to requests). Clients may also request a daily pick up/drop off service between their offices and those of the court clerks. Pricing will be competitive, based on the one other bicycle messenger service in Detroit.

PERSONNEL REQUIREMENTS

As founders of Legal Deliveries, Brad and Connie Deal will run the company. Brad will handle most deliveries, while Connie will run the office, scheduling staff and handling the financial aspects of Legal Deliveries. As the company client list grows, additional messengers will be hired to join Ed Mack, who is the only employee of the Deals. The fact that bicycle messengers in large cities like New York have been shown to move on quickly is not a problem because the job is not difficult and the training can be accomplished in a day of "shadowing" an experienced messenger, such as owner Brad Deal. Messengers will be paid on a per-run basis. At least one messenger will be on call in the office to step in and assume delivery duties should something unforeseen happen to another messenger on a run (e.g., flat tire).

LOCATION

The Deals have a two-room space on the first floor of a renovated loft apartment building in downtown Detroit near Grand Circus Park. The storefront is the office space, while a back entrance offers access to a room to store bicycles and make bicycle repairs as well as a place for messengers to wait for an assignment or just relax between deliveries.

STORE DESIGN AND EQUIPMENT

The headquarters for the company will be in a two-room office on the first floor of converted loft apartment building in Downtown Detroit. There will also be an area for employees to relax and enjoy lunch, and a unisex restroom.

The office will be in the front of the store, with a door opening onto the street. That space will contain the following:

- A desk and chair
- Bookshelves
- Filing cabinet
- Computer and AOI printer
- Copy machine

The back room, which has alley access, will provide bike storage for employees who do not ride their bikes to work. It will also serve as a repair shop where employees can oil their bikes, adjust brakes, repair or change tires, etc.

Cordoned off from the bike room will be an employee break room that will have the following:

- Table and chairs
- Small refrigerator
- Microwave
- Sink
- Cupboards

A unisex bathroom is in a corner of the bike room.

FINANCIAL

Startup costs will be minimal and include the following: rental for first floor office space, utilities, cell phones for all messengers, key man life insurance, liability insurance, property/casualty insurance, Wi-Fi, and web site maintenance.

Initial costs to set up the office will include the following:

- Two desks and two chairs, with floor mats
- One four-drawer filing cabinet
- Bookshelves
- A laptop and AOI printer
- A landline with two extensions
- A fax machine
- Brochure design and initial printing
- Business cards and letterhead design and printing
- Online invoice design template
- Legal fees to create the partnership
- Web site development
- T-shirts, ball caps, and outerwear with company logo for messengers
- Messenger bags with company logo

Costs for office supplies required for startup include the following:

- Paper, staplers, paper clips, pencils, pens, file folders

- Kitchen supplies (paper toweling, hand soap, dish soap, paper plates, plastic ware, paper cups)

- Bathroom supplies (toilet paper, soap, paper toweling, cleaning supplies)

The bike room will be stocked with the following:

- Repair tools and supplies

Other miscellaneous costs will include security deposits, fees for registering the name of the messenger service with state and local authorities, necessary licenses, taxes, and accounting fees.

PROFESSIONAL AND ADVISORY SUPPORT

Brad and Connie Deal will work with the SBA and loan officers at their Fifth Third bank branch for a line of credit to cover major start-up costs. The couple has committed $20,000 of their savings to cover other costs. They believe that minimal start-up costs and little competition will ensure profitability within six months of opening.

An attorney has been retained to handle all initial start-up requirements and lease arrangements, as well as develop a template for contracts with law firms and attorneys for both daily contract work and individual pickup and delivery service. In lieu of payment, the attorney has agreed to accept messenger services from Legal Deliveries for six months.

BUSINESS AND GROWTH STRATEGY

Legal Deliveries seeks to be the premier bicycle messenger service in Downtown Detroit for attorneys and law firms. Developing a customer base will be a key component of growth strategy, and is outlined under advertising and promotion.

Brad and Connie Deal plan to increase their client base 10 percent per quarter, which will result in hiring additional messengers. Repeat business will be important, so part of Connie's duties will be to contact clients regularly to ensure they have received professional, reliable, efficient service from the company.

Within three years, the Deals plan to expand to Mt. Clemens to serve the Macomb County court system and local law firms and attorneys. That expansion will be followed within two years by the opening of a branch in Pontiac to serve the Oakland County court system and its law firms and attorneys.

COMPETITION

In mid-2012 there is only one other bicycle messenger service in Detroit that serves the legal community. With the number of lawyers and the lengthy court dockets there is room for a second such service, which is what Legal Deliveries will provide. Other bicycle delivery services exist, but they expedite packages and food from area restaurants. The local pedicab service will not offer any competition to Legal Deliveries.

WEBSITE

Connie Deal will work on developing a company website with a family friend who is a web developer. The website will include contact information, background on the owners and staff, hours, and testimonials from clients. Prospective clients wanting additional information about Legal Deliveries' services will have the ability to send an immediate message to the Deals. In the future, the pair will add a live chat option to the site.

CONCLUSION

Brad and Connie Deal are creating a bicycle messenger service company for attorneys and law firms that will not only meet, but also exceed client expectations. Following their business plan, they project that they will build their client list 20 percent per year. The couple expects that by providing clients with an environmentally friendly, efficient, reliable messenger/delivery service, they will be profitable within the first quarter of operations.

Produce and Flower Market

Richmond Farmer's Market

123 Main St.
Richmond, MI 48062

Zuzu Enterprises

The Richmond Farmer's Market will offer a wide variety of fresh and locally grown fruits, vegetables, plants, flowers, herbs, Christmas trees, and holiday wreaths. Other, related items for sale include cider, honey, jams and jellies, maple syrup, fresh eggs, milk, and many varieties of fresh cheeses. Yarn produced from local sheep and alpacas may also be available for purchase.

PRODUCTS

The Market will offer a wide variety of fresh and locally grown fruits, vegetables, plants, flowers, herbs, Christmas trees, and holiday wreaths. Other, related items for sale include cider, honey, jams and jellies, maple syrup, fresh eggs, milk, and many varieties of fresh cheeses. Yarn produced from local sheep and alpacas may also be available for purchase.

All items for sale will be locally grown or produced. Customers will feel confident knowing their purchases are not only the freshest possible, but also that their money is going to support their neighbors and the local economy. Sourcing the inventory from nearby farms is environmentally friendly, thus an added bonus.

GROWING SEASON

The two major components of the growing season length are the dates of the last frost in spring and the first frost in fall. The surrounding area has the longest growing season in the state, or more than 160 days. Greenhouse-grown plants and flowers extend this season throughout the entire year.

Below are charts depicting the availability of fresh fruits, vegetables and other, related items. As you can see from the data, the vast majority of our product line will be available from May through October; these will be our busy months with approximately 80% of all income from the year being earning during this time. November and December will be somewhat busy with sales of Christmas trees, wreaths, and locally-made food gifts (jams, jellies, honey, etc.) We will be closed from January through April.

Michigan Farm Fresh Product Availability Calendars

Fruit

	Dates	January	February	March	April	May	June	July	August	September	October	November	December
Apples	8/15–2/28	■	■						■	■	■	■	■
Apricots	7/1–8/15							■	■				
Berries (black)	8/1–9/15								■	■			
Blueberries	7/13–9/15							■	■	■			
Cantaloupe	8/7–9/20								■	■			
Cherries (red tart)	7/1–7/31							■					
Cherries (sweet)	7/1–8/31							■	■				
Grapes	9/1–10/15									■	■		
Melons (watermelon, muskmelon)	8/10–frost								■	■	■		
Nectarines	8/20–9/10								■	■			
Peaches	7/15–9/20							■	■	■			
Pears	8/20–10/31								■	■	■		
Plums	8/6–9/20								■	■			
Raspberries	7/1–7/31, 8/25–9/30							■	■	■			
Rhubarb	5/1–5/31					■							
Strawberries	6/7–6/30						■						

Source: State of Michigan

Vegetables

	Dates	January	February	March	April	May	June	July	August	September	October	November	December
Asparagus	5/1–6/30					■	■						
Beans (snap, green, etc.)	7/1–9/30							■	■	■			
Beets	8/1–10/20								■	■	■		
Broccoli	7/10–10/15							■	■	■	■		
Brussels sprouts	10/1–11/15										■	■	
Cabbage	7/1–10/31							■	■	■	■		
Carrots	7/20–10/31							■	■	■	■		
Cauliflower	8/1–10/31								■	■	■		
Celery	7/1–12/31							■	■	■	■	■	■
Corn (sweet)	8/1–9/21								■	■			
Cucumbers (for pickles)	8/1–9/15								■	■			
Cucumbers (salad)	7/7–9/21							■	■	■			
Greens	6/1–10/10						■	■	■	■	■		
Eggplant	7/1–10/31							■	■	■	■		
Lettuce (head, leafy)	6/15–9/15						■	■	■	■			
Mushrooms	All year	■	■	■	■	■	■	■	■	■	■	■	■
Onions	8/25–1/31	■							■	■	■	■	■
Onions (green)	6/15–9/30						■	■	■	■			
Parsnips	9/1–10/15									■	■		
Peas (sugar)	6/1–6/30						■						
Peppers	6/15–10/15						■	■	■	■	■		
Potatoes (white)	8/1–3/31	■	■	■					■	■	■	■	■
Pumpkins	9/15–10/31									■	■		
Radishes	6/15–10/31						■	■	■	■	■		
Rutabagas	9/15–11/30									■	■	■	
Spinach	6/15–10/15						■	■	■	■	■		
Squash (yellow, zucchini)	7/15–9/15							■	■	■			
Squash (butternut, acorn)	9/15–12/31									■	■	■	■
Tomatoes (cherry, roma, slicers)	8/10–10/15								■	■	■		
Turnips	6/10–11/15						■	■	■	■	■	■	

Source: State of Michigan

Other

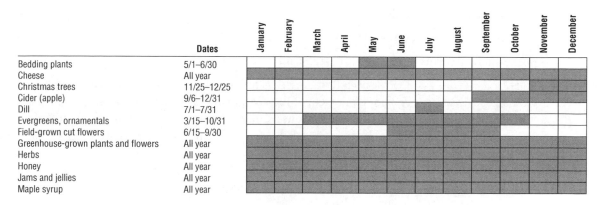

	Dates	January	February	March	April	May	June	July	August	September	October	November	December
Bedding plants	5/1–6/30												
Cheese	All year												
Christmas trees	11/25–12/25												
Cider (apple)	9/6–12/31												
Dill	7/1–7/31												
Evergreens, ornamentals	3/15–10/31												
Field-grown cut flowers	6/15–9/30												
Greenhouse-grown plants and flowers	All year												
Herbs	All year												
Honey	All year												
Jams and jellies	All year												
Maple syrup	All year												

Source: State of Michigan

Typical apple ripening dates in Michigan

Apple Varieties	Approximate ripening dates	Description & uses
Jersey (summer) Mac	Mid Aug–early Sept	Smaller and slightly sweeter than winter mac—eating, sauce, jelly.
Paula Red	Early Sept	Crunchy and juicy—good for pies, baking, sauce, drying, jelly.
Whitney Crab	Early Sept	Large-for spicing and jelly.
State Fair	Early Sept	Sweet/tart, not a real hard apple—eating sauce, jelly, baking, salads.
Early Gold	Early-mid Sept	Tart and crisp, a cross between transparent & a golden—eating, baking, pies, sauce.
Wealthy	Early-mid Sept	Tart and tangy, an antique apple that's excellent for pies, sauce and baking, tart for eating.
Jona-Mac	Mid-later Sept	Jonathan and Macintosh cross—eating, baking, sauce, jelly, pies.
Macintosh	Mid-late Sept	The perennial favorite!—eating, baking, pies (cooks down), sauce, jelly.
Cortland	Mid-late Sept	White flesh, crispy, a best seller! Excellent for eating, drying, pies, sauce, baking, jelly, salads.
Honeycrisp	Late September–early Oct	Large, firm, juicy dessert apple—our fastest selling eating apple (not recommended for baking).
Sweet 16	Late September–early Oct	Crunchy, juicy, sweet-similar to Honeycrisp (but not quite as hard or large)—eating, salads, can bake.
Snow Apples	Early Oct	Tiny, sweet, aromatic eating apple (an antique apple)—not a keeper!
Spartan	Early Oct	Crunchy, tart, juicy—eating, salads, pies, baking, keeper too!
Gala	Early Oct	Our sweetest apple! crunchy, non-acid eating apple, not large—good for lunch boxes, salads.
Wolf River	Early-mid Oct	Giant, sour old-time pie apple.
Empire	Early-mid Oct	Cross between a Mac and Red Delicious, juicy taste-test favorite!—eating, salads, sauce, drying, can bake.
Cameo	Early-mid Oct	Crisp, sweet/tart eating apple! Great for applesauce
Red Delicious	Mid Oct	A favorite old eating apple—salads and a good keeper.
Jonathan	Mid Oct	Tart and aromatic—eating, pies (does not "mush"), baking, jelly, applesauce!
Golden Delicious	Mid Oct	Sweet old favorite, stores well with moisture added—eating, salads, baking, pies, sauce.
Red Haralson	Mid Oct	Tart and juicy. Excellent flavor for pies (cooks down), drying, baking, eating.
Jona-gold	Mid Oct	Part Jonathan, part Golden Delicious-good eater, pies, baking, sauce, jelly, salads.
Ida Red	Mid-late Oct	All-purpose apple! super keeper—pies, baking, eating (tart), drying, frying!
Northern Spy	Mid-late Oct	Big and firm—pies, baking, drying, eating.
Double Red Stamen Winesap	Late Oct	"Wine-like" flavor, creamy interior, not a large apple in the north—pies, baking, eating.
Yellow Newton Pippen	Late Oct	Antique (Geo. Washington's favorite!) tart, crisp nutty flavor, good keeper and eater. Firm in pies and baking.

Source: http://www.pickyourown.org

PREFERRED SUPPLIERS

There are a number of different supplies that are considered "preferred" vendors. All have agreed to wholesale prices, have been in business for a number of years, and are within a 20-mile radius of the market.

- Bleat Dreams Farm, Allenton, MI—goat cheese and milk

- Brookwood Fruit Farm, Almont, MI—full line of fruits in the season, including apples, peaches, tart cherries, raspberries, blackberries, blueberries, strawberries, watermelon, rhubarb, and pears.

- Campau Farm, Lenox, MI—yarn from alpacas

- Country Bee, Inc., Goodells, MI—honey

- Red Barn Farm, Columbus, MI—yarn from sheep

- Woolyacreas Farms, Goodells, MI—eggs, milk, cheeses

- Ziehm Greenhouse & Produce, Romeo, MI—full line of vegetables in their season, including tomatoes, sweet peppers, hot chilies, cucumbers, eggplant, onions, pumpkins, spinach, salad greens, zucchini, broccoli, cauliflower, acorn squash, butternut squash, cabbage and potatoes. Winter vegetables are available year round. Fresh flowers, bedding plants, Christmas trees, and holiday wreaths are also available.

LOCATION

The Market will be located at 123 Main Street. This is an ideal location because it is at the center of town. This location intersects Main Street, or M-19, and 32 Mile Rd., which is a major throughway leading east to I-94 and west to M-53. This location is within walking distance to city government, local schools, the library, a youth recreation center, the city park with pool and skate park, downtown shopping, and local restaurants.

Building

The building itself is approximately 1,200 square feet and includes a small restroom and office/storage area. It has parking for approximately 10 vehicles and parking lot access from both M-19 and 32 Mile Rd. It was recently painted a rich, dark green with black trim, and the parking lot and roof were redone as well.

The building used to be a convenience store but has sat empty for a number of years. Recently the building was purchased by the Forrester Family, a prominent family in the town that owns a number of profitable businesses. One of their businesses includes the local BP gas station and convenience store located diagonally across from the vacant building. They purchased the building to ensure that no other convenience store could be opened in the immediate area to compete with their store, and have no other plans for the building. They are open to ideas for leasing the space as long as the business does not directly or indirectly impact the sales revenue of their other operations.

HOURS

- Monday—Friday: 9 am to 8 pm

- Saturday: 7 am to 8 pm

- Sunday: 7 am to 6 pm

The Market will be closed on major holidays. Restaurants wishing to purchase fresh produce and flowers may come by appointment if needed.

CUSTOMER BASE

Richmond and the surrounding communities boast over 20,000 residents. Historically, the biggest industry in the area was farming. In the late 1990s and early 2000s, several areas were converted from farmland to condominiums, site-condominiums, and luxury home developments. This building boom brought increased the population by luring commuters looking to live in a small town environment while still living relatively close to major highways and amenities.

COMPETITION

There is only one grocery store within the immediate area; it is a large chain store that sells fresh produce procured from around the world. Because it is the only store in the area, prices also tend to be 5-10% higher than the same chain store located 30 miles away that has more direct competition.

People will choose to purchase fresh produce at the Richmond Farmer's Market because they want the freshest of the fresh and because they want to support their local farmers and neighbors. Our prices are competitive with the big chain store and our convenient location and easy access make us a worthwhile alternative.

MARKETING & ADVERTISING

Several methods of advertising and marketing will be undertaken to encourage business.

- Newspaper advertisements, including coupons will be purchased in the *Macomb Daily*, *The Voice*, *The Jester*, and *The Times Herald*

- Membership in the local Chamber of Commerce—they offer a ribbon cutting ceremony, periodic press releases, and an aggressive "Buy Local, Shop Local" campaign

- Letter and follow up visit to local restaurants touting available fresh ingredients

- Grand Opening celebration to be held in conjunction with the ribbon-cutting ceremony

- Electronic sign advertising new produce, special prices, community messages

- Recipe giveaways incorporating fresh available ingredients

START-UP COSTS

	Cost
Advertisements	$ 1,500
Signage (inside and out)	$ 9,500
Grand opening celebration	$ 750
Legal fees	$ 750
Business and license fees	$ 750
Display tables	$ 5,000
Check-out counter	$ 1,750
Cash register	$ 500
Bags	$ 500
Office supplies	$ 250
Computer and software	$ 1,500
Utilities (start-up fees)	$ 900
Cleaning supplies	$ 300
Décor	$ 2,500
Lease deposit	$10,000
Inventory	$ 5,000
Total	**$41,450**

Retail Popcorn Store

Franklin's Popcorn Works

8379 Main View Dr.
Wintergreen Lake, IL 60102

Paul Greenland

Franklin's Popcorn Works is a popcorn retailer based in a popular tourist area.

EXECUTIVE SUMMARY

Franklin's Popcorn Works is a popcorn retailer based in Wintergreen Lake, Illinois, a popular tourist town. The business originated as a mobile vending operation and its owner, Peter Franklin, has prepared the following business plan to formally establish Franklin's Popcorn Works as a permanent business in Wintergreen Lake. Franklin is a resident of nearby Sycamore, Illinois. He earned an undergraduate business administration degree from Northern Illinois University in 2009, followed by his MBA in 2011.

Background & Development

After earning an undergraduate business degree from NIU in 2009, Peter Franklin was unable to find work during the prevailing economic downturn. Unfazed, he remained in school, pursuing his MBA. However, to satisfy his entrepreneurial spirit and earn a much-needed income, Franklin leased mobile concession equipment (a popcorn cart), secured a vending permit, and began selling popcorn in the popular tourist town of Wintergreen Lake. Using an old family recipe developed by his great-grandfather in the late 1800s, Franklin marketed his popcorn at Music on the Lake, the Wintergreen Carnival, and a number of other smaller events that year.

Franklin's signature "Old-Fashioned White" recipe popcorn was a hit. In 2010 he purchased his own popcorn machine/cart and continued marketing his single product throughout the tourist season, becoming a staple at Wintergreen Beach on weekends and at almost every festival. Toward the end of the 2010 tourist season, Franklin began to have difficulty keeping up with demand.

Faced with a "good problem" (strong demand for his product), Franklin considered his options at the end of the tourist season. The town of Wintergreen Lake would not allow him to operate his business from a semi-permanent concession trailer, which would have enabled him to cost-effectively expand operations. Unfortunately, no permanent storefronts were available for purchase or lease at that time.

Undeterred, Peter Franklin spent the winter of 2010 experimenting with more than 50 different potential variations of his popular popcorn recipe. Ultimately, he settled on a range of five new flavors (in addition to his signature "Old-Fashioned White") that generated the strongest response from informal test groups of friends and family:

- Kettle Corn

- Cajun

- Cheddar Cheese

- Sea Salt & Cracked Pepper

- Butter Toffee Peanut

Franklin purchased additional popcorn making equipment and made special arrangements with a local restaurant owner, who allowed him to utilize the restaurant's kitchen space (during off hours) for occasional batch production. Arrangements also were made with several popular retailers (restaurants, antique stores, etc.), who agreed to sell small, pre-packaged batches of his gourmet popcorn. In addition, Franklin also had small quantities of the new gourmet flavors available on his mobile cart, providing customers with additional options.

The 2011 tourist season was a tremendous success for Franklin. By this time his name had become established with both tourists and area residents, many of whom became repeat customers. Meeting demand was manageable, but still challenging at times.

A golden opportunity appeared in December of 2011 when, after 35 years, the owner of Bookends, a used bookstore, decided to close the business. He offered to lease the facility to Franklin. The storefront location, which is located adjacent to The Sundae Shoppe, a popular ice cream parlor, is in a prime location.

INDUSTRY ANALYSIS

Franklin's Popcorn Works competes within the larger restaurant industry, which was expected to generate sales of $631.8 billion in 2012, according to the National Restaurant Association. Specifically, our business operates within the smaller Retail, Vending, Recreation, Mobile segment, which was projected to produce sales of $61.2 billion in 2012. Popcorn-focused retail operations exist online and in other geographic markets, and some have been in business for nearly a century.

MARKET ANALYSIS

Our primary market is Wintergreen Lake, a small town in northern Illinois, located on the outskirts of the Chicago suburbs between the communities of DeKalb (home to Northern Illinois University) and Naperville. It is a popular tourist destination, offering an eclectic mix of antique stores, bed-and-breakfast operations, boutiques, diners, and restaurants. However, one key differential is 150-acre Wintergreen Lake, which offers several sandy beaches for swimming and sunbathing during the warmer months, as well as activities such as ice skating and ice fishing during the wintertime. Seasonal festivals, such as the Spring Fling, Music on the Lake (summer), Pumpkin Festival (fall), and the Wintergreen Carnival (winter) bring a steady stream of tourists from Chicagoland and other parts of Illinois in the Midwest year-round.

Wintergreen Lake's Main Street area includes approximately 150 establishments, including 19 snack shops and eating places. Of these, most are full-service or fast-food restaurants which pose no real direct competition. Our main competitors are Lynnie's Gift Shop, which sells a limited variety of pre-packaged old-fashioned candies and popcorn goods, as well as the Pretzel Shoppe, which concentrates on homemade salty snacks.

According to a survey conducted by the Wintergreen Lake Community Development Council, the Wintergreen Lake Business Owners Association, and the consulting firm TGG Partners, retail sales in Wintergreen Lake reached $17 million in 2011. This reflects a five-year annual growth rate of 3.5 percent. As the economy continues to recover, growth is expected to total 2.5 percent in 2012, 3.5 percent in 2013, and 4.5 percent in 2014.

Collectively, the Wintergreen Lake Community Development Council and the Wintergreen Lake Business Owners Association conduct an annual marketing campaign to attract tourists from the nearby Illinois cities of Rockford in Chicago, as well as Milwaukee, Wisconsin.

PERSONNEL

Peter Franklin (owner)

A resident of nearby Sycamore, Illinois, Peter Franklin began doing business in Wintergreen Lake since 2009. After earning an undergraduate degree in business administration from NIU that year, he was unable to find work during the prevailing economic downturn. Unfazed, Franklin remained in school, pursuing his MBA. However, to satisfy has entrepreneurial spirit and earn a much-needed income, he leased mobile concession equipment (a popcorn cart). Using an old family recipe developed by his great-grandfather in the late 1800s, he sold popcorn at Music on the Lake, the Wintergreen Carnival, and a number of other smaller events that year.

Franklin's signature "Old-Fashioned White" recipe popcorn was a hit. In 2010 he purchased his own popcorn machine/cart and continued marketing his single product throughout the tourist season, becoming a staple at Wintergreen Beach on weekends and at almost every festival. Toward the end of the 2010 tourist season, Franklin began to have difficulty keeping up with demand. Growth continued in 2011 after Franklin expanded his product line and made his gourmet popcorn selections available at several popular retailers (restaurants, antique stores, etc.).

Franklin, who completed his MBA in December of 2011, has been presented with an opportunity to operate Franklin's Popcorn Works from a permanent location.

Staff

In addition to Peter Franklin, the business will hire one part-time person to work the counter and help prepare popcorn during its first year of operations. Additional staff will be hired during subsequent years (see Growth Strategy section of this plan).

Professional & Advisory Support

Franklin's Popcorn Works has retained Holly Gendron, a local accountant, to provide bookkeeping and tax accounting assistance. A commercial checking account has been established with Wintergreen Lake Community Bank, which also has agreed to provide a merchant account for accepting credit card and debit card payments.

GROWTH STRATEGY

The following strategy outlines Peter Franklin's plans to grow the business during its first five years of operations. He has established aggressive, but attainable, annual sales goals, and is taking a long-term view of the business, in terms of establishing it as a regional chain or a national franchise.

Year One: Continue to Build the Franklin's Popcorn Works brand name. Focus on maximizing the efficiency of operations (e.g., inventory management, supplier relations, popcorn production). Hire one part-time employee to assist with daily operations. Generate gross sales of at least $100,000.

Year Two: Introduce five new popcorn flavors. Begin offering Internet sales. Hire an additional part-time employee to assist with regular store and Internet sales. Increase gross sales by 15 percent.

Year Three: Introduce five new popcorn flavors. Increase gross sales by 15 percent.

Year Four: Introduce five new popcorn flavors. Hire and train a full-time manager, allowing Peter Franklin to focus more closely on strategic matters in year five. Increase gross sales by 15 percent.

Year Five: Investigate the steps needed to establish Franklin's Popcorn Works as a regional chain (e.g., by establishing additional locations in other Midwestern tourist towns) or a national franchise. Identify potential investment partners. Increase sales by 15 percent.

PRODUCTS

The foundation of Franklin's businesses is his signature "Old-Fashioned White" popcorn. However, during his last year of operations as a mobile concession business, his product line was expanded to include the following selections:

- Butter Toffee Peanut
- Cajun
- Cheddar Cheese
- Kettle Corn
- Sea Salt & Cracked Pepper

Operating from a permanent location, Franklin will be able to expand his product line. The following 10 new varieties of popcorn will be offered during his first year in the permanent retail location:

- Caramel Apple
- Cinnamon & Sugar
- Honey Mustard
- Jalapeno Cheddar
- Parmesan & Garlic
- Pizza
- Ranch
- Salt & Vinegar
- Sour Cream & Chive
- White Cheddar

In addition to selling popcorn in individual (2 oz.) servings, Franklin also will offer occasional specialty items, such as popcorn balls, larger quantity tubs, and special gift tins (especially during the holiday season).

MARKETING & SALES

The following comprehensive marketing plan, which includes both short-term and long-term tactics, has been developed for Franklin's Popcorn Works.

Short-Term Tactics

Franklin's Popcorn Works will commence operations on Memorial Day weekend 2012 with a grand opening celebration. Customers will receive special offers, including buy-one-get-one-free popcorn on opening day. In order to encourage customers to visit the store, samples will be distributed to passersby in the Main Street tourist area.

Long-term/Ongoing Tactics

Website: Franklin's Popcorn Works will develop a website that lists our product selection, hours, and details about our customer loyalty program. The site eventually will accept online orders, allowing the business to expand its geographic reach.

Coupons and Specials: Daily specials will be offered to customers. In addition, we will include discount coupons at area hotels, and in the monthly Wintergreen Lake Tourist Guide, which is distributed at all area retailers.

Customer Loyalty Program: Franklin's Popcorn Works will reward repeat customers with special coupons, as well as a punch card entitling them to a free bag of popcorn every five purchases.

Social Media: We will maintain a presence on Facebook and Twitter in order to stay in touch with customers and build relationships with them.

Event Marketing: Free popcorn samples will be distributed to attendees at Wintergreen Lake's signature events, in order to encourage them to visit the store. These events include, but are not limited to, the following:

- Spring Fling
- Music on the Lake (summer)
- Pumpkin Festival (fall)
- Wintergreen Carnival (winter)

OPERATIONS

Facility and Location

Jim Stanfield has agreed to lease a 1,850-square-foot storefront to Franklin for five years and cover some of the costs needed to make the building suitable for the new business.

Suppliers

Franklin's Popcorn Works is very selective about the quality of the popcorn that it buys. When operating his vending business, Peter Franklin purchased organic popcorn from Iowa-based Johansson Farms. From time to time he also has purchased from several other family-owned popcorn suppliers in the Midwest. Moving forward, Johansson Farms has agreed to remain his primary supplier, and has provided assurance that it will be able to meet Franklin's Popcorn Works' needs as the business continues to grow.

In the event that, for some unforeseen reason, Johansson Farms is unable to meet our needs, the following national suppliers can provide quality popcorn at a moment's notice. Franklin's Popcorn

Works also will rely upon these national suppliers for general cooking supplies (e.g., popcorn bags, containers, oil, flavorings, sugar, etc.):

- Brooks Products Corp.

- Lexington Foods LLC

- Worldwide Food Supply Inc.

Hours

Franklin's Popcorn Works will operate Monday through Sunday from Memorial Day through December 24, which is Wintergreen Lake's peak tourist season. The business will be open on Tuesdays, Thursdays, and Saturdays during most of the off-season (January through late May). Typical hours of operation will be 10:00 a.m. to 6:30 p.m.

Equipment

In order to establish operations, Franklin's Popcorn Works will need to purchase a cash register and approximately $5,000 in commercial-grade kitchen equipment needed for popcorn preparation and production. A detailed listing of these items is available upon request. In addition, the business also will need to acquire the following store fixtures, at an estimated cost of $4,000:

- 5 product display cases

- Shelving for product display

- In-store speaker system

FINANCIAL ANALYSIS

Following is a projected three-year income statement for Franklin's Popcorn Works. Modest net income is projected during our first two fiscal years. However, by year three the business will have generated nearly $20,000.

Peter Franklin will invest $17,000 of his own capital, generated from the operation of his mobile popcorn operation over the last several years, into the establishment of Franklin's Popcorn Works. This will cover the aforementioned equipment costs, and provide funding for initial operations.

Fiscal year	2012–13	2013–14	2014–15
Income			
Total sales	**$106,106**	**$120,022**	**$140,325**
Cost of goods sold	$ 31,832	$ 36,007	$ 42,098
Labor cost	$ 46,000	$ 56,000	$ 60,000
Gross profit	$ 28,274	$ 28,015	$ 38,227
Expenses			
Advertising & marketing fee	$ 5,000	$ 5,000	$ 5,000
Accounting & legal	$ 2,000	$ 1,500	$ 1,500
Insurance	$ 800	$ 850	$ 900
Rent	$ 10,000	$ 10,000	$ 10,000
Sales tax	$ 1,279	$ 1,261	$ 1,976
Telephone	$ 900	$ 950	$ 1,000
Utilities	$ 4,250	$ 4,500	$ 5,000
Misc.	$ 500	$ 600	$ 700
Total expenses	**$ 24,729**	**$ 24,661**	**$ 26,076**
Net income	**$ 3,545**	**$ 3,354**	**$ 12,151**

Retro Gaming Systems
Fist Full of Quarters Gaming Systems

PO Box 23145
Clinton Township, MI 48035

Zuzu Enterprises

Fist Full of Quarters Gaming Systems (FFQ) creates retro gaming systems while utilizing modern technology.

EXECUTIVE SUMMARY

Ethan Michaels longed to have an arcade machine of his own and undertook the task of building one from scratch. Since that time, he has worked on another thirteen arcade gaming systems and is knowledgeable and experienced enough to start his own full-time business building systems for others.

PRODUCT

Cabinet
The most basic part of the gaming system is the cabinet. The traditional upright, two-person design is the most popular, but other designs can be accommodated as well. Other designs include a cocktail system (sit-down) and a table-top version.

Cabinet Graphics
Arcade machines have typically had graphics of the game it contained. Building a system that contains multiple games leaves the cabinet open to any number of possibilities. The cabinet can utilize new, colorful and fun graphic schemes in any combination of colors and themes. Or, it can be built to coordinate with other household furniture and decor.

Ethan can easily make the cabinet blend with other furniture styles and finishes utilizing trims, stains, and paints from the local hardware store. Customers can provide pictures of other furniture and decor they are trying to coordinate with, providing Ethan guidance for the plans.

Customers who prefer to have more traditional arcade graphics on their machine can have that as well. Ethan does not prepare these graphics on his own, but works with an artist known for his arcade designs. The customer chooses one of the existing designs or works with the artist to come up with something unique; the artist then prepares the graphics, and Ethan applies the graphics to the cabinet.

Components

There are any number of components available for the control panel. Customers may choose any combination of the components based on what they think they will use. It is recommended to incorporate at least one of most components so that all available games can be accommodated and played in the same way as the original versions.

The types of available components include the following:

- Buttons
- Joysticks
- Spinners
- Trackballs
- Steering wheels
- Flight yokes
- Guns
- Dance pads
- Pedals
- Gear shift

The placement of the components is another consideration. Once the exact components are decided upon, it must be determined where to place each component so that it can be easily accessed and not interfere with the play of the other components.

There are standard, predetermined components and control panel arrangements for people to easily and quickly choose, or a custom plan can be created to suit the individual needs.

Computer

The computer needed to run the games has very specific requirements to run optimally. These requirements include:

- CPU
- Mother board
- Operating System (Microsoft Windows XP)
- Hard drives
- Video card
- RAM
- Sound card
- DVD-ROM drive
- USB Ports
- Network adapter
- Keyboard
- Mouse
- Monitor
- Speakers

- Software

- Emulator

MAME

MAME, or Multiple Arcade Machine Emulator, is at the heart of the computer arcade. When used in conjunction with images of the original arcade game's ROM and disk data, MAME attempts to reproduce that game as faithfully as possible on a more modern general-purpose computer. MAME can currently emulate several thousand different classic arcade video games from the late 1970s through the modern era, although MAME is not intended to be a platform that competes with arcade games that are still being actively sold.

SIGHTS, SOUNDS, AND THEMES

The sights and sounds that appear on the computer screen before and after the games is another area that needs attention. Backgrounds, screensavers, mouse cursors, icons, and startup screens are all areas where you can be creative and really add fun and flair to the gaming experience. The right sights and sounds can really complete the illusion that you're playing a real arcade machine.

Again, clients can choose from a large selection of predetermined themes or, for a higher cost, opt to have something created and customized specifically for them.

SERVICES

Fist Full of Quarters offers several different types of services, including a complete build of the gaming system including cabinet and all computer components; partial jobs involving either the cabinet or the computer system; and service and repair of existing arcades.

Complete Build

A complete build is the most expensive option, but includes a complete and total arcade system configured to the client's specifications and delivered ready-to-go.

The cost for a complete build can vary greatly depending on the specific options chosen. For example, choosing from preexisting artwork is cheaper than having custom artwork made; including steering wheels and gearshifts is more expensive than joysticks or pushbuttons. The average cost for a complete build is $2,550.

Individual Components

A more affordable option is to have FFQ help with specific tasks. Oftentimes, clients will have the know-how and time to complete some aspects of the project, but need some help completing the entire thing. Clients that have building skills may just want help with the more technological parts of the projects; conversely, those with expertise in technology may want help with the carpentry tasks.

In either case, FFQ is willing and able to step in and help complete the project. Typical cabinets (including control panel) run from $1,500 - $2,000. Computers average $750 to $1,250. In both cases, the parts are delivered to clients complete and ready-to-go.

Service and Repair

Finally, FFQ is available to service and repair existing units, including either the cabinet or the computer. Time is billed on an hourly basis with materials and supplies charged in addition to these fees. The hourly rate is $50 per hour.

TARGET MARKET

The target market consists primarily of men ages 35-50. This demographic grew up before computers and gaming systems existed in every household; this type of entertainment was sought by going to the local arcade or candy store to play their favorite games with their pockets bursting with quarters.

Now reaching "middle age," these men long to play the games of their youth, but do so in the comfort of their own homes. They typically have established careers and the discretionary income to afford a customized gaming system.

PERSONNEL

Owner-Operator

Ethan Michaels is the owner-operator of Fist Full of Quarters Gaming Systems (FFQ). Ethan, now 43, recalls the days of being dropped off at the arcade and spending hours playing all of his favorite games—PacMan, Asteroids, Centipede, Mortal Combat, Sinistar, and Berserk—dropping quarter after quarter into the machines.

He decided to purchase an old arcade machine for his home, but couldn't decide which game he wanted most. Doing some research, he stumbled across game cabinets with computers that could run any number of different games and decided this was the way to go. He purchased manuals on how to build your own arcade machine and started intensive online research.

Ethan began to the long process of making his arcade machine by building and decorating the arcade cabinet and control panel. He was able to find suppliers for all of the various components he would need for the control panel (buttons, joysticks, trackballs, etc.) from a well-known source and incorporated them all so that any game could be played as it was once done on the original machines. He then began to work on the computer, or the brains of the arcade machine. Again, research was key to the success of the project and Ethan was able to use the CPU to house and run the games.

Friends and family of Ethan were duly impressed with his arcade and wanted one for themselves. They began to question him about the process and costs, and Ethan knew this may be a way for him to make some money while utilizing his new-found expertise. Best of all, he enjoyed what he was doing.

Since that time, Ethan has built 14 arcade systems. He is now ready to expand and make this his full-time job.

FINANCIAL INFORMATION

ASSETS

Mr. Michaels already owns the tools and supplies necessary to build the arcade cabinets. These assets have been valued below for insurance purposes and are considered assets to the company.

Table saw	$ 500
Router	$ 200
Nail gun	$ 175
Circular saw	$ 100
Jigsaw	$ 150
Drill	$ 50
Various bits (spade, forstner, countersink, slot cutter)	$ 100
Hole saw	$ 50
Power screwdriver	$ 75
High speed rotary tool	$ 100
Sander	$ 50
T-Square	$ 15
Level	$ 30
Straightedge	$ 10
Sawhorses	$ 50
Clamps	$ 60
Wood putty	$ 30
Sandpaper	$ 30
Protective gear	$ 35
Casters	$ 80
Soldering tools (gun, iron, removal tool)	$ 30
Multimeter	$ 40
Crimping tool	$ 25
Total	**$1,985**

START UP COSTS

Start-up costs for the business are relatively low because Mr. Michaels already owns the majority of the tools and supplies he needs to begin working. Costs primarily consist of marketing and advertising, insurance, legal fees, and a dedicated personal computer.

Website development	$1,000
Online advertising	$ 300
Insurance	$1,000
Workshop upgrades	$ 500
Inventory of components and artwork	$1,500
Computer (dedicated)	$ 500
Legal	$ 500
Total	**$5,300**

COSTS OF BUILDING THE MACHINE FROM SCRATCH (average)

Below is a breakdown of the average costs of the components to build an entire arcade system, including cabinet, control panel, artwork, and computer system/accessories. Time and labor costs are included as well.

Wood (Medium density fiberboard, or MDF)—4 sheets	$ 125
Trim	$ 20
Monitor (27 inch)	$ 200
Speakers	$ 30
Coin door	$ 50
Control panel components	$ 150 (average)
Buttons	$2–$4
Joysticks	$22–$60
Spinners	$ 70
Trackballs	$ 50
Steering wheels	$ 200
Flight yokes	$ 30
Guns	$ 100
Dance pads	$ 50
Pedals	$ 100
Gear shift	$ 35
Graphics	$ 350
Control panel	$ 75
Side art	$ 150
Bezel	$ 40
Marquees	$ 35
Kick plate	$ 50
PCBs	$ 10
Computer (motherboard, memory, processor, graphics card, hard drives, operating system)	$ 200
Keyboard	$ 25
Paint/primer/stain	$ 25
Screws	$ 5
L-brackets	$ 5
Glue	$ 5
Plans	$ 25
Wire	$ 5
Cable ties	$ 5
Wiring block	$ 5
Mouse	$20+5
Power supply strip	$ 10
Cords/adapters	$ 50
LED illumination	$ 30
Time and labor	$1,200
Total	**$2,550**

School Store

The Devil's Den

George Washington High School
7890 Main St.
Wyandotte, MI 48192

Zuzu Enterprises

A school store will be opened and run primarily by students enrolled in the business technology department's business cluster. The cross-curricular program will mix traditional classes with business classes and focus on the principles and techniques of successful entrepreneurship and its practical, real-world application.

EXECUTIVE SUMMARY

A school store will be opened and run primarily by students enrolled in the business technology department's business cluster. The cross-curricular program will mix traditional classes with business classes and focus on the principles and techniques of successful entrepreneurship and its practical, real-world application.

CLASSROOM CURRICULA

The school store will be a project of the business technology department and its students. The store will operate as a project for students enrolled in the business course cluster as a way to begin focusing on academic themes. Clusters are two courses taken during the same semester that add an interdisciplinary dimension to our curriculum and include the following classes:

- Intro to Business class—scheduling, training, customer service, store layout and design, store cleaning and maintenance

- Accounting/Advanced Accounting classes—pricing, payroll, accounts payable/accounts receivable

- Marketing/Advanced Marketing classes—product selection, surveys/polls, product assessment, advertising and promotion

- Computer Applications/Web Page Design classes—website design, creation, and maintenance; computerized cash register/scanner; computerized inventory program

- English class—copyediting advertising, website, and other published materials; preparing training manual

- Business Law class—contract and employment law

- Entrepreneurship class—write a business plan and annual report

- Business internship (all year)—store manager
- Business internship—cashiers

It is intended that students choose from the above classes and take two per semester for the six semesters in their junior and senior years, or a total of eight of the ten classes available. Students may also apply for a business internship to work in a paid position as store manager, a position that requires a year-long commitment, or as a cashier.

STUDENT ORGANIZATIONS

DECA

DECA is a student organization that prepares emerging leaders and entrepreneurs for careers in marketing, finance, hospitality and management in high schools and colleges around the globe. DECA coincides nicely with our course cluster system by providing co-curricular programs that integrate into classroom instruction, applying learning in the context of business, connecting to business and the community and promoting competition. DECA's High School Division includes 185,000 members in 5,000 schools.

Our school chapter of DECA will operate as a club open to students enrolled in any of the offered business classes. Students can retain their membership in DECA as long as they are actively pursuing courses in one of the content areas. The club will be advised by a faculty member from the Business Technology Department.

Junior Achievement

Another club open to students in the business department is Junior Achievement. Junior Achievement is an integral part of our plan to include community business as mentors and advisers to our student, as they can arrange for business people and local community leaders to visit the classroom to share their workforce experience with students, all while teaching sound economic principles and reinforcing class curricula.

MERCHANDISE

The school store will offer a wide range of merchandise to the student population, staff, and community. Products range from school spirit items to food to personal care products to school supplies. A complete list of proposed items for sale is included below.

School Spirit Items

Clothes

- T-shirts
- Polo shirts
- Sweatshirts
- Hoodies
- Warm-up jackets
- Letterman jackets
- Fleece jackets

- Shorts
- Sweatpants
- Flannel pants
- Flannel boxer shorts

Accessories
- Knee socks
- Flip flops
- Ties
- Hair ties/headbands
- Drawstring bags, backpacks, totes, messenger bags, laptop bags
- Scarves and mittens
- Hats—visors, baseball hats, knit hats

Home Goods
- Mugs and water bottles
- Blankets
- Christmas ornaments
- Coasters
- Blankets
- Lanyards
- Umbrellas
- Teddy bears

Automobile Accessories
- Automobile decals
- Bumper Stickers
- Key rings
- Blue and white window paint

Game Day Spirit
- Stadium chairs/bleacher pads
- Thunderstix
- Cow bells
- Pom Pons
- Horns, tails, and pitchforks
- Temporary tattoos
- Beads/necklaces

School Supplies
- Pencils
- Colored pencils

- Markers
- Tape
- Staplers and staples
- Paper clips
- Pens
- Printer paper
- Loose leaf paper
- Notebooks
- Binders
- Graph paper
- Highlighters
- Flash drives
- Poster board
- Calculators
- Protractors
- Blank CDs

Snacks/Beverages

- Cappuccino (French Vanilla or Irish Creme)
- Hot Chocolate
- Slushies
- Juices (apple or orange)
- Water
- Granola bars
- Cereal bars
- Fresh fruit (bananas, apples, etc.)
- Nuts
- Yogurt
- Candy
- Mints
- Gum

Other

- Gift cards—Thank You, Back to School, Birthday
- Extra copies of the school Yearbook
- Ear buds
- Mini sewing kits

- Hygiene products—toothbrushes, toothpaste, dental floss, deodorant, feminine products, combs, hairspray

- Prepaid lunch cards

- Selection of alumni paraphernalia

STAFFING

Staffing for the school store will be done primarily by students although school personnel and community leaders will serve as oversight and guides.

School Personnel
- Business technology educators to serve as teachers and mentors

- School administrative staff to serve as mentors

Students
- Student manager

- Cashiers

Students and teachers will complete marketing, advertising, website development, and other tasks as part of their classroom experience which is not part of the day-to-day staffing of the store.

HOURS

The proposed hours for the school store include the following:
- Before and after school, or 30 minutes prior to school beginning and 30 minutes after school is done for the day

- Throughout all three lunch periods

- Prior to and during sporting events

- During special events including conferences, open houses, school board meetings, etc.

- Special hours will also be arranged one week prior to school starting in the fall and one week after school is over in the spring

LOCATION

The store is conveniently located near the front entrance to the school as well as a short distance from the cafeteria and the adjacent gymnasium. It has entrances from both the outside of the school as well as from the inside of the school.

Its proximity to the lunch room and gymnasium makes it ideal for students to come throughout the day as well as during sporting events. The outside entrance is also perfect for community members to reach because they do not have to enter the school building proper to have access to the store.

WEBSITE/CATALOG ORDERS

A website will be designed and maintained by students enrolled in the web design class. It will feature all of the school spirit items such as t-shirts, stadium chairs, and the like.

Catalog orders will also be placed, one in August, one in November, and another in March. Leaflets containing specific merchandise for sale as well as an order form will be posted to the school district's website and delivered to all district students.

Website and catalog orders may be mailed to customers for a small charge, dropped off to one of the other local schools, or kept in the high school general office for pickup.

A special feature of the store dedicated to alumni information, including information on upcoming reunions, contact information for alumni class officers, etc. It is hoped that former students searching for this information may also be interested in purchasing spirit items from their alma mater.

PORTABLE SALES

Selection of t-shirts, sweatshirts, accessories, and other various merchandise will be available in a convenient and manageable display that can be moved from location to location as needed. The sales display will be used at other area schools during book fairs, conferences, spirit days, sporting events, concerts, and the like to maximize exposure to all community members. It may also be employed during the city art fair, carnival/fireworks celebration, boat races, and other community events.

MARKETING & ADVERTISING

Several avenues for marketing and advertising will be employed, including the following:

- School announcements
- School newspaper
- Website with links from schools' websites
- Flyers for other schools in the district to reach parents, students, teachers, and staff in all buildings to expand the potential client base
- Attend PTA meetings, open houses, teacher conferences, school board meetings

FUNDING

Funding for the opening of the store, including preparing the space, ordering inventory, and staffing will initially come from the school's operations budget. It is expected that the store will operate at a loss during the first year while revenue is used to maintain operations and reimburse the school for the initial loan.

Student Advocate

Student Support Services LLC

123 Pine Grove Ave.
Port Huron, MI 48062

Zuzu Enterprises

It is the mission of Student Support Services (SSS), LLC to help children with learning disabilities and their families by assisting parents in discovering the specific, unique challenges to their child and determine the best methods of dealing with them; and to work with the parents, child, teachers, and school administrators to implement these methods to help the child succeed both academically and socially.

MISSION

Students with learning disabilities have different learning styles and rates, strengths and weaknesses. The Individuals with Disabilities Education Act (IDEA) requires that an Individualized Education Program (IEP) be developed for each child with a disability so that these individual differences can be addressed. The process to get an effective IEP in place, however, can be a daunting task for most families.

It is the mission of Student Support Services, LLC to help children with learning disabilities and their families by assisting parents in discovering the specific, unique challenges to their child and determine the best methods of dealing with them; and to work with the parents, child, teachers, and school administrators to implement these methods to help the child succeed both academically and socially.

RATIONALE

For many students with disabilities, the key to success in the classroom lies in having appropriate adaptations, accommodations, and modifications made to the instruction and other classroom activities.

Some adaptations are as simple as moving a distractible student to the front of the class or away from the pencil sharpener or the window. Other modifications may involve changing the way that material is presented or the way that students respond to show their learning.

Accommodations and modifications need to be individualized for each particular student, based upon his or her needs and personal learning style and interests. However, it is not always readily apparent what accommodations or modifications would be beneficial for a particular student, or how changes to the curriculum, its presentation, the classroom setting, or student evaluation might be made. Because of this, often nothing is done, and the problems continue. At this point, several factors are occurring simultaneously, including the following:

- The frustration level is high for child, parents, and teachers alike

- The child is struggling academically

- Often, the child is struggling socially

- The child may suffer from depression

- There is a lack of understanding on the part of parents and teachers

- The child may exhibit inappropriate responses

- There may be behavior issues such as lashing out or acting inappropriately

- There may be a complete refusal to do work; the child may withdraw or be truant

As a former special education teacher, I saw this pattern repeat again and again. Because of this, I want to use my experience and knowledge to help children and their families get the help they need, put plans in place to alleviate the problems and find ways to help the child become successful. Specifically, I aim to do the following:

- Find a balance to help child succeed without coddling or enabling them

- Help parents know what help to ask for, or what is appropriate and what will lead to better results

- Improve the child's self-esteem

- Improve the child's behavior and social acuity

SERVICES

To achieve these goals, Student Support Services will provide comprehensive services to clients and their families. SSS will do the following:

- Provide a list of relevant books and reference materials

- Recommend a pediatrician, psychiatrist and psychologist

- Coordinate neuropsychological testing

- Provide information on different diet plans that may affect the child

- Propose a sleep study

- Find a local social skills group for the child

- Find a parental support group, either locally or online

- Suggest sensory integration activities that may be helpful

- Hold organization skills classes

- Hold study skills classes

- Work with different doctors and review test results to see "whole picture"

- Work with school to persuade them of the need for an IEP if they don't think one is necessary

- Determine specific, practical modifications that may benefit child to be included in IEP

- Attend IEP meeting to explain what is going on and the requested modifications that can address the issues. Ensure modifications are included in IEP, keeping in mind that specific wording is important

- Follow up with parent and teachers to make sure modifications are being observed appropriately and that results are being seen

- Attend special meetings with teachers or administrative staff to address issues as they arise

RELEVANT REFERENCE MATERIALS AND SOURCES

Books

A very short list of recommended reference materials follows. A more specific, targeted list will be provided to each family based on their child's exact needs.

- *Learning Outside The Lines: Two Ivy League Students with Learning Disabilities and ADHD Give You the Tools for Academic Success and Educational Revolution* by Jonathan Mooney, David Cole and Edward M. Hallowell

- *The Misunderstood Child, Fourth Edition: Understanding and Coping with Your Child's Learning Disabilities* by Larry B. Silver

- *Parenting Children with ADHD: 10 Lessons That Medicine Cannot Teach (APA Lifetools)* by Vincent J. Monastra

- *Smart Kids with Learning Difficulties: Overcoming Obstacles and Realizing Potential* by Rich Weinfeld, Sue Jeweler, Linda Barnes-Robinson and Betty Shevitz

- *A Special Education: One Family's Journey through the Maze of Learning Disabilities* by Dana Buchman

- *The Survival Guide for Kids with LD*: *(Learning Differences)* by Gary Fisher Ph.D. and Rhoda Cummings Ed.D.

- *Take Control of Asperger's Syndrome: The Official Strategy Guide for Teens With Asperger's Syndrome and Nonverbal Learning Disorders* by Janet Price and Jennifer Engel Fisher

Websites

Several recommended reference websites are listed below. Again, more specific resources will be provided to families based on their individual needs.

- ADDA provides information, resources and networking opportunities to help adults with Attention Deficit/Hyperactivity Disorder (AD/HD): http://www.add.org/

- Children and Adults with Attention-Deficit/Hyperactivity Disorder (CHADD) provides education, advocacy and support for individuals with AD/HD: http://www.chadd.org/

- Council for Learning Disabilities (CLD) provides services to professionals who work with individuals with learning disabilities. http://www.cldinternational.org/

- International Dyslexia Association (IDA) is a non-profit organization dedicated to helping individuals with dyslexia, their families and the communities that support them: http://www.interdys.org

- Learning Disabilities Association of America (LDA) is a national organization of parents, professionals and individuals with learning disabilities. LDA has state and local chapters in your area: http://www.ldaamerica.org/

- LD OnLine offers information for parents, teachers, and other interested professionals in the areas of learning disabilities, legal issues, current research, instructional strategies, and personal stories: http://www.LDOnline.org

- National Association for the Education of African American Children with Learning Disabilities includes information and resources provided by an established network of individuals and organizations experienced in minority research and special education. It also provides a parent resource network and publications for teachers, parents, and others: http://www.aacld.org/

- National Center for Learning Disabilities (NCLD) seeks to raise public awareness and understanding, furnish national information and referrals, and arrange educational programs and legislative advocacy: http://www.ld.org/

- National Coalition on Auditory Processing Disorders, Inc (NCAPD) includes a state-by-state referral network: http://www.audiologyonline.com/Articles/article_detail.asp?article_id=327

- National Information Center for Children and Youth with Disabilities (NICHCY): http://www.nichcy.org/

- National Joint Committee on Learning Disabilities

- ReadingRockets.org provides detailed information about learning to read and strategies for supporting struggling readers at home, at school, and in the community. It offers news, practical information, expert advice, and resources for parents, teachers, tutors, child care providers, and policy makers: http://www.readingrockets.org/

- Learning Ally (formerly Recording for the Blind & Dyslexic), provides information on over 80,000 recorded textbooks and other classroom materials, from 4th grade through postgraduate levels, available for loan. Individuals with learning disabilities are eligible to participate but must complete the certification requirements: http://www.learningally.org/

- SmartKidswithLD.org is the website of Smart Kids with Learning Disabilities, Inc., a non-profit organization dedicated to providing support to parents of children with learning disabilities and/or attention deficit disorders: http://www.smartkidswithld.org

PEDIATRICIANS, PSYCHIATRISTS, AND PSYCHOLOGISTS

Sometimes even a great doctor may not be a great fit with the child, and a new one might be more effective. When needed, Student Support Services can provide a list of competent, friendly pediatricians, psychiatrists, and/or psychologists to help diagnose and treat the child. Many factors are taken into consideration including reputation, openness to treatment, gender, and insurance.

NEUROPSYCHOLOGICAL TESTING

Neuropsychological testing is a method through which a neuropsychologist can acquire data about a child's cognitive, motor, behavioral, linguistic, and executive functioning. It can include testing of intelligence, attention, memory, and personality, as well as problem solving, language, perceptual, motor, academic, and learning abilities.

In the hands of a trained neuropsychologist, this data can provide information leading to the diagnosis of a cognitive deficit or to the confirmation of a diagnosis. Neuropsychological testing provides insight into the psychological functioning of an individual and is useful for measuring many function categories, including the following:

- Academic achievement
- Attention/concentration
- Executive functions
- Intellectual functioning
- Language processing
- Motivation/symptom validity
- Motor speed and strength
- Personality assessment
- Sensory-perceptual functions
- Speed of processing
- Verbal learning and memory
- Visual learning and memory
- Visuo-spatial processing

More specifically, neuropsychological tests provide quantifiable data about the following aspects of cognition:

- Ability to understand and express language
- Planning, synthesizing, and organizing abilities
- Processing speed
- Reasoning and problem-solving ability
- Short-term and long-term memory
- Visual-motor coordination
- Visual-spatial organization
- Working memory and attention

All of this information can help pinpoint exactly what is going on with the child. Once we know that, we can deal with the issues one by one to come up with helpful and effective solutions.

Examples of Commonly Used Neuropsychological Tests

Domain	Neuropsychological test
Academic achievement	Wechsler Individual Achievement Test (WIAT)
	Woodcock-Johnson Achievement Test
Attention/concentration	Cancellation Tasks (Letter and symbol)
	Digit Span Forward and Reversed
	IVA+Plus Continuous Performance Test
	Paced Auditory Serial Addition Test (PASAT)
	Trail Making Tests
Executive functions	Category Test
	Multiple Errands Test (MET)
	Porteus Maze Test
	Stroop Test
	Trail Making Test-B
	WAIS Subtests of Similarities and Block Design
	Wisconsin Card Sorting Test
Intellectual functioning	Stanford-Binet Intelligence Scale-IV
	Wechsler Adult Intelligence Scale-III (WAIS-III)
	Wechsler Adult Intelligence Scale-Revised (WAIS-R)
	Wechsler Intelligence Scale for Children-IV (WISC-IV)
	Wechsler Scales
Language processing	Boston Diagnostic Aphasia Examination
	Boston Naming Test
	Multilingual Aphasia Examination
	Token Test
Motivation	Dot Counting
	Forced-Choice Symptom Validity Testing
	Rey 15 Item Test
Motor speed and strength	Grooved Pegboard Task
	Hand Grip Strength
	Index Finger Tapping
	Thurstone Uni-and Bimanual Coordination Test
Personality assessment	Beck Depression Inventory (BDI)
	Millon Clinical Multiaxial Inventory
	Minnesota Multiphasic Personality Inventory (MMPI)
	Rorschach Test
	Thematic Apperception Test for Children or Adults
Sensory-perceptual functions	Halstead-Reitan Neuropsychological Battery (HRNB) Tactual Performance Test and Sensory Perceptual Examination
Speed of processing	Simple and Choice Reaction Time
	Symbol Digit Modalities Test-Written and oral
Verbal learning and memory	California Verbal Learning Test-Rote list learning (related words)
	Hopkins Verbal Learning Test
	Logical Memory I and II-Contextualized prose
	Rey Auditory Verbal Learning Test-Rote list learning (unrelated words)
	Verbal Paired-Associates
	Verbal Selective Reminding Test-Selective reminding (unrelated words)
	Wechsler Memory Scale (WMS)
	WMS-III Verbal Memory Index
Visual learning and memory	Continuous Recognition Memory Test
	Nonverbal Selective Reminding Test
	Rey-Osterrieth Complex Figure–Immediate and delayed recall
	Visual Reproduction I and II
	Visuo-Motor Integration Test-Block design
	WMS
	WMS-III Visual Memory Index
Visuo-spatial processing	Hooper Visual Organization Test
	Judgment of Line Orientation
	Rey-Osterrieth Complex Figure–Copy condition
	WAIS Block Design Subtest

In combination with the neuropsychological tests, many other factors are considered and recorded. The neuropsychologist will interview both the child and the parents, the child's educational and medical records will be reviewed, and both the parents and the child will complete questionnaires. All of this information, taken together, can provide a more detailed assessment of the exact learning issues a child may have.

Some common questionnaires used for parents and children include the following:

- Behavior Rating Inventory of Executive Function (BRIEF)

- Conners Comprehensive Behavior Rating Scale

At the end of testing and synthesizing all of the data collected, the neuropsychologist will present a detailed report of the findings as well as individualized recommendations including such varied topics as psychological intervention; occupational therapy; strategies to support executive functioning, learning, and social and emotional adjustment; educational and programming. This report is easy to read and helpful for parents as well as for school staff. It can be used to help diagnose the problems and help plan a course of treatment as well as establishes a baseline for future testing.

DIET PLANS

Many people believe that changes in diet can affect symptoms and behaviors of children with learning disabilities. Theories range from incorporating certain vitamins into the diet and promoting a more well-balance diet to excluding certain things from the diet, including sugar; gluten; and food additives such as artificial coloring, artificial flavoring, artificial preservatives such as BHA, BHT, and TBH, and artificial sweeteners such as Aspartame. Parents may wish to explore one or more of these dietary changes to see what affect it has on their child.

SLEEP STUDIES

Sleep problems in children can cause depression, low self-esteem, difficulty in concentration and/or focus, difficulty with critical thinking, problem solving and hyperactivity. Sleep deprivation that continues over an extended period of time may present as Attention Deficit Disorder, and increases a child's risk of obesity, diabetes and clinical depression.

Furthermore, children who suffer from sleep deprivation are at a greater risk for health, performance and safety problems. Sleep is an important and necessary component of a healthy lifestyle and the current research is proving time and again that our children are especially at risk when they are sleep deprived.

Students who are diagnosed with Attention Deficit Disorder may also suffer from low self-esteem, depression and/or anxiety. All of these things can be related to and exacerbated by sleep deprivation.

SOCIAL SKILLS GROUPS

Children with learning disabilities often lack necessary social skills. The child who lacks these social skills often experiences:

* Academic failures
* Aggressiveness
* Behavioral difficulties in school
* Bullying
* Concentration difficulties
* Delinquency
* Depression
* Difficulty in making friends
* Emotional difficulties

- Inattentiveness

- Isolation from peers

- Peer rejection

- Poor self-esteem

- Problems in interpersonal relationships

Social skills are the basis of successful interactions with other people. Children with learning disabilities, sensory integration difficulties, Asperger's Disorder, Autism Spectrum Disorder, neurological disorders, and emotional disabilities would often benefit from training in social skills groups led by trained professionals. In addition, a safe environment in which to practice newly learned the social skills is a recommended benefit.

A child who has Attention-Deficit/Hyperactivity Disorder (AD/HD) may be inattentive, impulsive, hyperactive—or any combination of these. When inattentive, he may not pay close attention to other people's speech and behavior; his mind may wander, or his attention may be drawn to some other distraction. When impulsive and/or hyperactive, he may interrupt others when they're speaking and find it difficult to wait his turn. While this behavior is not deliberate, others will likely be frustrated or offended by it.

The child with a learning problem, such as a language or auditory processing disorder, may have difficulty understanding what has been said to him. Expressing his own ideas in speech may also be problematic for him. Both of these issues can interfere with interpersonal communication.

To be an effective social participant, we must be able to hear, discriminate, and understand what is being communicated. Without this skill, the life of the child with learning impairments is filled with social blunders that are frustrating and embarrassing.

PARENTAL SUPPORT GROUPS

There are any number of parental support groups for parents of children with learning disabilities. Specific recommendations will be based on the particular child and his or her learning difficulties. Some examples of parental support groups include the following:

Children with ADHD

Attention Deficit Hyperactive Disorder in children is frustrating and exhausting to the child and the family. Schools find these kids generally a burden, and often lack the understanding, skills and training to effectively deal with and help kids with ADHD succeed.

NIDS (Neuro Immune Dysfunction Syndromes)

From Dr. Michael Goldberg, this information and support forum is for families affected by Neuro Immune Dysfunction Syndromes. Our focus includes: Autism / ASD, Asperger's / AS, PDD, ADD / ADHD, CF / CFIDS / ME and others—who are following or considering following the NIDS protocol.

Asperger

An excellent listserv for discussions of all aspects of Asperger Syndrome (AS) and other forms of high-functioning autism, including Pervasive Developmental Disorder (PDD). Subscription requires owner approval. This is a well-established, high volume autism support list.

Autism in Girls

This is a high quality list for parents and professionals who wish to exchange information regarding treatment of autism in girls, how autism effect females in the family, and any other issues dealing with autism and females and/or the comparison of males and females with autism.

GF CF Kids (Gluten-Free Casein-Free Kids)

This high volume, unmoderated list provides discussion forum for parents of children on the autism spectrum who are avoiding gluten and casein and other substances in their children's diets.

SENSORY INTEGRATION

Sensory experiences include touch, movement, body awareness, sight, sound, and the pull of gravity. The process of the brain organizing and interpreting this information is called sensory integration. Sensory integration provides a crucial foundation for later, more complex learning and behavior.

For most children, sensory integration develops in the course of ordinary childhood activities. Motor planning ability is a natural outcome of the process, as is the ability to adapt to incoming sensations. But for some children, sensory integration does not develop as efficiently as it should. When the process is disordered, a number of problems in learning, development, or behavior may become evident.

As many as 30% of school-aged children are estimated to have learning disabilities. Research indicates that a majority of these children, although normal in intelligence, are likely to have sensory integrative problems. These children are also more likely than their peers to have had a premature birth, early developmental problems, and poor motor coordination. Early intervention can improve sensory integration in these children, minimizing the possibility of school failure before it occurs. Adding sensory integration experiences for a child already experiencing school failure can also help alleviate the problems and lead to enhanced success.

CLASSES

Periodically, Student Support Services will offer organization skills and study skills classes for clients wishing to attend. Concrete, tried-and-true methods will be taught to the children so that they may participate in their education and feel confident in their ability to cope with their learning challenges.

INDIVIDUALIZED EDUCATION PROGRAM (IEP)

The Individualized Education Program, or IEP, is a written document developed by parents and educators itemizing the child's specific learning difficulties, goals the parent and educator team has for the child's learning, and any special support needed to achieve these goals. It can be an essential and indispensable tool to guide school staff in the best ways to help the child succeed, mapping out and itemizing all of the special modifications or accommodations that can be made in the classroom to address the specific child and his or her learning difficulties.

Modifications and Accommodations

The world is full of examples of accommodations that permit people with disabilities to perform specific tasks they might not otherwise be able to. Drivers with poor vision wear glasses or contacts, elevators mark the buttons in Braille, and voters with disabilities may be given assistance by the person of their choice.

Accommodations play an important role in educational settings, particularly for students whose disabilities interfere with performing learning tasks (such as reading a book, taking notes in class, or writing an essay) or testing tasks (such as getting through the items within the time limit or filling in the circles on a multiple-choice test). A critical part of teaching and assessing students with disabilities is providing them with accommodations that support learning and that support their ability to show what they know and can do.

Modifications or accommodations are most often made in the following areas:

Instruction
- Reducing the difficulty of assignments
- Reducing the reading level
- Using a student/peer tutor

Materials
- Providing audiotaped lectures or books
- Giving copies of teacher's lecture notes
- Giving copies of the textbooks for home use
- Using large print books, Braille, or books on CD (digital text)

Scheduling
- Giving the student extra time to complete assignments or tests
- Breaking up testing over several days
- Making sure parents and child have advance notice of tests dates and assignment due dates

Setting
- Working in a small group
- Working one-on-one with the teacher
- Working in a quiet environment away from the classroom

Student Response
- Allowing answers to be given orally or dictated
- Overlooking spelling and grammatical errors in other subject areas
- Using a word processor for written work
- Using sign language, a communication device, Braille, or native language if it is not English.

The challenge for educators and families is to decide which accommodations will help students learn new skills and knowledge—and which will help them demonstrate what they've learned. This is where the neuropsychological testing report and Student Support Services can really help. SSS will actively participate as part of the team to develop the student's IEP and list all of the appropriate modifications and accommodations, both in the classroom as well as in state-wide, district-wide, or national testing. As part of the team, SSS will advocate for the student and consider his or her specific strengths, challenges, and routines. This will help the team determine which accommodations will support the student across a range of school situations and activities as well as help the student access instruction designed to meet educational standards established by the district and state.

Students can also help inform these decisions by talking with the team about what works best for them. Involving students in the process of determining goals and respecting their voices about which accommodations might best help them achieve those goals recognizes them as valued participants and can ultimately lead to feelings of increased control and responsibility in their education.

When taken alone, accommodations themselves may not result in much of an impact, but when thoughtfully integrated with other components in the IEP and implemented in the classroom, they can help students reach and demonstrate their full potential. It is also important to note that accommodations are most effective when they are based on individual strengths and needs rather than disability type. In addition, accommodations chosen for testing situations can be most effective when they are adopted as an integral part of day-to-day instruction, to ensure that students have ample opportunity to practice their use prior to a mandated testing situation.

Choosing and Using Accommodations

The questions below are designed to serve as a tool to help the IEP team discuss and determine what accommodations a student needs in the classroom or in assessment.

- What kinds of instructional strategies (e.g., visual, tactile, auditory, combination) work best for the student?

- What learning strategies will help the student overcome challenges?

- What accommodations increase the student's access to instruction and assessment?

- What accommodations has the student tried in the past?

- What has worked well and in what situations?

- What does the student prefer?

- Are there ways to improve the student's use of the accommodation?

- Does the student still need the accommodation?

- What are the challenges of providing the student's preferred accommodations and how can these be overcome?

- Are there other accommodations that the student should try?

- Are there ways the student can use preferred accommodations outside of school (e.g., at home, on the job, in the community)?

- Are preferred accommodations allowed on state and district assessments of accountability?

- How can the student learn to request preferred accommodations (e.g., self-advocacy)?

- Are there opportunities for the student to use preferred accommodations on practice tests?

- What arrangements need to be made to make sure the student's preferred accommodations are available in assessment situations?

- How can actual use of accommodations be documented?

Possible Classroom Modifications

This list of classroom modifications and accommodations may be considered when developing the IEP:

- Additional time for reading assignments

- Additional time for test preparation

- Assignment notebooks

- Assistance with note taking

- Assistance with organization and planning of classwork and/or homework

- Behavior check cards

- Clearly defined limits

- Concrete, positive reinforcers
- Cooling-off period
- Credit for class participation, effort and attendance
- Emphasis on successes
- Extended time for completion of assignments or tests
- Fewer repetitive test items
- Frequent breaks
- Functional level materials
- Grade only on completed classwork
- Highlighted textbooks
- Instructions/directions given in different channels (written, spoken, demonstration)
- Large print material
- Manuscript writing rather than cursive
- Mnemonic aids/devices
- One-to-one contact for at least 10-20 minutes daily
- Oral, short-answer, modified tests
- Overhead/outline for desk use
- Presentation of material in small steps
- Read or paraphrase subject matter
- Reduction of paper/pencil tasks
- Review/testing matched to student pace
- Seating to reduce distractions
- Self-testing
- Shortened assignments
- Small groups
- Study sheets/summary sheets/outlines of most important facts
- Supplemental aids (vocabulary, multiplication cards, etc.)
- Taped lectures
- Taped textbooks
- Test directions read/explained thoroughly
- Test format allowing more space
- Time for repeated review or drill
- Tutoring assistance (peer, pal, teacher, etc.)
- Visual demonstrations
- Visual or multisensory materials
- Word processor/spell checker; calculator

This list is by no means exhaustive, and specific points determined to be relevant for the particular circumstances will need to be fleshed out in more detail. Explicit language regarding what should be done to accommodate the student should be included to avoid miscommunication and aid in applying them to daily assignments and activities.

FOLLOW UP

Once the IEP is written and adequately address the unique concerns of the child, it may be necessary to follow up with parents and teachers to make sure it is being followed. Compliance may happen at first, but may wane as time goes on. The child should be encouraged to be his or her own advocate and request that the accommodations be made, but oftentimes parents may need to get involved. In some cases, results are still not forthcoming, and Student Support Services can intercede to help get back on track.

LEGAL BASIS

When Congress enacted Public Law 94-142 as the Education for All Handicapped Children's Act in 1975, they included a system of procedural safeguards designed to protect the rights of children with disabilities and their parents. During subsequent reauthorizations of the law, now known as the Individuals with Disabilities Education Act, Congress maintained and added to these safeguards.

The Individuals with Disabilities Education Act requires that public schools provide a free, appropriate education to students with disabilities. If there is a disagreement between parents and their school district, either party my request a special education due process hearing.

Procedural safeguards include the right to participate in all meetings, to examine all educational records, and to obtain an independent educational evaluation (IEE) of the child. Parents have the right to written notice when the school proposes to change or refuses to change the identification, evaluation or placement of a child.

The law includes several ways to resolve disputes including mediation, a "Resolution Session" and due process hearings. Procedural safeguards include legally binding written mediation agreements and confidentiality.

State of Michigan

The State of Michigan website contains all forms and procedures relating to the Individuals with Disabilities Education Act at: http://www.michigan.gov/mde/0,4615,7-140-6530_6598_36168---,00.html.

The Procedural Safeguards Notice for the State of Michigan can also be found on this website; it is a whopping 44 pages and covers various topics including parental consent, confidentiality, mediation, and complaint procedures.

Although this document provides parents with a description of the procedures and processes to follow, some parents may find it confusing. Also, while it is important, it does not tell parents the practical, day-to-day things that can be done to significantly help their child succeed. It can help a parent get an IEP, but it does nothing to help guide them when they get there.

504 PLAN

The "504" in 504 plan refers to Section 504 of the Rehabilitation Act and the Americans with Disabilities Act, which specifies that no one with a disability can be excluded from participating in federally funded programs or activities, including elementary, secondary or postsecondary schooling.

"Disability" in this context refers to a "physical or mental impairment which substantially limits one or more major life activities." This can include physical impairments; illnesses or injuries; communicable diseases; chronic conditions like asthma, allergies and diabetes; and learning problems. A 504 plan spells out the modifications and accommodations that will be needed for these students to have an opportunity perform at the same level as their peers, and might include such things as wheelchair ramps, blood sugar monitoring, an extra set of textbooks, a peanut-free lunch environment, home instruction, or a tape recorder or keyboard for taking notes.

The 504 Plan is similar to the IEP in that it is a document intended to help children deal with disabilities in a positive way to be successful in the academic environment.

The difference between and IEP and a 504 Plan is the way a student qualifies for services and what avenues must be taken when there is a problem or dispute.

From the parents and child's perspective, it does not really matter how the services are classified, just that services are forthcoming. Student Support Services is able to help children receive these services no matter how they are classified by the school.

PERSONNEL

Liza Osbourne is a former special education teacher for the Port Huron Area School District. She decided to open Student Support Services after witnessing first-hand how frustrated parents were in dealing with their learning disabled child and not knowing what to do to help them. Another major incentive to opening SSS was dealing with children who failed to receive basic considerations from their classroom teachers, simply because of a lack of knowledge or an unwillingness to go above and beyond for any one student. She felt her experience and knowledge would be better spent helping a larger pool of students across the area instead of only being able to help those students directly under her care at school.

PAYMENT

Parents will be required to pay the standard fee of $25 per hour. Insurance will not cover this cost. In some cases, Student Support Services, LLC will be willing to work with the families on a reduced rate or even pro bono.

SSS is also looking into receiving funding from local youth organizations and/or social service organizations to offset costs to families. Two grant applications for this purpose have already been submitted and I am awaiting final notification.

BUSINESS PLAN TEMPLATE

USING THIS TEMPLATE

A business plan carefully spells out a company's projected course of action over a period of time, usually the first two to three years after the start-up. In addition, banks, lenders, and other investors examine the information and financial documentation before deciding whether or not to finance a new business venture. Therefore, a business plan is an essential tool in obtaining financing and should describe the business itself in detail as well as all important factors influencing the company, including the market, industry, competition, operations and management policies, problem solving strategies, financial resources and needs, and other vital information. The plan enables the business owner to anticipate costs, plan for difficulties, and take advantage of opportunities, as well as design and implement strategies that keep the company running as smoothly as possible.

This template has been provided as a model to help you construct your own business plan. Please keep in mind that there is no single acceptable format for a business plan, and that this template is in no way comprehensive, but serves as an example.

The business plans provided in this section are fictional and have been used by small business agencies as models for clients to use in compiling their own business plans.

GENERIC BUSINESS PLAN

Main headings included below are topics that should be covered in a comprehensive business plan. They include:

Business Summary

Purpose
Provides a brief overview of your business, succinctly highlighting the main ideas of your plan.

Includes

- Name and Type of Business
- Description of Product/Service
- Business History and Development
- Location
- Market
- Competition
- Management
- Financial Information
- Business Strengths and Weaknesses
- Business Growth

Table of Contents

Purpose
Organized in an Outline Format, the Table of Contents illustrates the selection and arrangement of information contained in your plan.

Includes

- Topic Headings and Subheadings
- Page Number References

Business History and Industry Outlook

Purpose

Examines the conception and subsequent development of your business within an industry specific context.

Includes

- Start-up Information
- Owner/Key Personnel Experience
- Location
- Development Problems and Solutions
- Investment/Funding Information
- Future Plans and Goals
- Market Trends and Statistics
- Major Competitors
- Product/Service Advantages
- National, Regional, and Local Economic Impact

Product/Service

Purpose

Introduces, defines, and details the product and/or service that inspired the information of your business.

Includes

- Unique Features
- Niche Served
- Market Comparison
- Stage of Product/Service Development
- Production
- Facilities, Equipment, and Labor
- Financial Requirements
- Product/Service Life Cycle
- Future Growth

Market Examination

Purpose

Assessment of product/service applications in relation to consumer buying cycles.

Includes

- Target Market
- Consumer Buying Habits
- Product/Service Applications
- Consumer Reactions
- Market Factors and Trends
- Penetration of the Market
- Market Share
- Research and Studies
- Cost
- Sales Volume and Goals

Competition

Purpose

Analysis of Competitors in the Marketplace.

Includes

- Competitor Information
- Product/Service Comparison
- Market Niche
- Product/Service Strengths and Weaknesses
- Future Product/Service Development

Marketing

Purpose

Identifies promotion and sales strategies for your product/service.

Includes

- Product/Service Sales Appeal
- Special and Unique Features
- Identification of Customers
- Sales and Marketing Staff
- Sales Cycles
- Type of Advertising/ Promotion
- Pricing
- Competition
- Customer Services

Operations

Purpose

Traces product/service development from production/inception to the market environment.

Includes

- Cost Effective Production Methods
- Facility
- Location
- Equipment
- Labor
- Future Expansion

Administration and Management

Purpose

Offers a statement of your management philosophy with an in-depth focus on processes and procedures.

Includes

- Management Philosophy
- Structure of Organization
- Reporting System
- Methods of Communication
- Employee Skills and Training
- Employee Needs and Compensation
- Work Environment
- Management Policies and Procedures
- Roles and Responsibilities

Key Personnel

Purpose

Describes the unique backgrounds of principle employees involved in business.

Includes

- Owner(s)/Employee Education and Experience
- Positions and Roles
- Benefits and Salary
- Duties and Responsibilities
- Objectives and Goals

Potential Problems and Solutions

Purpose

Discussion of problem solving strategies that change issues into opportunities.

Includes

- Risks
- Litigation
- Future Competition
- Economic Impact
- Problem Solving Skills

Financial Information

Purpose

Secures needed funding and assistance through worksheets and projections detailing financial plans, methods of repayment, and future growth opportunities.

Includes

- Financial Statements
- Bank Loans
- Methods of Repayment
- Tax Returns

- Start-up Costs
- Projected Income (3 years)
- Projected Cash Flow (3 Years)
- Projected Balance Statements (3 years)

Appendices

Purpose

Supporting documents used to enhance your business proposal.

Includes

- Photographs of product, equipment, facilities, etc.
- Copyright/Trademark Documents
- Legal Agreements
- Marketing Materials
- Research and or Studies

- Operation Schedules
- Organizational Charts
- Job Descriptions
- Resumes
- Additional Financial Documentation

Fictional Food Distributor

Commercial Foods, Inc.

3003 Avondale Ave.
Knoxville, TN 37920

This plan demonstrates how a partnership can have a positive impact on a new business. It demonstrates how two individuals can carve a niche in the specialty foods market by offering gourmet foods to upscale restaurants and fine hotels. This plan is fictional and has not been used to gain funding from a bank or other lending institution.

STATEMENT OF PURPOSE

Commercial Foods, Inc. seeks a loan of $75,000 to establish a new business. This sum, together with $5,000 equity investment by the principals, will be used as follows:

- Merchandise inventory $25,000

- Office fixture/equipment $12,000

- Warehouse equipment $14,000

- One delivery truck $10,000

- Working capital $39,000

- Total $100,000

DESCRIPTION OF THE BUSINESS

Commercial Foods, Inc. will be a distributor of specialty food service products to hotels and upscale restaurants in the geographical area of a 50 mile radius of Knoxville. Richard Roberts will direct the sales effort and John Williams will manage the warehouse operation and the office. One delivery truck will be used initially with a second truck added in the third year. We expect to begin operation of the business within 30 days after securing the requested financing.

MANAGEMENT

A. Richard Roberts is a native of Memphis, Tennessee. He is a graduate of Memphis State University with a Bachelor's degree from the School of Business. After graduation, he worked for a major manufacturer of specialty food service products as a detail sales person for five years, and, for the past three years, he has served as a product sales manager for this firm.

B. John Williams is a native of Nashville, Tennessee. He holds a B.S. Degree in Food Technology from the University of Tennessee. His career includes five years as a product development chemist in gourmet food products and five years as operations manager for a food service distributor.

Both men are healthy and energetic. Their backgrounds complement each other, which will ensure the success of Commercial Foods, Inc. They will set policies together and personnel decisions will be made jointly. Initial salaries for the owners will be $1,000 per month for the first few years. The spouses of both principals are successful in the business world and earn enough to support the families.

They have engaged the services of Foster Jones, CPA, and William Hale, Attorney, to assist them in an advisory capacity.

PERSONNEL

The firm will employ one delivery truck driver at a wage of $8.00 per hour. One office worker will be employed at $7.50 per hour. One part-time employee will be used in the office at $5.00 per hour. The driver will load and unload his own trucks. Mr. Williams will assist in the warehouse operation as needed to assist one stock person at $7.00 per hour. An additional delivery truck and driver will be added the third year.

LOCATION

The firm will lease a 20,000 square foot building at 3003 Avondale Ave., in Knoxville, which contains warehouse and office areas equipped with two-door truck docks. The annual rental is $9,000. The building was previously used as a food service warehouse and very little modification to the building will be required.

PRODUCTS AND SERVICES

The firm will offer specialty food service products such as soup bases, dessert mixes, sauce bases, pastry mixes, spices, and flavors, normally used by upscale restaurants and nice hotels. We are going after a niche in the market with high quality gourmet products. There is much less competition in this market than in standard run of the mill food service products. Through their work experiences, the principals have contacts with supply sources and with local chefs.

THE MARKET

We know from our market survey that there are over 200 hotels and upscale restaurants in the area we plan to serve. Customers will be attracted by a direct sales approach. We will offer samples of our products and product application data on use of our products in the finished prepared foods. We will cultivate the chefs in these establishments. The technical background of John Williams will be especially useful here.

COMPETITION

We find that we will be only distributor in the area offering a full line of gourmet food service products. Other foodservice distributors offer only a few such items in conjunction with their standard product line. Our survey shows that many of the chefs are ordering products from Atlanta and Memphis because of a lack of adequate local supply.

SUMMARY

Commercial Foods, Inc. will be established as a foodservice distributor of specialty food in Knoxville. The principals, with excellent experience in the industry, are seeking a $75,000 loan to establish the business. The principals are investing $25,000 as equity capital.

The business will be set up as an S Corporation with each principal owning 50% of the common stock in the corporation.

FICTIONAL HARDWARE STORE
OSHKOSH HARDWARE, Inc.

123 Main St.
Oshkosh, WI 54901

The following plan outlines how a small hardware store can survive competition from large discount chains by offering products and providing expert advice in the use of any product it sells. This plan is fictional and has not been used to gain funding from a bank or other lending institution.

EXECUTIVE SUMMARY

Oshkosh Hardware, Inc. is a new corporation that is going to establish a retail hardware store in a strip mall in Oshkosh, Wisconsin. The store will sell hardware of all kinds, quality tools, paint, and housewares. The business will make revenue and a profit by servicing its customers not only with needed hardware but also with expert advice in the use of any product it sells.

Oshkosh Hardware, Inc. will be operated by its sole shareholder, James Smith. The company will have a total of four employees. It will sell its products in the local market. Customers will buy our products because we will provide free advice on the use of all of our products and will also furnish a full refund warranty.

Oshkosh Hardware, Inc. will sell its products in the Oshkosh store staffed by three sales representatives. No additional employees will be needed to achieve its short and long range goals. The primary short range goal is to open the store by October 1, 1994. In order to achieve this goal a lease must be signed by July 1, 1994 and the complete inventory ordered by August 1, 1994.

Mr. James Smith will invest $30,000 in the business. In addition, the company will have to borrow $150,000 during the first year to cover the investment in inventory, accounts receivable, and furniture and equipment. The company will be profitable after six months of operation and should be able to start repayment of the loan in the second year.

THE BUSINESS

The business will sell hardware of all kinds, quality tools, paint, and housewares. We will purchase our products from three large wholesale buying groups.

In general our customers are homeowners who do their own repair and maintenance, hobbyists, and housewives. Our business is unique in that we will have a complete line of all hardware items and will be able to get special orders by overnight delivery. The business makes revenue and profits by servicing our customers not only with needed hardware but also with expert advice in the use of any product we sell. Our major costs for bringing our products to market are cost of merchandise of 36%, salaries of $45,000, and occupancy costs of $60,000.

163

Oshkosh Hardware, Inc.'s retail outlet will be located at 1524 Frontage Road, which is in a newly developed retail center of Oshkosh. Our location helps facilitate accessibility from all parts of town and reduces our delivery costs. The store will occupy 7500 square feet of space. The major equipment involved in our business is counters and shelving, a computer, a paint mixing machine, and a truck.

THE MARKET

Oshkosh Hardware, Inc. will operate in the local market. There are 15,000 potential customers in this market area. We have three competitors who control approximately 98% of the market at present. We feel we can capture 25% of the market within the next four years. Our major reason for believing this is that our staff is technically competent to advise our customers in the correct use of all products we sell.

After a careful market analysis, we have determined that approximately 60% of our customers are men and 40% are women. The percentage of customers that fall into the following age categories are:

Under 16: 0%
17-21: 5%
22-30: 30%
31-40: 30%
41-50: 20%
51-60: 10%
61-70: 5%
Over 70: 0%

The reasons our customers prefer our products is our complete knowledge of their use and our full refund warranty.

We get our information about what products our customers want by talking to existing customers. There seems to be an increasing demand for our product. The demand for our product is increasing in size based on the change in population characteristics.

SALES

At Oshkosh Hardware, Inc. we will employ three sales people and will not need any additional personnel to achieve our sales goals. These salespeople will need several years experience in home repair and power tool usage. We expect to attract 30% of our customers from newspaper ads, 5% of our customers from local directories, 5% of our customers from the yellow pages, 10% of our customers from family and friends, and 50% of our customers from current customers. The most cost effect source will be current customers. In general our industry is growing.

MANAGEMENT

We would evaluate the quality of our management staff as being excellent. Our manager is experienced and very motivated to achieve the various sales and quality assurance objectives we have set. We will use a management information system that produces key inventory, quality assurance, and sales data on a weekly basis. All data is compared to previously established goals for that week, and deviations are the primary focus of the management staff.

GOALS IMPLEMENTATION

The short term goals of our business are:

1. Open the store by October 1, 1994
2. Reach our breakeven point in two months
3. Have sales of $100,000 in the first six months

In order to achieve our first short term goal we must:

1. Sign the lease by July 1, 1994
2. Order a complete inventory by August 1, 1994

In order to achieve our second short term goal we must:

1. Advertise extensively in Sept. and Oct.
2. Keep expenses to a minimum

In order to achieve our third short term goal we must:

1. Promote power tool sales for the Christmas season
2. Keep good customer traffic in Jan. and Feb.

The long term goals for our business are:

1. Obtain sales volume of $600,000 in three years
2. Become the largest hardware dealer in the city
3. Open a second store in Fond du Lac

The most important thing we must do in order to achieve the long term goals for our business is to develop a highly profitable business with excellent cash flow.

FINANCE

Oshkosh Hardware, Inc. Faces some potential threats or risks to our business. They are discount house competition. We believe we can avoid or compensate for this by providing quality products complimented by quality advice on the use of every product we sell. The financial projections we have prepared are located at the end of this document.

JOB DESCRIPTION-GENERAL MANAGER

The General Manager of the business of the corporation will be the president of the corporation. He will be responsible for the complete operation of the retail hardware store which is owned by the corporation. A detailed description of his duties and responsibilities is as follows.

Sales

Train and supervise the three sales people. Develop programs to motivate and compensate these employees. Coordinate advertising and sales promotion effects to achieve sales totals as outlined in budget. Oversee purchasing function and inventory control procedures to insure adequate merchandise at all times at a reasonable cost.

Finance

Prepare monthly and annual budgets. Secure adequate line of credit from local banks. Supervise office personnel to insure timely preparation of records, statements, all government reports, control of receivables and payables, and monthly financial statements.

Administration

Perform duties as required in the areas of personnel, building leasing and maintenance, licenses and permits, and public relations.

Organizations, Agencies, & Consultants

A listing of Associations and Consultants of interest to entrepreneurs, followed by the ten Small Business Administration Regional Offices, Small Business Development Centers, Service Corps of Retired Executives offices, and Venture Capital and Finance Companies.

Associations

This section contains a listing of associations and other agencies of interest to the small business owner. Entries are listed alphabetically by organization name.

American Business Women's Association
9100 Ward Pkwy.
PO Box 8728
Kansas City, MO 64114-0728
(800)228-0007
E-mail: abwa@abwa.org
Website: http://www.abwa.org
Jeanne Banks, National President

American Franchisee Association
53 W Jackson Blvd., Ste. 1157
Chicago, IL 60604
(312)431-0545
E-mail: info@franchisee.org
Website: http://www.franchisee.org
Susan P. Kezios, President

American Independent Business Alliance
222 S Black Ave.
Bozeman, MT 59715
(406)582-1255
E-mail: info@amiba.net
Website: http://www.amiba.net
Jennifer Rockne, Director

American Small Businesses Association
206 E College St., Ste. 201
Grapevine, TX 76051
800-942-2722
E-mail: info@asbaonline.org
Website: http://www.asbaonline.org/

American Women's Economic Development Corporation
216 East 45th St., 10th Floor
New York, NY 10017
(917)368-6100

Fax: (212)986-7114
E-mail: info@awed.org
Website: http://www.awed.org
Roseanne Antonucci, Exec. Dir.

Association for Enterprise Opportunity
1601 N Kent St., Ste. 1101
Arlington, VA 22209
(703)841-7760
Fax: (703)841-7748
E-mail: aeo@assoceo.org
Website: http://www.micro enterpriseworks.org
Bill Edwards, Exec.Dir.

Association of Small Business Development Centers
c/o Don Wilson
8990 Burke Lake Rd.
Burke, VA 22015
(703)764-9850
Fax: (703)764-1234
E-mail: info@asbdc-us.org
Website: http://www.asbdc-us.org
Don Wilson, Pres./CEO

BEST Employers Association
2505 McCabe Way
Irvine, CA 92614
(949)253-4080
800-433-0088
Fax: (714)553-0883
E-mail: info@bestlife.com
Website: http://www.bestlife.com
Donald R. Lawrenz, CEO

Center for Family Business
PO Box 24219
Cleveland, OH 44124
(440)460-5409
E-mail: grummi@aol.com
Dr. Leon A. Danco, Chm.

Coalition for Government Procurement
1990 M St. NW, Ste. 400
Washington, DC 20036
(202)331-0975
E-mail: info@thecgp.org
Website: http://www.coalgovpro.org
Paul Caggiano, Pres.

Employers of America
PO Box 1874
Mason City, IA 50402-1874
(641)424-3187
800-728-3187
Fax: (641)424-1673
E-mail: employer@employerhelp.org
Website: http://www.employerhelp.org
Jim Collison, Pres.

Family Firm Institute
200 Lincoln St., Ste. 201
Boston, MA 02111
(617)482-3045
Fax: (617)482-3049
E-mail: ffi@ffi.org
Website: http://www.ffi.org
Judy L. Green, Ph.D., Exec.Dir.

Independent Visually Impaired Enterprisers
500 S 3rd St., Apt. H
Burbank, CA 91502
(818)238-9321
E-mail: abazyn@bazyn communications.com
http://www.acb.org/affiliates
Adris Bazyn, Pres.

International Association for Business Organizations
3 Woodthorn Ct., Ste. 12
Owings Mills, MD 21117
(410)581-1373
E-mail: nahbb@msn.com
Rudolph Lewis, Exec. Officer

International Council for Small Business
The George Washington University
School of Business and Public
Management
2115 G St. NW, Ste. 403
Washington, DC 20052
(202)994-0704
Fax: (202)994-4930
E-mail: icsb@gwu.edu
Website: http://www.icsb.org
Susan G. Duffy. Admin.

International Small Business Consortium
3309 Windjammer St.
Norman, OK 73072
E-mail: sb@isbc.com
Website: http://www.isbc.com

Kauffman Center for Entrepreneurial Leadership
4801 Rockhill Rd.
Kansas City, MO 64110-2046
(816)932-1000
E-mail: info@kauffman.org
Website: http://www.entreworld.org

National Alliance for Fair Competition
3 Bethesda Metro Center, Ste. 1100
Bethesda, MD 20814
(410)235-7116
Fax: (410)235-7116
E-mail: ampesq@aol.com
Tony Ponticelli, Exec.Dir.

National Association for the Self-Employed
PO Box 612067
DFW Airport
Dallas, TX 75261-2067
(800)232-6273
E-mail: mpetron@nase.org
Website: http://www.nase.org
Robert Hughes, Pres.

National Association of Business Leaders
4132 Shoreline Dr., Ste. J & H
Earth City, MO 63045
Fax: (314)298-9110
E-mail: nabl@nabl.com
Website: http://www.nabl.com/
Gene Blumenthal, Contact

National Association of Private Enterprise
PO Box 15550
Long Beach, CA 90815
888-224-0953

Fax: (714)844-4942
Website: http://www.napeonline.net
Laura Squiers, Exec.Dir.

National Association of Small Business Investment Companies
666 11th St. NW, Ste. 750
Washington, DC 20001
(202)628-5055
Fax: (202)628-5080
E-mail: nasbic@nasbic.org
Website: http://www.nasbic.org
Lee W. Mercer, Pres.

National Business Association
PO Box 700728
5151 Beltline Rd., Ste. 1150
Dallas, TX 75370
(972)458-0900
800-456-0440
Fax: (972)960-9149
E-mail: info@nationalbusiness.org
Website: http://www.national
business.org
Raj Nisankarao, Pres.

National Business Owners Association
PO Box 111
Stuart, VA 24171
(276)251-7500
(866)251-7505
Fax: (276)251-2217
E-mail: membershipservices@nboa.org
Website: http://www.rvmdb.com.nboa
Paul LaBarr, Pres.

National Center for Fair Competition
PO Box 220
Annandale, VA 22003
(703)280-4622
Fax: (703)280-0942
E-mail: kentonp1@aol.com
Kenton Pattie, Pres.

National Family Business Council
1640 W. Kennedy Rd.
Lake Forest, IL 60045
(847)295-1040
Fax: (847)295-1898
E-mail: lmsnfbc@email.msn.com
Jogn E. Messervey, Pres.

National Federation of Independent Business
53 Century Blvd., Ste. 250
Nashville, TN 37214
(615)872-5800
800-NFIBNOW
Fax: (615)872-5353
Website: http://www.nfib.org
Jack Faris, Pres. and CEO

National Small Business Association
1156 15th St. NW, Ste. 1100
Washington, DC 20005
(202)293-8830
800-345-6728
Fax: (202)872-8543
E-mail: press@nsba.biz
Website: http://www.nsba.biz
Rob Yunich, Dir. of Communications

PUSH Commercial Division
930 E 50th St.
Chicago, IL 60615-2702
(773)373-3366
Fax: (773)373-3571
E-mail: info@rainbowpush.org
Website: http://www.rainbowpush.org
Rev. Willie T. Barrow, Co-Chm.

Research Institute for Small and Emerging Business
722 12th St. NW
Washington, DC 20005
(202)628-8382
Fax: (202)628-8392
E-mail: info@riseb.org
Website: http://www.riseb.org
Allan Neece, Jr., Chm.

Sales Professionals USA
PO Box 149
Arvada, CO 80001
(303)534-4937
888-736-7767
E-mail: salespro@salesprofessionals-usa.com
Website: http://www.salesprofessionals-usa.com
Sharon Herbert, Natl. Pres.

Score Association - Service Corps of Retired Executives
409 3rd St. SW, 6th Fl.
Washington, DC 20024
(202)205-6762
800-634-0245
Fax: (202)205-7636
E-mail: media@score.org
Website: http://www.score.org
W. Kenneth Yancey, Jr., CEO

Small Business and Entrepreneurship Council
1920 L St. NW, Ste. 200
Washington, DC 20036
(202)785-0238
Fax: (202)822-8118
E-mail: membership@sbec.org
Website: http://www.sbecouncil.org
Karen Kerrigan, Pres./CEO

Small Business in Telecommunications
1331 H St. NW, Ste. 500
Washington, DC 20005
(202)347-4511
Fax: (202)347-8607
E-mail: sbt@sbthome.org
Website: http://www.sbthome.org
Lonnie Danchik, Chm.

Small Business Legislative Council
1010 Massachusetts Ave. NW, Ste. 540
Washington, DC 20005
(202)639-8500
Fax: (202)296-5333
E-mail: email@sblc.org
Website: http://www.sblc.org
John Satagaj, Pres.

Small Business Service Bureau
554 Main St.
PO Box 15014
Worcester, MA 01615-0014
(508)756-3513
800-343-0939
Fax: (508)770-0528
E-mail: membership@sbsb.com
Website: http://www.sbsb.com
Francis R. Carroll, Pres.

**Small Publishers Association
of North America**
1618 W COlorado Ave.
Colorado Springs, CO 80904
(719)475-1726
Fax: (719)471-2182
E mail: span@spannet.org
Website: http://www.spannet.org
Scott Flora, Exec. Dir.

SOHO America
PO Box 941
Hurst, TX 76053-0941
800-495-SOHO
E-mail: soho@1sas.com
Website: http://www.soho.org

**Structured Employment Economic
Development Corporation**
915 Broadway, 17th Fl.
New York, NY 10010
(212)473-0255
Fax: (212)473-0357
E-mail: info@seedco.org
Website: http://www.seedco.org
William Grinker, CEO

Support Services Alliance
107 Prospect St.
Schoharie, NY 12157
800-836-4772

E-mail: info@ssamembers.com
Website: http://www.ssainfo.com
Steve COle, Pres.

**United States Association for Small
Business and Entrepreneurship**
975 University Ave., No. 3260
Madison, WI 53706
(608)262-9982
Fax: (608)263-0818
E-mail: jgillman@wisc.edu
Website: http://www.ususbe.org
Joan Gillman, Exec. Dir.

Consultants

This section contains a listing of consultants specializing in small business development. It is arranged alphabetically by country, then by state or province, then by city, then by firm name.

Canada

Alberta

Common Sense Solutions
3405 16A Ave.
Edmonton, AB, Canada
(403)465-7330
Fax: (403)465-7380
E-mail: gcoulson@comsense
solutions.com
Website: http://www.comsense
solutions.com

Varsity Consulting Group
School of Business
University of Alberta
Edmonton, AB, Canada T6G 2R6
(780)492-2994
Fax: (780)492-5400
Website: http://www.bus.ualberta.ca/vcg

Viro Hospital Consulting
42 Commonwealth Bldg., 9912 - 106
St. NW
Edmonton, AB, Canada T5K 1C5
(403)425-3871
Fax: (403)425-3871
E-mail: rpb@freenet.edmonton.ab.ca

British Columbia

SRI Strategic Resources Inc.
4330 Kingsway, Ste. 1600
Burnaby, BC, Canada V5H 4G7
(604)435 0627
Fax: (604)435-2782

E-mail: inquiry@sri.bc.ca
Website: http://www.sri.com

Andrew R. De Boda Consulting
1523 Milford Ave.
Coquitlam, BC, Canada V3J 2V9
(604)936-4527
Fax: (604)936-4527
E-mail: deboda@intergate.bc.ca
Website: http://www.ourworld.
compuserve.com/homepages/deboda

The Sage Group Ltd.
980 - 355 Burrard St.
744 W Haistings, Ste. 410
Vancouver, BC, Canada V6C 1A5
(604)669-9269
Fax: (604)669-6622

Tikkanen-Bradley
1345 Nelson St., Ste. 202
Vancouver, BC, Canada V6E 1J8
(604)669-0583
E-mail: webmaster@tikkanen
bradley.com
Website: http://www.tikkanenbradley.com

Ontario

The Cynton Co.
17 Massey St.
Brampton, ON, Canada L6S 2V6
(905)792-7769
Fax: (905)792-8116
E-mail: cynton@home.com
Website: http://www.cynton.com

Begley & Associates
RR 6
Cambridge, ON, Canada N1R 5S7
(519)740-3629
Fax: (519)740-3629
E-mail: begley@in.on.ca
Website: http://www.in.on.ca/~begley/
index.htm

CRO Engineering Ltd.
1895 William Hodgins Ln.
Carp, ON, Canada K0A 1L0
(613)839-1108
Fax: (613)839-1406
E-mail: J.Grefford@ieee.ca
Website: http://www.geocities.com/
WallStreet/District/7401/

Task Enterprises
Box 69, RR 2 Hamilton
Flamborough, ON, Canada L8N 2Z7
(905)659-0153
Fax: (905)659-0861

HST Group Ltd.
430 Gilmour St.
Ottawa, ON, Canada K2P 0R8
(613)236-7303
Fax: (613)236-9893

Harrison Associates
BCE Pl.
181 Bay St., Ste. 3740
PO Box 798
Toronto, ON, Canada M5J 2T3
(416)364-5441
Fax: (416)364-2875

TCI Convergence Ltd. Management Consultants
99 Crown's Ln.
Toronto, ON, Canada M5R 3P4
(416)515-4146
Fax: (416)515-2097
E-mail: tci@inforamp.net
Website: http://tciconverge.com/index.1.html

Ken Wyman & Associates Inc.
64B Shuter St., Ste. 200
Toronto, ON, Canada M5B 1B1
(416)362-2926
Fax: (416)362-3039
E-mail: kenwyman@compuserve.com

JPL Business Consultants
82705 Metter Rd.
Wellandport, ON, Canada L0R 2J0
(905)386-7450
Fax: (905)386-7450
E-mail: plamarch@freenet.npiec.on.ca

Quebec

The Zimmar Consulting Partnership Inc.
Westmount
PO Box 98
Montreal, QC, Canada H3Z 2T1
(514)484-1459
Fax: (514)484-3063

Saskatchewan

Trimension Group
No. 104-110 Research Dr.
Innovation Place, SK, Canada S7N 3R3
(306)668-2560
Fax: (306)975-1156
E-mail: trimension@trimension.ca
Website: http://www.trimension.ca

Corporate Management Consultants
40 Government Road - PO Box 185
Prud Homme, SK, Canada, S0K 3K0
(306)654-4569
Fax: (650)618-2742

E-mail: cmccorporatemanagement@shaw.ca
Website: http://www.Corporatemanagementconsultants.com
Gerald Rekve

United States

Alabama

Business Planning Inc.
300 Office Park Dr.
Birmingham, AL 35223-2474
(205)870-7090
Fax: (205)870-7103

Tradebank of Eastern Alabama
546 Broad St., Ste. 3
Gadsden, AL 35901
(205)547-8700
Fax: (205)547-8718
E-mail: mansion@webex.com
Website: http://www.webex.com/~tea

Alaska

AK Business Development Center
3335 Arctic Blvd., Ste. 203
Anchorage, AK 99503
(907)562-0335
Free: 800-478-3474
Fax: (907)562-6988
E-mail: abdc@gci.net
Website: http://www.abdc.org

Business Matters
PO Box 287
Fairbanks, AK 99707
(907)452-5650

Arizona

Carefree Direct Marketing Corp.
8001 E Serene St.
PO Box 3737
Carefree, AZ 85377-3737
(480)488-4227
Fax: (480)488-2841

Trans Energy Corp.
1739 W 7th Ave.
Mesa, AZ 85202
(480)827-7915
Fax: (480)967-6601
E-mail: aha@clean-air.org
Website: http://www.clean-air.org

CMAS
5125 N 16th St.
Phoenix, AZ 85016

(602)395-1001
Fax: (602)604-8180

Comgate Telemanagement Ltd.
706 E Bell Rd., Ste. 105
Phoenix, AZ 85022
(602)485-5708
Fax: (602)485-5709
E-mail: comgate@netzone.com
Website: http://www.comgate.com

Moneysoft Inc.
1 E Camelback Rd. #550
Phoenix, AZ 85012
Free: 800-966-7797
E-mail: mbray@moneysoft.com

Harvey C. Skoog
PO Box 26439
Prescott Valley, AZ 86312
(520)772-1714
Fax: (520)772-2814

LMC Services
8711 E Pinnacle Peak Rd., No. 340
Scottsdale, AZ 85255-3555
(602)585-7177
Fax: (602)585-5880
E-mail: louws@earthlink.com

Sauerbrun Technology Group Ltd.
7979 E Princess Dr., Ste. 5
Scottsdale, AZ 85255-5878
(602)502-4950
Fax: (602)502-4292
E-mail: info@sauerbrun.com
Website: http://www.sauerbrun.com

Gary L. McLeod
PO Box 230
Sonoita, AZ 85637
Fax: (602)455-5661

Van Cleve Associates
6932 E 2nd St.
Tucson, AZ 85710
(520)296-2587
Fax: (520)296-3358

California

Acumen Group Inc.
(650)949-9349
Fax: (650)949-4845
E-mail: acumen-g@ix.netcom.com
Website: http://pw2.netcom.com/~janed/acumen.html

On-line Career and Management Consulting
420 Central Ave., No. 314
Alameda, CA 94501

(510)864-0336
Fax: (510)864-0336
E-mail: career@dnai.com
Website: http://www.dnai.com/~career

Career Paths-Thomas E. Church & Associates Inc.
PO Box 2439
Aptos, CA 95001
(408)662-7950
Fax: (408)662-7955
E-mail: church@ix.netcom.com
Website: http://www.careerpaths-tom.com

Keck & Co. Business Consultants
410 Walsh Rd.
Atherton, CA 94027
(650)854-9588
Fax: (650)854-7240
E-mail: info@keckco.com
Website: http://www.keckco.com

Ben W. Laverty III, PhD, REA, CEI
4909 Stockdale Hwy., Ste. 132
Bakersfield, CA 93309
(661)283-8300
Free: 800-833-0373
Fax: (661)283-8313
E-mail: cstc@cstcsafety.com
Website: http://www.cstcsafety.com/cstc

Lindquist Consultants-Venture Planning
225 Arlington Ave.
Berkeley, CA 94707
(510)524-6685
Fax: (510)527-6604

Larson Associates
PO Box 9005
Brea, CA 92822
(714)529-4121
Fax: (714)572-3606
E-mail: ray@consultlarson.com
Website: http://www.consultlarson.com

Kremer Management Consulting
PO Box 500
Carmel, CA 93921
(408)626-8311
Fax: (408)624-2663
E-mail: ddkremer@aol.com

W and J PARTNERSHIP
PO Box 2499
18876 Edwin Markham Dr.
Castro Valley, CA 94546
(510)583-7751
Fax: (510)583-7645
E-mail: wamorgan@wjpartnership.com
Website: http://www.wjpartnership.com

JB Associates
21118 Gardena Dr.
Cupertino, CA 95014
(408)257-0214
Fax: (408)257-0216
E-mail: semarang@sirius.com

House Agricultural Consultants
PO Box 1615
Davis, CA 95617-1615
(916)753-3361
Fax: (916)753-0464
E-mail: infoag@houseag.com
Website: http://www.houseag.com/

3C Systems Co.
16161 Ventura Blvd., Ste. 815
Encino, CA 91436
(818)907-1302
Fax: (818)907-1357
E-mail: mark@3CSysCo.com
Website: http://www.3CSysCo.com

Technical Management Consultants
3624 Westfall Dr.
Encino, CA 91436-4154
(818)784-0626
Fax: (818)501-5575
E-mail: tmcrs@aol.com

RAINWATER-GISH & Associates, Business Finance & Development
317 3rd St., Ste. 3
Eureka, CA 95501
(707)443-0030
Fax: (707)443-5683

Global Tradelinks
451 Pebble Beach Pl.
Fullerton, CA 92835
(714)441-2280
Fax: (714)441-2281
E-mail: info@globaltradelinks.com
Website: http://www.globaltradelinks.com

Strategic Business Group
800 Cienaga Dr.
Fullerton, CA 92835-1248
(714)449-1040
Fax: (714)525-1631

Burnes Consulting
20537 Wolf Creek Rd.
Grass Valley, CA 95949
(530)346-8188
Free: 800-949-9021
Fax: (530)346-7704
E-mail: kent@burnesconsulting.com
Website: http://www.burnesconsulting.com

Pioneer Business Consultants
9042 Garfield Ave., Ste. 312
Huntington Beach, CA 92646
(714)964-7600

Beblie, Brandt & Jacobs Inc.
16 Technology, Ste. 164
Irvine, CA 92618
(714)450-8790
Fax: (714)450-8799
E-mail: darcy@bbjinc.com
Website: http://198.147.90.26

Fluor Daniel Inc.
3353 Michelson Dr.
Irvine, CA 92612-0650
(949)975-2000
Fax: (949)975-5271
E-mail: sales.consulting@fluordaniel.com
Website: http://www.fluordaniel
consulting.com

MCS Associates
18300 Von Karman, Ste. 710
Irvine, CA 92612
(949)263-8700
Fax: (949)263-0770
E-mail: info@mcsassociates.com
Website: http://www.mcsassociates.com

Inspired Arts Inc.
4225 Executive Sq., Ste. 1160
La Jolla, CA 92037
(619)623-3525
Free: 800-851-4394
Fax: (619)623-3534
E-mail: info@inspiredarts.com
Website: http://www.inspiredarts.com

The Laresis Companies
PO Box 3284
La Jolla, CA 92038
(619)452-2720
Fax: (619)452-8744

RCL & Co.
PO Box 1143
737 Pearl St., Ste. 201
La Jolla, CA 92038
(619)454-8883
Fax: (619)454-8880

Comprehensive Business Services
3201 Lucas Cir.
Lafayette, CA 94549
(925)283-8272
Fax: (925)283-8272

The Ribble Group
27601 Forbes Rd., Ste. 52
Laguna Niguel, CA 92677

(714)582-1085
Fax: (714)582-6420
E-mail: ribble@deltanet.com

Norris Bernstein, CMC
9309 Marina Pacifica Dr. N
Long Beach, CA 90803
(562)493-5458
Fax: (562)493-5459
E-mail: norris@ctecomputer.com
Website: http://foodconsultants.com/
bernstein/

Horizon Consulting Services
1315 Garthwick Dr.
Los Altos, CA 94024
(415)967-0906
Fax: (415)967-0906

Brincko Associates Inc.
1801 Avenue of the Stars, Ste. 1054
Los Angeles, CA 90067
(310)553-4523
Fax: (310)553-6782

Rubenstein/Justman Management Consultants
2049 Century Park E, 24th Fl.
Los Angeles, CA 90067
(310)282-0800
Fax: (310)282-0400
E-mail: info@rjmc.net
Website: http://www.rjmc.net

F.J. Schroeder & Associates
1926 Westholme Ave.
Los Angeles, CA 90025
(310)470-2655
Fax: (310)470-6378
E-mail: fjsacons@aol.com
Website: http://www.mcninet.com/
GlobalLook/Fjschroe.html

Western Management Associates
5959 W Century Blvd., Ste. 565
Los Angeles, CA 90045-6506
(310)645-1091
Free: (888)788-6534
Fax: (310)645-1092
E-mail: gene@cfoforrent.com
Website: http://www.cfoforrent.com

Darrell Sell and Associates
Los Gatos, CA 95030
(408)354-7794
E-mail: darrell@netcom.com

Leslie J. Zambo
3355 Michael Dr.
Marina, CA 93933
(408)384-7086

Fax: (408)647-4199
E-mail: 104776.1552@compuserve.com

Marketing Services Management
PO Box 1377
Martinez, CA 94553
(510)370-8527
Fax: (510)370-8527
E-mail: markserve@biotechnet.com

William M. Shine Consulting Service
PO Box 127
Moraga, CA 94556-0127
(510)376-6516

Palo Alto Management Group Inc.
2672 Bayshore Pky., Ste. 701
Mountain View, CA 94043
(415)968-4374
Fax: (415)968-4245
E-mail: mburwen@pamg.com

BizplanSource
1048 Irvine Ave., Ste. 621
Newport Beach, CA 92660
Free: 888-253-0974
Fax: 800-859-8254
E-mail: info@bizplansource.com
Website: http://www.bizplansource.com
Adam Greengrass, President

The Market Connection
4020 Birch St., Ste. 203
Newport Beach, CA 92660
(714)731-6273
Fax: (714)833-0253

Muller Associates
PO Box 7264
Newport Beach, CA 92658
(714)646-1169
Fax: (714)646-1169

International Health Resources
PO Box 329
North San Juan, CA 95960-0329
(530)292-1266
Fax: (530)292-1243
Website: http://www.futureof
healthcare.com

NEXUS - Consultants to Management
PO Box 1531
Novato, CA 94948
(415)897-4400
Fax: (415)898-2252
E-mail: jimnexus@aol.com

Aerospcace.Org
PO Box 28831
Oakland, CA 94604-8831

(510)530-9169
Fax: (510)530-3411
Website: http://www.aerospace.org

Intelequest Corp.
722 Gailen Ave.
Palo Alto, CA 94303
(415)968-3443
Fax: (415)493-6954
E-mail: frits@iqix.com

McLaughlin & Associates
66 San Marino Cir.
Rancho Mirage, CA 92270
(760)321-2932
Fax: (760)328-2474
E-mail: jackmcla@msn.com

Carrera Consulting Group, a division of Maximus
2110 21st St., Ste. 400
Sacramento, CA 95818
(916)456-3300
Fax: (916)456-3306
E-mail: central@carreraconsulting.com
Website: http://www.carreraconsulting.com

Bay Area Tax Consultants and Bayhill Financial Consultants
1150 Bayhill Dr., Ste. 1150
San Bruno, CA 94066-3004
(415)952-8786
Fax: (415)588-4524
E-mail: baytax@compuserve.com
Website: http://www.baytax.com/

AdCon Services, LLC
8871 Hillery Dr.
Dan Diego, CA 92126
(858)433-1411
E-mail: adam@adconservices.com
Website: http://www.adconservices.com
Adam Greengrass

California Business Incubation Network
101 W Broadway, No. 480
San Diego, CA 92101
(619)237-0559
Fax: (619)237-0521

G.R. Gordetsky Consultants Inc.
11414 Windy Summit Pl.
San Diego, CA 92127
(619)487-4939
Fax: (619)487-5587
E-mail: gordet@pacbell.net

Freeman, Sullivan & Co.
131 Steuart St., Ste. 500
San Francisco, CA 94105
(415)777-0707

Free: 800-777-0737
Fax: (415)777-2420
Website: http://www.fsc-research.com

Ideas Unlimited
2151 California St., Ste. 7
San Francisco, CA 94115
(415)931-0641
Fax: (415)931-0880

Russell Miller Inc.
300 Montgomery St., Ste. 900
San Francisco, CA 94104
(415)956-7474
Fax: (415)398-0620
E-mail: rmi@pacbell.net
Website: http://www.rmisf.com

PKF Consulting
425 California St., Ste. 1650
San Francisco, CA 94104
(415)421-5378
Fax: (415)956-7708
E-mail: callahan@pkfc.com
Website: http://www.pkfonline.com

Welling & Woodard Inc.
1067 Broadway
San Francisco, CA 94133
(415)776-4500
Fax: (415)776-5067

Highland Associates
16174 Highland Dr.
San Jose, CA 95127
(408)272-7008
Fax: (408)272-4040

ORDIS Inc.
6815 Trinidad Dr.
San Jose, CA 95120-2056
(408)268-3321
Free: 800-446-7347
Fax: (408)268-3582
E-mail: ordis@ordis.com
Website: http://www.ordis.com

Stanford Resources Inc.
20 Great Oaks Blvd., Ste. 200
San Jose, CA 95119
(408)360-8400
Fax: (408)360-8410
E-mail: sales@stanfordsources.com
Website: http://www.stanfordresources.com

Technology Properties Ltd. Inc.
PO Box 20250
San Jose, CA 95160
(408)243-9898
Fax: (408)296-6637
E-mail: sanjose@tplnet.com

Helfert Associates
1777 Borel Pl., Ste. 508
San Mateo, CA 94402-3514
(650)377-0540
Fax: (650)377-0472

Mykytyn Consulting Group Inc.
185 N Redwood Dr., Ste. 200
San Rafael, CA 94903
(415)491-1770
Fax: (415)491-1251
E-mail: info@mcgi.com
Website: http://www.mcgi.com

Omega Management Systems Inc.
3 Mount Darwin Ct.
San Rafael, CA 94903-1109
(415)499-1300
Fax: (415)492-9490
E-mail: omegamgt@ix.netcom.com

The Information Group Inc.
4675 Stevens Creek Blvd., Ste. 100
Santa Clara, CA 95051
(408)985-7877
Fax: (408)985-2945
E-mail: dvincent@tig-usa.com
Website: http://www.tig-usa.com

Cast Management Consultants
1620 26th St., Ste. 2040N
Santa Monica, CA 90404
(310)828-7511
Fax: (310)453-6831

Cuma Consulting Management
Box 724
Santa Rosa, CA 95402
(707)785-2477
Fax: (707)785-2478

The E-Myth Academy
131B Stony Cir., Ste. 2000
Santa Rosa, CA 95401
(707)569-5600
Free: 800-221-0266
Fax: (707)569-5700
E-mail: info@e-myth.com
Website: http://www.e-myth.com

Reilly, Connors & Ray
1743 Canyon Rd.
Spring Valley, CA 91977
(619)698-4808
Fax: (619)460-3892
E-mail: davidray@adnc.com

Management Consultants
Sunnyvale, CA 94087-4700
(408)773-0321

RJR Associates
1639 Lewiston Dr.
Sunnyvale, CA 94087
(408)737-7720
E-mail: bobroy@rjrassoc.com
Website: http://www.rjrassoc.com

Schwafel Associates
333 Cobalt Way, Ste. 21
Sunnyvale, CA 94085
(408)720-0649
Fax: (408)720-1796
E-mail: schwafel@ricochet.net
Website: http://www.patca.org

Staubs Business Services
23320 S Vermont Ave.
Torrance, CA 90502-2940
(310)830-9128
Fax: (310)830-9128
E-mail: Harry_L_Staubs@Lamg.com

Out of Your Mind...and Into the Marketplace
13381 White Sands Dr.
Tustin, CA 92780-4565
(714)544-0248
Free: 800-419-1513
Fax: (714)730-1414
E-mail: lpinson@aol.com
Website: http://www.business-plan.com

Independent Research Services
PO Box 2426
Van Nuys, CA 91404-2426
(818)993-3622

Ingman Company Inc.
7949 Woodley Ave., Ste. 120
Van Nuys, CA 91406-1232
(818)375-5027
Fax: (818)894-5001

Innovative Technology Associates
3639 E Harbor Blvd., Ste. 203E
Ventura, CA 93001
(805)650-9353

Grid Technology Associates
20404 Tufts Cir.
Walnut, CA 91789
(909)444-0922
Fax: (909)444-0922
E-mail: grid_technology@msn.com

Ridge Consultants Inc.
100 Pringle Ave., Ste. 580
Walnut Creek, CA 94596
(925)274-1990
Fax: (510)274-1956
E-mail: info@ridgecon.com
Website: http://www.ridgecon.com

Bell Springs Publishing
PO Box 1240
Willits, CA 95490
(707)459-6372
E-mail: bellsprings@sabernet
Website: http://www.bellsprings.com

Hutchinson Consulting and Appraisal
23245 Sylvan St., Ste. 103
Woodland Hills, CA 91367
(818)888-8175
Free: 800-977-7548
Fax: (818)888-8220
E-mail: r.f.hutchinson-cpa@worldnet.
att.net

Colorado

Sam Boyer & Associates
4255 S Buckley Rd., No. 136
Aurora, CO 80013
Free: 800-785-0485
Fax: (303)766-8740
E-mail: samboyer@samboyer.com
Website: http://www.samboyer.com/

Ameriwest Business Consultants Inc.
PO Box 26266
Colorado Springs, CO 80936
(719)380-7096
Fax: (719)380-7096
E-mail: email@abchelp.com
Website: http://www.abchelp.com

GVNW Consulting Inc.
2270 La Montana Way
Colorado Springs, CO 80936
(719)594-5800
Fax: (719)594-5803
Website: http://www.gvnw.com

M-Squared Inc.
755 San Gabriel Pl.
Colorado Springs, CO 80906
(719)576-2554
Fax: (719)576-2554

Thornton Financial FNIC
1024 Centre Ave., Bldg. E
Fort Collins, CO 80526-1849
(970)221-2089
Fax: (970)484-5206

TenEyck Associates
1760 Cherryville Rd.
Greenwood Village, CO 80121-1503
(303)758-6129
Fax: (303)761-8286

Associated Enterprises Ltd.
13050 W Ceder Dr., Unit 11
Lakewood, CO 80228

(303)988-6695
Fax: (303)988-6739
E-mail: ael1@classic.msn.com

The Vincent Company Inc.
200 Union Blvd., Ste. 210
Lakewood, CO 80228
(303)989-7271
Free: 800-274-0733
Fax: (303)989-7570
E-mail: vincent@vincentco.com
Website: http://www.vincentco.com

Johnson & West Management Consultants Inc.
7612 S Logan Dr.
Littleton, CO 80122
(303)730-2810
Fax: (303)730-3219

Western Capital Holdings Inc.
10050 E Applwood Dr.
Parker, CO 80138
(303)841-1022
Fax: (303)770-1945

Connecticut

Stratman Group Inc.
40 Tower Ln.
Avon, CT 06001-4222
(860)677-2898
Free: 800-551-0499
Fax: (860)677-8210

Cowherd Consulting Group Inc.
106 Stephen Mather Rd.
Darien, CT 06820
(203)655-2150
Fax: (203)655-6427

Greenwich Associates
8 Greenwich Office Park
Greenwich, CT 06831-5149
(203)629-1200
Fax: (203)629-1229
E-mail: lisa@greenwich.com
Website: http://www.greenwich.com

Follow-up News
185 Pine St., Ste. 818
Manchester, CT 06040
(860)647-7542
Free: 800-708-0696
Fax: (860)646-6544
E-mail: Followupnews@aol.com

Lovins & Associates Consulting
309 Edwards St.
New Haven, CT 06511
(203)787-3367

Fax: (203)624-7599
E-mail: Alovinsphd@aol.com
Website: http://www.lovinsgroup.com

JC Ventures Inc.
4 Arnold St.
Old Greenwich, CT 06870-1203
(203)698-1990
Free: 800-698-1997
Fax: (203)698-2638

Charles L. Hornung Associates
52 Ned's Mountain Rd.
Ridgefield, CT 06877
(203)431-0297

Manus
100 Prospect St., S Tower
Stamford, CT 06901
(203)326-3880
Free: 800-445-0942
Fax: (203)326-3890
E-mail: manus1@aol.com
Website: http://www.RightManus.com

RealBusinessPlans.com
156 Westport Rd.
Wilton, CT 06897
(914)837-2886
E-mail: ct@realbusinessplans.com
Website: http://www.RealBusinessPlans.com
Tony Tecce

Delaware

Focus Marketing
61-7 Habor Dr.
Claymont, DE 19703
(302)793-3064

Daedalus Ventures Ltd.
PO Box 1474
Hockessin, DE 19707
(302)239-6758
Fax: (302)239-9991
E-mail: daedalus@mail.del.net

The Formula Group
PO Box 866
Hockessin, DE 19707
(302)456-0952
Fax: (302)456-1354
E-mail: formula@netaxs.com

Selden Enterprises Inc.
2502 Silverside Rd., Ste. 1
Wilmington, DE 19810-3740
(302)529-7113
Fax: (302)529-7442
E-mail: selden2@bellatlantic.net
Website: http://www.seldenenterprises.com

District of Columbia

Bruce W. McGee and Associates
7826 Eastern Ave. NW, Ste. 30
Washington, DC 20012
(202)726-7272
Fax: (202)726-2946

McManis Associates Inc.
1900 K St. NW, Ste. 700
Washington, DC 20006
(202)466-7680
Fax: (202)872-1898
Website: http://www.mcmanis-mmi.com

Smith, Dawson & Andrews Inc.
1000 Connecticut Ave., Ste. 302
Washington, DC 20036
(202)835-0740
Fax: (202)775-8526
E-mail: webmaster@sda-inc.com
Website: http://www.sda-inc.com

Florida

BackBone, Inc.
20404 Hacienda Court
Boca Raton, FL 33498
(561)470-0965
Fax: 516-908-4038
E-mail: BPlans@backboneinc.com
Website: http://www.backboneinc.com
Charles Epstein, President

Whalen & Associates Inc.
4255 Northwest 26 Ct.
Boca Raton, FL 33434
(561)241-5950
Fax: (561)241-7414
E-mail: drwhalen@ix.nctcom.com

E.N. Rysso & Associates
180 Bermuda Petrel Ct.
Daytona Beach, FL 32119
(386)760-3028
E-mail: erysso@aol.com

Virtual Technocrats LLC
560 Lavers Circle, #146
Delray Beach, FL 33444
(561)265-3509
E-mail: josh@virtualtechnocrats.com;
info@virtualtechnocrats.com
Website: http://www.virtualtechno
crats.com
Josh Eikov, Managing Director

Eric Sands Consulting Services
6193 Rock Island Rd., Ste. 412
Fort Lauderdale, FL 33319
(954)721-4767

Fax: (954)720-2815
E-mail: easands@aol.com
Website: http://www.ericsandsconsultig.com

Professional Planning Associates, Inc.
1975 E. Sunrise Blvd. Suite 607
Fort Lauderdale, FL 33304
(954)764-5204
Fax: 954-463-4172
E-mail: Mgoldstein@proplana.com
Website: http://proplana.com
Michael Goldstein, President

Host Media Corp.
3948 S 3rd St., Ste. 191
Jacksonville Beach, FL 32250
(904)285-3239
Fax: (904)285-5618
E-mail: msconsulting@compuserve.com
Website: http://www.media
servicesgroup.com

William V. Hall
1925 Brickell, Ste. D-701
Miami, FL 33129
(305)856-9622
Fax: (305)856-4113
E-mail: williamvhall@compuserve.com

F.A. McGee Inc.
800 Claughton Island Dr., Ste. 401
Miami, FL 33131
(305)377-9123

Taxplan Inc.
Mirasol International Ctr.
2699 Collins Ave.
Miami Beach, FL 33140
(305)538-3303

T.C. Brown & Associates
8415 Excalibur Cir., Apt. B1
Naples, FL 34108
(941)594-1949
Fax: (941)594-0611
E-mail: tcater@naples.net.com

RLA International Consulting
713 Lagoon Dr.
North Palm Beach, FL 33408
(407)626-4258
Fax: (407)626-5772

Comprehensive Franchising Inc.
2465 Ridgecrest Ave.
Orange Park, FL 32065
(904)272-6567
Free: 800-321-6567
Fax: (904)272-6750
E-mail: theimp@cris.com
Website: http://www.franchise411.com

Hunter G. Jackson Jr. - Consulting Environmental Physicist
PO Box 618272
Orlando, FL 32861-8272
(407)295-4188
E-mail: hunterjackson@juno.com

F. Newton Parks
210 El Brillo Way
Palm Beach, FL 33480
(561)833-1727
Fax: (561)833-4541

Avery Business Development Services
2506 St. Michel Ct.
Ponte Vedra Beach, FL 32082
(904)285-6033
Fax: (904)285-6033

Strategic Business Planning Co.
PO Box 821006
South Florida, FL 33082-1006
(954)704-9100
Fax: (954)438-7333
E-mail: info@bizplan.com
Website: http://www.bizplan.com

Dufresne Consulting Group Inc.
10014 N Dale Mabry, Ste. 101
Tampa, FL 33618-4426
(813)264-4775
Fax: (813)264-9300
Website: http://www.dcgconsult.com

Agrippa Enterprises Inc.
PO Box 175
Venice, FL 34284-0175
(941)355-7876
E-mail: webservices@agrippa.com
Website: http://www.agrippa.com

Center for Simplified Strategic Planning Inc.
PO Box 3324
Vero Beach, FL 32964-3324
(561)231-3636
Fax: (561)231-1099
Website: http://www.cssp.com

Georgia

Marketing Spectrum Inc.
115 Perimeter Pl., Ste. 440
Atlanta, GA 30346
(770)395-7244
Fax: (770)393-4071

Business Ventures Corp.
1650 Oakbrook Dr., Ste. 405
Norcross, GA 30093
(770)729-8000
Fax: (770)729-8028

Informed Decisions Inc.
100 Falling Cheek
Sautee Nacoochee, GA 30571
(706)878-1905
Fax: (706)878-1802
E-mail: skylake@compuserve.com

Tom C. Davis & Associates, P.C.
3189 Perimeter Rd.
Valdosta, GA 31602
(912)247-9801
Fax: (912)244-7704
E-mail: mail@tcdcpa.com
Website: http://www.tcdcpa.com/

Illinois

TWD and Associates
431 S Patton
Arlington Heights, IL 60005
(847)398-6410
Fax: (847)255-5095
E-mail: tdoo@aol.com

Management Planning Associates Inc.
2275 Half Day Rd., Ste. 350
Bannockburn, IL 60015-1277
(847)945-2421
Fax: (847)945-2425

Phil Faris Associates
86 Old Mill Ct.
Barrington, IL 60010
(847)382-4888
Fax: (847)382-4890
E-mail: pfaris@meginsnet.net

Seven Continents Technology
787 Stonebridge
Buffalo Grove, IL 60089
(708)577-9653
Fax: (708)870-1220

Grubb & Blue Inc.
2404 Windsor Pl.
Champaign, IL 61820
(217)366-0052
Fax: (217)356-0117

ACE Accounting Service Inc.
3128 N Bernard St.
Chicago, IL 60618
(773)463-7854
Fax: (773)463-7854

AON Consulting Worldwide
200 E Randolph St., 10th Fl.
Chicago, IL 60601
(312)381-4800
Free: 800-438-6487
Fax: (312)381-0240
Website: http://www.aon.com

FMS Consultants
5801 N Sheridan Rd., Ste. 3D
Chicago, IL 60660
(773)561-7362
Fax: (773)561-6274

Grant Thornton
800 1 Prudential Plz.
130 E Randolph St.
Chicago, IL 60601
(312)856-0001
Fax: (312)861-1340
E-mail: gtinfo@gt.com
Website: http://www.grantthornton.com

Kingsbury International Ltd.
5341 N Glenwood Ave.
Chicago, IL 60640
(773)271-3030
Fax: (773)728-7080
E-mail: jetlag@mcs.com
Website: http://www.kingbiz.com

MacDougall & Blake Inc.
1414 N Wells St., Ste. 311
Chicago, IL 60610-1306
(312)587-3330
Fax: (312)587-3699
E-mail: jblake@compuserve.com

James C. Osburn Ltd.
6445 N. Western Ave., Ste. 304
Chicago, IL 60645
(773)262-4428
Fax: (773)262-6755
E-mail: osburnltd@aol.com

Tarifero & Tazewell Inc.
211 S Clark
Chicago, IL 60690
(312)665-9714
Fax: (312)665-9716

Human Energy Design Systems
620 Roosevelt Dr.
Edwardsville, IL 62025
(618)692-0258
Fax: (618)692-0819

China Business Consultants Group
931 Dakota Cir.
Naperville, IL 60563
(630)778-7992
Fax: (630)778-7915
E-mail: cbcq@aol.com

Center for Workforce Effectiveness
500 Skokie Blvd., Ste. 222
Northbrook, IL 60062
(847)559-8777
Fax: (847)559-8778

E-mail: office@cwelink.com
Website: http://www.cwelink.com

Smith Associates
1320 White Mountain Dr.
Northbrook, IL 60062
(847)480-7200
Fax: (847)480-9828

Francorp Inc.
20200 Governors Dr.
Olympia Fields, IL 60461
(708)481-2900
Free: 800-372-6244
Fax: (708)481-5885
E-mail: francorp@aol.com
Website: http://www.francorpinc.com

Camber Business Strategy Consultants
1010 S Plum Tree Ct
Palatine, IL 60078-0986
(847)202-0101
Fax: (847)705-7510
E-mail: camber@ameritech.net

Partec Enterprise Group
5202 Keith Dr.
Richton Park, IL 60471
(708)503-4047
Fax: (708)503-9468

Rockford Consulting Group Ltd.
Century Plz., Ste. 206
7210 E State St.
Rockford, IL 61108
(815)229-2900
Free: 800-667-7495
Fax: (815)229-2612
E-mail: rligus@RockfordConsulting.com
Website: http://www.Rockford
Consulting.com

RSM McGladrey Inc.
1699 E Woodfield Rd., Ste. 300
Schaumburg, IL 60173-4969
(847)413-6900
Fax: (847)517-7067
Website: http://www.rsmmcgladrey.com

A.D. Star Consulting
320 Euclid
Winnetka, IL 60093
(847)446-7827
Fax: (847)446-7827
E-mail: startwo@worldnet.att.net

Indiana

Modular Consultants Inc.
3109 Crabtree Ln.
Elkhart, IN 46514

(219)264-5761
Fax: (219)264-5761
E-mail: sasabo5313@aol.com

Midwest Marketing Research
PO Box 1077
Goshen, IN 46527
(219)533-0548
Fax: (219)533-0540
E-mail: 103365.654@compuserve

Ketchum Consulting Group
8021 Knue Rd., Ste. 112
Indianapolis, IN 46250
(317)845-5411
Fax: (317)842-9941

**MDI Management
Consulting**
1519 Park Dr.
Munster, IN 46321
(219)838-7909
Fax: (219)838-7909

Iowa

McCord Consulting Group Inc.
4533 Pine View Dr. NE
PO Box 11024
Cedar Rapids, IA 52410
(319)378-0077
Fax: (319)378-1577
E-mail: smmccord@hom.com
Website: http://www.mccordgroup.com

Management Solutions L.C.
3815 Lincoln Pl. Dr.
Des Moines, IA 50312
(515)277-6408
Fax: (515)277-3506
E-mail: wasunimers@uswest.net

Grandview Marketing
15 Red Bridge Dr.
Sioux City, IA 51104
(712)239-3122
Fax: (712)258-7578
E-mail: eandrews@pionet.net

Kansas

Assessments in Action
513A N Mur-Len
Olathe, KS 66062
(913)764-6270
Free: (888)548-1504
Fax: (913)764-6495
E-mail: lowdene@qni.com
Website: http://www.assessments
in-action.com

Maine

Edgemont Enterprises
PO Box 8354
Portland, ME 04104
(207)871-8964
Fax: (207)871-8964

Pan Atlantic Consultants
5 Milk St.
Portland, ME 04101
(207)871-8622
Fax: (207)772-4842
E-mail: pmurphy@maine.rr.com
Website: http://www.panatlantic.net

Maryland

Clemons & Associates Inc.
5024-R Campbell Blvd.
Baltimore, MD 21236
(410)931-8100
Fax: (410)931-8111
E-mail: info@clemonsmgmt.com
Website: http://www.clemonsmgmt.com

Imperial Group Ltd.
305 Washington Ave., Ste. 204
Baltimore, MD 21204-6009
(410)337-8500
Fax: (410)337-7641

Leadership Institute
3831 Yolando Rd.
Baltimore, MD 21218
(410)366-9111
Fax: (410)243-8478
E-mail: behconsult@aol.com

Burdeshaw Associates Ltd.
4701 Sangamore Rd.
Bethesda, MD 20816-2508
(301)229-5800
Fax: (301)229-5045
E-mail: jstacy@burdeshaw.com
Website: http://www.burdeshaw.com

Michael E. Cohen
5225 Pooks Hill Rd., Ste. 1119 S
Bethesda, MD 20814
(301)530-5738
Fax: (301)530-2988
E-mail: mecohen@crosslink.net

World Development Group Inc.
5272 River Rd., Ste. 650
Bethesda, MD 20816-1405
(301)652-1818
Fax: (301)652-1250
E-mail: wdg@has.com
Website: http://www.worlddg.com

Swartz Consulting
PO Box 4301
Crofton, MD 21114-4301
(301)262-6728

Software Solutions International Inc.
9633 Duffer Way
Gaithersburg, MD 20886
(301)330-4136
Fax: (301)330-4136

Strategies Inc.
8 Park Center Ct., Ste. 200
Owings Mills, MD 21117
(410)363-6669
Fax: (410)363-1231
E-mail: strategies@strat1.com
Website: http://www.strat1.com

Hammer Marketing Resources
179 Inverness Rd.
Severna Park, MD 21146
(410)544-9191
Fax: (305)675-3277
E-mail: info@gohammer.com
Website: http://www.gohammer.com

Andrew Sussman & Associates
13731 Kretsinger
Smithsburg, MD 21783
(301)824-2943
Fax: (301)824-2943

Massachusetts

Geibel Marketing and Public Relations
PO Box 611
Belmont, MA 02478-0005
(617)484-8285
Fax: (617)489-3567
E-mail: jgeibel@geibelpr.com
Website: http://www.geibelpr.com

Bain & Co.
2 Copley Pl.
Boston, MA 02116
(617)572-2000
Fax: (617)572-2427
E-mail: corporate.inquiries@bain.com
Website: http://www.bain.com

Mehr & Co.
62 Kinnaird St.
Cambridge, MA 02139
(617)876-3311
Fax: (617)876-3023
E-mail: mehrco@aol.com

Monitor Company Inc.
2 Canal Park
Cambridge, MA 02141

(617)252-2000
Fax: (617)252-2100
Website: http://www.monitor.com

Information & Research Associates
PO Box 3121
Framingham, MA 01701
(508)788-0784

Walden Consultants Ltd.
252 Pond St.
Hopkinton, MA 01748
(508)435-4882
Fax: (508)435-3971
Website: http://www.waldencon
sultants.com

Jeffrey D. Marshall
102 Mitchell Rd.
Ipswich, MA 01938-1219
(508)356-1113
Fax: (508)356-2989

Consulting Resources Corp.
6 Northbrook Park
Lexington, MA 02420
(781)863-1222
Fax: (781)863-1441
E-mail: res@consultingresources.net
Website: http://www.consulting
resources.net

Planning Technologies Group L.L.C.
92 Hayden Ave.
Lexington, MA 02421
(781)778-4678
Fax: (781)861-1099
E-mail: ptg@plantech.com
Website: http://www.plantech.com

Kalba International Inc.
23 Sandy Pond Rd.
Lincoln, MA 01773
(781)259-9589
Fax: (781)259-1460
E-mail: info@kalbainternational.com
Website: http://www.kalbainter
national.com

VMB Associates Inc.
115 Ashland St.
Melrose, MA 02176
(781)665-0623
Fax: (425)732-7142
E-mail: vmbinc@aol.com

The Company Doctor
14 Pudding Stone Ln.
Mendon, MA 01756
(508)478-1747
Fax: (508)478-0520

Data and Strategies Group Inc.
190 N Main St.
Natick, MA 01760
(508)653-9990
Fax: (508)653-7799
E-mail: dsginc@dsggroup.com
Website: http://www.dsggroup.com

The Enterprise Group
73 Parker Rd.
Needham, MA 02494
(617)444-6631
Fax: (617)433-9991
E-mail: lsacco@world.std.com
Website: http://www.enterprise-group.com

PSMJ Resources Inc.
10 Midland Ave.
Newton, MA 02458
(617)965-0055
Free: 800-537-7765
Fax: (617)965-5152
E-mail: psmj@tiac.net
Website: http://www.psmj.com

Scheur Management Group Inc.
255 Washington St., Ste. 100
Newton, MA 02458-1611
(617)969-7500
Fax: (617)969-7508
E-mail: smgnow@scheur.com
Website: http://www.scheur.com

I.E.E.E., Boston Section
240 Bear Hill Rd., 202B
Waltham, MA 02451-1017
(781)890-5294
Fax: (781)890-5290

Business Planning and Consulting Services
20 Beechwood Ter.
Wellesley, MA 02482
(617)237-9151
Fax: (617)237-9151

Michigan

Walter Frederick Consulting
1719 South Blvd.
Ann Arbor, MI 48104
(313)662-4336
Fax: (313)769-7505

Fox Enterprises
6220 W Freeland Rd.
Freeland, MI 48623
(517)695-9170
Fax: (517)695-9174
E-mail: foxjw@concentric.net
Website: http://www.cris.com/~foxjw

G.G.W. and Associates
1213 Hampton
Jackson, MI 49203
(517)782-2255
Fax: (517)782-2255

Altamar Group Ltd.
6810 S Cedar, Ste. 2-B
Lansing, MI 48911
(517)694-0910
Free: 800-443-2627
Fax: (517)694-1377

Sheffieck Consultants Inc.
23610 Greening Dr.
Novi, MI 48375-3130
(248)347-3545
Fax: (248)347-3530
E-mail: cfsheff@concentric.net

Rehmann, Robson PC
5800 Gratiot
Saginaw, MI 48605
(517)799-9580
Fax: (517)799-0227
Website: http://www.rrpc.com

Francis & Co.
17200 W 10 Mile Rd., Ste. 207
Southfield, MI 48075
(248)559-7600
Fax: (248)559-5249

Private Ventures Inc.
16000 W 9 Mile Rd., Ste. 504
Southfield, MI 48075
(248)569-1977
Free: 800-448-7614
Fax: (248)569-1838
E-mail: pventuresi@aol.com

JGK Associates
14464 Kerner Dr.
Sterling Heights, MI 48313
(810)247-9055
Fax: (248)822-4977
E-mail: kozlowski@home.com

Minnesota

Health Fitness Corp.
3500 W 80th St., Ste. 130
Bloomington, MN 55431
(612)831-6830
Fax: (612)831-7264

Consatech Inc.
PO Box 1047
Burnsville, MN 55337
(612)953-1088
Fax: (612)435-2966

Robert F. Knotek
14960 Ironwood Ct.
Eden Prairie, MN 55346
(612)949-2875

DRI Consulting
7715 Stonewood Ct.
Edina, MN 55439
(612)941-9656
Fax: (612)941-2693
E-mail: dric@dric.com
Website: http://www.dric.com

Markin Consulting
12072 87th Pl. N
Maple Grove, MN 55369
(612)493-3568
Fax: (612)493-5744
E-mail: markin@markinconsulting.com
Website: http://www.markin
consulting.com

Minnesota Cooperation Office for Small Business & Job Creation Inc.
5001 W 80th St., Ste. 825
Minneapolis, MN 55437
(612)830-1230
Fax: (612)830-1232
E-mail: mncoop@msn.com
Website: http://www.mnco.org

Enterprise Consulting Inc.
PO Box 1111
Minnetonka, MN 55345
(612)949-5909
Fax: (612)906-3965

Amdahl International
724 1st Ave. SW
Rochester, MN 55902
(507)252-0402
Fax: (507)252-0402
E-mail: amdahl@best-service.com
Website: http://www.wp.com/amdahl_int

Power Systems Research
1365 Corporate Center Curve, 2nd Fl.
St. Paul, MN 55121
(612)905-8400
Free: (888)625-8612
Fax: (612)454-0760
E-mail: Barb@Powersys.com
Website: http://www.powersys.com

Missouri

Business Planning and Development Corp.
4030 Charlotte St.
Kansas City, MO 64110
(816)753-0495

E-mail: humph@bpdev.demon.co.uk
Website: http://www.bpdev.demon.co.uk

CFO Service
10336 Donoho
St. Louis, MO 63131
(314)750-2940
E-mail: jskae@cfoservice.com
Website: http://www.cfoservice.com

Nebraska

International Management Consulting Group Inc.
1309 Harlan Dr., Ste. 205
Bellevue, NE 68005
(402)291-4545
Free: 800-665-IMCG
Fax: (402)291-4343
E-mail: imcg@neonramp.com
Website: http://www.mgtcon
sulting.com

Heartland Management Consulting Group
1904 Barrington Pky.
Papillion, NE 68046
(402)339-2387
Fax: (402)339-1319

Nevada

The DuBois Group
865 Tahoe Blvd., Ste. 108
Incline Village, NV 89451
(775)832-0550
Free: 800-375-2935
Fax: (775)832-0556
E-mail: DuBoisGrp@aol.com

New Hampshire

Wolff Consultants
10 Buck Rd.
Hanover, NH 03755
(603)643-6015

BPT Consulting Associates Ltd.
12 Parmenter Rd., Ste. B-6
Londonderry, NH 03053
(603)437-8484
Free: (888)278-0030
Fax: (603)434-5388
E-mail: bptcons@tiac.net
Website: http://www.bptconsulting.com

New Jersey

Bedminster Group Inc.
1170 Rte. 22 E
Bridgewater, NJ 08807

(908)500-4155
Fax: (908)766-0780
E-mail: info@bedminstergroup.com
Website: http://www.bedminster
group.com
Fax: (202)806-1777
Terry Strong, Acting Regional Dir.

Delta Planning Inc.
PO Box 425
Denville, NJ 07834
(913)625-1742
Free: 800-672-0762
Fax: (973)625-3531
E-mail: DeltaP@worldnet.att.net
Website: http://deltaplanning.com

Kumar Associates Inc.
1004 Cumbermeade Rd.
Fort Lee, NJ 07024
(201)224-9480
Fax: (201)585-2343
E-mail: mail@kumarassociates.com
Website: http://kumarassociates.com

John Hall & Company Inc.
PO Box 187
Glen Ridge, NJ 07028
(973)680-4449
Fax: (973)680-4581
E-mail: jhcompany@aol.com

Market Focus
PO Box 402
Maplewood, NJ 07040
(973)378-2470
Fax: (973)378-2470
E-mail: mcss66@marketfocus.com

Vanguard Communications Corp.
100 American Rd.
Morris Plains, NJ 07950
(973)605-8000
Fax: (973)605-8329
Website: http://www.vanguard.net/

ConMar International Ltd.
1901 US Hwy. 130
North Brunswick, NJ 08902
(732)940-8347
Fax: (732)274-1199

KLW New Products
156 Cedar Dr.
Old Tappan, NJ 07675
(201)358-1300
Fax: (201)664-2594
E-mail: lrlarsen@usa.net
Website: http://www.klwnew
products.com

PA Consulting Group
315A Enterprise Dr.
Plainsboro, NJ 08536
(609)936-8300
Fax: (609)936-8811
E-mail: info@paconsulting.com
Website: http://www.pa-consulting.com

Aurora Marketing Management Inc.
66 Witherspoon St., Ste. 600
Princeton, NJ 08542
(908)904-1125
Fax: (908)359-1108
E-mail: aurora2@voicenet.com
Website: http://www.auroramarketing.net

Smart Business Supersite
88 Orchard Rd., CN-5219
Princeton, NJ 08543
(908)321-1924
Fax: (908)321-5156
E-mail: irv@smartbiz.com
Website: http://www.smartbiz.com

Tracelin Associates
1171 Main St., Ste. 6K
Rahway, NJ 07065
(732)381-3288

Schkeeper Inc.
130-6 Bodman Pl.
Red Bank, NJ 07701
(732)219-1965
Fax: (732)530-3703

Henry Branch Associates
2502 Harmon Cove Twr.
Secaucus, NJ 07094
(201)866-2008
Fax: (201)601-0101
E-mail: hbranch161@home.com

Robert Gibbons & Company Inc.
46 Knoll Rd.
Tenafly, NJ 07670-1050
(201)871-3933
Fax: (201)871-2173
E-mail: crisisbob@aol.com

PMC Management Consultants Inc.
6 Thistle Ln.
Three Bridges, NJ 08887-0332
(908)788-1014
Free: 800-PMC-0250
Fax: (908)806-7287
E-mail: int@pmc-management.com
Website: http://www.pmc-management.com

R.W. Bankart & Associates
20 Valley Ave., Ste. D-2

Westwood, NJ 07675-3607
(201)664-7672

New Mexico

Vondle & Associates Inc.
4926 Calle de Tierra, NE
Albuquerque, NM 87111
(505)292-8961
Fax: (505)296-2790
E-mail: vondle@aol.com

InfoNewMexico
2207 Black Hills Rd., NE
Rio Rancho, NM 87124
(505)891-2462
Fax: (505)896-8971

New York

Powers Research and Training Institute
PO Box 78
Bayville, NY 11709
(516)628-2250
Fax: (516)628-2252
E-mail: powercocch@compuserve.com
Website: http://www.nancypowers.com

Consortium House
296 Wittenberg Rd.
Bearsville, NY 12409
(845)679-8867
Fax: (845)679-9248
E-mail: eugenegs@aol.com
Website: http://www.chpub.com

Progressive Finance Corp.
3549 Tiemann Ave.
Bronx, NY 10469
(718)405-9029
Free: 800-225-8381
Fax: (718)405-1170

Wave Hill Associates Inc.
2621 Palisade Ave., Ste. 15-C
Bronx, NY 10463
(718)549-7368
Fax: (718)601-9670
E-mail: pepper@compuserve.com

Management Insight
96 Arlington Rd.
Buffalo, NY 14221
(716)631-3319
Fax: (716)631-0203
E-mail: michalski@foodservice insight.com
Website: http://www.foodservice insight.com

Samani International Enterprises, Marions Panyaught Consultancy
2028 Parsons
Flushing, NY 11357-3436
(917)287-8087
Fax: 800-873-8939
E-mail: vjp2@biostrategist.com
Website: http://www.biostrategist.com

Marketing Resources Group
71-58 Austin St.
Forest Hills, NY 11375
(718)261-8882

Mangabay Business Plans & Development Subsidiary of Innis Asset Allocation
125-10 Queens Blvd., Ste. 2202
Kew Gardens, NY 11415
(905)527-1947
Fax: 509-472-1935
E-mail: mangabay@mangabay.com
Website: http://www.mangabay.com
Lee Toh, Managing Partner

ComputerEase Co.
1301 Monmouth Ave.
Lakewood, NY 08701
(212)406-9464
Fax: (914)277-5317
E-mail: crawfordc@juno.com

Boice Dunham Group
30 W 13th St.
New York, NY 10011
(212)924-2200
Fax: (212)924-1108

Elizabeth Capen
27 E 95th St.
New York, NY 10128
(212)427-7654
Fax: (212)876-3190

Haver Analytics
60 E 42nd St., Ste. 2424
New York, NY 10017
(212)986-9300
Fax: (212)986-5857
E-mail: data@haver.com
Website: http://www.haver.com

The Jordan, Edmiston Group Inc.
150 E 52nd Ave., 18th Fl.
New York, NY 10022
(212)754-0710
Fax: (212)754-0337

KPMG International
345 Park Ave.
New York, NY 10154-0102
(212)758-9700

Fax: (212)758-9819
Website: http://www.kpmg.com

Mahoney Cohen Consulting Corp.
111 W 40th St., 12th Fl.
New York, NY 10018
(212)490-8000
Fax: (212)790-5913

Management Practice Inc.
342 Madison Ave.
New York, NY 10173-1230
(212)867-7948
Fax: (212)972-5188
Website: http://www.mpiweb.com

Moseley Associates Inc.
342 Madison Ave., Ste. 1414
New York, NY 10016
(212)213-6673
Fax: (212)687-1520

Practice Development Counsel
60 Sutton Pl. S
New York, NY 10022
(212)593-1549
Fax: (212)980-7940
E-mail: pwhaserot@pdcounsel.com
Website: http://www.pdcounsel.com

Unique Value International Inc.
575 Madison Ave., 10th Fl.
New York, NY 10022-1304
(212)605-0590
Fax: (212)605-0589

The Van Tulleken Co.
126 E 56th St.
New York, NY 10022
(212)355-1390
Fax: (212)755-3061
E-mail: newyork@vantulleken.com

Vencon Management Inc.
301 W 53rd St.
New York, NY 10019
(212)581-8787
Fax: (212)397-4126
Website: http://www.venconinc.com

Werner International Inc.
55 E 52nd, 29th Fl.
New York, NY 10055
(212)909-1260
Fax: (212)909-1273
E-mail: richard.downing@rgh.com
Website: http://www.wernertex.com

Zimmerman Business Consulting Inc.
44 E 92nd St., Ste. 5-B
New York, NY 10128

(212)860-3107
Fax: (212)860-7730
E-mail: ljzzbci@aol.com
Website: http://www.zbcinc.com

Overton Financial
7 Allen Rd.
Peekskill, NY 10566
(914)737-4649
Fax: (914)737-4696

Stromberg Consulting
2500 Westchester Ave.
Purchase, NY 10577
(914)251-1515
Fax: (914)251-1562
E-mail: strategy@stromberg_consul
ting.com
Website: http://www.stromberg_
consulting.com

Innovation Management Consulting Inc.
209 Dewitt Rd.
Syracuse, NY 13214-2006
(315)425-5144
Fax: (315)445-8989
E-mail: missonneb@axess.net

M. Clifford Agress
891 Fulton St.
Valley Stream, NY 11580
(516)825-8955
Fax: (516)825-8955

Destiny Kinal Marketing Consultancy
105 Chemung St.
Waverly, NY 14892
(607)565-8317
Fax: (607)565-4083

Valutis Consulting Inc.
5350 Main St., Ste. 7
Williamsville, NY 14221-5338
(716)634-2553
Fax: (716)634-2554
E-mail: valutis@localnet.com
Website: http://www.valutisconsulting.com

North Carolina

Best Practices L.L.C.
6320 Quadrangle Dr., Ste. 200
Chapel Hill, NC 27514
(919)403-0251
Fax: (919)403-0144
E-mail: best@best:in/class
Website: http://www.best-in-class.com

Norelli & Co.
Bank of America Corporate Ctr.
100 N Tyron St., Ste. 5160

Charlotte, NC 28202-4000
(704)376-5484
Fax: (704)376-5485
E-mail: consult@norelli.com
Website: http://www.norelli.com

North Dakota

Center for Innovation
4300 Dartmouth Dr.
PO Box 8372
Grand Forks, ND 58202
(701)777-3132
Fax: (701)777-2339
E-mail: bruce@innovators.net
Website: http://www.innovators.net

Ohio

Transportation Technology Services
208 Harmon Rd.
Aurora, OH 44202
(330)562-3596

Empro Systems Inc.
4777 Red Bank Expy., Ste. 1
Cincinnati, OH 45227-1542
(513)271-2042
Fax: (513)271-2042

Alliance Management International Ltd.
1440 Windrow Ln.
Cleveland, OH 44147-3200
(440)838-1922
Fax: (440)838-0979
E-mail: bgruss@amiltd.com
Website: http://www.amiltd.com

Bozell Kamstra Public Relations
1301 E 9th St., Ste. 3400
Cleveland, OH 44114
(216)623-1511
Fax: (216)623-1501
E-mail: jfeniger@cleveland.bozellk
amstra.com
Website: http://www.bozellk
amstra.com

Cory Dillon Associates
111 Schreyer Pl. E
Columbus, OH 43214
(614)262-8211
Fax: (614)262-3806

Holcomb Gallagher Adams
300 Marconi, Ste. 303
Columbus, OH 43215
(614)221-3343
Fax: (614)221-3367
E-mail: riadams@acme.freenet.oh.us

Young & Associates
PO Box 711
Kent, OH 44240
(330)678-0524
Free: 800-525-9775
Fax: (330)678-6219
E-mail: online@younginc.com
Website: http://www.younginc.com

Robert A. Westman & Associates
8981 Inversary Dr. SE
Warren, OH 44484-2551
(330)856-4149
Fax: (330)856-2564

Oklahoma

Innovative Partners L.L.C.
4900 Richmond Sq., Ste. 100
Oklahoma City, OK 73118
(405)840-0033
Fax: (405)843-8359
E-mail: ipartners@juno.com

Oregon

INTERCON - The International Converting Institute
5200 Badger Rd.
Crooked River Ranch, OR 97760
(541)548-1447
Fax: (541)548-1618
E-mail: johnbowler@
crookedriverranch.com

Talbott ARM
HC 60, Box 5620
Lakeview, OR 97630
(541)635-8587
Fax: (503)947-3482

Management Technology Associates Ltd.
2768 SW Sherwood Dr, Ste. 105
Portland, OR 97201-2251
(503)224-5220
Fax: (503)224-5334
E-mail: lcuster@mta-ltd.com
Website: http://www.mgmt-tech.com

Pennsylvania

Healthscope Inc.
400 Lancaster Ave.
Devon, PA 19333
(610)687-6199
Fax: (610)687-6376
E-mail: health@voicenet.com
Website: http://www.healthscope.net/

Elayne Howard & Associates Inc.
3501 Masons Mill Rd., Ste. 501

Huntingdon Valley, PA 19006-3509
(215)657-9550

GRA Inc.
115 West Ave., Ste. 201
Jenkintown, PA 19046
(215)884-7500
Fax: (215)884-1385
E-mail: gramail@gra-inc.com
Website: http://www.gra-inc.com

Mifflin County Industrial Development Corp.
Mifflin County Industrial Plz.
6395 SR 103 N
Bldg. 50
Lewistown, PA 17044
(717)242-0393
Fax: (717)242-1842
E-mail: mcide@acsworld.net

Autech Products
1289 Revere Rd.
Morrisville, PA 19067
(215)493-3759
Fax: (215)493-9791
E-mail: autech4@yahoo.com

Advantage Associates
434 Avon Dr.
Pittsburgh, PA 15228
(412)343-1558
Fax: (412)362-1684
E-mail: ecocba1@aol.com

Regis J. Sheehan & Associates
Pittsburgh, PA 15220
(412)279-1207

James W. Davidson Company Inc.
23 Forest View Rd.
Wallingford, PA 19086
(610)566-1462

Puerto Rico

Diego Chevere & Co.
Metro Parque 7, Ste. 204
Metro Office
Caparra Heights, PR 00920
(787)774-9595
Fax: (787)774-9566
E-mail: dcco@coqui.net

Manuel L. Porrata and Associates
898 Munoz Rivera Ave., Ste. 201
San Juan, PR 00927
(787)765-2140
Fax: (787)754-3285
E-mail: m_porrata@manuelporrata.com
Website: http://manualporrata.com

South Carolina

Aquafood Business Associates
PO Box 13267
Charleston, SC 29422
(843)795-9506
Fax: (843)795-9477
E-mail: rraba@aol.com

Profit Associates Inc.
PO Box 38026
Charleston, SC 29414
(803)763-5718
Fax: (803)763-5719
E-mail: bobrog@awod.com
Website: http://www.awod.com/gallery/
business/proasc

Strategic Innovations International
12 Executive Ct.
Lake Wylie, SC 29710
(803)831-1225
Fax: (803)831-1177
E-mail: stratinnov@aol.com
Website: http://www.
strategicinnovations.com

Minus Stage
Box 4436
Rock Hill, SC 29731
(803)328-0705
Fax: (803)329-9948

Tennessee

Daniel Petchers & Associates
8820 Fernwood CV
Germantown, TN 38138
(901)755-9896

Business Choices
1114 Forest Harbor, Ste. 300
Hendersonville, TN 37075-9646
(615)822-8692
Free: 800-737-8382
Fax: (615)822-8692
E-mail: bz-ch@juno.com

RCFA Healthcare Management Services L.L.C.
9648 Kingston Pke., Ste. 8
Knoxville, TN 37922
(865)531-0176
Free: 800-635-4040
Fax: (865)531-0722
E-mail: info@rcfa.com
Website: http://www.rcfa.com

Growth Consultants of America
3917 Trimble Rd.
Nashville, TN 37215

(615)383-0550
Fax: (615)269-8940
E-mail: 70244.451@compuserve.com

Texas

Integrated Cost Management Systems Inc.
2261 Brookhollow Plz. Dr., Ste. 104
Arlington, TX 76006
(817)633-2873
Fax: (817)633-3781
E-mail: abm@icms.net
Website: http://www.icms.net

Lori Williams
1000 Leslie Ct.
Arlington, TX 76012
(817)459-3934
Fax: (817)459-3934

Business Resource Software Inc.
2013 Wells Branch Pky., Ste. 305
Austin, TX 78728
Free: 800-423-1228
Fax: (512)251-4401
E-mail: info@brs-inc.com
Website: http://www.brs-inc.com

Erisa Adminstrative Services Inc.
12325 Hymeadow Dr., Bldg. 4
Austin, TX 78750-1847
(512)250-9020
Fax: (512)250-9487
Website: http://www.cserisa.com

R. Miller Hicks & Co.
1011 W 11th St.
Austin, TX 78703
(512)477-7000
Fax: (512)477-9697
E-mail: millerhicks@rmhicks.com
Website: http://www.rmhicks.com

Pragmatic Tactics Inc.
3303 Westchester Ave.
College Station, TX 77845
(409)696-5294
Free: 800-570-5294
Fax: (409)696-4994
E-mail: ptactics@aol.com
Website: http://www.ptatics.com

Perot Systems
12404 Park Central Dr.
Dallas, TX 75251
(972)340-5000
Free: 800-688-4333
Fax: (972)455-4100
E-mail: corp.comm@ps.net
Website: http://www.perotsystems.com

ReGENERATION Partners
3838 Oak Lawn Ave.
Dallas, TX 75219
(214)559-3999
Free: 800-406-1112
E-mail: info@regeneration-partner.com
Website: http://www.regeneration-partners.com

High Technology Associates - Division of Global Technologies Inc.
1775 St. James Pl., Ste. 105
Houston, TX 77056
(713)963-9300
Fax: (713)963-8341
E-mail: hta@infohwy.com

MasterCOM
103 Thunder Rd.
Kerrville, TX 78028
(830)895-7990
Fax: (830)443-3428
E-mail: jmstubblefield@master training.com
Website: http://www.mastertraining.com

PROTEC
4607 Linden Pl.
Pearland, TX 77584
(281)997-9872
Fax: (281)997-9895
E-mail: p.oman@ix.netcom.com

Alpha Quadrant Inc.
10618 Auldine
San Antonio, TX 78230
(210)344-3330
Fax: (210)344-8151
E-mail: mbussone@sbcglobal.net
Website:http://www.a-quadrant.com
Michele Bussone

Bastian Public Relations
614 San Dizier
San Antonio, TX 78232
(210)404-1839
E-mail: lisa@bastianpr.com
Website: http://www.bastianpr.com
Lisa Bastian CBC

Business Strategy Development Consultants
PO Box 690365
San Antonio, TX 78269
(210)696-8000
Free: 800-927-BSDC
Fax: (210)696-8000

Tom Welch, CPC
6900 San Pedro Ave., Ste. 147
San Antonio, TX 78216-6207

(210)737-7022
Fax: (210)737-7022
E-mail: bplan@iamerica.net
Website: http://www.moneywords.com

Utah

Business Management Resource
PO Box 521125
Salt Lake City, UT 84152-1125
(801)272-4668
Fax: (801)277-3290
E-mail: pingfong@worldnet.att.net

Virginia

Tindell Associates
209 Oxford Ave.
Alexandria, VA 22301
(703)683-0109
Fax: 703-783-0219
E-mail: scott@tindell.net
Website: http://www.tindell.net
Scott Lockett, President

Elliott B. Jaffa
2530-B S Walter Reed Dr.
Arlington, VA 22206
(703)931-0040
E-mail: thetrainingdoctor@excite.com
Website: http://www.tregistry.com/jaffa.htm

Koach Enterprises - USA
5529 N 18th St.
Arlington, VA 22205
(703)241-8361
Fax: (703)241-8623

Federal Market Development
5650 Chapel Run Ct.
Centreville, VA 20120-3601
(703)502-8930
Free: 800-821-5003
Fax: (703)502-8929

Huff, Stuart & Carlton
2107 Graves Mills Rd., Ste. C
Forest, VA 24551
(804)316-9356
Free: (888)316-9356
Fax: (804)316-9357
Website: http://www.wealthmgt.net

AMX International Inc.
1420 Spring Hill Rd. , Ste. 600
McLean, VA 22102-3006
(703)690-4100
Fax: (703)643-1279
E-mail: amxmail@amxi.com
Website: http://www.amxi.com

Charles Scott Pugh (Investor)
4101 Pittaway Dr.
Richmond, VA 23235-1022
(804)560-0979
Fax: (804)560-4670

John C. Randall and Associates Inc.
PO Box 15127
Richmond, VA 23227
(804)746-4450
Fax: (804)730-8933
E-mail: randalljcx@aol.com
Website: http://www.johncrandall.com

McLeod & Co.
410 1st St.
Roanoke, VA 24011
(540)342-6911
Fax: (540)344-6367
Website: http://www.mcleodco.com/

Salzinger & Company Inc.
8000 Towers Crescent Dr., Ste. 1350
Vienna, VA 22182
(703)442-5200
Fax: (703)442-5205
E-mail: info@salzinger.com
Website: http://www.salzinger.com

The Small Business Counselor
12423 Hedges Run Dr., Ste. 153
Woodbridge, VA 22192
(703)490-6755
Fax: (703)490-1356

Washington

Burlington Consultants
10900 NE 8th St., Ste. 900
Bellevue, WA 98004
(425)688-3060
Fax: (425)454-4383
E-mail: partners@burlington
consultants.com
Website: http://www.burlington
consultants.com

Perry L. Smith Consulting
800 Bellevue Way NE, Ste. 400
Bellevue, WA 98004-4208
(425)462-2072
Fax: (425)462-5638

St. Charles Consulting Group
1420 NW Gilman Blvd.
Issaquah, WA 98027
(425)557-8708
Fax: (425)557-8731
E-mail: info@stcharlesconsulting.com
Website: http://www.stcharlescon
sulting.com

Independent Automotive Training Services
PO Box 334
Kirkland, WA 98083
(425)822-5715
E-mail: ltunney@autosvccon.com
Website: http://www.autosvccon.com

Kahle Associate Inc.
6203 204th Dr. NE
Redmond, WA 98053
(425)836-8763
Fax: (425)868-3770
E-mail: randykahle@kahleassociates.com
Website: http://www.kahleassociates.com

Dan Collin
3419 Wallingord Ave N, No. 2
Seattle, WA 98103
(206)634-9469
E-mail: dc@dancollin.com
Website: http://members.home.net/
dcollin/

ECG Management Consultants Inc.
1111 3rd Ave., Ste. 2700
Seattle, WA 98101-3201
(206)689-2200
Fax: (206)689-2209
E-mail: ecg@ecgmc.com
Website: http://www.ecgmc.com

Northwest Trade Adjustment Assistance Center
900 4th Ave., Ste. 2430
Seattle, WA 98164-1001
(206)622-2730
Free: 800-667-8087
Fax: (206)622-1105
E-mail: matchingfunds@nwtaac.org
Website: http://www.taacenters.org

Business Planning Consultants
S 3510 Ridgeview Dr.
Spokane, WA 99206
(509)928-0332
Fax: (509)921-0842
E-mail: bpci@nextdim.com

West Virginia

**Stanley & Associates Inc./
BusinessandMarketingPlans.com**
1687 Robert C. Byrd Dr.
Beckley, WV 25801
(304)252-0324
Free: 888-752-6720
Fax: (304)252-0470
E-mail: cclay@charterinternet.com

Website: http://www.Businessand
MarketingPlans.com
Christopher Clay

Wisconsin

White & Associates Inc.
5349 Somerset Ln. S
Greenfield, WI 53221
(414)281-7373
Fax: (414)281-7006
E-mail: wnaconsult@aol.com

Small business administration regional offices

This section contains a listing of Small Business Administration offices arranged numerically by region. Service areas are provided. Contact the appropriate office for a referral to the nearest field office, or visit the Small Business Administration online at www.sba.gov.

Region 1

U.S. Small Business Administration
Region I Office
10 Causeway St., Ste. 812
Boston, MA 02222-1093
Phone: (617)565-8415
Fax: (617)565-8420
Serves Connecticut, Maine, Massachusetts, New Hampshire, Rhode Island, and Vermont.

Region 2

U.S. Small Business Administration
Region II Office
26 Federal Plaza, Ste. 3108
New York, NY 10278
Phone: (212)264-1450
Fax: (212)264-0038
Serves New Jersey, New York, Puerto Rico, and the Virgin Islands.

Region 3

U.S. Small Business Administration
Region III Office
Robert N C Nix Sr. Federal Building
900 Market St., 5th Fl.
Philadelphia, PA 19107
(215)580-2807
Serves Delaware, the District of Columbia, Maryland, Pennsylvania, Virginia, and West Virginia.

Region 4

U.S. Small Business Administration
Region IV Office
233 Peachtree St. NE
Harris Tower 1800
Atlanta, GA 30303
Phone: (404)331-4999
Fax: (404)331-2354
Serves Alabama, Florida, Georgia, Kentucky, Mississippi, North Carolina, South Carolina, and Tennessee.

Region 5

U.S. Small Business Administration
Region V Office
500 W. Madison St.
Citicorp Center, Ste. 1240
Chicago, IL 60661-2511
Phone: (312)353-0357
Fax: (312)353-3426
Serves Illinois, Indiana, Michigan, Minnesota, Ohio, and Wisconsin.

Region 6

U.S. Small Business Administration
Region VI Office
4300 Amon Carter Blvd., Ste. 108
Fort Worth, TX 76155
Phone: (817)684-5581
Fax: (817)684-5588
Serves Arkansas, Louisiana, New Mexico, Oklahoma, and Texas.

Region 7

U.S. Small Business Administration
Region VII Office
323 W. 8th St., Ste. 307
Kansas City, MO 64105-1500
Phone: (816)374-6380
Fax: (816)374-6339
Serves Iowa, Kansas, Missouri, and Nebraska.

Region 8

U.S. Small Business Administration
Region VIII Office
721 19th St., Ste. 400
Denver, CO 80202
Phone: (303)844-0500
Fax: (303)844-0506
Serves Colorado, Montana, North Dakota, South Dakota, Utah, and Wyoming.

Region 9

U.S. Small Business Administration
Region IX Office
330 N Brand Blvd., Ste. 1270
Glendale, CA 91203-2304
Phone: (818)552-3434
Fax: (818)552-3440
Serves American Samoa, Arizona, California, Guam, Hawaii, Nevada, and the Trust Territory of the Pacific Islands.

Region 10

U.S. Small Business Administration
Region X Office
2401 Fourth Ave., Ste. 400
Seattle, WA 98121
Phone: (206)553-5676
Fax: (206)553-4155
Serves Alaska, Idaho, Oregon, and Washington.

Small business development centers

This section contains a listing of all Small Business Development Centers, organized alphabetically by state/U.S. territory, then by city, then by agency name.

Alabama

Alabama SBDC
UNIVERSITY OF ALABAMA
2800 Milan Court Suite 124
Birmingham, AL 35211-6908
Phone: 205-943-6750
Fax: 205-943-6752
E-Mail: wcampbell@provost.uab.edu
Website: http://www.asbdc.org
Mr. William Campbell Jr, State Director

Alaska

Alaska SBDC
UNIVERSITY OF ALASKA - ANCHORAGE
430 West Seventh Avenue, Suite 110
Anchorage, AK 99501
Phone: 907-274 -7232
Fax: 907-274-9524
E-Mail: anerw@uaa.alaska.edu
Website: http://www.aksbdc.org
Ms. Jean R. Wall, State Director

American Samoa

American Samoa SBDC
AMERICAN SAMOA COMMUNITY COLLEGE
P.O. Box 2609
Pago Pago, American Samoa 96799
Phone: 011-684-699-4830
Fax: 011-684-699-6132
E-Mail: htalex@att.net
Mr. Herbert Thweatt, Director

Arizona

Arizona SBDC
MARICOPA COUNTY COMMUNITY COLLEGE
2411 West 14th Street, Suite 132
Tempe, AZ 85281
Phone: 480-731-8720
Fax: 480-731-8729
E-Mail: mike.york@domail.maricopa.edu
Website: http://www.dist.maricopa.edu.sbdc
Mr. Michael York, State Director

Arkansas

Arkansas SBDC
UNIVERSITY OF ARKANSAS
2801 South University Avenue
Little Rock, AR 72204
Phone: 501-324-9043
Fax: 501-324-9049
E-Mail: jmroderick@ualr.edu
Website: http://asbdc.ualr.edu
Ms. Janet M. Roderick, State Director

California

California - San Francisco SBDC
Northern California SBDC Lead Center
HUMBOLDT STATE UNIVERSITY
Office of Economic Development
1 Harpst Street 2006A, Siemens Hall
Arcata, CA, 95521
Phone: 707-826-3922
Fax: 707-826-3206
E-Mail: gainer@humboldt.edu
Ms. Margaret A. Gainer, Regional Director

California - Sacramento SBDC
CALIFORNIA STATE UNIVERSITY - CHICO
Chico, CA 95929-0765
Phone: 530-898-4598
Fax: 530-898-4734

E-Mail: dripke@csuchico.edu
Website: http://gsbdc.csuchico.edu
Mr. Dan Ripke, Interim Regional Director

California - San Diego SBDC
SOUTHWESTERN COMMUNITY
COLLEGE DISTRICT
900 Otey Lakes Road
Chula Vista, CA 91910
Phone: 619-482-6388
Fax: 619-482-6402
E-Mail: dtrujillo@swc.cc.ca.us
Website: http://www.sbditc.org
Ms. Debbie P. Trujillo, Regional Director

California - Fresno SBDC
UC Merced Lead Center
UNIVERSITY OF CALIFORNIA -
MERCED
550 East Shaw, Suite 105A
Fresno, CA 93710
Phone: 559-241-6590
Fax: 559-241-7422
E-Mail: crosander@ucmerced.edu
Website: http://sbdc.ucmerced.edu
Mr. Chris Rosander, State Director

California - Santa Ana SBDC
Tri-County Lead SBDC
CALIFORNIA STATE UNIVERSITY -
FULLERTON
800 North State College Boulevard, LH640
Fullerton, CA 92834
Phone: 714-278-2719
Fax: 714-278-7858
E-Mail: vpham@fullerton.edu
Website: http://www.leadsbdc.org
Ms. Vi Pham, Lead Center Director

California - Los Angeles Region SBDC
LONG BEACH COMMUNITY
COLLEGE DISTRICT
3950 Paramount Boulevard, Ste 101
Lakewood, CA 90712
Phone: 562-938-5004
Fax: 562-938-5030
E-Mail: ssloan@lbcc.edu
Ms. Sheneui Sloan, Interim Lead Center
Director

Colorado

Colorado SBDC
OFFICE OF ECONOMIC
DEVELOPMENT
1625 Broadway, Suite 170
Denver, CO 80202
Phone: 303-892-3864
Fax: 303-892-3848
E-Mail: Kelly.Manning@state.co.us

Website: http://www.state.co.us/oed/sbdc
Ms. Kelly Manning, State Director

Connecticut

Connecticut SBDC
UNIVERSITY OF CONNECTICUT
1376 Storrs Road, Unit 4094
Storrs, CT 06269-1094
Phone: 860-870-6370
Fax: 860-870-6374
E-Mail: richard.cheney@uconn.edu
Website: http://www.sbdc.uconn.edu
Mr. Richard Cheney, Interim State Director

Delaware

Delaware SBDC
DELAWARE TECHNOLOGY PARK
1 Innovation Way, Suite 301
Newark, DE 19711
Phone: 302-831-2747
Fax: 302-831-1423
E-Mail: Clinton.tymes@mvs.udel.edu
Website: http://www.delawaresbdc.org
Mr. Clinton Tymes, State Director

District of Columbia

District of Columbia SBDC
HOWARD UNIVERSITY
2600 6th Street, NW Room 128
Washington, DC 20059
Phone: 202-806-1550
Fax: 202-806-1777
E-Mail: hturner@howard.edu
Website: http://www.dcsbdc.com/
Mr. Henry Turner, Executive Director

Florida

Florida SBDC
UNIVERSITY OF WEST FLORIDA
401 East Chase Street, Suite 100
Pensacola, FL 32502
Phone: 850-473-7800
Fax: 850-473-7813
E-Mail: jcartwri@uwf.edu
Website: http://www.floridasbdc.com
Mr. Jerry Cartwright, State Director

Georgia

Georgia SBDC
UNIVERSITY OF GEORGIA
1180 East Broad Street
Athens, GA 30602
Phone: 706-542-6762
Fax: 706-542-6776
E-mail: aadams@sbdc.uga.edu

Website: http://www.sbdc.uga.edu
Mr. Allan Adams, Interim State Director

Guam

Guam Small Business Development
Center
UNIVERSITY OF GUAM
Pacific Islands SBDC
P.O. Box 5014 - U.O.G. Station
Mangilao, GU 96923
Phone: 671-735-2590
Fax: 671-734-2002
E-mail: casey@pacificsbdc.com
Website: http://www.uog.edu/sbdc
Mr. Casey Jeszenka, Director

Hawaii

Hawaii SBDC
UNIVERSITY OF HAWAII - HILO
308 Kamehameha Avenue, Suite 201
Hilo, HI 96720
Phone: 808-974-7515
Fax: 808-974-7683
E-Mail: darrylm@interpac.net
Website: http://www.hawaii-sbdc.org
Mr. Darryl Mleynek, State Director

Idaho

Idaho SBDC
BOISE STATE UNIVERSITY
1910 University Drive
Boise, ID 83725
Phone: 208-426-3799
Fax: 208-426-3877
E-mail: jhogge@boisestate.edu
Website: http://www.idahosbdc.org
Mr. Jim Hogge, State Director

Illinois

Illinois SBDC
DEPARTMENT OF COMMERCE
AND ECONOMIC OPPORTUNITY
620 E. Adams, S-4
Springfield, IL 62701
Phone: 217-524-5700
Fax: 217-524-0171
E-mail: mpatrilli@ildceo.net
Website: http://www.ilsbdc.biz
Mr. Mark Petrilli, State Director

Indiana

Indiana SBDC
INDIANA ECONOMIC
DEVELOPMENT CORPORATION
One North Capitol, Suite 900
Indianapolis, IN 46204

Phone: 317-234-8872
Fax: 317-232-8874
E-mail: dtrocha@isbdc.org
Website: http://www.isbdc.org
Ms. Debbie Bishop Trocha, State
Director

Iowa

Iowa SBDC
IOWA STATE UNIVERSITY
340 Gerdin Business Bldg.
Ames, IA 50011-1350
Phone: 515-294-2037
Fax: 515-294-6522
E-mail: jonryan@iastate.edu
Website: http://www.iabusnet.org
Mr. Jon Ryan, State Director

Kansas

Kansas SBDC
FORT HAYS STATE UNIVERSITY
214 SW Sixth Street, Suite 301
Topeka, KS 66603
Phone: 785-296-6514
Fax: 785-291-3261
E-mail: ksbdc.wkearns@fhsu.edu
Website: http://www.fhsu.edu/ksbdc
Mr. Wally Kearns, State Director

Kentucky

Kentucky SBDC
UNIVERSITY OF KENTUCKY
225 Gatton College of Business
Economics Building
Lexington, KY 40506 0034
Phone: 859-257-7668
Fax: 859-323-1907
E-mail: lrnaug0@pop.uky.edu
Website: http://www.ksbdc.org
Ms. Becky Naugle, State Director

Louisiana

Louisiana SBDC
**UNIVERSITY OF LOUISIANA -
MONROE**
College of Business Administration
700 University Avenue
Monroe, LA 71209
Phone: 318-342-5506
Fax: 318-342-5510
E-mail: wilkerson@ulm.edu
Website: http://www.lsbdc.org
Ms. Mary Lynn Wilkerson, State
Director

Maine

Maine SBDC
**UNIVERSITY OF SOUTHERN
MAINE**
96 Falmouth Street P.O. Box 9300
Portland, ME 04103
Phone: 207-780-4420
Fax: 207-780-4810
E-mail: jrmassaua@maine.edu
Website: http://www.mainesbdc.org
Mr. John Massaua, State Director

Maryland

Maryland SBDC
UNIVERSITY OF MARYLAND
7100 Baltimore Avenue, Suite 401
College Park, MD 20742
Phone: 301-403-8300
Fax: 301-403-8303
E-mail: rsprow@mdsbdc.umd.edu
Website: http://www.mdsbdc.umd.edu
Ms. Renee Sprow, State Director

Massachusetts

Massachusetts SBDC
UNIVERSITY OF MASSACHUSETTS
School of Management, Room 205
Amherst, MA 01003-4935
Phone: 413-545-6301
Fax: 413-545-1273
E-mail: gep@msbdc.umass.edu
Website: http://msbdc.som.umass.edu
Ms. Georgianna Parkin, State Director

Michigan

Michigan SBTDC
**GRAND VALLEY STATE
UNIVERSITY**
510 West Fulton Avenue
Grand Rapids, MI 49504
Phone: 616-331-7485
Fax: 616-331-7389
E-mail: lopuckic@gvsu.edu
Website: http://www.misbtdc.org
Ms. Carol Lopucki, State Director

Minnesota

Minnesota SBDC
**MINNESOTA SMALL BUSINESS
DEVELOPMENT CENTER**
1st National Bank Building
332 Minnesota Street, Suite E200
St. Paul, MN 55101-1351
Phone: 651-297-5773
Fax: 651-296-5287

E-mail: michacl.myhre@state.mn.us
Website: http://www.mnsbdc.com
Mr. Michael Myhre, State Director

Mississippi

Mississippi SBDC
UNIVERSITY OF MISSISSIPPI
B-19 Jeanette Phillips Drive
P.O. Box 1848
University, MS 38677
Phone: 662-915-5001
Fax: 662-915-5650
E-mail: wgurley@olemiss.edu
Website: http://www.olemiss.edu/depts/
mssbdc
Mr. Doug Gurley, Jr., State Director

Missouri

Missouri SBDC
UNIVERSITY OF MISSOURI
1205 University Avenue, Suite 300
Columbia, MO 65211
Phone: 573-882-1348
Fax: 573-884-4297
E-mail: summersm@missouri.edu
Website: http://www.mo-sbdc.org/
index.shtml
Mr. Max Summers, State Director

Montana

Montana SBDC
DEPARTMENT OF COMMERCE
301 South Park Avenue, Room 114 /
P.O. Box 200505
Helena, MT 59620
Phone: 406-841-2746
Fax: 406-444-1872
E-mail: adesch@state.mt.us
Website: http://commerce.state.mt.us/
brd/BRD_SBDC.html
Ms. Ann Desch, State Director

Nebraska

Nebraska SBDC
**UNIVERSITY OF NEBRASKA -
OMAHA**
60th & Dodge Street, CBA Room 407
Omaha, NE 68182
Phone: 402-554-2521
Fax: 402-554-3473
E-mail: rbernier@unomaha.edu
Website: http://nbdc.unomaha.edu
Mr. Robert Bernier, State Director

Nevada

Nevada SBDC
UNIVERSITY OF NEVADA - RENO
Reno College of Business
Administration, Room 411
Reno, NV 89557-0100
Phone: 775-784-1717
Fax: 775-784-4337
E-mail: males@unr.edu
Website: http://www.nsbdc.org
Mr. Sam Males, State Director

New Hampshire

New Hampshire SBDC
UNIVERSITY OF NEW HAMPSHIRE
108 McConnell Hall
Durham, NH 03824-3593
Phone: 603-862-4879
Fax: 603-862-4876
E-mail: Mary.Collins@unh.edu
Website: http://www.nhsbdc.org
Ms. Mary Collins, State Director

New Jersey

New Jersey SBDC
RUTGERS UNIVERSITY
49 Bleeker Street
Newark, NJ 07102-1993
Phone: 973-353-5950
Fax: 973-353-1110
E-mail: bhopper@njsbdc.com
Website: http://www.njsbdc.com/home
Ms. Brenda Hopper, State Director

New Mexico

New Mexico SBDC
SANTA FE COMMUNITY COLLEGE
6401 Richards Avenue
Santa Fe, NM 87505
Phone: 505-428-1362
Fax: 505-471-9469
E-mail: rmiller@santa-fe.cc.nm.us
Website: http://www.nmsbdc.org
Mr. Roy Miller, State Director

New York

New York SBDC
STATE UNIVERSITY OF NEW YORK
SUNY Plaza, S-523
Albany, NY 12246
Phone: 518-443-5398
Fax: 518-443-5275
E-mail: j.king@nyssbdc.org
Website: http://www.nyssbdc.org
Mr. Jim King, State Director

North Carolina

North Carolina SBDTC
UNIVERSITY OF NORTH CAROLINA
5 West Hargett Street, Suite 600
Raleigh, NC 27601
Phone: 919-715-7272
Fax: 919-715-7777
E-mail: sdaugherty@sbtdc.org
Website: http://www.sbtdc.org
Mr. Scott Daugherty, State Director

North Dakota

North Dakota SBDC
UNIVERSITY OF NORTH DAKOTA
1600 E. Century Avenue, Suite 2
Bismarck, ND 58503
Phone: 701-328-5375
Fax: 701-328-5320
E-mail: christine.martin@und.nodak.edu
Website: http://www.ndsbdc.org
Ms. Christine Martin-Goldman, State
Director

Ohio

Ohio SBDC
OHIO DEPARTMENT
OF DEVELOPMENT
77 South High Street
Columbus, OH 43216
Phone: 614-466-5102
Fax: 614-466-0829
E-mail: mabraham@odod.state.oh.us
Website: http://www.ohiosbdc.org
Ms. Michele Abraham, State Director

Oklahoma

Oklahoma SBDC
SOUTHEAST OKLAHOMA STATE
UNIVERSITY
517 University, Box 2584, Station A
Durant, OK 74701
Phone: 580-745-7577
Fax: 580-745-7471
E-mail: gpennington@sosu.edu
Website: http://www.osbdc.org
Mr. Grady Pennington, State Director

Oregon

Oregon SBDC
LANE COMMUNITY COLLEGE
99 West Tenth Avenue, Suite 390
Eugene, OR 97401-3021
Phone: 541-463-5250
Fax: 541-345-6006
E-mail: carterb@lanecc.edu

Website: http://www.bizcenter.org
Mr. William Carter, State Director

Pennsylvania

Pennsylvania SBDC
UNIVERSITY OF PENNSYLVANIA
The Wharton School
3733 Spruce Street
Philadelphia, PA 19104-6374
Phone: 215-898-1219
Fax: 215-573-2135
E-mail: ghiggins@wharton.upenn.edu
Website: http://pasbdc.org
Mr. Gregory Higgins, State Director

Puerto Rico

Puerto Rico SBDC
INTER-AMERICAN UNIVERSITY
OF PUERTO RICO
416 Ponce de Leon Avenue, Union Plaza,
Seventh Floor
Hato Rey, PR 00918
Phone: 787-763-6811
Fax: 787-763-4629
E-mail: cmarti@prsbdc.org
Website: http://www.prsbdc.org
Ms. Carmen Marti, Executive Director

Rhode Island

Rhode Island SBDC
BRYANT UNIVERSITY
1150 Douglas Pike
Smithfield, RI 02917
Phone: 401-232-6923
Fax: 401-232-6933
E-mail: adawson@bryant.edu
Website: http://www.risbdc.org
Ms. Diane Fournaris, Interim State Director

South Carolina

South Carolina SBDC
UNIVERSITY OF SOUTH CAROLINA
College of Business Administration
1710 College Street
Columbia, SC 29208
Phone: 803-777-4907
Fax: 803-777-4403
E-mail: lenti@moore.sc.edu
Website: http://scsbdc.moore.sc.edu
Mr. John Lenti, State Director

South Dakota

South Dakota SBDC
UNIVERSITY OF SOUTH DAKOTA
414 East Clark Street, Patterson Hall
Vermillion, SD 57069

Phone: 605-677-6256
Fax: 605-677-5427
E-mail: jshemmin@usd.edu
Website: http://www.sdsbdc.org
Mr. John S. Hemmingstad, State
Director

Tennessee

Tennessee SBDC
TENNESSEE BOARD OF REGENTS
1415 Murfressboro Road, Suite 540
Nashville, TN 37217-2833
Phone: 615-898-2745
Fax: 615-893-7089
E-mail: pgeho@mail.tsbdc.org
Website: http://www.tsbdc.org
Mr. Patrick Geho, State Director

Texas

Texas-North SBDC
**DALLAS COUNTY COMMUNITY
COLLEGE**
1402 Corinth Street
Dallas, TX 75215
Phone: 214-860-5835
Fax: 214-860-5813
E-mail: emk9402@dcccd.edu
Website: http://www.ntsbdc.org
Ms. Liz Klimback, Region Director

Texas-Houston SBDC
UNIVERSITY OF HOUSTON
2302 Fannin, Suite 200
Houston, TX 77002
Phone: 713-752-8425
Fax: 713-756-1500
E-mail: fyoung@uh.edu
Website: http://sbdcnetwork.uh.edu
Mr. Mike Young, Executive Director

Texas-NW SBDC
TEXAS TECH UNIVERSITY
2579 South Loop 289, Suite 114
Lubbock, TX 79423
Phone: 806-745-3973
Fax: 806-745-6207
E-mail: c.bean@nwtsbdc.org
Website: http://www.nwtsbdc.org
Mr. Craig Bean, Executive Director

**Texas-South-West Texas Border
Region SBDC**
**UNIVERSITY OF TEXAS -
SAN ANTONIO**
501 West Durango Boulevard
San Antonio, TX 78207-4415
Phone: 210-458-2742
Fax: 210-458-2464

E-mail: albert.salgado@utsa.edu
Website: http://www.iedtexas.org
Mr. Alberto Salgado, Region Director

Utah

Utah SBDC
SALT LAKE COMMUNITY COLLEGE
9750 South 300 West
Sandy, UT 84070
Phone: 801-957-3493
Fax: 801-957-3488
E-mail: Greg.Panichello@slcc.edu
Website: http://www.slcc.edu/sbdc
Mr. Greg Panichello, State Director

Vermont

Vermont SBDC
VERMONT TECHNICAL COLLEGE
PO Box 188, 1 Main Street
Randolph Center, VT 05061-0188
Phone: 802-728-9101
Fax: 802-728-3026
E-mail: lquillen@vtc.edu
Website: http://www.vtsbdc.org
Ms. Lenae Quillen-Blume, State Director

Virgin Islands

Virgin Islands SBDC
**UNIVERSITY OF THE VIRGIN
ISLANDS**
8000 Nisky Center, Suite 720
St. Thomas, VI 00802-5804
Phone: 340-776-3206
Fax: 340-775-3756
E-mail: wbush@webmail.uvi.edu
Website: http://rps.uvi.edu/SBDC
Mr. Warren Bush, State Director

Virginia

Virginia SBDC
GEORGE MASON UNIVERSITY
4031 University Drive, Suite 200
Fairfax, VA 22030-3409
Phone: 703-277-7727
Fax: 703-352-8515
E-mail: jkeenan@gmu.edu
Website: http://www.virginiasbdc.org
Ms. Jody Keenan, Director

Washington

Washington SBDC
WASHINGTON STATE UNIVERSITY
534 E. Trent Avenue
P.O. Box 1495
Spokane, WA 99210-1495

Phone: 509-358-7765
Fax: 509-358-7764
E-mail: barogers@wsu.edu
Website: http://www.wsbdc.org
Mr. Brett Rogers, State Director

West Virginia

West Virginia SBDC
**WEST VIRGINIA DEVELOPMENT
OFFICE**
Capital Complex, Building 6, Room 652
Charleston, WV 25301
Phone: 304-558-2960
Fax: 304-558-0127
E-mail: csalyer@wvsbdc.org
Website: http://www.wvsbdc.org
Mr. Conley Salyor, State Director

Wisconsin

Wisconsin SBDC
UNIVERSITY OF WISCONSIN
432 North Lake Street, Room 423
Madison, WI 53706
Phone: 608-263-7794
Fax: 608-263-7830
E-mail: erica.kauten@uwex.edu
Website: http://www.wisconsinsbdc.org
Ms. Erica Kauten, State Director

Wyoming

Wyoming SBDC
UNIVERSITY OF WYOMING
P.O. Box 3922
Laramie, WY 82071-3922
Phone: 307-766-3505
Fax: 307-766-3406
E-mail: DDW@uwyo.edu
Website: http://www.uwyo.edu/sbdc
Ms. Debbie Popp, Acting State Director

Service corps of retired executives (score) offices

*This section contains a listing of all
SCORE offices organized alphabetically by
state/U.S. territory, then by city, then by
agency name.*

Alabama

SCORE Office (Northeast Alabama)
1330 Quintard Ave.
Anniston, AL 36202
(256)237-3536

SCORE Office (North Alabama)
901 South 15th St, Rm. 201
Birmingham, AL 35294-2060
(205)934-6868
Fax: (205)934-0538

SCORE Office (Baldwin County)
29750 Larry Dee Cawyer Dr.
Daphne, AL 36526
(334)928-5838

SCORE Office (Shoals)
612 S. COurt
Florence, AL 35630
(256)764-4661
Fax: (256)766-9017
E-mail: shoals@shoalschamber.com

SCORE Office (Mobile)
600 S Court St.
Mobile, AL 36104
(334)240-6868
Fax: (334)240-6869

SCORE Office (Alabama Capitol City)
600 S. Court St.
Montgomery, AL 36104
(334)240-6868
Fax: (334)240-6869

SCORE Office (East Alabama)
601 Ave. A
Opelika, AL 36801
(334)745-4861
E-mail: score636@hotmail.com
Website: http://www.angelfire.com/sc/
score636/

SCORE Office (Tuscaloosa)
2200 University Blvd.
Tuscaloosa, AL 35402
(205)758-7588

Alaska

SCORE Office (Anchorage)
510 L St., Ste. 310
Anchorage, AK 99501
(907)271-4022
Fax: (907)271-4545

Arizona

SCORE Office (Lake Havasu)
10 S. Acoma Blvd.
Lake Havasu City, AZ 86403
(520)453-5951
E-mail: SCORE@ctaz.com
Website: http://www.scorearizona.org/
lake_havasu/

SCORE Office (East Valley)
Federal Bldg., Rm. 104
26 N. MacDonald St.
Mesa, AZ 85201
(602)379-3100
Fax: (602)379-3143
E-mail: 402@aol.com
Website: http://www.scorearizona.
org/mesa/

SCORE Office (Phoenix)
2828 N. Central Ave., Ste. 800
Central & One Thomas
Phoenix, AZ 85004
(602)640-2329
Fax: (602)640-2360
E-mail: e-mail@SCORE-phoenix.org
Website: http://www.score-phoenix.org/

SCORE Office (Prescott Arizona)
1228 Willow Creek Rd., Ste. 2
Prescott, AZ 86301
(520)778-7438
Fax: (520)778-0812
E-mail: score@northlink.com
Website: http://www.scorearizona.org/
prescott/

SCORE Office (Tucson)
110 E. Pennington St.
Tucson, AZ 85702
(520)670-5008
Fax: (520)670-5011
E-mail: score@azstarnet.com
Website: http://www.scorearizona.org/
tucson/

SCORE Office (Yuma)
281 W. 24th St., Ste. 116
Yuma, AZ 85364
(520)314-0480
E-mail: score@C2i2.com
Website: http://www.scorearizona.org/
yuma

Arkansas

SCORE Office (South Central)
201 N. Jackson Ave.
El Dorado, AR 71730-5803
(870)863-6113
Fax: (870)863-6115

SCORE Office (Ozark)
Fayetteville, AR 72701
(501)442-7619

SCORE Office (Northwest Arkansas)
Glenn Haven Dr., No. 4
Ft. Smith, AR 72901
(501)783-3556

SCORE Office (Garland County)
Grand & Ouachita
PO Box 6012
Hot Springs Village, AR 71902
(501)321-1700

SCORE Office (Little Rock)
2120 Riverfront Dr., Rm. 100
Little Rock, AR 72202-1747
(501)324-5893
Fax: (501)324-5199

SCORE Office (Southeast Arkansas)
121 W. 6th
Pine Bluff, AR 71601
(870)535-7189
Fax: (870)535-1643

California

SCORE Office (Golden Empire)
1706 Chester Ave., No. 200
Bakersfield, CA 93301
(805)322-5881
Fax: (805)322-5663

SCORE Office (Greater Chico Area)
1324 Mangrove St., Ste. 114
Chico, CA 95926
(916)342-8932
Fax: (916)342-8932

SCORE Office (Concord)
2151-A Salvio St., Ste. B
Concord, CA 94520
(510)685-1181
Fax: (510)685-5623

SCORE Office (Covina)
935 W. Badillo St.
Covina, CA 91723
(818)967-4191
Fax: (818)966-9660

SCORE Office (Rancho Cucamonga)
8280 Utica, Ste. 160
Cucamonga, CA 91730
(909)987-1012
Fax: (909)987-5917

SCORE Office (Culver City)
PO Box 707
Culver City, CA 90232-0707
(310)287-3850
Fax: (310)287-1350

SCORE Office (Danville)
380 Diablo Rd., Ste. 103
Danville, CA 94526
(510)837-4400

SCORE Office (Downey)
11131 Brookshire Ave.
Downey, CA 90241
(310)923-2191
Fax: (310)864-0461

SCORE Office (El Cajon)
109 Rea Ave.
El Cajon, CA 92020
(619)444-1327
Fax: (619)440-6164

SCORE Office (El Centro)
1100 Main St.
El Centro, CA 92243
(619)352-3681
Fax: (619)352-3246

SCORE Office (Escondido)
720 N. Broadway
Escondido, CA 92025
(619)745-2125
Fax: (619)745-1183

SCORE Office (Fairfield)
1111 Webster St.
Fairfield, CA 94533
(707)425-4625
Fax: (707)425-0826

SCORE Office (Fontana)
17009 Valley Blvd., Ste. B
Fontana, CA 92335
(909)822-4433
Fax: (909)822-6238

SCORE Office (Foster City)
1125 E. Hillsdale Blvd.
Foster City, CA 94404
(415)573-7600
Fax: (415)573-5201

SCORE Office (Fremont)
2201 Walnut Ave., Ste. 110
Fremont, CA 94538
(510)795-2244
Fax: (510)795-2240

SCORE Office (Central California)
2719 N. Air Fresno Dr., Ste. 200
Fresno, CA 93727-1547
(559)487-5605
Fax: (559)487-5636

SCORE Office (Gardena)
1204 W. Gardena Blvd.
Gardena, CA 90247
(310)532-9905
Fax: (310)515-4893

SCORE Office (Lompoc)
330 N. Brand Blvd., Ste. 190
Glendale, CA 91203-2304

(818)552-3206
Fax: (818)552-3323

SCORE Office (Los Angeles)
330 N. Brand Blvd., Ste. 190
Glendale, CA 91203-2304
(818)552-3206
Fax: (818)552-3323

SCORE Office (Glendora)
131 E. Foothill Blvd.
Glendora, CA 91740
(818)963-4128
Fax: (818)914-4822

SCORE Office (Grover Beach)
177 S. 8th St.
Grover Beach, CA 93433
(805)489-9091
Fax: (805)489-9091

SCORE Office (Hawthorne)
12477 Hawthorne Blvd.
Hawthorne, CA 90250
(310)676-1163
Fax: (310)676-7661

SCORE Office (Hayward)
22300 Foothill Blvd., Ste. 303
Hayward, CA 94541
(510)537-2424

SCORE Office (Hemet)
1700 E. Florida Ave.
Hemet, CA 92544-4679
(909)652-4390
Fax: (909)929-8543

SCORE Office (Hesperia)
16367 Main St.
PO Box 403656
Hesperia, CA 92340
(619)244-2135

SCORE Office (Holloster)
321 San Felipe Rd., No. 11
Hollister, CA 95023

SCORE Office (Hollywood)
7018 Hollywood Blvd.
Hollywood, CA 90028
(213)469-8311
Fax: (213)469-2805

SCORE Office (Indio)
82503 Hwy. 111
PO Drawer TTT
Indio, CA 92202
(619)347-0676

SCORE Office (Inglewood)
330 Queen St.

Inglewood, CA 90301
(818)552-3206

SCORE Office (La Puente)
218 N. Grendanda St. D.
La Puente, CA 91744
(818)330-3216
Fax: (818)330-9524

SCORE Office (La Verne)
2078 Bonita Ave.
La Verne, CA 91750
(909)593-5265
Fax: (714)929-8475

SCORE Office (Lake Elsinore)
132 W. Graham Ave.
Lake Elsinore, CA 92530
(909)674-2577

SCORE Office (Lakeport)
PO Box 295
Lakeport, CA 95453
(707)263-5092

SCORE Office (Lakewood)
5445 E. Del Amo Blvd., Ste. 2
Lakewood, CA 90714
(213)920-7737

SCORE Office (Long Beach)
1 World Trade Center
Long Beach, CA 90831

SCORE Office (Los Alamitos)
901 W. Civic Center Dr., Ste. 160
Los Alamitos, CA 90720

SCORE Office (Los Altos)
321 University Ave.
Los Altos, CA 94022
(415)948-1455

SCORE Office (Manhattan Beach)
PO Box 3007
Manhattan Beach, CA 90266
(310)545-5313
Fax: (310)545-7203

SCORE Office (Merced)
1632 N. St.
Merced, CA 95340
(209)725-3800
Fax: (209)383-4959

SCORE Office (Milpitas)
75 S. Milpitas Blvd., Ste. 205
Milpitas, CA 95035
(408)262-2613
Fax: (408)262-2823

SCORE Office (Yosemite)
1012 11th St., Ste. 300
Modesto, CA 95354
(209)521-9333

SCORE Office (Montclair)
5220 Benito Ave.
Montclair, CA 91763

SCORE Office (Monterey Bay)
380 Alvarado St.
PO Box 1770
Monterey, CA 93940-1770
(408)649-1770

SCORE Office (Moreno Valley)
25480 Alessandro
Moreno Valley, CA 92553

SCORE Office (Morgan Hill)
25 W. 1st St.
PO Box 786
Morgan Hill, CA 95038
(408)779-9444
Fax: (408)778-1786

SCORE Office (Morro Bay)
880 Main St.
Morro Bay, CA 93442
(805)772-4467

SCORE Office (Mountain View)
580 Castro St.
Mountain View, CA 94041
(415)968-8378
Fax: (415)968-5668

SCORE Office (Napa)
1556 1st St.
Napa, CA 94559
(707)226-7455
Fax: (707)226-1171

SCORE Office (North Hollywood)
5019 Lankershim Blvd.
North Hollywood, CA 91601
(818)552-3206

SCORE Office (Northridge)
8801 Reseda Blvd.
Northridge, CA 91324
(818)349-5676

SCORE Office (Novato)
807 De Long Ave.
Novato, CA 94945
(415)897-1164
Fax: (415)898-9097

SCORE Office (East Bay)
519 17th St.
Oakland, CA 94612

(510)273-6611
Fax: (510)273-6015
E-mail: webmaster@eastbayscore.org
Website: http://www.eastbayscore.org

SCORE Office (Oceanside)
928 N. Coast Hwy.
Oceanside, CA 92054
(619)722-1534

SCORE Office (Ontario)
121 West B. St.
Ontario, CA 91762
Fax: (714)984-6439

SCORE Office (Oxnard)
PO Box 867
Oxnard, CA 93032
(805)385-8860
Fax: (805)487-1763

SCORE Office (Pacifica)
450 Dundee Way, Ste. 2
Pacifica, CA 94044
(415)355-4122

SCORE Office (Palm Desert)
72990 Hwy. 111
Palm Desert, CA 92260
(619)346-6111
Fax: (619)346-3463

SCORE Office (Palm Springs)
650 E. Tahquitz Canyon Way Ste. D
Palm Springs, CA 92262-6706
(760)320-6682
Fax: (760)323-9426

SCORE Office (Lakeside)
2150 Low Tree
Palmdale, CA 93551
(805)948-4518
Fax: (805)949-1212

SCORE Office (Palo Alto)
325 Forest Ave.
Palo Alto, CA 94301
(415)324-3121
Fax: (415)324-1215

SCORE Office (Pasadena)
117 E. Colorado Blvd., Ste. 100
Pasadena, CA 91105
(818)795-3355
Fax: (818)795-5663

SCORE Office (Paso Robles)
1225 Park St.
Paso Robles, CA 93446-2234
(805)238-0506
Fax: (805)238-0527

SCORE Office (Petaluma)
799 Baywood Dr., Ste. 3
Petaluma, CA 94954
(707)762-2785
Fax: (707)762-4721

SCORE Office (Pico Rivera)
9122 E. Washington Blvd.
Pico Rivera, CA 90660

SCORE Office (Pittsburg)
2700 E. Leland Rd.
Pittsburg, CA 94565
(510)439-2181
Fax: (510)427-1599

SCORE Office (Pleasanton)
777 Peters Ave.
Pleasanton, CA 94566
(510)846-9697

SCORE Office (Monterey Park)
485 N. Garey
Pomona, CA 91769

SCORE Office (Pomona)
485 N. Garey Ave.
Pomona, CA 91766
(909)622-1256

SCORE Office (Antelope Valley)
4511 West Ave. M-4
Quartz Hill, CA 93536
(805)272-0087
E-mail: avscore@ptw.com
Website: http://www.score.av.org/

SCORE Office (Shasta)
737 Auditorium Dr.
Redding, CA 96099
(916)225-2770

SCORE Office (Redwood City)
1675 Broadway
Redwood City, CA 94063
(415)364-1722
Fax: (415)364-1729

SCORE Office (Richmond)
3925 MacDonald Ave.
Richmond, CA 94805

SCORE Office (Ridgecrest)
PO Box 771
Ridgecrest, CA 93555
(619)375-8331
Fax: (619)375-0365

SCORE Office (Riverside)
3685 Main St., Ste. 350
Riverside, CA 92501
(909)683-7100

SCORE Office (Sacramento)
9845 Horn Rd., 260-B
Sacramento, CA 95827
(916)361-2322
Fax: (916)361-2164
E-mail: sacchapter@directcon.net

SCORE Office (Salinas)
PO Box 1170
Salinas, CA 93902
(408)424-7611
Fax: (408)424-8639

SCORE Office (Inland Empire)
777 E. Rialto Ave.
Purchasing
San Bernardino, CA 92415-0760
(909)386-8278

SCORE Office (San Carlos)
San Carlos Chamber of Commerce
PO Box 1086
San Carlos, CA 94070
(415)593-1068
Fax: (415)593-9108

SCORE Office (Encinitas)
550 W. C St., Ste. 550
San Diego, CA 92101-3540
(619)557-7272
Fax: (619)557-5894

SCORE Office (San Diego)
550 West C. St., Ste. 550
San Diego, CA 92101-3540
(619)557-7272
Fax: (619)557-5894
Website: http://www.score-sandiego.org

SCORE Office (Menlo Park)
1100 Merrill St.
San Francisco, CA 94105
(415)325-2818
Fax: (415)325-0920

SCORE Office (San Francisco)
455 Market St., 6th Fl.
San Francisco, CA 94105
(415)744-6827
Fax: (415)744-6750
E-mail: sfscore@sfscore.
Website: http://www.sfscore.com

SCORE Office (San Gabriel)
401 W. Las Tunas Dr.
San Gabriel, CA 91776
(818)576-2525
Fax: (818)289-2901

SCORE Office (San Jose)
Deanza College
208 S. 1st. St., Ste. 137
San Jose, CA 95113
(408)288-8479
Fax: (408)535-5541

SCORE Office (Silicon Valley)
84 W. Santa Clara St., Ste. 100
San Jose, CA 95113
(408)288-8479
Fax: (408)535-5541
E-mail: info@svscore.org
Website: http://www.svscore.org

SCORE Office (San Luis Obispo)
3566 S. Hiquera, No. 104
San Luis Obispo, CA 93401
(805)547-0779

SCORE Office (San Mateo)
1021 S. El Camino, 2nd Fl.
San Mateo, CA 94402
(415)341-5679

SCORE Office (San Pedro)
390 W. 7th St.
San Pedro, CA 90731
(310)832-7272

SCORE Office (Orange County)
200 W. Santa Anna Blvd., Ste. 700
Santa Ana, CA 92701
(714)550-7369
Fax: (714)550-0191
Website: http://www.score114.org

SCORE Office (Santa Barbara)
3227 State St.
Santa Barbara, CA 93130
(805)563-0084

SCORE Office (Central Coast)
509 W. Morrison Ave.
Santa Maria, CA 93454
(805)347-7755

SCORE Office (Santa Maria)
614 S. Broadway
Santa Maria, CA 93454-5111
(805)925-2403
Fax: (805)928-7559

SCORE Office (Santa Monica)
501 Colorado, Ste. 150
Santa Monica, CA 90401
(310)393-9825
Fax: (310)394-1868

SCORE Office (Santa Rosa)
777 Sonoma Ave., Rm. 115E
Santa Rosa, CA 95404

(707)571-8342
Fax: (707)541-0331
Website: http://www.pressdemo.com/community/score/score.html

SCORE Office (Scotts Valley)
4 Camp Evers Ln.
Scotts Valley, CA 95066
(408)438-1010
Fax: (408)438-6544

SCORE Office (Simi Valley)
40 W. Cochran St., Ste. 100
Simi Valley, CA 93065
(805)526-3900
Fax: (805)526-6234

SCORE Office (Sonoma)
453 1st St. E
Sonoma, CA 95476
(707)996-1033

SCORE Office (Los Banos)
222 S. Shepard St.
Sonora, CA 95370
(209)532-4212

SCORE Office (Tuolumne County)
39 North Washington St.
Sonora, CA 95370
(209)588-0128
E-mail: score@mlode.com

SCORE Office (South San Francisco)
445 Market St., Ste. 6th Fl.
South San Francisco, CA 94105
(415)744-6827
Fax: (415)744-6812

SCORE Office (Stockton)
401 N. San Joaquin St., Rm. 215
Stockton, CA 95202
(209)946-6293

SCORE Office (Taft)
314 4th St.
Taft, CA 93268
(805)765-2165
Fax: (805)765-6639

SCORE Office (Conejo Valley)
625 W. Hillcrest Dr.
Thousand Oaks, CA 91360
(805)499-1993
Fax: (805)498-7264

SCORE Office (Torrance)
3400 Torrance Blvd., Ste. 100
Torrance, CA 90503
(310)540-5858
Fax: (310)540-7662

SCORE Office (Truckee)
PO Box 2757
Truckee, CA 96160
(916)587-2757
Fax: (916)587-2439

SCORE Office (Visalia)
113 S. M St,
Tulare, CA 93274
(209)627-0766
Fax: (209)627-8149

SCORE Office (Upland)
433 N. 2nd Ave.
Upland, CA 91786
(909)931-4108

SCORE Office (Vallejo)
2 Florida St.
Vallejo, CA 94590
(707)644-5551
Fax: (707)644-5590

SCORE Office (Van Nuys)
14540 Victory Blvd.
Van Nuys, CA 91411
(818)989-0300
Fax: (818)989-3836

SCORE Office (Ventura)
5700 Ralston St., Ste. 310
Ventura, CA 93001
(805)658-2688
Fax: (805)658-2252
E-mail: scoreven@jps.net
Website: http://www.jps.net/scoreven

SCORE Office (Vista)
201 E. Washington St.
Vista, CA 92084
(619)726-1122
Fax: (619)226-8654

SCORE Office (Watsonville)
PO Box 1748
Watsonville, CA 95077
(408)724-3849
Fax: (408)728-5300

SCORE Office (West Covina)
811 S. Sunset Ave.
West Covina, CA 91790
(818)338-8496
Fax: (818)960-0511

SCORE Office (Westlake)
30893 Thousand Oaks Blvd.
Westlake Village, CA 91362
(805)496-5630
Fax: (818)991-1754

Colorado

SCORE Office (Colorado Springs)
2 N. Cascade Ave., Ste. 110
Colorado Springs, CO 80903
(719)636-3074
Website: http://www.cscc.org/score02/
index.html

SCORE Office (Denver)
US Custom's House, 4th Fl.
721 19th St.
Denver, CO 80201-0660
(303)844-3985
Fax: (303)844-6490
E-mail: score62@csn.net
Website: http://www.sni.net/score62

SCORE Office (Tri-River)
1102 Grand Ave.
Glenwood Springs, CO 81601
(970)945-6589

SCORE Office (Grand Junction)
2591 B & 3/4 Rd.
Grand Junction, CO 81503
(970)243-5242

SCORE Office (Gunnison)
608 N. 11th
Gunnison, CO 81230
(303)641-4422

SCORE Office (Montrose)
1214 Peppertree Dr.
Montrose, CO 81401
(970)249-6080

SCORE Office (Pagosa Springs)
PO Box 4381
Pagosa Springs, CO 81157
(970)731-4890

SCORE Office (Rifle)
0854 W. Battlement Pky., Apt. C106
Parachute, CO 81635
(970)285-9390

SCORE Office (Pueblo)
302 N. Santa Fe
Pueblo, CO 81003
(719)542-1704
Fax: (719)542-1624
E-mail: mackey@iex.net
Website: http://www.pueblo.org/score

SCORE Office (Ridgway)
143 Poplar Pl.
Ridgway, CO 81432

SCORE Office (Silverton)
PO Box 480

Silverton, CO 81433
(303)387-5430

SCORE Office (Minturn)
PO Box 2066
Vail, CO 81658
(970)476-1224

Connecticut

SCORE Office (Greater Bridgeport)
230 Park Ave.
Bridgeport, CT 06601-0999
(203)576-4369
Fax: (203)576-4388

SCORE Office (Bristol)
10 Main St. 1st. Fl.
Bristol, CT 06010
(203)584-4718
Fax: (203)584-4722

SCORE office (Greater Danbury)
246 Federal Rd.
Unit LL2, Ste. 7
Brookfield, CT 06804
(203)775-1151

SCORE Office (Greater Danbury)
246 Federal Rd., Unit LL2, Ste. 7
Brookfield, CT 06804
(203)775-1151

SCORE Office (Eastern Connecticut)
Administration Bldg., Rm. 313
PO 625
61 Main St. (Chapter 579)
Groton, CT 06475
(203)388-9508

SCORE Office (Greater Hartford County)
330 Main St.
Hartford, CT 06106
(860)548-1749
Fax: (860)240-4659
Website: http://www.score56.org

SCORE Office (Manchester)
20 Hartford Rd.
Manchester, CT 06040
(203)646-2223
Fax: (203)646-5871

SCORE Office (New Britain)
185 Main St., Ste. 431
New Britain, CT 06051
(203)827-4492
Fax: (203)827-4480

SCORE Office (New Haven)
25 Science Pk., Bldg. 25, Rm. 366

New Haven, CT 06511
(203)865-7645

SCORE Office (Fairfield County)
24 Beldon Ave., 5th Fl.
Norwalk, CT 06850
(203)847-7348
Fax: (203)849-9308

SCORE Office (Old Saybrook)
146 Main St.
Old Saybrook, CT 06475
(860)388-9508

SCORE Office (Simsbury)
Box 244
Simsbury, CT 06070
(203)651-7307
Fax: (203)651-1933

SCORE Office (Torrington)
23 North Rd.
Torrington, CT 06791
(203)482-6586

Delaware

SCORE Office (Dover)
Treadway Towers
PO Box 576
Dover, DE 19903
(302)678-0892
Fax: (302)678-0189

SCORE Office (Lewes)
PO Box 1
Lewes, DE 19958
(302)645-8073
Fax: (302)645-8412

SCORE Office (Milford)
204 NE Front St.
Milford, DE 19963
(302)422-3301

SCORE Office (Wilmington)
824 Market St., Ste. 610
Wilmington, DE 19801
(302)573-6652
Fax: (302)573-6092
Website: http://www.scoredelaware.com

District of Columbia

SCORE Office (George Mason University)
409 3rd St. SW, 4th Fl.
Washington, DC 20024
800-634-0245

SCORE Office (Washington DC)
1110 Vermont Ave. NW, 9th Fl.

Washington, DC 20043
(202)606-4000
Fax: (202)606-4225
E-mail: dcscore@hotmail.com
Website: http://www.scoredc.org/

Florida

SCORE Office (Desota County Chamber of Commerce)
16 South Velucia Ave.
Arcadia, FL 34266
(941)494-4033

SCORE Office (Suncoast/Pinellas)
Airport Business Ctr.
4707 - 140th Ave. N, No. 311
Clearwater, FL 33755
(813)532-6800
Fax: (813)532-6800

SCORE Office (DeLand)
336 N. Woodland Blvd.
DeLand, FL 32720
(904)734-4331
Fax: (904)734-4333

SCORE Office (South Palm Beach)
1050 S. Federal Hwy., Ste. 132
Delray Beach, FL 33483
(561)278-7752
Fax: (561)278-0288

SCORE Office (Ft. Lauderdale)
Federal Bldg., Ste. 123
299 E. Broward Blvd.
Ft. Lauderdale, FL 33301
(954)356-7263
Fax: (954)356-7145

SCORE Office (Southwest Florida)
The Renaissance
8695 College Pky., Ste. 345 & 346
Ft. Myers, FL 33919
(941)489-2935
Fax: (941)489-1170

SCORE Office (Treasure Coast)
Professional Center, Ste. 2
3220 S. US, No. 1
Ft. Pierce, FL 34982
(561)489-0548

SCORE Office (Gainesville)
101 SE 2nd Pl., Ste. 104
Gainesville, FL 32601
(904)375-8278

SCORE Office (Hialeah Dade Chamber)
59 W. 5th St.
Hialeah, FL 33010

(305)887-1515
Fax: (305)887-2453

SCORE Office (Daytona Beach)
921 Nova Rd., Ste. A
Holly Hills, FL 32117
(904)255-6889
Fax: (904)255-0229
E-mail: score87@dbeach.com

SCORE Office (South Broward)
3475 Sheridian St., Ste. 203
Hollywood, FL 33021
(305)966-8415

SCORE Office (Citrus County)
5 Poplar Ct.
Homosassa, FL 34446
(352)382-1037

SCORE Office (Jacksonville)
7825 Baymeadows Way, Ste. 100-B
Jacksonville, FL 32256
(904)443-1911
Fax: (904)443-1980
E-mail: scorejax@juno.com
Website: http://www.scorejax.org/

SCORE Office (Jacksonville Satellite)
3 Independent Dr.
Jacksonville, FL 32256
(904)366-6600
Fax: (904)632-0617

SCORE Office (Central Florida)
5410 S. Florida Ave., No. 3
Lakeland, FL 33801
(941)687-5783
Fax: (941)687-6225

SCORE Office (Lakeland)
100 Lake Morton Dr.
Lakeland, FL 33801
(941)686-2168

SCORE Office (St. Petersburg)
800 W. Bay Dr., Ste. 505
Largo, FL 33712
(813)585-4571

SCORE Office (Leesburg)
9501 US Hwy. 441
Leesburg, FL 34788-8751
(352)365-3556
Fax: (352)365-3501

SCORE Office (Cocoa)
1600 Farno Rd., Unit 205
Melbourne, FL 32935
(407)254-2288

SCORE Office (Melbourne)
Melbourne Professional Complex
1600 Sarno, Ste. 205
Melbourne, FL 32935
(407)254-2288
Fax: (407)245-2288

SCORE Office (Merritt Island)
1600 Sarno Rd., Ste. 205
Melbourne, FL 32935
(407)254-2288
Fax: (407)254-2288

SCORE Office (Space Coast)
Melbourn Professional Complex
1600 Sarno, Ste. 205
Melbourne, FL 32935
(407)254-2288
Fax: (407)254-2288

SCORE Office (Dade)
49 NW 5th St.
Miami, FL 33128
(305)371-6889
Fax: (305)374-1882
E-mail: score@netrox.net
Website: http://www.netrox.net/~score/

SCORE Office (Naples of Collier)
International College
2654 Tamiami Trl. E
Naples, FL 34112
(941)417-1280
Fax: (941)417-1281
E-mail: score@naples.net
Website: http://www.naples.net/clubs/
score/index.htm

SCORE Office (Pasco County)
6014 US Hwy. 19, Ste. 302
New Port Richey, FL 34652
(813)842-4638

SCORE Office (Southeast Volusia)
115 Canal St.
New Smyrna Beach, FL 32168
(904)428-2449
Fax: (904)423-3512

SCORE Office (Ocala)
110 E. Silver Springs Blvd.
Ocala, FL 34470
(352)629-5959

Clay County SCORE Office
Clay County Chamber of Commerce
1734 Kingsdey Ave.
PO Box 1441
Orange Park, FL 32073
(904)264-2651
Fax: (904)269-0363

SCORE Office (Orlando)
80 N. Hughey Ave.
Rm. 445 Federal Bldg.
Orlando, FL 32801
(407)648-6476
Fax: (407)648-6425

SCORE Office (Emerald Coast)
19 W. Garden St., No. 325
Pensacola, FL 32501
(904)444-2060
Fax: (904)444-2070

SCORE Office (Charlotte County)
201 W. Marion Ave., Ste. 211
Punta Gorda, FL 33950
(941)575-1818
E-mail: score@gls3c.com
Website: http://www.charlotte-
florida.com/business/scorepg01.htm

SCORE Office (St. Augustine)
1 Riberia St.
St. Augustine, FL 32084
(904)829-5681
Fax: (904)829-6477

SCORE Office (Bradenton)
2801 Fruitville, Ste. 280
Sarasota, FL 34237
(813)955-1029

SCORE Office (Manasota)
2801 Fruitville Rd., Ste. 280
Sarasota, FL 34237
(941)955-1029
Fax: (941)955-5581
E-mail: score116@gte.net
Website: http://www.score-suncoast.org/

SCORE Office (Tallahassee)
200 W. Park Ave.
Tallahassee, FL 32302
(850)487-2665

SCORE Office (Hillsborough)
4732 Dale Mabry Hwy. N, Ste. 400
Tampa, FL 33614-6509
(813)870-0125

SCORE Office (Lake Sumter)
122 E. Main St.
Tavares, FL 32778-3810
(352)365-3556

SCORE Office (Titusville)
2000 S. Washington Ave.
Titusville, FL 32780
(407)267-3036
Fax: (407)264-0127

SCORE Office (Venice)
257 N. Tamiami Trl.
Venice, FL 34285
(941)488-2236
Fax: (941)484-5903

SCORE Office (Palm Beach)
500 Australian Ave. S, Ste. 100
West Palm Beach, FL 33401
(561)833-1672
Fax: (561)833-1712

SCORE Office (Wildwood)
103 N. Webster St.
Wildwood, FL 34785

Georgia

SCORE Office (Atlanta)
Harris Tower, Suite 1900
233 Peachtree Rd., NE
Atlanta, GA 30309
(404)347-2442
Fax: (404)347-1227

SCORE Office (Augusta)
3126 Oxford Rd.
Augusta, GA 30909
(706)869-9100

SCORE Office (Columbus)
School Bldg.
PO Box 40
Columbus, GA 31901
(706)327-3654

SCORE Office (Dalton-Whitfield)
305 S. Thorton Ave.
Dalton, GA 30720
(706)279-3383

SCORE Office (Gainesville)
PO Box 374
Gainesville, GA 30503
(770)532-6206
Fax: (770)535-8419

SCORE Office (Macon)
711 Grand Bldg.
Macon, GA 31201
(912)751-6160

SCORE Office (Brunswick)
4 Glen Ave.
St. Simons Island, GA 31520
(912)265-0620
Fax: (912)265-0629

SCORE Office (Savannah)
111 E. Liberty St., Ste. 103
Savannah, GA 31401
(912)652-4335

Fax: (912)652-4184
E-mail: info@scoresav.org
Website: http://www.coastalempire.com/
score/index.htm

Guam

SCORE Office (Guam)
Pacific News Bldg., Rm. 103
238 Archbishop Flores St.
Agana, GU 96910-5100
(671)472-7308

Hawaii

SCORE Office (Hawaii, Inc.)
1111 Bishop St., Ste. 204
PO Box 50207
Honolulu, HI 96813
(808)522-8132
Fax: (808)522-8135
E-mail: hnlscore@juno.com

SCORE Office (Kahului)
250 Alamaha, Unit N16A
Kahului, HI 96732
(808)871-7711

SCORE Office (Maui, Inc.)
590 E. Lipoa Pkwy., Ste. 227
Kihei, III 96753
(808)875-2380

Idaho

SCORE Office (Treasure Valley)
1020 Main St., No. 290
Boise, ID 83702
(208)334-1696
Fax: (208)334-9353

SCORE Office (Eastern Idaho)
2300 N. Yellowstone, Ste. 119
Idaho Falls, ID 83401
(208)523-1022
Fax: (208)528-7127

Illinois

SCORE Office (Fox Valley)
40 W. Downer Pl.
PO Box 277
Aurora, IL 60506
(630)897-9214
Fax: (630)897-7002

SCORE Office (Greater Belvidere)
419 S. State St.
Belvidere, IL 61008
(815)544-4357
Fax: (815)547-7654

SCORE Office (Bensenville)
1050 Busse Hwy. Suite 100
Bensenville, IL 60106
(708)350-2944
Fax: (708)350-2979

SCORE Office (Central Illinois)
402 N. Hershey Rd.
Bloomington, IL 61704
(309)644-0549
Fax: (309)663-8270
E-mail: webmaster@central-illinois-
score.org
Website: http://www.central-illinois-
score.org/

SCORE Office (Southern Illinois)
150 E. Pleasant Hill Rd.
Box 1
Carbondale, IL 62901
(618)453-6654
Fax: (618)453-5040

SCORE Office (Chicago)
Northwest Atrium Ctr.
500 W. Madison St., No. 1250
Chicago, IL 60661
(312)353-7724
Fax: (312)886-5688
Website: http://www.mcs.net/~bic/

SCORE Office (Chicago–Oliver Harvey College)
Pullman Bldg.
1000 E. 11th St., 7th Fl.
Chicago, IL 60628
Fax: (312)468-8086

SCORE Office (Danville)
28 W. N. Street
Danville, IL 61832
(217)442-7232
Fax: (217)442-6228

SCORE Office (Decatur)
Milliken University
1184 W. Main St.
Decatur, IL 62522
(217)424-6297
Fax: (217)424-3993
E-mail: charding@mail.millikin.edu
Website: http://www.millikin.edu/
academics/Tabor/score.html

SCORE Office (Downers Grove)
925 Curtis
Downers Grove, IL 60515
(708)968-4050
Fax: (708)968-8368

SCORE Office (Elgin)
24 E. Chicago, 3rd Fl.
PO Box 648
Elgin, IL 60120
(847)741-5660
Fax: (847)741-5677

SCORE Office (Freeport Area)
26 S. Galena Ave.
Freeport, IL 61032
(815)233-1350
Fax: (815)235-4038

SCORE Office (Galesburg)
292 E. Simmons St.
PO Box 749
Galesburg, IL 61401
(309)343-1194
Fax: (309)343-1195

SCORE Office (Glen Ellyn)
500 Pennsylvania
Glen Ellyn, IL 60137
(708)469-0907
Fax: (708)469-0426

SCORE Office (Greater Alton)
Alden Hall
5800 Godfrey Rd.
Godfrey, IL 62035-2466
(618)467-2280
Fax: (618)466-8289
Website: http://www.altonweb.com/
score/

SCORE Office (Grayslake)
19351 W. Washington St.
Grayslake, IL 60030
(708)223-3633
Fax: (708)223-9371

SCORE Office (Harrisburg)
303 S. Commercial
Harrisburg, IL 62946-1528
(618)252-8528
Fax: (618)252-0210

SCORE Office (Joliet)
100 N. Chicago
Joliet, IL 60432
(815)727-5371
Fax: (815)727-5374

SCORE Office (Kankakee)
101 S. Schuyler Ave.
Kankakee, IL 60901
(815)933-0376
Fax: (815)933-0380

SCORE Office (Macomb)
216 Seal Hall, Rm. 214

Macomb, IL 61455
(309)298-1128
Fax: (309)298-2520

SCORE Office (Matteson)
210 Lincoln Mall
Matteson, IL 60443
(708)709-3750
Fax: (708)503-9322

SCORE Office (Mattoon)
1701 Wabash Ave.
Mattoon, IL 61938
(217)235-5661
Fax: (217)234-6544

SCORE Office (Quad Cities)
622 19th St.
Moline, IL 61265
(309)797-0082
Fax: (309)757-5435
E-mail: score@qconline.com
Website: http://www.qconline.com/
business/score/

SCORE Office (Naperville)
131 W. Jefferson Ave.
Naperville, IL 60540
(708)355-4141
Fax: (708)355-8355

SCORE Office (Northbrook)
2002 Walters Ave.
Northbrook, IL 60062
(847)498-5555
Fax: (847)498-5510

SCORE Office (Palos Hills)
10900 S. 88th Ave.
Palos Hills, IL 60465
(847)974-5468
Fax: (847)974-0078

SCORE Office (Peoria)
124 SW Adams, Ste. 300
Peoria, IL 61602
(309)676-0755
Fax: (309)676-7534

SCORE Office (Prospect Heights)
1375 Wolf Rd.
Prospect Heights, IL 60070
(847)537-8660
Fax: (847)537-7138

SCORE Office (Quincy Tri-State)
300 Civic Center Plz., Ste. 245
Quincy, IL 62301
(217)222-8093
Fax: (217)222-3033

SCORE Office (River Grove)
2000 5th Ave.
River Grove, IL 60171
(708)456-0300
Fax: (708)583-3121

SCORE Office (Northern Illinois)
515 N. Court St.
Rockford, IL 61103
(815)962-0122
Fax: (815)962-0122

SCORE Office (St. Charles)
103 N. 1st Ave.
St. Charles, IL 60174-1982
(847)584-8384
Fax: (847)584-6065

SCORE Office (Springfield)
511 W. Capitol Ave., Ste. 302
Springfield, IL 62704
(217)492-4416
Fax: (217)492-4867

SCORE Office (Sycamore)
112 Somunak St.
Sycamore, IL 60178
(815)895-3456
Fax: (815)895-0125

SCORE Office (University)
Hwy. 50 & Stuenkel Rd. Ste. C3305
University Park, IL 60466
(708)534-5000
Fax: (708)534-8457

Indiana

SCORE Office (Anderson)
205 W. 11th St.
Anderson, IN 46015
(317)642-0264

SCORE Office (Bloomington)
Star Center
216 W. Allen
Bloomington, IN 47403
(812)335-7334
E-mail: wtfische@indiana.edu
Website: http://www.brainfreezemedia.
com/score527/

SCORE Office (South East Indiana)
500 Franklin St.
Box 29
Columbus, IN 47201
(812)379-4457

SCORE Office (Corydon)
310 N. Elm St.
Corydon, IN 47112

(812)738-2137
Fax: (812)738-6438

SCORE Office (Crown Point)
Old Courthouse Sq. Ste. 206
PO Box 43
Crown Point, IN 46307
(219)663-1800

SCORE Office (Elkhart)
418 S. Main St.
Elkhart, IN 46515
(219)293-1531
Fax: (219)294-1859

SCORE Office (Evansville)
1100 W. Lloyd Expy., Ste. 105
Evansville, IN 47708
(812)426-6144

SCORE Office (Fort Wayne)
1300 S. Harrison St.
Ft. Wayne, IN 46802
(219)422-2601
Fax: (219)422-2601

SCORE Office (Gary)
973 W. 6th Ave., Rm. 326
Gary, IN 46402
(219)882-3918

SCORE Office (Hammond)
7034 Indianapolis Blvd.
Hammond, IN 46324
(219)931-1000
Fax: (219)845-9548

SCORE Office (Indianapolis)
429 N. Pennsylvania St., Ste. 100
Indianapolis, IN 46204-1873
(317)226-7264
Fax: (317)226-7259
E-mail: inscore@indy.net
Website: http://www.score-
indianapolis.org/

SCORE Office (Jasper)
PO Box 307
Jasper, IN 47547-0307
(812)482-6866

SCORE Office (Kokomo/Howard Counties)
106 N. Washington St.
Kokomo, IN 46901
(765)457-5301
Fax: (765)452-4564

SCORE Office (Logansport)
300 E. Broadway, Ste. 103
Logansport, IN 46947
(219)753-6388

SCORE Office (Madison)
301 E. Main St.
Madison, IN 47250
(812)265-3135
Fax: (812)265-2923

SCORE Office (Marengo)
Rt. 1 Box 224D
Marengo, IN 47140
Fax: (812)365-2793

SCORE Office (Marion/Grant Counties)
215 S. Adams
Marion, IN 46952
(765)664-5107

SCORE Office (Merrillville)
255 W. 80th Pl.
Merrillville, IN 46410
(219)769-8180
Fax: (219)736-6223

SCORE Office (Michigan City)
200 E. Michigan Blvd.
Michigan City, IN 46360
(219)874-6221
Fax: (219)873-1204

SCORE Office (South Central Indiana)
4100 Charleston Rd.
New Albany, IN 47150-9538
(812)945-0066

SCORE Office (Rensselaer)
104 W. Washington
Rensselaer, IN 47978

SCORE Office (Salem)
210 N. Main St.
Salem, IN 47167
(812)883-4303
Fax: (812)883-1467

SCORE Office (South Bend)
300 N. Michigan St.
South Bend, IN 46601
(219)282-4350
E-mail: chair@southbend-score.org
Website: http://www.southbend-score.org/

SCORE Office (Valparaiso)
150 Lincolnway
Valparaiso, IN 46383
(219)462-1105
Fax: (219)469-5710

SCORE Office (Vincennes)
27 N. 3rd
PO Box 553
Vincennes, IN 47591
(812)882-6440
Fax: (812)882-6441

SCORE Office (Wabash)
PO Box 371
Wabash, IN 46992
(219)563-1168
Fax: (219)563-6920

Iowa

SCORE Office (Burlington)
Federal Bldg.
300 N. Main St.
Burlington, IA 52601
(319)752-2967

SCORE Office (Cedar Rapids)
2750 1st Ave. NE, Ste 350
Cedar Rapids, IA 52401-1806
(319)362-6405
Fax: (319)362-7861
E:mail: score@scorecr.org
Website: http://www.scorecr.org

SCORE Office (Illowa)
333 4th Ave. S
Clinton, IA 52732
(319)242-5702

SCORE Office (Council Bluffs)
7 N. 6th St.
Council Bluffs, IA 51502
(712)325-1000

SCORE Office (Northeast Iowa)
3404 285th St.
Cresco, IA 52136
(319)547-3377

SCORE Office (Des Moines)
Federal Bldg., Rm. 749
210 Walnut St.
Des Moines, IA 50309-2186
(515)284-4760

SCORE Office (Ft. Dodge)
Federal Bldg., Rm. 436
205 S. 8th St.
Ft. Dodge, IA 50501
(515)955-2622

SCORE Office (Independence)
110 1st. St. east
Independence, IA 50644
(319)334-7178
Fax: (319)334-7179

SCORE Office (Iowa City)
210 Federal Bldg.
PO Box 1853
Iowa City, IA 52240-1853
(319)338-1662

SCORE Office (Keokuk)
401 Main St.
Pierce Bldg., No. 1
Keokuk, IA 52632
(319)524-5055

SCORE Office (Central Iowa)
Fisher Community College
709 S. Center
Marshalltown, IA 50158
(515)753-6645

SCORE Office (River City)
15 West State St.
Mason City, IA 50401
(515)423-5724

SCORE Office (South Central)
SBDC, Indian Hills Community College
525 Grandview Ave.
Ottumwa, IA 52501
(515)683-5127
Fax: (515)683-5263

SCORE Office (Dubuque)
10250 Sundown Rd.
Peosta, IA 52068
(319)556-5110

SCORE Office (Southwest Iowa)
614 W. Sheridan
Shenandoah, IA 51601
(712)246-3260

SCORE Office (Sioux City)
Federal Bldg.
320 6th St.
Sioux City, IA 51101
(712)277-2324
Fax: (712)277-2325

SCORE Office (Iowa Lakes)
122 W. 5th St.
Spencer, IA 51301
(712)262-3059

SCORE Office (Vista)
119 W. 6th St.
Storm Lake, IA 50588
(712)732-3780

SCORE Office (Waterloo)
215 E. 4th
Waterloo, IA 50703
(319)233-8431

Kansas

SCORE Office (Southwest Kansas)
501 W. Spruce
Dodge City, KS 67801
(316)227-3119

SCORE Office (Emporia)
811 Homewood
Emporia, KS 66801
(316)342-1600

SCORE Office (Golden Belt)
1307 Williams
Great Bend, KS 67530
(316)792-2401

SCORE Office (Hays)
PO Box 400
Hays, KS 67601
(913)625-6595

SCORE Office (Hutchinson)
1 E. 9th St.
Hutchinson, KS 67501
(316)665-8468
Fax: (316)665-7619

SCORE Office (Southeast Kansas)
404 Westminster Pl.
PO Box 886
Independence, KS 67301
(316)331-4741

SCORE Office (McPherson)
306 N. Main
PO Box 616
McPherson, KS 67460
(316)241-3303

SCORE Office (Salina)
120 Ash St.
Salina, KS 67401
(785)243-4290
Fax: (785)243-1833

SCORE Office (Topeka)
1700 College
Topeka, KS 66621
(785)231-1010

SCORE Office (Wichita)
100 E. English, Ste. 510
Wichita, KS 67202
(316)269-6273
Fax: (316)269-6499

SCORE Office (Ark Valley)
205 E. 9th St.
Winfield, KS 67156
(316)221-1617

Kentucky

SCORE Office (Ashland)
PO Box 830
Ashland, KY 41105
(606)329-8011
Fax: (606)325-4607

SCORE Office (Bowling Green)
812 State St.
PO Box 51
Bowling Green, KY 42101
(502)781-3200
Fax: (502)843-0458

SCORE Office (Tri-Lakes)
508 Barbee Way
Danville, KY 40422-1548
(606)231-9902

SCORE Office (Glasgow)
301 W. Main St.
Glasgow, KY 42141
(502)651-3161
Fax: (502)651-3122

SCORE Office (Hazard)
B & I Technical Center
100 Airport Gardens Rd.
Hazard, KY 41701
(606)439-5856
Fax: (606)439-1808

SCORE Office (Lexington)
410 W. Vine St., Ste. 290, Civic C
Lexington, KY 40507
(606)231-9902
Fax: (606)253-3190
E-mail: scorelex@uky.campus.mci.net

SCORE Office (Louisville)
188 Federal Office Bldg.
600 Dr. Martin L. King Jr. Pl.
Louisville, KY 40202
(502)582-5976

SCORE Office (Madisonville)
257 N. Main
Madisonville, KY 42431
(502)825-1399
Fax: (502)825-1396

SCORE Office (Paducah)
Federal Office Bldg.
501 Broadway, Rm. B-36
Paducah, KY 42001
(502)442-5685

Louisiana

SCORE Office (Central Louisiana)
802 3rd St.
Alexandria, LA 71309
(318)442-6671

SCORE Office (Baton Rouge)
564 Laurel St.
PO Box 3217
Baton Rouge, LA 70801

(504)381-7130
Fax: (504)336-4306

SCORE Office (North Shore)
2 W. Thomas
Hammond, LA 70401
(504)345-4457
Fax: (504)345-4749

SCORE Office (Lafayette)
804 St. Mary Blvd.
Lafayette, LA 70505-1307
(318)233-2705
Fax: (318)234-8671
E-mail: score302@aol.com

SCORE Office (Lake Charles)
120 W. Pujo St.
Lake Charles, LA 70601
(318)433-3632

SCORE Office (New Orleans)
365 Canal St., Ste. 3100
New Orleans, LA 70130
(504)589-2356
Fax: (504)589-2339

SCORE Office (Shreveport)
400 Edwards St.
Shreveport, LA 71101
(318)677-2536
Fax: (318)677-2541

Maine

SCORE Office (Augusta)
40 Western Ave.
Augusta, ME 04330
(207)622-8509

SCORE Office (Bangor)
Peabody Hall, Rm. 229
One College Cir.
Bangor, ME 04401
(207)941-9707

SCORE Office (Central & Northern Arroostock)
111 High St.
Caribou, ME 04736
(207)492-8010
Fax: (207)492-8010

SCORE Office (Penquis)
South St.
Dover Foxcroft, ME 04426
(207)564-7021

SCORE Office (Maine Coastal)
Mill Mall
Box 1105
Ellsworth, ME 04605-1105

(207)667-5800

E-mail: score@arcadia.net

SCORE Office (Lewiston-Auburn)

BIC of Maine-Bates Mill Complex

35 Canal St.

Lewiston, ME 04240-7764

(207)782-3708

Fax: (207)783-7745

SCORE Office (Portland)

66 Pearl St., Rm. 210

Portland, ME 04101

(207)772-1147

Fax: (207)772-5581

E-mail: Score53@score.maine.org

Website: http://www.score.maine.org/

chapter53/

SCORE Office (Western Mountains)

255 River St.

PO Box 252

Rumford, ME 04257-0252

(207)369-9976

SCORE Office (Oxford Hills)

166 Main St.

South Paris, ME 04281

(207)743-0499

Maryland

SCORE Office (Southern Maryland)

2525 Riva Rd., Ste. 110

Annapolis, MD 21401

(410)266-9553

Fax: (410)573-0981

E-mail: score390@aol.com

Website: http://members.aol.com/

score390/index.htm

SCORE Office (Baltimore)

The City Crescent Bldg., 6th Fl.

10 S. Howard St.

Baltimore, MD 21201

(410)962-2233

Fax: (410)962-1805

SCORE Office (Bel Air)

108 S. Bond St.

Bel Air, MD 21014

(410)838-2020

Fax: (410)893-4715

SCORE Office (Bethesda)

7910 Woodmont Ave., Ste. 1204

Bethesda, MD 20814

(301)652-4900

Fax: (301)657-1973

SCORE Office (Bowie)

6670 Race Track Rd.

Bowie, MD 20715

(301)262-0920

Fax: (301)262-0921

SCORE Office (Dorchester County)

203 Sunburst Hwy.

Cambridge, MD 21613

(410)228-3575

SCORE Office (Upper Shore)

210 Marlboro Ave.

Easton, MD 21601

(410)822-4606

Fax: (410)822-7922

SCORE Office (Frederick County)

43A S. Market St.

Frederick, MD 21701

(301)662-8723

Fax: (301)846-4427

SCORE Office (Gaithersburg)

9 Park Ave.

Gaithersburg, MD 20877

(301)840-1400

Fax: (301)963-3918

SCORE Office (Glen Burnie)

103 Crain Hwy. SE

Glen Burnie, MD 21061

(410)766-8282

Fax: (410)766-9722

SCORE Office (Hagerstown)

111 W. Washington St.

Hagerstown, MD 21740

(301)739-2015

Fax: (301)739-1278

SCORE Office (Laurel)

7901 Sandy Spring Rd. Ste. 501

Laurel, MD 20707

(301)725-4000

Fax: (301)725-0776

SCORE Office (Salisbury)

300 E. Main St.

Salisbury, MD 21801

(410)749-0185

Fax: (410)860-9925

Massachusetts

SCORE Office (NE Massachusetts)

100 Cummings Ctr., Ste. 101 K

Beverly, MA 01923

(978)922-9441

Website: http://www1.shore.net/~score/

SCORE Office (Boston)

10 Causeway St., Rm. 265

Boston, MA 02222-1093

(617)565-5591

Fax: (617)565-5598

E-mail: boston-score-20@worldnet.att.net

Website: http://www.scoreboston.org/

SCORE office (Bristol/Plymouth County)

53 N. 6th St., Federal Bldg.

Bristol, MA 02740

(508)994-5093

SCORE Office (SE Massachusetts)

60 School St.

Brockton, MA 02401

(508)587-2673

Fax: (508)587-1340

Website: http://www.metrosouth

chamber.com/score.html

SCORE Office (North Adams)

820 N. State Rd.

Cheshire, MA 01225

(413)743-5100

SCORE Office (Clinton Satellite)

1 Green St.

Clinton, MA 01510

Fax: (508)368-7689

SCORE Office (Greenfield)

PO Box 898

Greenfield, MA 01302

(413)773-5463

Fax: (413)773-7008

SCORE Office (Haverhill)

87 Winter St.

Haverhill, MA 01830

(508)373-5663

Fax: (508)373-8060

SCORE Office (Hudson Satellite)

PO Box 578

Hudson, MA 01749

(508)568-0360

Fax: (508)568-0360

SCORE Office (Cape Cod)

Independence Pk., Ste. 5B

270 Communications Way

Hyannis, MA 02601

(508)775-4884

Fax: (508)790-2540

SCORE Office (Lawrence)

264 Essex St.

Lawrence, MA 01840

(508)686-0900

Fax: (508)794-9953

SCORE Office (Leominster Satellite)
110 Erdman Way
Leominster, MA 01453
(508)840-4300
Fax: (508)840-4896

SCORE Office (Bristol/Plymouth Counties)
53 N. 6th St., Federal Bldg.
New Bedford, MA 02740
(508)994-5093

SCORE Office (Newburyport)
29 State St.
Newburyport, MA 01950
(617)462-6680

SCORE Office (Pittsfield)
66 West St.
Pittsfield, MA 01201
(413)499-2485

SCORE Office (Haverhill-Salem)
32 Derby Sq.
Salem, MA 01970
(508)745-0330
Fax: (508)745-3855

SCORE Office (Springfield)
1350 Main St.
Federal Bldg.
Springfield, MA 01103
(413)785-0314

SCORE Office (Carver)
12 Taunton Green, Ste. 201
Taunton, MA 02780
(508)824-4068
Fax: (508)824-4069

SCORE Office (Worcester)
33 Waldo St.
Worcester, MA 01608
(508)753-2929
Fax: (508)754-8560

Michigan

SCORE Office (Allegan)
PO Box 338
Allegan, MI 49010
(616)673-2479

SCORE Office (Ann Arbor)
425 S. Main St., Ste. 103
Ann Arbor, MI 48104
(313)665-4433

SCORE Office (Battle Creek)
34 W. Jackson Ste. 4A
Battle Creek, MI 49017-3505

(616)962-4076
Fax: (616)962-6309

SCORE Office (Cadillac)
222 Lake St.
Cadillac, MI 49601
(616)775-9776
Fax: (616)768-4255

SCORE Office (Detroit)
477 Michigan Ave., Rm. 515
Detroit, MI 48226
(313)226-7947
Fax: (313)226-3448

SCORE Office (Flint)
708 Root Rd., Rm. 308
Flint, MI 48503
(810)233-6846

SCORE Office (Grand Rapids)
111 Pearl St. NW
Grand Rapids, MI 49503-2831
(616)771-0305
Fax: (616)771-0328
E-mail: scoreone@iserv.net
Website: http://www.iserv.net/
~scoreone/

SCORE Office (Holland)
480 State St.
Holland, MI 49423
(616)396-9472

SCORE Office (Jackson)
209 East Washington
PO Box 80
Jackson, MI 49204
(517)782-8221
Fax: (517)782-0061

SCORE Office (Kalamazoo)
345 W. Michigan Ave.
Kalamazoo, MI 49007
(616)381-5382
Fax: (616)384-0096
E-mail: score@nucleus.net

SCORE Office (Lansing)
117 E. Allegan
PO Box 14030
Lansing, MI 48901
(517)487-6340
Fax: (517)484-6910

SCORE Office (Livonia)
15401 Farmington Rd.
Livonia, MI 48154
(313)427-2122
Fax: (313)427-6055

SCORE Office (Madison Heights)
26345 John R
Madison Heights, MI 48071
(810)542-5010
Fax: (810)542-6821

SCORE Office (Monroe)
111 E. 1st
Monroe, MI 48161
(313)242-3366
Fax: (313)242-7253

SCORE Office (Mt. Clemens)
58 S/B Gratiot
Mt. Clemens, MI 48043
(810)463-1528
Fax: (810)463-6541

SCORE Office (Muskegon)
PO Box 1087
230 Terrace Plz.
Muskegon, MI 49443
(616)722-3751
Fax: (616)728-7251

SCORE Office (Petoskey)
401 E. Mitchell St.
Petoskey, MI 49770
(616)347-4150

SCORE Office (Pontiac)
Executive Office Bldg.
1200 N. Telegraph Rd.
Pontiac, MI 48341
(810)975-9555

SCORE Office (Pontiac)
PO Box 430025
Pontiac, MI 48343
(810)335-9600

SCORE Office (Port Huron)
920 Pinegrove Ave.
Port Huron, MI 48060
(810)985-7101

SCORE Office (Rochester)
71 Walnut Ste. 110
Rochester, MI 48307
(810)651-6700
Fax: (810)651-5270

SCORE Office (Saginaw)
901 S. Washington Ave.
Saginaw, MI 48601
(517)752-7161
Fax: (517)752-9055

SCORE Office (Upper Peninsula)
2581 I-75 Business Spur
Sault Ste. Marie, MI 49783
(906)632-3301

SCORE Office (Southfield)
21000 W. 10 Mile Rd.
Southfield, MI 48075
(810)204-3050
Fax: (810)204-3099

SCORE Office (Traverse City)
202 E. Grandview Pkwy.
PO Box 387
Traverse City, MI 49685
(616)947-5075
Fax: (616)946-2565

SCORE Office (Warren)
30500 Van Dyke, Ste. 118
Warren, MI 48093
(810)751-3939

Minnesota

SCORE Office (Aitkin)
Aitkin, MN 56431
(218)741-3906

SCORE Office (Albert Lea)
202 N. Broadway Ave.
Albert Lea, MN 56007
(507)373-7487

SCORE Office (Austin)
PO Box 864
Austin, MN 55912
(507)437-4561
Fax: (507)437-4869

SCORE Office (South Metro)
Ames Business Ctr.
2500 W. County Rd., No. 42
Burnsville, MN 55337
(612)898-5645
Fax: (612)435-6972
E-mail: southmetro@scoreminn.org
Website: http://www.scoreminn.org/
southmetro/

SCORE Office (Duluth)
1717 Minnesota Ave.
Duluth, MN 55802
(218)727-8286
Fax: (218)727-3113
E-mail: duluth@scoreminn.org
Website: http://www.scoreminn.org

SCORE Office (Fairmont)
PO Box 826
Fairmont, MN 56031
(507)235-5547
Fax: (507)235-8411

SCORE Office (Southwest Minnesota)
112 Riverfront St.

Box 999
Mankato, MN 56001
(507)345-4519
Fax: (507)345-4451
Website: http://www.scoreminn.org/

SCORE Office (Minneapolis)
North Plaza Bldg., Ste. 51
5217 Wayzata Blvd.
Minneapolis, MN 55416
(612)591-0539
Fax: (612)544-0436
Website: http://www.scoreminn.org/

SCORE Office (Owatonna)
PO Box 331
Owatonna, MN 55060
(507)451-7970
Fax: (507)451-7972

SCORE Office (Red Wing)
2000 W. Main St., Ste. 324
Red Wing, MN 55066
(612)388-4079

SCORE Office (Southeastern Minnesota)
220 S. Broadway, Ste. 100
Rochester, MN 55901
(507)288-1122
Fax: (507)282-8960
Website: http://www.scorcminn.org/

SCORE Office (Brainerd)
St. Cloud, MN 56301

SCORE Office (Central Area)
1527 Northway Dr.
St. Cloud, MN 56301
(320)240-1332
Fax: (320)255 9050
Website: http://www.scoreminn.org/

SCORE Office (St. Paul)
350 St. Peter St., No. 295
Lowry Professional Bldg.
St. Paul, MN 55102
(651)223-5010
Fax: (651)223-5048
Website: http://www.scoreminn.org/

SCORE Office (Winona)
Box 870
Winona, MN 55987
(507)452-2272
Fax: (507)454-8814

SCORE Office (Worthington)
1121 3rd Ave.
Worthington, MN 56187
(507)372-2919
Fax: (507)372-2827

Mississippi

SCORE Office (Delta)
915 Washington Ave.
PO Box 933
Greenville, MS 38701
(601)378-3141

SCORE Office (Gulfcoast)
1 Government Plaza
2909 13th St., Ste. 203
Gulfport, MS 39501
(228)863-0054

SCORE Office (Jackson)
1st Jackson Center, Ste. 400
101 W. Capitol St.
Jackson, MS 39201
(601)965-5533

SCORE Office (Meridian)
5220 16th Ave.
Meridian, MS 39305
(601)482-4412

Missouri

SCORE Office (Lake of the Ozark)
University Extension
113 Kansas St.
PO Box 1405
Camdenton, MO 65020
(573)346-2644
Fax: (573)346-2694
E-mail: score@cdoc.net
Website: http://sites.cdoc.net/score/

Chamber of Commerce (Cape Girardeau)
PO Box 98
Cape Girardeau, MO 63702-0098
(314)335-3312

SCORE Office (Mid-Missouri)
1705 Halstead Ct.
Columbia, MO 65203
(573)874-1132

SCORE Office (Ozark-Gateway)
1486 Glassy Rd.
Cuba, MO 65453-1640
(573)885-4954

SCORE Office (Kansas City)
323 W. 8th St., Ste. 104
Kansas City, MO 64105
(816)374-6675
Fax: (816)374-6692
E-mail: SCOREBIC@AOL.COM
Website: http://www.crn.org/score/

SCORE Office (Sedalia)
Lucas Place
323 W. 8th St., Ste.104
Kansas City, MO 64105
(816)374-6675

SCORE office (Tri-Lakes)
PO Box 1148
Kimberling, MO 65686
(417)739-3041

SCORE Office (Tri-Lakes)
HCRI Box 85
Lampe, MO 65681
(417)858-6798

SCORE Office (Mexico)
111 N. Washington St.
Mexico, MO 65265
(314)581-2765

SCORE Office (Southeast Missouri)
Rte. 1, Box 280
Neelyville, MO 63954
(573)989-3577

SCORE office (Poplar Bluff Area)
806 Emma St.
Poplar Bluff, MO 63901
(573)686-8892

SCORE Office (St. Joseph)
3003 Frederick Ave.
St. Joseph, MO 64506
(816)232-4461

SCORE Office (St. Louis)
815 Olive St., Rm. 242
St. Louis, MO 63101-1569
(314)539-6970
Fax: (314)539-3785
E-mail: info@stlscore.org
Website: http://www.stlscore.org/

SCORE Office (Lewis & Clark)
425 Spencer Rd.
St. Peters, MO 63376
(314)928-2900
Fax: (314)928-2900
E-mail: score01@mail.win.org

SCORE Office (Springfield)
620 S. Glenstone, Ste. 110
Springfield, MO 65802-3200
(417)864-7670
Fax: (417)864-4108

SCORE office (Southeast Kansas)
1206 W. First St.
Webb City, MO 64870
(417)673-3984

Montana

SCORE Office (Billings)
815 S. 27th St.
Billings, MT 59101
(406)245-4111

SCORE Office (Bozeman)
1205 E. Main St.
Bozeman, MT 59715
(406)586-5421

SCORE Office (Butte)
1000 George St.
Butte, MT 59701
(406)723-3177

SCORE Office (Great Falls)
710 First Ave. N
Great Falls, MT 59401
(406)761-4434
E-mail: scoregtf@in.tch.com

SCORE Office (Havre, Montana)
518 First St.
Havre, MT 59501
(406)265-4383

SCORE Office (Helena)
Federal Bldg.
301 S. Park
Helena, MT 59626-0054
(406)441-1081

SCORE Office (Kalispell)
2 Main St.
Kalispell, MT 59901
(406)756-5271
Fax: (406)752-6665

SCORE Office (Missoula)
723 Ronan
Missoula, MT 59806
(406)327-8806
E-mail: score@safeshop.com
Website: http://missoula.bigsky.net/
score/

Nebraska

SCORE Office (Columbus)
Columbus, NE 68601
(402)564-2769

SCORE Office (Fremont)
92 W. 5th St.
Fremont, NE 68025
(402)721-2641

SCORE Office (Hastings)
Hastings, NE 68901
(402)463-3447

SCORE Office (Lincoln)
8800 O St.
Lincoln, NE 68520
(402)437-2409

SCORE Office (Panhandle)
150549 CR 30
Minatare, NE 69356
(308)632-2133
Website: http://www.tandt.com/
SCORE

SCORE Office (Norfolk)
3209 S. 48th Ave.
Norfolk, NE 68106
(402)564-2769

SCORE Office (North Platte)
3301 W. 2nd St.
North Platte, NE 69101
(308)532-4466

SCORE Office (Omaha)
11145 Mill Valley Rd.
Omaha, NE 68154
(402)221-3606
Fax: (402)221-3680
E-mail: infoctr@ne.uswest.net
Website: http://www.tandt.com/score/

Nevada

SCORE Office (Incline Village)
969 Tahoe Blvd.
Incline Village, NV 89451
(702)831-7327
Fax: (702)832-1605

SCORE Office (Carson City)
301 E. Stewart
PO Box 7527
Las Vegas, NV 89125
(702)388-6104

SCORE Office (Las Vegas)
300 Las Vegas Blvd. S, Ste. 1100
Las Vegas, NV 89101
(702)388-6104

SCORE Office (Northern Nevada)
SBDC, College of Business
Administration
Univ. of Nevada
Reno, NV 89557-0100
(702)784-4436
Fax: (702)784-4337

New Hampshire

SCORE Office (North Country)
PO Box 34

Berlin, NH 03570
(603)752-1090

SCORE Office (Concord)
143 N. Main St., Rm. 202A
PO Box 1258
Concord, NH 03301
(603)225-1400
Fax: (603)225-1409

SCORE Office (Dover)
299 Central Ave.
Dover, NH 03820
(603)742-2218
Fax: (603)749-6317

SCORE Office (Monadnock)
34 Mechanic St.
Keene, NH 03431-3421
(603)352-0320

SCORE Office (Lakes Region)
67 Water St., Ste. 105
Laconia, NH 03246
(603)524-9168

SCORE Office (Upper Valley)
Citizens Bank Bldg., Rm. 310
20 W. Park St.
Lebanon, NH 03766
(603)448-3491
Fax: (603)448-1908
E-mail: billt@valley.net
Website: http://www.valley.net/~score/

SCORE Office (Merrimack Valley)
275 Chestnut St., Rm. 618
Manchester, NH 03103
(603)666-7561
Fax: (603)666-7925

SCORE Office (Mt. Washington Valley)
PO Box 1066
North Conway, NH 03818
(603)383-0800

SCORE Office (Seacoast)
195 Commerce Way, Unit-A
Portsmouth, NH 03801-3251
(603)433-0575

New Jersey

SCORE Office (Somerset)
Paritan Valley Community College,
Rte. 28
Branchburg, NJ 08807
(908)218-8874
E-mail: nj-score@grizbiz.com.
Website: http://www.nj-score.org/

SCORE Office (Chester)
5 Old Mill Rd.
Chester, NJ 07930
(908)879-7080

**SCORE Office
(Greater Princeton)**
4 A George Washington Dr.
Cranbury, NJ 08512
(609)520-1776

SCORE Office (Freehold)
36 W. Main St.
Freehold, NJ 07728
(908)462-3030
Fax: (908)462-2123

SCORE Office (North West)
Picantinny Innovation Ctr.
3159 Schrader Rd.
Hamburg, NJ 07419
(973)209-8525
Fax: (973)209-7252
E-mail: nj-score@grizbiz.com
Website: http://www.nj-score.org/

SCORE Office (Monmouth)
765 Newman Springs Rd.
Lincroft, NJ 07738
(908)224-2573
E-mail: nj-score@grizbiz.com
Website: http://www.nj-score.org/

SCORE Office (Manalapan)
125 Symmes Dr.
Manalapan, NJ 07726
(908)431-7220

SCORE Office (Jersey City)
2 Gateway Ctr., 4th Fl.
Newark, NJ 07102
(973)645-3982
Fax: (973)645-2375

SCORE Office (Newark)
2 Gateway Center, 15th Fl.
Newark, NJ 07102-5553
(973)645-3982
Fax: (973)645-2375
E-mail: nj-score@grizbiz.com
Website: http://www.nj-score.org

SCORE Office (Bergen County)
327 E. Ridgewood Ave.
Paramus, NJ 07652
(201)599-6090
E-mail: nj-score@grizbiz.com
Website: http://www.nj-score.org/

SCORE Office (Pennsauken)
4900 Rte. 70

Pennsauken, NJ 08109
(609)486-3421

SCORE Office (Southern New Jersey)
4900 Rte. 70
Pennsauken, NJ 08109
(609)486-3421
E-mail: nj-score@grizbiz.com
Website: http://www.nj-score.org/

SCORE Office (Greater Princeton)
216 Rockingham Row
Princeton Forrestal Village
Princeton, NJ 08540
(609)520-1776
Fax: (609)520-9107
E-mail: nj-score@grizbiz.com
Website: http://www.nj-score.org/

SCORE Office (Shrewsbury)
Hwy. 35
Shrewsbury, NJ 07702
(908)842-5995
Fax: (908)219-6140

SCORE Office (Ocean County)
33 Washington St.
Toms River, NJ 08754
(732)505-6033
E-mail: nj-score@grizbiz.com
Website: http://www.nj-score.org/

SCORE Office (Wall)
2700 Allaire Rd.
Wall, NJ 07719
(908)449-8877

SCORE Office (Wayne)
2055 Hamburg Tpke.
Wayne, NJ 07470
(201)831-7788
Fax: (201)831-9112

New Mexico

SCORE Office (Albuquerque)
525 Buena Vista, SE
Albuquerque, NM 87106
(505)272-7999
Fax: (505)272-7963

SCORE Office (Las Cruces)
Loretto Towne Center
505 S. Main St., Ste. 125
Las Cruces, NM 88001
(505)523-5627
Fax: (505)524-2101
E-mail: score.397@zianet.com

SCORE Office (Roswell)
Federal Bldg., Rm. 237

Roswell, NM 88201
(505)625-2112
Fax: (505)623-2545

SCORE Office (Santa Fe)
Montoya Federal Bldg.
120 Federal Place, Rm. 307
Santa Fe, NM 87501
(505)988-6302
Fax: (505)988-6300

New York

SCORE Office (Northeast)
1 Computer Dr. S
Albany, NY 12205
(518)446-1118
Fax: (518)446-1228

SCORE Office (Auburn)
30 South St.
PO Box 675
Auburn, NY 13021
(315)252-7291

SCORE Office (South Tier Binghamton)
Metro Center, 2nd Fl.
49 Court St.
PO Box 995
Binghamton, NY 13902
(607)772-8860

SCORE Office (Queens County City)
12055 Queens Blvd., Rm. 333
Borough Hall, NY 11424
(718)263-8961

SCORE Office (Buffalo)
Federal Bldg., Rm. 1311
111 W. Huron St.
Buffalo, NY 14202
(716)551-4301
Website: http://www2.pcom.net/score/
buf45.html

SCORE Office (Canandaigua)
Chamber of Commerce Bldg.
113 S. Main St.
Canandaigua, NY 14424
(716)394-4400
Fax: (716)394-4546

SCORE Office (Chemung)
333 E. Water St., 4th Fl.
Elmira, NY 14901
(607)734-3358

SCORE Office (Geneva)
Chamber of Commerce Bldg.
PO Box 587

Geneva, NY 14456
(315)789-1776
Fax: (315)789-3993

SCORE Office (Glens Falls)
84 Broad St.
Glens Falls, NY 12801
(518)798-8463
Fax: (518)745-1433

SCORE Office (Orange County)
40 Matthews St.
Goshen, NY 10924
(914)294-8080
Fax: (914)294-6121

SCORE Office (Huntington Area)
151 W. Carver St.
Huntington, NY 11743
(516)423-6100

SCORE Office (Tompkins County)
904 E. Shore Dr.
Ithaca, NY 14850
(607)273-7080

SCORE Office (Long Island City)
120-55 Queens Blvd.
Jamaica, NY 11424
(718)263-8961
Fax: (718)263-9032

SCORE Office (Chatauqua)
101 W. 5th St.
Jamestown, NY 14701
(716)484-1103

SCORE Office (Westchester)
2 Caradon Ln.
Katonah, NY 10536
(914)948-3907
Fax: (914)948-4645
E-mail: score@w-w-w.com
Website: http://w-w-w.com/score/

SCORE Office (Queens County)
Queens Borough Hall
120-55 Queens Blvd. Rm. 333
Kew Gardens, NY 11424
(718)263-8961
Fax: (718)263-9032

SCORE Office (Brookhaven)
3233 Rte. 112
Medford, NY 11763
(516)451-6563
Fax: (516)451-6925

SCORE Office (Melville)
35 Pinelawn Rd., Rm. 207-W
Melville, NY 11747
(516)454-0771

SCORE Office (Nassau County)
400 County Seat Dr., No. 140
Mineola, NY 11501
(516)571-3303
E-mail: Counse1998@aol.com
Website: http://members.aol.com/
Counse1998/Default.htm

SCORE Office (Mt. Vernon)
4 N. 7th Ave.
Mt. Vernon, NY 10550
(914)667-7500

SCORE Office (New York)
26 Federal Plz., Rm. 3100
New York, NY 10278
(212)264-4507
Fax: (212)264-4963
E-mail: score1000@erols.com
Website: http://users.erols.com/
score-nyc/

SCORE Office (Newburgh)
47 Grand St.
Newburgh, NY 12550
(914)562-5100

SCORE Office (Owego)
188 Front St.
Owego, NY 13827
(607)687-2020

SCORE Office (Peekskill)
1 S. Division St.
Peekskill, NY 10566
(914)737-3600
Fax: (914)737-0541

SCORE Office (Penn Yan)
2375 Rte. 14A
Penn Yan, NY 14527
(315)536-3111

SCORE Office (Dutchess)
110 Main St.
Poughkeepsie, NY 12601
(914)454-1700

SCORE Office (Rochester)
601 Keating Federal Bldg., Rm. 410
100 State St.
Rochester, NY 14614
(716)263-6473
Fax: (716)263-3146
Website: http://www.ggw.org/score/

SCORE Office (Saranac Lake)
30 Main St.
Saranac Lake, NY 12983
(315)448-0415

SCORE Office (Suffolk)
286 Main St.
Setauket, NY 11733
(516)751-3886

SCORE Office (Staten Island)
130 Bay St.
Staten Island, NY 10301
(718)727-1221

SCORE Office (Ulster)
Clinton Bldg., Rm. 107
Stone Ridge, NY 12484
(914)687-5035
Fax: (914)687-5015
Website: http://www.scoreulster.org/

SCORE Office (Syracuse)
401 S. Salina, 5th Fl.
Syracuse, NY 13202
(315)471-9393

SCORE Office (Utica)
SUNY Institute of Technology, Route 12
Utica, NY 13504-3050
(315)792-7553

SCORE Office (Watertown)
518 Davidson St.
Watertown, NY 13601
(315)788-1200
Fax: (315)788-8251

North Carolina

SCORE office (Asheboro)
317 E. Dixie Dr.
Asheboro, NC 27203
(336)626-2626
Fax: (336)626-7077

SCORE Office (Asheville)
Federal Bldg., Rm. 259
151 Patton
Asheville, NC 28801-5770
(828)271-4786
Fax: (828)271-4009

SCORE Office (Chapel Hill)
104 S. Estes Dr.
PO Box 2897
Chapel Hill, NC 27514
(919)967-7075

SCORE Office (Coastal Plains)
PO Box 2897
Chapel Hill, NC 27515
(919)967-7075
Fax: (919)968-6874

SCORE Office (Charlotte)
200 N. College St., Ste. A-2015

Charlotte, NC 28202
(704)344-6576
Fax: (704)344-6769
E-mail: CharlotteSCORE47@AOL.com
Website: http://www.charweb.org/
business/score/

SCORE Office (Durham)
411 W. Chapel Hill St.
Durham, NC 27707
(919)541-2171

SCORE Office (Gastonia)
PO Box 2168
Gastonia, NC 28053
(704)864-2621
Fax: (704)854-8723

SCORE Office (Greensboro)
400 W. Market St., Ste. 103
Greensboro, NC 27401-2241
(910)333-5399

SCORE Office (Henderson)
PO Box 917
Henderson, NC 27536
(919)492-2061
Fax: (919)430-0460

SCORE Office (Hendersonville)
Federal Bldg., Rm. 108
W. 4th Ave. & Church St.
Hendersonville, NC 28792
(828)693-8702
E-mail: score@circle.net
Website: http://www.wncguide.com/
score/Welcome.html

SCORE Office (Unifour)
PO Box 1828
Hickory, NC 28603
(704)328-6111

SCORE Office (High Point)
1101 N. Main St.
High Point, NC 27262
(336)882-8625
Fax: (336)889-9499

SCORE Office (Outer Banks)
Collington Rd. and Mustain
Kill Devil Hills, NC 27948
(252)441-8144

SCORE Office (Down East)
312 S. Front St., Ste. 6
New Bern, NC 28560
(252)633-6688
Fax: (252)633-9608

SCORE Office (Kinston)
PO Box 95

New Bern, NC 28561
(919)633-6688

SCORE Office (Raleigh)
Century Post Office Bldg., Ste. 306
300 Federal St. Mall
Raleigh, NC 27601
(919)856-4739
E-mail: jendres@ibm.net
Website: http://www.intrex.net/score96/
score96.htm

SCORE Office (Sanford)
1801 Nash St.
Sanford, NC 27330
(919)774-6442
Fax: (919)776-8739

SCORE Office (Sandhills Area)
1480 Hwy. 15-501
PO Box 458
Southern Pines, NC 28387
(910)692-3926

SCORE Office (Wilmington)
Corps of Engineers Bldg.
96 Darlington Ave., Ste. 207
Wilmington, NC 28403
(910)815-4576
Fax: (910)815-4658

North Dakota

**SCORE Office
(Bismarck-Mandan)**
700 E. Main Ave., 2nd Fl.
PO Box 5509
Bismarck, ND 58506-5509
(701)250-4303

SCORE Office (Fargo)
657 2nd Ave., Rm. 225
Fargo, ND 58108-3083
(701)239-5677

SCORE Office (Upper Red River)
4275 Technology Dr., Rm. 156
Grand Forks, ND 58202-8372
(701)777-3051

SCORE Office (Minot)
100 1st St. SW
Minot, ND 58701-3846
(701)852-6883
Fax: (701)852-6905

Ohio

SCORE Office (Akron)
1 Cascade Plz., 7th Fl.
Akron, OH 44308

(330)379-3163
Fax: (330)379-3164

SCORE Office (Ashland)
Gill Center
47 W. Main St.
Ashland, OH 44805
(419)281-4584

SCORE Office (Canton)
116 Cleveland Ave. NW, Ste. 601
Canton, OH 44702-1720
(330)453-6047

SCORE Office (Chillicothe)
165 S. Paint St.
Chillicothe, OH 45601
(614)772-4530

SCORE Office (Cincinnati)
Ameritrust Bldg., Rm. 850
525 Vine St.
Cincinnati, OH 45202
(513)684-2812
Fax: (513)684-3251
Website: http://www.score.
chapter34.org/

SCORE Office (Cleveland)
Eaton Center, Ste. 620
1100 Superior Ave.
Cleveland, OH 44114-2507
(216)522-4194
Fax: (216)522-4844

SCORE Office (Columbus)
2 Nationwide Plz., Ste. 1400
Columbus, OH 43215-2542
(614)469-2357
Fax: (614)469-2391
E-mail: info@scorecolumbus.org
Website: http://www.scorecolumbus.org/

SCORE Office (Dayton)
Dayton Federal Bldg., Rm. 505
200 W. Second St.
Dayton, OH 45402-1430
(513)225-2887
Fax: (513)225-7667

SCORE Office (Defiance)
615 W. 3rd St.
PO Box 130
Defiance, OH 43512
(419)782-7946

SCORE Office (Findlay)
123 E. Main Cross St.
PO Box 923
Findlay, OH 45840
(419)422-3314

SCORE Office (Lima)
147 N. Main St.
Lima, OH 45801
(419)222-6045
Fax: (419)229-0266

SCORE Office (Mansfield)
55 N. Mulberry St.
Mansfield, OH 44902
(419)522-3211

SCORE Office (Marietta)
Thomas Hall
Marietta, OH 45750
(614)373-0268

SCORE Office (Medina)
County Administrative Bldg.
144 N. Broadway
Medina, OH 44256
(216)764-8650

SCORE Office (Licking County)
50 W. Locust St.
Newark, OH 43055
(614)345-7458

SCORE Office (Salem)
2491 State Rte. 45 S
Salem, OH 44460
(216)332-0361

SCORE Office (Tiffin)
62 S. Washington St.
Tiffin, OH 44883
(419)447-4141
Fax: (419)447-5141

SCORE Office (Toledo)
608 Madison Ave, Ste. 910
Toledo, OH 43624
(419)259-7598
Fax: (419)259-6460

SCORE Office (Heart of Ohio)
377 W. Liberty St.
Wooster, OH 44691
(330)262-5735
Fax: (330)262-5745

SCORE Office (Youngstown)
306 Williamson Hall
Youngstown, OH 44555
(330)746-2687

Oklahoma

SCORE Office (Anadarko)
PO Box 366
Anadarko, OK 73005
(405)247-6651

SCORE Office (Ardmore)
410 W. Main
Ardmore, OK 73401
(580)226-2620

SCORE Office (Northeast Oklahoma)
210 S. Main
Grove, OK 74344
(918)787-2796
Fax: (918)787-2796
E-mail: Score595@greencis.net

SCORE Office (Lawton)
4500 W. Lee Blvd., Bldg. 100, Ste. 107
Lawton, OK 73505
(580)353-8727
Fax: (580)250-5677

SCORE Office (Oklahoma City)
210 Park Ave., No. 1300
Oklahoma City, OK 73102
(405)231-5163
Fax: (405)231-4876
E-mail: score212@usa.net

SCORE Office (Stillwater)
439 S. Main
Stillwater, OK 74074
(405)372-5573
Fax: (405)372-4316

SCORE Office (Tulsa)
616 S. Boston, Ste. 406
Tulsa, OK 74119
(918)581-7462
Fax: (918)581-6908
Website: http://www.ionet.net/~tulscore/

Oregon

SCORE Office (Bend)
63085 N. Hwy. 97
Bend, OR 97701
(541)923-2849
Fax: (541)330-6900

SCORE Office (Willamette)
1401 Willamette St.
PO Box 1107
Eugene, OR 97401-4003
(541)465-6600
Fax: (541)484-4942

SCORE Office (Florence)
3149 Oak St.
Florence, OR 97439
(503)997-8444
Fax: (503)997-8448

SCORE Office (Southern Oregon)
33 N. Central Ave., Ste. 216

Medford, OR 97501
(541)776-4220
E-mail: pgr134f@prodigy.com

SCORE Office (Portland)
1515 SW 5th Ave., Ste. 1050
Portland, OR 97201
(503)326-3441
Fax: (503)326-2808
E-mail: gr134@prodigy.com

SCORE Office (Salem)
416 State St. (corner of Liberty)
Salem, OR 97301
(503)370-2896

Pennsylvania

SCORE Office (Altoona-Blair)
1212 12th Ave.
Altoona, PA 16601-3493
(814)943-8151

SCORE Office (Lehigh Valley)
Rauch Bldg. 37
Lehigh University
621 Taylor St.
Bethlehem, PA 18015
(610)758-4496
Fax: (610)758-5205

SCORE Office (Butler County)
100 N. Main St.
PO Box 1082
Butler, PA 16003
(412)283-2222
Fax: (412)283-0224

SCORE Office (Harrisburg)
4211 Trindle Rd.
Camp Hill, PA 17011
(717)761-4304
Fax: (717)761-4315

SCORE Office (Cumberland Valley)
75 S. 2nd St.
Chambersburg, PA 17201
(717)264-2935

SCORE Office (Monroe County-Stroudsburg)
556 Main St.
East Stroudsburg, PA 18301
(717)421-4433

SCORE Office (Erie)
120 W. 9th St.
Erie, PA 16501
(814)871-5650
Fax: (814)871-7530

SCORE Office (Bucks County)
409 Hood Blvd.
Fairless Hills, PA 19030
(215)943-8850
Fax: (215)943-7404

SCORE Office (Hanover)
146 Broadway
Hanover, PA 17331
(717)637-6130
Fax: (717)637-9127

SCORE Office (Harrisburg)
100 Chestnut, Ste. 309
Harrisburg, PA 17101
(717)782-3874

SCORE Office (East Montgomery County)
Baederwood Shopping Center
1653 The Fairways, Ste. 204
Jenkintown, PA 19046
(215)885-3027

SCORE Office (Kittanning)
2 Butler Rd.
Kittanning, PA 16201
(412)543-1305
Fax: (412)543-6206

SCORE Office (Lancaster)
118 W. Chestnut St.
Lancaster, PA 17603
(717)397-3092

SCORE Office (Westmoreland County)
300 Fraser Purchase Rd.
Latrobe, PA 15650-2690
(412)539-7505
Fax: (412)539-1850

SCORE Office (Lebanon)
252 N. 8th St.
PO Box 899
Lebanon, PA 17042-0899
(717)273-3727
Fax: (717)273-7940

SCORE Office (Lewistown)
3 W. Monument Sq., Ste. 204
Lewistown, PA 17044
(717)248-6713
Fax: (717)248-6714

SCORE Office (Delaware County)
602 E. Baltimore Pike
Media, PA 19063
(610)565-3677
Fax: (610)565-1606

SCORE Office (Milton Area)
112 S. Front St
Milton, PA 17847

(717)742-7341
Fax: (717)792-2008

SCORE Office (Mon-Valley)
435 Donner Ave.
Monessen, PA 15062
(412)684-4277
Fax: (412)684-7688

SCORE Office (Monroeville)
William Penn Plaza
2790 Mosside Blvd., Ste. 295
Monroeville, PA 15146
(412)856-0622
Fax: (412)856-1030

SCORE Office (Airport Area)
986 Brodhead Rd.
Moon Township, PA 15108-2398
(412)264-6270
Fax: (412)264-1575

SCORE Office (Northeast)
8601 E. Roosevelt Blvd.
Philadelphia, PA 19152
(215)332-3400
Fax: (215)332-6050

SCORE Office (Philadelphia)
1315 Walnut St., Ste. 500
Philadelphia, PA 19107
(215)790-5050
Fax: (215)790-5057
E-mail: score46@bellatlantic.net
Website: http://www.pgweb.net/score46/

SCORE Office (Pittsburgh)
1000 Liberty Ave., Rm. 1122
Pittsburgh, PA 15222
(412)395-6560
Fax: (412)395-6562

SCORE Office (Tri-County)
801 N. Charlotte St.
Pottstown, PA 19464
(610)327-2673

SCORE Office (Reading)
601 Penn St.
Reading, PA 19601
(610)376-3497

SCORE Office (Scranton)
Oppenheim Bldg.
116 N. Washington Ave., Ste. 650
Scranton, PA 18503
(717)347-4611
Fax: (717)347-4611

SCORE Office (Central Pennsylvania)
200 Innovation Blvd., Ste. 242-B
State College, PA 16803

(814)234-9415
Fax: (814)238-9686
Website: http://countrystore.org/
business/score.htm

SCORE Office (Monroe-Stroudsburg)
556 Main St.
Stroudsburg, PA 18360
(717)421-4433

SCORE Office (Uniontown)
Federal Bldg.
Pittsburg St.
PO Box 2065 DTS
Uniontown, PA 15401
(412)437-4222
E-mail: uniontownscore@lcsys.net

SCORE Office (Warren County)
315 2nd Ave.
Warren, PA 16365
(814)723-9017

SCORE Office (Waynesboro)
323 E. Main St.
Waynesboro, PA 17268
(717)762-7123
Fax: (717)962-7124

SCORE Office (Chester County)
Government Service Center, Ste. 281
601 Westtown Rd.
West Chester, PA 19382-4538
(610)344-6910
Fax: (610)344-6919
E-mail: score@locke.ccil.org

SCORE Office (Wilkes-Barre)
7 N. Wilkes-Barre Blvd.
Wilkes Barre, PA 18702-5241
(717)826-6502
Fax: (717)826-6287

SCORE Office (North Central Pennsylvania)
240 W. 3rd St., Rm. 227
PO Box 725
Williamsport, PA 17703
(717)322-3720
Fax: (717)322-1607
E-mail: score234@mail.csrlink.net
Website: http://www.lycoming.org/
score/

SCORE Office (York)
Cyber Center
2101 Pennsylvania Ave.
York, PA 17404
(717)845-8830
Fax: (717)854-9333

Puerto Rico

SCORE Office (Puerto Rico & Virgin Islands)
PO Box 12383-96
San Juan, PR 00914-0383
(787)726-8040
Fax: (787)726-8135

Rhode Island

SCORE Office (Barrington)
281 County Rd.
Barrington, RI 02806
(401)247-1920
Fax: (401)247-3763

SCORE Office (Woonsocket)
640 Washington Hwy.
Lincoln, RI 02865
(401)334-1000
Fax: (401)334-1009

SCORE Office (Wickford)
8045 Post Rd.
North Kingstown, RI 02852
(401)295-5566
Fax: (401)295-8987

SCORE Office (J.G.E. Knight)
380 Westminster St.
Providence, RI 02903
(401)528-4571
Fax: (401)528-4539
Website: http://www.riscore.org

SCORE Office (Warwick)
3288 Post Rd.
Warwick, RI 02886
(401)732-1100
Fax: (401)732-1101

SCORE Office (Westerly)
74 Post Rd.
Westerly, RI 02891
(401)596-7761
800-732-7636
Fax: (401)596-2190

South Carolina

SCORE Office (Aiken)
PO Box 892
Aiken, SC 29802
(803)641-1111
800-542-4536
Fax: (803)641-4174

SCORE Office (Anderson)
Anderson Mall
3130 N. Main St.

Anderson, SC 29621
(864)224-0453

SCORE Office (Coastal)
284 King St.
Charleston, SC 29401
(803)727-4778
Fax: (803)853-2529

SCORE Office (Midlands)
Strom Thurmond Bldg., Rm. 358
1835 Assembly St., Rm 358
Columbia, SC 29201
(803)765-5131
Fax: (803)765-5962
Website: http://www.scoremid
lands.org/

SCORE Office (Piedmont)
Federal Bldg., Rm. B-02
300 E. Washington St.
Greenville, SC 29601
(864)271-3638

SCORE Office (Greenwood)
PO Drawer 1467
Greenwood, SC 29648
(864)223-8357

SCORE Office (Hilton Head Island)
52 Savannah Trail
Hilton Head, SC 29926
(803)785-7107
Fax: (803)785-7110

SCORE Office (Grand Strand)
937 Broadway
Myrtle Beach, SC 29577
(803)918-1079
Fax: (803)918-1083
E-mail: score381@aol.com

SCORE Office (Spartanburg)
PO Box 1636
Spartanburg, SC 29304
(864)594-5000
Fax: (864)594-5055

South Dakota

SCORE Office (West River)
Rushmore Plz. Civic Ctr.
444 Mount Rushmore Rd., No. 209
Rapid City, SD 57701
(605)394-5311
E-mail: score@gwtc.net

SCORE Office (Sioux Falls)
First Financial Center
110 S. Phillips Ave., Ste. 200
Sioux Falls, SD 57104-6727

(605)330-4231
Fax: (605)330-4231

Tennessee

SCORE Office (Chattanooga)
Federal Bldg., Rm. 26
900 Georgia Ave.
Chattanooga, TN 37402
(423)752-5190
Fax: (423)752-5335

SCORE Office (Cleveland)
PO Box 2275
Cleveland, TN 37320
(423)472-6587
Fax: (423)472-2019

SCORE Office (Upper Cumberland Center)
1225 S. Willow Ave.
Cookeville, TN 38501
(615)432-4111
Fax: (615)432-6010

SCORE Office (Unicoi County)
PO Box 713
Erwin, TN 37650
(423)743-3000
Fax: (423)743-0942

SCORE Office (Greeneville)
115 Academy St.
Greeneville, TN 37743
(423)638-4111
Fax: (423)638-5345

SCORE Office (Jackson)
194 Auditorium St.
Jackson, TN 38301
(901)423-2200

SCORE Office (Northeast Tennessee)
1st Tennessee Bank Bldg.
2710 S. Roan St., Ste. 584
Johnson City, TN 37601
(423)929-7686
Fax: (423)461-8052

SCORE Office (Kingsport)
151 E. Main St.
Kingsport, TN 37662
(423)392-8805

SCORE Office (Greater Knoxville)
Farragot Bldg., Ste. 224
530 S. Gay St.
Knoxville, TN 37902
(423)545-4203
E-mail: scoreknox@ntown.com
Website: http://www.scoreknox.org/

SCORE Office (Maryville)
201 S. Washington St.
Maryville, TN 37804-5728
(423)983-2241
800-525-6834
Fax: (423)984-1386

SCORE Office (Memphis)
Federal Bldg., Ste. 390
167 N. Main St.
Memphis, TN 38103
(901)544-3588

SCORE Office (Nashville)
50 Vantage Way, Ste. 201
Nashville, TN 37228-1500
(615)736-7621

Texas

SCORE Office (Abilene)
2106 Federal Post Office and Court Bldg.
Abilene, TX 79601
(915)677-1857

SCORE Office (Austin)
2501 S. Congress
Austin, TX 78701
(512)442-7235
Fax: (512)442-7528

SCORE Office (Golden Triangle)
450 Boyd St.
Beaumont, TX 77704
(409)838-6581
Fax: (409)833-6718

SCORE Office (Brownsville)
3505 Boca Chica Blvd., Ste. 305
Brownsville, TX 78521
(210)541-4508

SCORE Office (Brazos Valley)
3000 Briarcrest, Ste. 302
Bryan, TX 77802
(409)776-8876
E-mail: 102633.2612@compuserve.com

SCORE Office (Cleburne)
Watergarden Pl., 9th Fl., Ste. 400
Cleburne, TX 76031
(817)871-6002

SCORE Office (Corpus Christi)
651 Upper North Broadway, Ste. 654
Corpus Christi, TX 78477
(512)888-4322
Fax: (512)888-3418

SCORE Office (Dallas)
6260 E. Mockingbird
Dallas, TX 75214-2619

(214)828-2471
Fax: (214)821-8033

SCORE Office (El Paso)
10 Civic Center Plaza
El Paso, TX 79901
(915)534-0541
Fax: (915)534-0513

SCORE Office (Bedford)
100 E. 15th St., Ste. 400
Ft. Worth, TX 76102
(817)871-6002

SCORE Office (Ft. Worth)
100 E. 15th St., No. 24
Ft. Worth, TX 76102
(817)871-6002
Fax: (817)871-6031
E-mail: fwbac@onramp.net

SCORE Office (Garland)
2734 W. Kingsley Rd.
Garland, TX 75041
(214)271-9224

SCORE Office (Granbury Chamber of Commerce)
416 S. Morgan
Granbury, TX 76048
(817)573-1622
Fax: (817)573-0805

SCORE Office (Lower Rio Grande Valley)
222 E. Van Buren, Ste. 500
Harlingen, TX 78550
(956)427-8533
Fax: (956)427-8537

SCORE Office (Houston)
9301 Southwest Fwy., Ste. 550
Houston, TX 77074
(713)773-6565
Fax: (713)773-6550

SCORE Office (Irving)
3333 N. MacArthur Blvd., Ste. 100
Irving, TX 75062
(214)252-8484
Fax: (214)252-6710

SCORE Office (Lubbock)
1205 Texas Ave., Rm. 411D
Lubbock, TX 79401
(806)472-7462
Fax: (806)472-7487

SCORE Office (Midland)
Post Office Annex
200 E. Wall St., Rm. P121
Midland, TX 79701
(915)687-2649

SCORE Office (Orange)
1012 Green Ave.
Orange, TX 77630-5620
(409)883-3536
800-528-4906
Fax: (409)886-3247

SCORE Office (Plano)
1200 E. 15th St.
PO Drawer 940287
Plano, TX 75094-0287
(214)424-7547
Fax: (214)422-5182

SCORE Office (Port Arthur)
4749 Twin City Hwy., Ste. 300
Port Arthur, TX 77642
(409)963-1107
Fax: (409)963-3322

SCORE Office (Richardson)
411 Belle Grove
Richardson, TX 75080
(214)234-4141
800-777-8001
Fax: (214)680-9103

SCORE Office (San Antonio)
Federal Bldg., Rm. A527
727 E. Durango
San Antonio, TX 78206
(210)472-5931
Fax: (210)472-5935

SCORE Office (Texarkana State College)
819 State Line Ave.
Texarkana, TX 75501
(903)792-7191
Fax: (903)793-4304

SCORE Office (East Texas)
RTDC
1530 SSW Loop 323, Ste. 100
Tyler, TX 75701
(903)510-2975
Fax: (903)510-2978

SCORE Office (Waco)
401 Franklin Ave.
Waco, TX 76701
(817)754-8898
Fax: (817)756-0776
Website: http://www.brc-waco.com/

SCORE Office (Wichita Falls)
Hamilton Bldg.
900 8th St.
Wichita Falls, TX 76307
(940)723-2741
Fax: (940)723-8773

Utah

SCORE Office (Northern Utah)
160 N. Main
Logan, UT 84321
(435)746-2269

SCORE Office (Ogden)
1701 E. Windsor Dr.
Ogden, UT 84604
(801)629-8613
E-mail: score158@netscape.net

SCORE Office (Central Utah)
1071 E. Windsor Dr.
Provo, UT 84604
(801)373-8660

SCORE Office (Southern Utah)
225 South 700 East
St. George, UT 84770
(435)652-7751

SCORE Office (Salt Lake)
310 S Main St.
Salt Lake City, UT 84101
(801)746-2269
Fax: (801)746-2273

Vermont

SCORE Office (Champlain Valley)
Winston Prouty Federal Bldg.
11 Lincoln St., Rm. 106
Essex Junction, VT 05452
(802)951-6762

SCORE Office (Montpelier)
87 State St., Rm. 205
PO Box 605
Montpelier, VT 05601
(802)828-4422
Fax: (802)828-4485

SCORE Office (Marble Valley)
256 N. Main St.
Rutland, VT 05701-2413
(802)773-9147

SCORE Office (Northeast Kingdom)
20 Main St.
PO Box 904
St. Johnsbury, VT 05819
(802)748-5101

Virgin Islands

SCORE Office (St. Croix)
United Plaza Shopping Center
PO Box 4010, Christiansted
St. Croix, VI 00822
(809)778-5380

SCORE Office (St. Thomas-St. John)
Federal Bldg., Rm. 21
Veterans Dr.
St. Thomas, VI 00801
(809)774-8530

Virginia

SCORE Office (Arlington)
2009 N. 14th St., Ste. 111
Arlington, VA 22201
(703)525-2400

SCORE Office (Blacksburg)
141 Jackson St.
Blacksburg, VA 24060
(540)552-4061

SCORE Office (Bristol)
20 Volunteer Pkwy.
Bristol, VA 24203
(540)989-4850

SCORE Office (Central Virginia)
1001 E. Market St., Ste. 101
Charlottesville, VA 22902
(804)295-6712
Fax: (804)295-7066

SCORE Office (Alleghany Satellite)
241 W. Main St.
Covington, VA 24426
(540)962-2178
Fax: (540)962-2179

SCORE Office (Central Fairfax)
3975 University Dr., Ste. 350
Fairfax, VA 22030
(703)591-2450

SCORE Office (Falls Church)
PO Box 491
Falls Church, VA 22040
(703)532-1050
Fax: (703)237-7904

SCORE Office (Glenns)
Glenns Campus
Box 287
Glenns, VA 23149
(804)693-9650

SCORE Office (Peninsula)
6 Manhattan Sq.
PO Box 7269
Hampton, VA 23666
(757)766-2000
Fax: (757)865-0339
E-mail: score100@seva.net

SCORE Office (Tri-Cities)
108 N. Main St.

Hopewell, VA 23860
(804)458-5536

SCORE Office (Lynchburg)
Federal Bldg.
1100 Main St.
Lynchburg, VA 24504-1714
(804)846-3235

SCORE Office (Greater Prince William)
8963 Center St
Manassas, VA 20110
(703)368-4813
Fax: (703)368-4733

SCORE Office (Martinsvile)
115 Broad St.
Martinsville, VA 24112-0709
(540)632-6401
Fax: (540)632-5059

SCORE Office (Hampton Roads)
Federal Bldg., Rm. 737
200 Grandby St.
Norfolk, VA 23510
(757)441-3733
Fax: (757)441-3733
E-mail: scorehr60@juno.com

SCORE Office (Norfolk)
Federal Bldg., Rm. 737
200 Granby St.
Norfolk, VA 23510
(757)441-3733
Fax: (757)441-3733

SCORE Office (Virginia Beach)
Chamber of Commerce
200 Grandby St., Rm 737
Norfolk, VA 23510
(804)441-3733

SCORE Office (Radford)
1126 Norwood St.
Radford, VA 24141
(540)639-2202

SCORE Office (Richmond)
Federal Bldg.
400 N. 8th St., Ste. 1150
PO Box 10126
Richmond, VA 23240-0126
(804)771-2400
Fax: (804)771-8018
E-mail: scorechapter12@yahoo.com
Website: http://www.cvco.org/score/

SCORE Office (Roanoke)
Federal Bldg., Rm. 716
250 Franklin Rd.
Roanoke, VA 24011

(540)857-2834
Fax: (540)857-2043
E-mail: scorerva@juno.com
Website: http://hometown.aol.com/
scorerv/Index.html

SCORE Office (Fairfax)
8391 Old Courthouse Rd., Ste. 300
Vienna, VA 22182
(703)749-0400

SCORE Office (Greater Vienna)
513 Maple Ave. West
Vienna, VA 22180
(703)281-1333
Fax: (703)242-1482

SCORE Office (Shenandoah Valley)
301 W. Main St.
Waynesboro, VA 22980
(540)949-8203
Fax: (540)949-7740
E-mail: score427@intelos.net

SCORE Office (Williamsburg)
201 Penniman Rd.
Williamsburg, VA 23185
(757)229-6511
E-mail: wacc@williamsburgcc.com

SCORE Office (Northern Virginia)
1360 S. Pleasant Valley Rd.
Winchester, VA 22601
(540)662-4118

Washington

SCORE Office (Gray's Harbor)
506 Duffy St.
Aberdeen, WA 98520
(360)532-1924
Fax: (360)533-7945

SCORE Office (Bellingham)
101 E. Holly St.
Bellingham, WA 98225
(360)676-3307

SCORE Office (Everett)
2702 Hoyt Ave.
Everett, WA 98201-3556
(206)259-8000

SCORE Office (Gig Harbor)
3125 Judson St.
Gig Harbor, WA 98335
(206)851-6865

SCORE Office (Kennewick)
PO Box 6986
Kennewick, WA 99336
(509)736-0510

SCORE Office (Puyallup)
322 2nd St. SW
PO Box 1298
Puyallup, WA 98371
(206)845-6755
Fax: (206)848-6164

SCORE Office (Seattle)
1200 6th Ave., Ste. 1700
Seattle, WA 98101
(206)553-7320
Fax: (206)553-7044
E-mail: score55@aol.com
Website: http://www.scn.org/civic/score-online/index55.html

SCORE Office (Spokane)
801 W. Riverside Ave., No. 240
Spokane, WA 99201
(509)353-2820
Fax: (509)353-2600
E-mail: score@dmi.net
Website: http://www.dmi.net/score/

SCORE Office (Clover Park)
PO Box 1933
Tacoma, WA 98401-1933
(206)627-2175

SCORE Office (Tacoma)
1101 Pacific Ave.
Tacoma, WA 98402
(253)274-1288
Fax: (253)274-1289

SCORE Office (Fort Vancouver)
1701 Broadway, S-1
Vancouver, WA 98663
(360)699-1079

SCORE Office (Walla Walla)
500 Tausick Way
Walla Walla, WA 99362
(509)527-4681

SCORE Office (Mid-Columbia)
1113 S. 14th Ave.
Yakima, WA 98907
(509)574-4944
Fax: (509)574-2943
Website: http://www.ellensburg.com/
~score/

West Virginia

SCORE Office (Charleston)
1116 Smith St.
Charleston, WV 25301
(304)347-5463
E-mail: score256@juno.com

SCORE Office (Virginia Street)
1116 Smith St., Ste. 302
Charleston, WV 25301
(304)347-5463

SCORE Office (Marion County)
PO Box 208
Fairmont, WV 26555-0208
(304)363-0486

SCORE Office (Upper Monongahela Valley)
1000 Technology Dr., Ste. 1111
Fairmont, WV 26555
(304)363-0486
E-mail: score537@hotmail.com

SCORE Office (Huntington)
1101 6th Ave., Ste. 220
Huntington, WV 25701-2309
(304)523-4092

SCORE Office (Wheeling)
1310 Market St.
Wheeling, WV 26003
(304)233-2575
Fax: (304)233-1320

Wisconsin

SCORE Office (Fox Cities)
227 S. Walnut St.
Appleton, WI 54913
(920)734-7101
Fax: (920)734-7161

SCORE Office (Beloit)
136 W. Grand Ave., Ste. 100
PO Box 717
Beloit, WI 53511
(608)365-8835
Fax: (608)365-9170

SCORE Office (Eau Claire)
Federal Bldg., Rm. B11
510 S. Barstow St.
Eau Claire, WI 54701
(715)834-1573
E-mail: score@ecol.net
Website: http://www.ecol.net/~score/

SCORE Office (Fond du Lac)
207 N. Main St.
Fond du Lac, WI 54935
(414)921-9500
Fax: (414)921-9559

SCORE Office (Green Bay)
835 Potts Ave.
Green Bay, WI 54304
(414)496-8930
Fax: (414)496-6009

SCORE Office (Janesville)
20 S. Main St., Ste. 11
PO Box 8008
Janesville, WI 53547
(608)757-3160
Fax: (608)757-3170

SCORE Office (La Crosse)
712 Main St.
La Crosse, WI 54602-0219
(608)784-4880

SCORE Office (Madison)
505 S. Rosa Rd.
Madison, WI 53719
(608)441-2820

SCORE Office (Manitowoc)
1515 Memorial Dr.
PO Box 903
Manitowoc, WI 54221-0903
(414)684-5575
Fax: (414)684-1915

SCORE Office (Milwaukee)
310 W. Wisconsin Ave., Ste. 425
Milwaukee, WI 53203
(414)297-3942
Fax: (414)297-1377

SCORE Office (Central Wisconsin)
1224 Lindbergh Ave.
Stevens Point, WI 54481
(715)344-7729

SCORE Office (Superior)
Superior Business Center Inc.
1423 N. 8th St.
Superior, WI 54880
(715)394-7388
Fax: (715)393-7414

SCORE Office (Waukesha)
223 Wisconsin Ave.
Waukesha, WI 53186-4926
(414)542-4249

SCORE Office (Wausau)
300 3rd St., Ste. 200
Wausau, WI 54402-6190
(715)845-6231

SCORE Office (Wisconsin Rapids)
2240 Kingston Rd.
Wisconsin Rapids, WI 54494
(715)423-1830

Wyoming

SCORE Office (Casper)
Federal Bldg., No. 2215
100 East B St.

Casper, WY 82602
(307)261-6529
Fax: (307)261-6530

Venture capital & financing companies

This section contains a listing of financing and loan companies in the United States and Canada. These listing are arranged alphabetically by country, then by state or province, then by city, then by organization name.

Canada

Alberta

Launchworks Inc.
1902J 11th St., S.E.
Calgary, AB, Canada T2G 3G2
(403)269-1119
Fax: (403)269-1141
Website: http://www.launchworks.com

Native Venture Capital Company, Inc.
21 Artist View Point, Box 7
Site 25, RR 12
Calgary, AB, Canada T3E 6W3
(903)208-5380

Miralta Capital Inc.
4445 Calgary Trail South
888 Terrace Plaza Alberta
Edmonton, AB, Canada T6H 5R7
(780)438-3535
Fax: (780)438-3129

Vencap Equities Alberta Ltd.
10180-101st St., Ste. 1980
Edmonton, AB, Canada T5J 3S4
(403)420-1171
Fax: (403)429-2541

British Columbia

Discovery Capital
5th Fl., 1199 West Hastings
Vancouver, BC, Canada V6E 3T5
(604)683-3000
Fax: (604)662-3457
E-mail: info@discoverycapital.com
Website: http://www.discoverycapital.com

Greenstone Venture Partners
1177 West Hastings St.
Ste. 400
Vancouver, BC, Canada V6E 2K3
(604)717-1977
Fax: (604)717-1976
Website: http://www.greenstonevc.com

Growthworks Capital
2600-1055 West Georgia St.
Box 11170 Royal Centre
Vancouver, BC, Canada V6E 3R5
(604)895-7259
Fax: (604)669-7605
Website: http://www.wofund.com

MDS Discovery Venture Management, Inc.
555 W. Eighth Ave., Ste. 305
Vancouver, BC, Canada V5Z 1C6
(604)872-8464
Fax: (604)872-2977
E-mail: info@mds-ventures.com

Ventures West Management Inc.
1285 W. Pender St., Ste. 280
Vancouver, BC, Canada V6E 4B1
(604)688-9495
Fax: (604)687-2145
Website: http://www.ventureswest.com

Nova Scotia

ACF Equity Atlantic Inc.
Purdy's Wharf Tower II
Ste. 2106
Halifax, NS, Canada B3J 3R7
(902)421-1965
Fax: (902)421-1808

Montgomerie, Huck & Co.
146 Bluenose Dr.
PO Box 538
Lunenburg, NS, Canada B0J 2C0
(902)634-7125
Fax: (902)634-7130

Ontario

IPS Industrial Promotion Services Ltd.
60 Columbia Way, Ste. 720
Markham, ON, Canada L3R 0C9
(905)475-9400
Fax: (905)475-5003

Betwin Investments Inc.
Box 23110
Sault Ste. Marie, ON, Canada P6A 6W6
(705)253-0744
Fax: (705)253-0744

Bailey & Company, Inc.
594 Spadina Ave.
Toronto, ON, Canada M5S 2H4
(416)921-6930
Fax: (416)925-4670

BCE Capital
200 Bay St.

South Tower, Ste. 3120
Toronto, ON, Canada M5J 2J2
(416)815-0078
Fax: (416)941-1073
Website: http://www.bcecapital.com

Castlehill Ventures
55 University Ave., Ste. 500
Toronto, ON, Canada M5J 2H7
(416)862-8574
Fax: (416)862-8875

CCFL Mezzanine Partners of Canada
70 University Ave.
Ste. 1450
Toronto, ON, Canada M5J 2M4
(416)977-1450
Fax: (416)977-6764
E-mail: info@ccfl.com
Website: http://www.ccfl.com

Celtic House International
100 Simcoe St., Ste. 100
Toronto, ON, Canada M5H 3G2
(416)542-2436
Fax: (416)542-2435
Website: http://www.celtic-house.com

Clairvest Group Inc.
22 St. Clair Ave. East
Ste. 1700
Toronto, ON, Canada M4T 2S3
(416)925-9270
Fax: (416)925-5753

Crosbie & Co., Inc.
One First Canadian Place
9th Fl.
PO Box 116
Toronto, ON, Canada M5X 1A4
(416)362-7726
Fax: (416)362-3447
E-mail: info@crosbieco.com
Website: http://www.crosbieco.com

Drug Royalty Corp.
Eight King St. East
Ste. 202
Toronto, ON, Canada M5C 1B5
(416)863-1865
Fax: (416)863-5161

Grieve, Horner, Brown & Asculai
8 King St. E, Ste. 1704
Toronto, ON, Canada M5C 1B5
(416)362-7668
Fax: (416)362-7660

Jefferson Partners
77 King St. West
Ste. 4010

PO Box 136
Toronto, ON, Canada M5K 1H1
(416)367-1533
Fax: (416)367-5827
Website: http://www.jefferson.com

J.L. Albright Venture Partners
Canada Trust Tower, 161 Bay St.
Ste. 4440
PO Box 215
Toronto, ON, Canada M5J 2S1
(416)367-2440
Fax: (416)367-4604
Website: http://www.jlaventures.com

McLean Watson Capital Inc.
One First Canadian Place
Ste. 1410
PO Box 129
Toronto, ON, Canada M5X 1A4
(416)363-2000
Fax: (416)363-2010
Website: http://www.mcleanwatson.com

Middlefield Capital Fund
One First Canadian Place
85th Fl.
PO Box 192
Toronto, ON, Canada M5X 1A6
(416)362-0714
Fax: (416)362-7925
Website: http://www.middlefield.com

Mosaic Venture Partners
24 Duncan St.
Ste. 300
Toronto, ON, Canada M5V 3M6
(416)597-8889
Fax: (416)597-2345

Onex Corp.
161 Bay St.
PO Box 700
Toronto, ON, Canada M5J 2S1
(416)362-7711
Fax: (416)362-5765

Penfund Partners Inc.
145 King St. West
Ste. 1920
Toronto, ON, Canada M5H 1J8
(416)865-0300
Fax: (416)364-6912
Website: http://www.penfund.com

Primaxis Technology Ventures Inc.
1 Richmond St. West, 8th Fl.
Toronto, ON, Canada M5H 3W4
(416)313-5210
Fax: (416)313-5218
Website: http://www.primaxis.com

Priveq Capital Funds
240 Duncan Mill Rd., Ste. 602
Toronto, ON, Canada M3B 3P1
(416)447-3330
Fax: (416)447-3331
E-mail: priveq@sympatico.ca

Roynat Ventures
40 King St. West, 26th Fl.
Toronto, ON, Canada M5H 1H1
(416)933-2667
Fax: (416)933-2783
Website: http://www.roynatcapital.com

Tera Capital Corp.
366 Adelaide St. East, Ste. 337
Toronto, ON, Canada M5A 3X9
(416)368-1024
Fax: (416)368-1427

Working Ventures Canadian Fund Inc.
250 Bloor St. East, Ste. 1600
Toronto, ON, Canada M4W 1E6
(416)934-7718
Fax: (416)929-0901
Website: http://www.workingventures.ca

Quebec

Altamira Capital Corp.
202 University
Niveau de Maisoneuve, Bur. 201
Montreal, QC, Canada H3A 2A5
(514)499-1656
Fax: (514)499-9570

Federal Business Development Bank
Venture Capital Division
Five Place Ville Marie, Ste. 600
Montreal, QC, Canada H3B 5E7
(514)283-1896
Fax: (514)283-5455

Hydro-Quebec Capitech Inc.
75 Boul, Rene Levesque Quest
Montreal, QC, Canada H2Z 1A4
(514)289-4783
Fax: (514)289-5420
Website: http://www.hqcapitech.com

Investissement Desjardins
2 complexe Desjardins
C.P. 760
Montreal, QC, Canada H5B 1B8
(514)281-7131
Fax: (514)281-7808
Website: http://www.desjardins.com/id

Marleau Lemire Inc.
One Place Ville-Marie, Ste. 3601
Montreal, QC, Canada H3B 3P2

(514)877-3800
Fax: (514)875-6415

Speirs Consultants Inc.
365 Stanstead
Montreal, QC, Canada H3R 1X5
(514)342-3858
Fax: (514)342-1977

Tecnocap Inc.
4028 Marlowe
Montreal, QC, Canada H4A 3M2
(514)483-6009
Fax: (514)483-6045
Website: http://www.technocap.com

Telsoft Ventures
1000, Rue de la Gauchetiere
Quest, 25eme Etage
Montreal, QC, Canada H3B 4W5
(514)397-8450
Fax: (514)397-8451

Saskatchewan

Saskatchewan Government Growth Fund
1801 Hamilton St., Ste. 1210
Canada Trust Tower
Regina, SK, Canada S4P 4B4
(306)787-2994
Fax: (306)787-2086

United states

Alabama

FHL Capital Corp.
600 20th Street North
Suite 350
Birmingham, AL 35203
(205)328-3098
Fax: (205)323-0001

Harbert Management Corp.
One Riverchase Pkwy. South
Birmingham, AL 35244
(205)987-5500
Fax: (205)987-5707
Website: http://www.harbert.net

Jefferson Capital Fund
PO Box 13129
Birmingham, AL 35213
(205)324-7709

Private Capital Corp.
100 Brookwood Pl., 4th Fl.
Birmingham, AL 35209
(205)879-2722
Fax: (205)879-5121

21st Century Health Ventures
One Health South Pkwy.
Birmingham, AL 35243
(256)268-6250
Fax: (256)970-8928

FJC Growth Capital Corp.
200 W. Side Sq., Ste. 340
Huntsville, AL 35801
(256)922-2918
Fax: (256)922-2909

Hickory Venture Capital Corp.
301 Washington St. NW
Suite 301
Huntsville, AL 35801
(256)539-1931
Fax: (256)539-5130
E-mail: hvcc@hvcc.com
Website: http://www.hvcc.com

Southeastern Technology Fund
7910 South Memorial Pkwy., Ste. F
Huntsville, AL 35802
(256)883-8711
Fax: (256)883-8558

Cordova Ventures
4121 Carmichael Rd., Ste. 301
Montgomery, AL 36106
(334)271-6011
Fax: (334)260-0120
Website: http://www.cordova
ventures.com

**Small Business Clinic of Alabama/AG
Bartholomew & Associates**
PO Box 231074
Montgomery, AL 36123-1074
(334)284-3640

Arizona

Miller Capital Corp.
4909 E. McDowell Rd.
Phoenix, AZ 85008
(602)225-0504
Fax: (602)225-9024
Website: http://www.themiller
group.com

The Columbine Venture Funds
9449 North 90th St., Ste. 200
Scottsdale, AZ 85258
(602)661-9222
Fax: (602)661-6262

Koch Ventures
17767 N. Perimeter Dr., Ste. 101
Scottsdale, AZ 85255
(480)419-3600

Fax: (480)419-3606

Website: http://www.kochventures.com

McKee & Co.

7702 E. Doubletree Ranch Rd.

Suite 230

Scottsdale, AZ 85258

(480)368-0333

Fax: (480)607-7446

Merita Capital Ltd.

7350 E. Stetson Dr., Ste. 108-A

Scottsdale, AZ 85251

(480)947-8700

Fax: (480)947-8766

Valley Ventures / Arizona Growth Partners L.P.

6720 N. Scottsdale Rd., Ste. 208

Scottsdale, AZ 85253

(480)661-6600

Fax: (480)661-6262

Estreetcapital.com

660 South Mill Ave., Ste. 315

Tempe, AZ 85281

(480)968-8400

Fax: (480)968-8480

Website: http://www.estreetcapital.com

Coronado Venture Fund

PO Box 65420

Tucson, AZ 85728-5420

(520)577-3764

Fax: (520)299-8491

Arkansas

Arkansas Capital Corp.

225 South Pulaski St.

Little Rock, AR 72201

(501)374-9247

Fax: (501)374-9425

Website: http://www.arcapital.com

California

Sundance Venture Partners, L.P.

100 Clocktower Place, Ste. 130

Carmel, CA 93923

(831)625-6500

Fax: (831)625-6590

Westar Capital (Costa Mesa)

949 South Coast Dr., Ste. 650

Costa Mesa, CA 92626

(714)481-5160

Fax: (714)481-5166

E-mail: mailbox@westarcapital.com

Website: http://www.westarcapital.com

Alpine Technology Ventures

20300 Stevens Creek Boulevard, Ste. 495

Cupertino, CA 95014

(408)725-1810

Fax: (408)725-1207

Website: http://www.alpineventures.com

Bay Partners

10600 N. De Anza Blvd.

Cupertino, CA 95014-2031

(408)725-2444

Fax: (408)446-4502

Website: http://www.baypartners.com

Novus Ventures

20111 Stevens Creek Blvd., Ste. 130

Cupertino, CA 95014

(408)252-3900

Fax: (408)252-1713

Website: http://www.novusventures.com

Triune Capital

19925 Stevens Creek Blvd., Ste. 200

Cupertino, CA 95014

(310)284-6800

Fax: (310)284-3290

Acorn Ventures

268 Bush St., Ste. 2829

Daly City, CA 94014

(650)994-7801

Fax: (650)994-3305

Website: http://www.acornventures.com

Digital Media Campus

2221 Park Place

El Segundo, CA 90245

(310)426-8000

Fax: (310)426-8010

E-mail: info@thecampus.com

Website: http://www.digital
mediacampus.com

BankAmerica Ventures / BA Venture Partners

950 Tower Ln., Ste. 700

Foster City, CA 94404

(650)378-6000

Fax: (650)378-6040

Website: http://
www.baventurepartners.com

Starting Point Partners

666 Portofino Lane

Foster City, CA 94404

(650)722-1035

Website: http://www.startingpoint
partners.com

Opportunity Capital Partners

2201 Walnut Ave., Ste. 210

Fremont, CA 94538

(510)795-7000

Fax: (510)494-5439

Website: http://www.ocpcapital.com

Imperial Ventures Inc.

9920 S. La Cienega Boulevar, 14th Fl.

Inglewood, CA 90301

(310)417-5409

Fax: (310)338-6115

Ventana Global (Irvine)

18881 Von Karman Ave., Ste. 1150

Irvine, CA 92612

(949)476-2204

Fax: (949)752-0223

Website: http://www.ventanaglobal.com

Integrated Consortium Inc.

50 Ridgecrest Rd.

Kentfield, CA 94904

(415)925-0386

Fax: (415)461-2726

Enterprise Partners

979 Ivanhoe Ave., Ste. 550

La Jolla, CA 92037

(858)454-8833

Fax: (858)454-2489

Website: http://www.epvc.com

Domain Associates

28202 Cabot Rd., Ste. 200

Laguna Niguel, CA 92677

(949)347-2446

Fax: (949)347-9720

Website: http://www.domainvc.com

Cascade Communications Ventures

60 E. Sir Francis Drake Blvd., Ste. 300

Larkspur, CA 94939

(415)925-6500

Fax: (415)925-6501

Allegis Capital

One First St., Ste. Two

Los Altos, CA 94022

(650)917-5900

Fax: (650)917-5901

Website: http://www.allegiscapital.com

Aspen Ventures

1000 Fremont Ave., Ste. 200

Los Altos, CA 94024

(650)917-5670

Fax: (650)917-5677

Website: http://www.aspenventures.com

AVI Capital L.P.

1 First St., Ste. 2

Los Altos, CA 94022

(650)949-9862
Fax: (650)949-8510
Website: http://www.avicapital.com

Bastion Capital Corp.
1999 Avenue of the Stars, Ste. 2960
Los Angeles, CA 90067
(310)788-5700
Fax: (310)277-7582
E-mail: ga@bastioncapital.com
Website: http://www.bastioncapital.com

Davis Group
PO Box 69953
Los Angeles, CA 90069-0953
(310)659-6327
Fax: (310)659-6337

Developers Equity Corp.
1880 Century Park East, Ste. 211
Los Angeles, CA 90067
(213)277-0300

Far East Capital Corp.
350 S. Grand Ave., Ste. 4100
Los Angeles, CA 90071
(213)687-1361
Fax: (213)617-7939
E-mail: free@fareastnationalbank.com

Kline Hawkes & Co.
11726 San Vicente Blvd., Ste. 300
Los Angeles, CA 90049
(310)442-4700
Fax: (310)442-4707
Website: http://www.klinehawkes.com

Lawrence Financial Group
701 Teakwood
PO Box 491773
Los Angeles, CA 90049
(310)471-4060
Fax: (310)472-3155

Riordan Lewis & Haden
300 S. Grand Ave., 29th Fl.
Los Angeles, CA 90071
(213)229-8500
Fax: (213)229-8597

Union Venture Corp.
445 S. Figueroa St., 9th Fl.
Los Angeles, CA 90071
(213)236-4092
Fax: (213)236-6329

Wedbush Capital Partners
1000 Wilshire Blvd.
Los Angeles, CA 90017
(213)688-4545
Fax: (213)688-6642
Website: http://www.wedbush.com

Advent International Corp.
2180 Sand Hill Rd., Ste. 420
Menlo Park, CA 94025
(650)233-7500
Fax: (650)233-7515
Website: http://www.adventinter
national.com

Altos Ventures
2882 Sand Hill Rd., Ste. 100
Menlo Park, CA 94025
(650)234-9771
Fax: (650)233-9821
Website: http://www.altosvc.com

Applied Technology
1010 El Camino Real, Ste. 300
Menlo Park, CA 94025
(415)326-8622
Fax: (415)326-8163

APV Technology Partners
535 Middlefield, Ste. 150
Menlo Park, CA 94025
(650)327-7871
Fax: (650)327-7631
Website: http://www.apvtp.com

August Capital Management
2480 Sand Hill Rd., Ste. 101
Menlo Park, CA 94025
(650)234-9900
Fax: (650)234-9910
Website: http://www.augustcap.com

Baccharis Capital Inc.
2420 Sand Hill Rd., Ste. 100
Menlo Park, CA 94025
(650)324-6844
Fax: (650)854-3025

Benchmark Capital
2480 Sand Hill Rd., Ste. 200
Menlo Park, CA 94025
(650)854-8180
Fax: (650)854-8183
E-mail: info@benchmark.com
Website: http://www.benchmark.com

Bessemer Venture Partners (Menlo Park)
535 Middlefield Rd., Ste. 245
Menlo Park, CA 94025
(650)853-7000
Fax: (650)853-7001
Website: http://www.bvp.com

The Cambria Group
1600 El Camino Real Rd., Ste. 155
Menlo Park, CA 94025
(650)329-8600

Fax: (650)329-8601
Website: http://www.cambriagroup.com

Canaan Partners
2884 Sand Hill Rd., Ste. 115
Menlo Park, CA 94025
(650)854-8092
Fax: (650)854-8127
Website: http://www.canaan.com

Capstone Ventures
3000 Sand Hill Rd., Bldg. One, Ste. 290
Menlo Park, CA 94025
(650)854-2523
Fax: (650)854-9010
Website: http://www.capstonevc.com

Comdisco Venture Group (Silicon Valley)
3000 Sand Hill Rd., Bldg. 1, Ste. 155
Menlo Park, CA 94025
(650)854-9484
Fax: (650)854-4026

Commtech International
535 Middlefield Rd., Ste. 200
Menlo Park, CA 94025
(650)328-0190
Fax: (650)328-6442

Compass Technology Partners
1550 El Camino Real, Ste. 275
Menlo Park, CA 94025-4111
(650)322-7595
Fax: (650)322-0588
Website: http://www.compass
techpartners.com

Convergence Partners
3000 Sand Hill Rd., Ste. 235
Menlo Park, CA 94025
(650)854-3010
Fax: (650)854-3015
Website: http://www.conver
gencepartners.com

The Dakota Group
PO Box 1025
Menlo Park, CA 94025
(650)853-0600
Fax: (650)851-4899
E-mail: info@dakota.com

Delphi Ventures
3000 Sand Hill Rd.
Bldg. One, Ste. 135
Menlo Park, CA 94025
(650)854-9650
Fax: (650)854-2961
Website: http://www.delphiventures.com

El Dorado Ventures
2884 Sand Hill Rd., Ste. 121
Menlo Park, CA 94025
(650)854-1200
Fax: (650)854-1202
Website: http://www.eldorado
ventures.com

Glynn Ventures
3000 Sand Hill Rd., Bldg. 4, Ste. 235
Menlo Park, CA 94025
(650)854-2215

Indosuez Ventures
2180 Sand Hill Rd., Ste. 450
Menlo Park, CA 94025
(650)854-0587
Fax: (650)323-5561
Website: http://www.indosuez
ventures.com

Institutional Venture Partners
3000 Sand Hill Rd., Bldg. 2, Ste. 290
Menlo Park, CA 94025
(650)854-0132
Fax: (650)854-5762
Website: http://www.ivp.com

Interwest Partners (Menlo Park)
3000 Sand Hill Rd., Bldg. 3, Ste. 255
Menlo Park, CA 94025-7112
(650)854-8585
Fax: (650)854-4706
Website: http://www.interwest.com

**Kleiner Perkins Caufield & Byers
(Menlo Park)**
2750 Sand Hill Rd.
Menlo Park, CA 94025
(650)233-2750
Fax: (650)233-0300
Website: http://www.kpcb.com

Magic Venture Capital LLC
1010 El Camino Real, Ste. 300
Menlo Park, CA 94025
(650)325-4149

Matrix Partners
2500 Sand Hill Rd., Ste. 113
Menlo Park, CA 94025
(650)854-3131
Fax: (650)854-3296
Website: http://www.matrixpartners.com

Mayfield Fund
2800 Sand Hill Rd.
Menlo Park, CA 94025
(650)854-5560
Fax: (650)854-5712
Website: http://www.mayfield.com

**McCown De Leeuw and Co. (Menlo
Park)**
3000 Sand Hill Rd., Bldg. 3, Ste. 290
Menlo Park, CA 94025-7111
(650)854-6000
Fax: (650)854-0853
Website: http://www.mdcpartners.com

Menlo Ventures
3000 Sand Hill Rd., Bldg. 4, Ste. 100
Menlo Park, CA 94025
(650)854-8540
Fax: (650)854-7059
Website: http://www.menloventures.com

Merrill Pickard Anderson & Eyre
2480 Sand Hill Rd., Ste. 200
Menlo Park, CA 94025
(650)854-8600
Fax: (650)854-0345

**New Enterprise Associates (Menlo
Park)**
2490 Sand Hill Rd.
Menlo Park, CA 94025
(650)854-9499
Fax: (650)854-9397
Website: http://www.nea.com

Onset Ventures
2400 Sand Hill Rd., Ste. 150
Menlo Park, CA 94025
(650)529-0700
Fax: (650)529-0777
Website: http://www.onset.com

Paragon Venture Partners
3000 Sand Hill Rd., Bldg. 1, Ste. 275
Menlo Park, CA 94025
(650)854-8000
Fax: (650)854-7260

**Pathfinder Venture Capital Funds
(Menlo Park)**
3000 Sand Hill Rd., Bldg. 3, Ste. 255
Menlo Park, CA 94025
(650)854-0650
Fax: (650)854-4706

Rocket Ventures
3000 Sandhill Rd., Bldg. 1, Ste. 170
Menlo Park, CA 94025
(650)561-9100
Fax: (650)561-9183
Website: http://www.rocketventures.com

Sequoia Capital
3000 Sand Hill Rd., Bldg. 4, Ste. 280
Menlo Park, CA 94025
(650)854 3927
Fax: (650)854-2977

E-mail: scquoia@sequoiacap.com
Website: http://www.sequoiacap.com

Sierra Ventures
3000 Sand Hill Rd., Bldg. 4, Ste. 210
Menlo Park, CA 94025
(650)854-1000
Fax: (650)854-5593
Website: http://www.sierraventures.com

Sigma Partners
2884 Sand Hill Rd., Ste. 121
Menlo Park, CA 94025-7022
(650)853-1700
Fax: (650)853-1717
E-mail: info@sigmapartners.com
Website: http://www.sigmapartners.com

Sprout Group (Menlo Park)
3000 Sand Hill Rd.
Bldg. 3, Ste. 170
Menlo Park, CA 94025
(650)234-2700
Fax: (650)234-2779
Website: http://www.sproutgroup.com

TA Associates (Menlo Park)
70 Willow Rd., Ste. 100
Menlo Park, CA 94025
(650)328-1210
Fax: (650)326-4933
Website: http://www.ta.com

Thompson Clive & Partners Ltd.
3000 Sand Hill Rd., Bldg. 1, Ste. 185
Menlo Park, CA 94025-7102
(650)854-0314
Fax: (650)854-0670
E-mail: mail@tcvc.com
Website: http://www.tcvc.com

Trinity Ventures Ltd.
3000 Sand Hill Rd., Bldg. 1, Ste. 240
Menlo Park, CA 94025
(650)854-9500
Fax: (650)854-9501
Website: http://www.trinityventures.com

U.S. Venture Partners
2180 Sand Hill Rd., Ste. 300
Menlo Park, CA 94025
(650)854-9080
Fax: (650)854-3018
Website: http://www.usvp.com

USVP-Schlein Marketing Fund
2180 Sand Hill Rd., Ste. 300
Menlo Park, CA 94025
(415)854-9080
Fax: (415)854-3018
Website: http://www.usvp.com

Venrock Associates
2494 Sand Hill Rd., Ste. 200
Menlo Park, CA 94025
(650)561-9580
Fax: (650)561-9180
Website: http://www.venrock.com

Brad Peery Capital Inc.
145 Chapel Pkwy.
Mill Valley, CA 94941
(415)389-0625
Fax: (415)389-1336

Dot Edu Ventures
650 Castro St., Ste. 270
Mountain View, CA 94041
(650)575-5638
Fax: (650)325-5247
Website: http://www.dotedu
ventures.com

Forrest, Binkley & Brown
840 Newport Ctr. Dr., Ste. 480
Newport Beach, CA 92660
(949)729-3222
Fax: (949)729-3226
Website: http://www.fbbvc.com

Marwit Capital LLC
180 Newport Center Dr., Ste. 200
Newport Beach, CA 92660
(949)640-6234
Fax: (949)720-8077
Website: http://www.marwit.com

Kaiser Permanente / National Venture Development
1800 Harrison St., 22nd Fl.
Oakland, CA 94612
(510)267-4010
Fax: (510)267-4036
Website: http://www.kpventures.com

Nu Capital Access Group, Ltd.
7677 Oakport St., Ste. 105
Oakland, CA 94621
(510)635-7345
Fax: (510)635-7068

Inman and Bowman
4 Orinda Way, Bldg. D, Ste. 150
Orinda, CA 94563
(510)253-1611
Fax: (510)253-9037

Accel Partners (San Francisco)
428 University Ave.
Palo Alto, CA 94301
(650)614-4800
Fax: (650)614-4880
Website: http://www.accel.com

Advanced Technology Ventures
485 Ramona St., Ste. 200
Palo Alto, CA 94301
(650)321-8601
Fax: (650)321-0934
Website: http://www.atvcapital.com

Anila Fund
400 Channing Ave.
Palo Alto, CA 94301
(650)833-5790
Fax: (650)833-0590
Website: http://www.anila.com

Asset Management Company Venture Capital
2275 E. Bayshore, Ste. 150
Palo Alto, CA 94303
(650)494-7400
Fax: (650)856-1826
E-mail: postmaster@assetman.com
Website: http://www.assetman.com

BancBoston Capital / BancBoston Ventures
435 Tasso St., Ste. 250
Palo Alto, CA 94305
(650)470-4100
Fax: (650)853-1425
Website: http://www.bancboston
capital.com

Charter Ventures
525 University Ave., Ste. 1400
Palo Alto, CA 94301
(650)325-6953
Fax: (650)325-4762
Website: http://www.charterventures.com

Communications Ventures
505 Hamilton Avenue, Ste. 305
Palo Alto, CA 94301
(650)325-9600
Fax: (650)325-9608
Website: http://www.comven.com

HMS Group
2468 Embarcadero Way
Palo Alto, CA 94303-3313
(650)856-9862
Fax: (650)856-9864

Jafco America Ventures, Inc.
505 Hamilton Ste. 310
Palto Alto, CA 94301
(650)463-8800
Fax: (650)463-8801
Website: http://www.jafco.com

New Vista Capital
540 Cowper St., Ste. 200

Palo Alto, CA 94301
(650)329-9333
Fax: (650)328-9434
E-mail: fgreene@nvcap.com
Website: http://www.nvcap.com

Norwest Equity Partners (Palo Alto)
245 Lytton Ave., Ste. 250
Palo Alto, CA 94301-1426
(650)321-8000
Fax: (650)321-8010
Website: http://www.norwestvp.com

Oak Investment Partners
525 University Ave., Ste. 1300
Palo Alto, CA 94301
(650)614-3700
Fax: (650)328-6345
Website: http://www.oakinv.com

Patricof & Co. Ventures, Inc. (Palo Alto)
2100 Geng Rd., Ste. 150
Palo Alto, CA 94303
(650)494-9944
Fax: (650)494-6751
Website: http://www.patricof.com

RWI Group
835 Page Mill Rd.
Palo Alto, CA 94304
(650)251-1800
Fax: (650)213-8660
Website: http://www.rwigroup.com

Summit Partners (Palo Alto)
499 Hamilton Ave., Ste. 200
Palo Alto, CA 94301
(650)321-1166
Fax: (650)321-1188
Website: http://www.summit
partners.com

Sutter Hill Ventures
755 Page Mill Rd., Ste. A-200
Palo Alto, CA 94304
(650)493-5600
Fax: (650)858-1854
E-mail: shv@shv.com

Vanguard Venture Partners
525 University Ave., Ste. 600
Palo Alto, CA 94301
(650)321-2900
Fax: (650)321-2902
Website: http://www.vanguard
ventures.com

Venture Growth Associates
2479 East Bayshore St., Ste. 710
Palo Alto, CA 94303

(650)855-9100
Fax: (650)855-9104

Worldview Technology Partners
435 Tasso St., Ste. 120
Palo Alto, CA 94301
(650)322-3800
Fax: (650)322-3880
Website: http://www.worldview.com

Draper, Fisher, Jurvetson / Draper Associates
400 Seaport Ct., Ste.250
Redwood City, CA 94063
(415)599-9000
Fax: (415)599-9726
Website: http://www.dfj.com

Gabriel Venture Partners
350 Marine Pkwy., Ste. 200
Redwood Shores, CA 94065
(650)551-5000
Fax: (650)551-5001
Website: http://www.gabrielvp.com

Hallador Venture Partners, L.L.C.
740 University Ave., Ste. 110
Sacramento, CA 95825-6710
(916)920-0191
Fax: (916)920-5188
E-mail: chris@hallador.com

Emerald Venture Group
12396 World Trade Dr., Ste. 116
San Diego, CA 92128
(858)451-1001
Fax: (858)451-1003
Website: http://www.emerald
venture.com

Forward Ventures
9255 Towne Centre Dr.
San Diego, CA 92121
(858)677-6077
Fax: (858)452-8799
E-mail: info@forwardventure.com
Website: http://www.forward
venture.com

Idanta Partners Ltd.
4660 La Jolla Village Dr., Ste. 850
San Diego, CA 92122
(619)452-9690
Fax: (619)452-2013
Website: http://www.idanta.com

Kingsbury Associates
3655 Nobel Dr., Ste. 490
San Diego, CA 92122
(858)677-0600
Fax: (858)677-0800

Kyocera International Inc.
Corporate Development
8611 Balboa Ave.
San Diego, CA 92123
(858)576-2600
Fax: (858)492-1456

Sorrento Associates, Inc.
4370 LaJolla Village Dr., Ste. 1040
San Diego, CA 92122
(619)452-3100
Fax: (619)452-7607
Website: http://www.sorrento
ventures.com

Western States Investment Group
9191 Towne Ctr. Dr., Ste. 310
San Diego, CA 92122
(619)678-0800
Fax: (619)678-0900

Aberdare Ventures
One Embarcadero Center, Ste. 4000
San Francisco, CA 94111
(415)392-7442
Fax: (415)392-4264
Website: http://www.aberdare.com

Acacia Venture Partners
101 California St., Ste. 3160
San Francisco, CA 94111
(415)433-4200
Fax: (415)433-4250
Website: http://www.acaciavp.com

Access Venture Partners
319 Laidley St.
San Francisco, CA 94131
(415)586-0132
Fax: (415)392 6310
Website: http://www.access
venturepartners.com

Alta Partners
One Embarcadero Center, Ste. 4050
San Francisco, CA 94111
(415)362-4022
Fax: (415)362-6178
E-mail: alta@altapartners.com
Website: http://www.altapartners.com

Bangert Dawes Reade Davis & Thom
220 Montgomery St., Ste. 424
San Francisco, CA 94104
(415)954-9900
Fax: (415)954-9901
E-mail: bdrdt@pacbell.net

Berkeley International Capital Corp.
650 California St., Ste. 2800
San Francisco, CA 94108-2609

(415)249-0450
Fax: (415)392-3929
Website: http://www.berkeleyvc.com

Blueprint Ventures LLC
456 Montgomery St., 22nd Fl.
San Francisco, CA 94104
(415)901-4000
Fax: (415)901-4035
Website: http://www.blue
printventures.com

Blumberg Capital Ventures
580 Howard St., Ste. 401
San Francisco, CA 94105
(415)905-5007
Fax: (415)357-5027
Website: http://www.blumberg-
capital.com

Burr, Egan, Deleage, and Co. (San Francisco)
1 Embarcadero Center, Ste. 4050
San Francisco, CA 94111
(415)362-4022
Fax: (415)362-6178

Burrill & Company
120 Montgomery St., Ste. 1370
San Francisco, CA 94104
(415)743-3160
Fax: (415)743-3161
Website: http://www.burrillandco.com

CMEA Ventures
235 Montgomery St., Ste. 920
San Francisco, CA 94401
(415)352-1520
Fax: (415)352-1524
Website: http://www.cmeaventures.com

Crocker Capital
1 Post St., Ste. 2500
San Francisco, CA 94101
(415)956-5250
Fax: (415)959-5710

Dominion Ventures, Inc.
44 Montgomery St., Ste. 4200
San Francisco, CA 94104
(415)362-4890
Fax: (415)394-9245

Dorset Capital
Pier 1
Bay 2
San Francisco, CA 94111
(415)398-7101
Fax: (415)398-7141
Website: http://www.dorsetcapital.com

Gatx Capital
Four Embarcadero Center, Ste. 2200
San Francisco, CA 94904
(415)955-3200
Fax: (415)955-3449

IMinds
135 Main St., Ste. 1350
San Francisco, CA 94105
(415)547-0000
Fax: (415)227-0300
Website: http://www.iminds.com

LF International Inc.
360 Post St., Ste. 705
San Francisco, CA 94108
(415)399-0110
Fax: (415)399-9222
Website: http://www.lfvc.com

Newbury Ventures
535 Pacific Ave., 2nd Fl.
San Francisco, CA 94133
(415)296-7408
Fax: (415)296-7416
Website: http://www.newburyven.com

Quest Ventures (San Francisco)
333 Bush St., Ste. 1750
San Francisco, CA 94104
(415)782-1414
Fax: (415)782-1415

Robertson-Stephens Co.
555 California St., Ste. 2600
San Francisco, CA 94104
(415)781-9700
Fax: (415)781-2556
Website: http://www.omegaad
ventures.com

Rosewood Capital, L.P.
One Maritime Plaza, Ste. 1330
San Francisco, CA 94111-3503
(415)362-5526
Fax: (415)362-1192
Website: http://www.rosewoodvc.com

Ticonderoga Capital Inc.
555 California St., No. 4950
San Francisco, CA 94104
(415)296-7900
Fax: (415)296-8956

21st Century Internet Venture Partners
Two South Park
2nd Floor
San Francisco, CA 94107
(415)512-1221
Fax: (415)512-2650
Website: http://www.21vc.com

VK Ventures
600 California St., Ste.1700
San Francisco, CA 94111
(415)391-5600
Fax: (415)397-2744

Walden Group of Venture Capital Funds
750 Battery St., Seventh Floor
San Francisco, CA 94111
(415)391-7225
Fax: (415)391-7262

Acer Technology Ventures
2641 Orchard Pkwy.
San Jose, CA 95134
(408)433-4945
Fax: (408)433-5230

Authosis
226 Airport Pkwy., Ste. 405
San Jose, CA 95110
(650)814-3603
Website: http://www.authosis.com

Western Technology Investment
2010 N. First St., Ste. 310
San Jose, CA 95131
(408)436-8577
Fax: (408)436-8625
E-mail: mktg@westerntech.com

Drysdale Enterprises
177 Bovet Rd., Ste. 600
San Mateo, CA 94402
(650)341-6336
Fax: (650)341-1329
E-mail: drysdale@aol.com

Greylock
2929 Campus Dr., Ste. 400
San Mateo, CA 94401
(650)493-5525
Fax: (650)493-5575
Website: http://www.greylock.com

Technology Funding
2000 Alameda de las Pulgas, Ste. 250
San Mateo, CA 94403
(415)345-2200
Fax: (415)345-1797

2M Invest Inc.
1875 S. Grant St.
Suite 750
San Mateo, CA 94402
(650)655-3765
Fax: (650)372-9107
E-mail: 2minfo@2minvest.com
Website: http://www.2minvest.com

Phoenix Growth Capital Corp.
2401 Kerner Blvd.
San Rafael, CA 94901
(415)485-4569
Fax: (415)485-4663

NextGen Partners LLC
1705 East Valley Rd.
Santa Barbara, CA 93108
(805)969-8540
Fax: (805)969-8542
Website: http://www.nextgen
partners.com

Denali Venture Capital
1925 Woodland Ave.
Santa Clara, CA 95050
(408)690-4838
Fax: (408)247-6979
E-mail: wael@denaliventurecapital.com
Website: http://www.denali
venturecapital.com

Dotcom Ventures LP
3945 Freedom Circle, Ste. 740
Santa Clara, CA 95045
(408)919-9855
Fax: (408)919-9857
Website: http://www.dotcom
venturesatl.com

Silicon Valley Bank
3003 Tasman
Santa Clara, CA 95054
(408)654-7400
Fax: (408)727-8728

Al Shugart International
920 41st Ave.
Santa Cruz, CA 95062
(831)479-7852
Fax: (831)479-7852
Website: http://www.alshugart.com

Leonard Mautner Associates
1434 Sixth St.
Santa Monica, CA 90401
(213)393-9788
Fax: (310)459-9918

Palomar Ventures
100 Wilshire Blvd., Ste. 450
Santa Monica, CA 90401
(310)260-6050
Fax: (310)656-4150
Website: http://www.palomar
ventures.com

Medicus Venture Partners
12930 Saratoga Ave., Ste. D8
Saratoga, CA 95070

(408)447-8600
Fax: (408)447-8599
Website: http://www.medicusvc.com

Redleaf Venture Management
14395 Saratoga Ave., Ste. 130
Saratoga, CA 95070
(408)868-0800
Fax: (408)868-0810
E-mail: nancy@redleaf.com
Website: http://www.redleaf.com

Artemis Ventures
207 Second St., Ste. E
3rd Fl.
Sausalito, CA 94965
(415)289-2500
Fax: (415)289-1789
Website: http://www.artemisventures.com

Deucalion Venture Partners
19501 Brooklime
Sonoma, CA 95476
(707)938-4974
Fax: (707)938-8921

Windward Ventures
PO Box 7688
Thousand Oaks, CA 91359-7688
(805)497-3332
Fax: (805)497-9331

National Investment Management, Inc.
2601 Airport Dr., Ste.210
Torrance, CA 90505
(310)784-7600
Fax: (310)784-7605

Southern California Ventures
406 Amapola Ave. Ste. 125
Torrance, CA 90501
(310)787-4381
Fax: (310)787-4382

Sandton Financial Group
21550 Oxnard St., Ste. 300
Woodland Hills, CA 91367
(818)702-9283

Woodside Fund
850 Woodside Dr.
Woodside, CA 94062
(650)368-5545
Fax: (650)368-2416
Website: http://www.woodsidefund.com

Colorado

Colorado Venture Management
Ste. 300
Boulder, CO 80301

(303)440-4055
Fax: (303)440-4636

Dean & Associates
4362 Apple Way
Boulder, CO 80301
Fax: (303)473-9900

Roser Ventures LLC
1105 Spruce St.
Boulder, CO 80302
(303)443-6436
Fax: (303)443-1885
Website: http://www.roserventures.com

Sequel Venture Partners
4430 Arapahoe Ave., Ste. 220
Boulder, CO 80303
(303)546-0400
Fax: (303)546-9728
E-mail: tom@sequelvc.com
Website: http://www.sequelvc.com

New Venture Resources
445C E. Cheyenne Mtn. Blvd.
Colorado Springs, CO 80906-4570
(719)598-9272
Fax: (719)598-9272

The Centennial Funds
1428 15th St.
Denver, CO 80202-1318
(303)405-7500
Fax: (303)405-7575
Website: http://www.centennial.com

Rocky Mountain Capital Partners
1125 17th St., Ste. 2260
Denver, CO 80202
(303)291-5200
Fax: (303)291-5327

Sandlot Capital LLC
600 South Cherry St., Ste. 525
Denver, CO 80246
(303)893-3400
Fax: (303)893-3403
Website: http://www.sandlotcapital.com

Wolf Ventures
50 South Steele St., Ste. 777
Denver, CO 80209
(303)321-4800
Fax: (303)321-4848
E-mail: businessplan@wolf
ventures.com
Website: http://www.wolfventures.com

The Columbine Venture Funds
5460 S. Quebec St., Ste. 270
Englewood, CO 80111

(303)694-3222
Fax: (303)694-9007

Investment Securities of Colorado, Inc.
4605 Denice Dr.
Englewood, CO 80111
(303)796-9192

Kinship Partners
6300 S. Syracuse Way, Ste. 484
Englewood, CO 80111
(303)694-0268
Fax: (303)694-1707
E-mail: block@vailsys.com

Boranco Management, L.L.C.
1528 Hillside Dr.
Fort Collins, CO 80524-1969
(970)221-2297
Fax: (970)221-4787

Aweida Ventures
890 West Cherry St., Ste. 220
Louisville, CO 80027
(303)664-9520
Fax: (303)664-9530
Website: http://www.aweida.com

Access Venture Partners
8787 Turnpike Dr., Ste. 260
Westminster, CO 80030
(303)426-8899
Fax: (303)426-8828

Medmax Ventures LP
1 Northwestern Dr., Ste. 203
Bloomfield, CT 06002
(860)286-2960
Fax: (860)286-9960

James B. Kobak & Co.
Four Mansfield Place
Darien, CT 06820
(203)656-3471
Fax: (203)655-2905

Orien Ventures
1 Post Rd.
Fairfield, CT 06430
(203)259-9933
Fax: (203)259-5288

ABP Acquisition Corporation
115 Maple Ave.
Greenwich, CT 06830
(203)625-8287
Fax: (203)447-6187

Catterton Partners
9 Greenwich Office Park
Greenwich, CT 06830
(203)629-4901

Fax: (203)629-4903
Website: http://www.cpequity.com

Consumer Venture Partners
3 Pickwick Plz.
Greenwich, CT 06830
(203)629-8800
Fax: (203)629-2019

Insurance Venture Partners
31 Brookside Dr., Ste. 211
Greenwich, CT 06830
(203)861-0030
Fax: (203)861-2745

The NTC Group
Three Pickwick Plaza
Ste. 200
Greenwich, CT 06830
(203)862-2800
Fax: (203)622-6538

Regulus International Capital Co., Inc.
140 Greenwich Ave.
Greenwich, CT 06830
(203)625-9700
Fax: (203)625-9706

Axiom Venture Partners
City Place II
185 Asylum St., 17th Fl.
Hartford, CT 06103
(860)548-7799
Fax: (860)548-7797
Website: http://www.axiomventures.com

Conning Capital Partners
City Place II
185 Asylum St.
Hartford, CT 06103-4105
(860)520-1289
Fax: (860)520-1299
E-mail: pe@conning.com
Website: http://www.conning.com

First New England Capital L.P.
100 Pearl St.
Hartford, CT 06103
(860)293-3333
Fax: (860)293-3338
E-mail: info@firstnewenglandcapital.com
Website: http://www.firstnewengland
capital.com

Northeast Ventures
One State St., Ste. 1720
Hartford, CT 06103
(860)547-1414
Fax: (860)246-8755

Windward Holdings
38 Sylvan Rd.
Madison, CT 06443
(203)245-6870
Fax: (203)245-6865

Advanced Materials Partners, Inc.
45 Pine St.
PO Box 1022
New Canaan, CT 06840
(203)966-6415
Fax: (203)966-8448
E-mail: wkb@amplink.com

RFE Investment Partners
36 Grove St.
New Canaan, CT 06840
(203)966-2800
Fax: (203)966-3109
Website: http://www.rfeip.com

Connecticut Innovations, Inc.
999 West St.
Rocky Hill, CT 06067
(860)563-5851
Fax: (860)563-4877
E-mail: pamela.hartley@ctin
novations.com
Website: http://www.ctinnovations.com

Canaan Partners
105 Rowayton Ave.
Rowayton, CT 06853
(203)855-0400
Fax: (203)854-9117
Website: http://www.canaan.com

Landmark Partners, Inc.
10 Mill Pond Ln.
Simsbury, CT 06070
(860)651-9760
Fax: (860)651-8890
Website: http://
www.landmarkpartners.com

Sweeney & Company
PO Box 567
Southport, CT 06490
(203)255-0220
Fax: (203)255-0220
E-mail: sweeney@connix.com

Baxter Associates, Inc.
PO Box 1333
Stamford, CT 06904
(203)323-3143
Fax: (203)348-0622

Beacon Partners Inc.
6 Landmark Sq., 4th Fl.
Stamford, CT 06901-2792

(203)359-5776
Fax: (203)359-5876

Collinson, Howe, and Lennox, LLC
1055 Washington Blvd., 5th Fl.
Stamford, CT 06901
(203)324-7700
Fax: (203)324-3636
E-mail: info@chlmedical.com
Website: http://www.chlmedical.com

Prime Capital Management Co.
550 West Ave.
Stamford, CT 06902
(203)964-0642
Fax: (203)964-0862

Saugatuck Capital Co.
1 Canterbury Green
Stamford, CT 06901
(203)348-6669
Fax: (203)324-6995
Website: http://www.sauga
tuckcapital.com

Soundview Financial Group Inc.
22 Gatehouse Rd.
Stamford, CT 06902
(203)462-7200
Fax: (203)462-7350
Website: http://www.sndv.com

TSG Ventures, L.L.C.
177 Broad St., 12th Fl.
Stamford, CT 06901
(203)406-1500
Fax: (203)406-1590

Whitney & Company
177 Broad St.
Stamford, CT 06901
(203)973-1400
Fax: (203)973-1422
Website: http://www.jhwhitney.com

Cullinane & Donnelly Venture Partners L.P.
970 Farmington Ave.
West Hartford, CT 06107
(860)521-7811

The Crestview Investment and Financial Group
431 Post Rd. E, Ste. 1
Westport, CT 06880-4403
(203)222-0333
Fax: (203)222-0000

Marketcorp Venture Associates, L.P. (MCV)
274 Riverside Ave.
Westport, CT 06880

(203)222-3030
Fax: (203)222-3033

Oak Investment Partners (Westport)
1 Gorham Island
Westport, CT 06880
(203)226-8346
Fax: (203)227-0372
Website: http://www.oakinv.com

Oxford Bioscience Partners
315 Post Rd. W
Westport, CT 06880-5200
(203)341-3300
Fax: (203)341-3309
Website: http://www.oxbio.com

Prince Ventures (Westport)
25 Ford Rd.
Westport, CT 06880
(203)227-8332
Fax: (203)226-5302

LTI Venture Leasing Corp.
221 Danbury Rd.
Wilton, CT 06897
(203)563-1100
Fax: (203)563-1111
Website: http://www.ltileasing.com

Delaware

Blue Rock Capital
5803 Kennett Pike, Ste. A
Wilmington, DE 19807
(302)426-0981
Fax: (302)426-0982
Website: http://www.bluerockcapital.com

District of Columbia

Allied Capital Corp.
1919 Pennsylvania Ave. NW
Washington, DC 20006-3434
(202)331-2444
Fax: (202)659-2053
Website: http://www.alliedcapital.com

Atlantic Coastal Ventures, L.P.
3101 South St. NW
Washington, DC 20007
(202)293-1166
Fax: (202)293-1181
Website: http://www.atlanticcv.com

Columbia Capital Group, Inc.
1660 L St. NW, Ste. 308
Washington, DC 20036
(202)775-8815
Fax: (202)223-0544

Core Capital Partners
901 15th St., NW
9th Fl.
Washington, DC 20005
(202)589-0090
Fax: (202)589-0091
Website: http://www.core-capital.com

Next Point Partners
701 Pennsylvania Ave. NW, Ste. 900
Washington, DC 20004
(202)661-8703
Fax: (202)434-7400
E-mail: mf@nextpoint.vc
Website: http://www.nextpointvc.com

Telecommunications Development Fund
2020 K. St. NW
Ste. 375
Washington, DC 20006
(202)293-8840
Fax: (202)293-8850
Website: http://www.tdfund.com

Wachtel & Co., Inc.
1101 4th St. NW
Washington, DC 20005-5680
(202)898-1144

Winslow Partners LLC
1300 Connecticut Ave. NW
Washington, DC 20036-1703
(202)530-5000
Fax: (202)530-5010
E-mail: winslow@winslowpartners.com

Women's Growth Capital Fund
1054 31st St., NW
Ste. 110
Washington, DC 20007
(202)342-1431
Fax: (202)341-1203
Website: http://www.wgcf.com

Sigma Capital Corp.
22668 Caravelle Circle
Boca Raton, FL 33433
(561)368-9783

North American Business Development Co., L.L.C.
111 East Las Olas Blvd.
Ft. Lauderdale, FL 33301
(305)463-0681
Fax: (305)527-0904
Website: http://www.northamericanfund.com

Chartwell Capital Management Co. Inc.
1 Independent Dr., Ste. 3120

Jacksonville, FL 32202
(904)355-3519
Fax: (904)353-5833
E-mail: info@chartwellcap.com

CEO Advisors
1061 Maitland Center Commons
Ste. 209
Maitland, FL 32751
(407)660-9327
Fax: (407)660-2109

Henry & Co.
8201 Peters Rd., Ste. 1000
Plantation, FL 33324
(954)797-7400

Avery Business Development Services
2506 St. Michel Ct.
Ponte Vedra, FL 32082
(904)285-6033

New South Ventures
5053 Ocean Blvd.
Sarasota, FL 34242
(941)358-6000
Fax: (941)358-6078
Website: http://www.newsouthventures.com

Venture Capital Management Corp.
PO Box 2626
Satellite Beach, FL 32937
(407)777-1969

Florida Capital Venture Ltd.
325 Florida Bank Plaza
100 W. Kennedy Blvd.
Tampa, FL 33602
(813)229-2294
Fax: (813)229-2028

Quantum Capital Partners
339 South Plant Ave.
Tampa, FL 33606
(813)250-1999
Fax: (813)250-1998
Website: http://www.quantumcapitalpartners.com

South Atlantic Venture Fund
614 W. Bay St.
Tampa, FL 33606-2704
(813)253-2500
Fax: (813)253-2360
E-mail: venture@southatlantic.com
Website: http://www.southatlantic.com

LM Capital Corp.
120 S. Olive, Ste. 400
West Palm Beach, FL 33401

(561)833-9700
Fax: (561)655-6587
Website: http://www.lmcapital
securities.com

Georgia

Venture First Associates
4811 Thornwood Dr.
Acworth, GA 30102
(770)928-3733
Fax: (770)928-6455

Alliance Technology Ventures
8995 Westside Pkwy., Ste. 200
Alpharetta, GA 30004
(678)336-2000
Fax: (678)336-2001
E-mail: info@atv.com
Website: http://www.atv.com

Cordova Ventures
2500 North Winds Pkwy., Ste. 475
Alpharetta, GA 30004
(678)942-0300
Fax: (678)942-0301
Website: http://www.cordovaventures.
com

**Advanced Technology Development
Fund**
1000 Abernathy, Ste. 1420
Atlanta, GA 30328-5614
(404)668-2333
Fax: (404)668-2333

CGW Southeast Partners
12 Piedmont Center, Ste. 210
Atlanta, GA 30305
(404)816-3255
Fax: (404)816-3258
Website: http://www.cgwlp.com

Cyberstarts
1900 Emery St., NW
3rd Fl.
Atlanta, GA 30318
(404)267-5000
Fax: (404)267-5200
Website: http://www.cyberstarts.com

EGL Holdings, Inc.
10 Piedmont Center, Ste. 412
Atlanta, GA 30305
(404)949-8300
Fax: (404)949-8311

Equity South
1790 The Lenox Bldg.
3399 Peachtree Rd. NE
Atlanta, GA 30326

(404)237-6222
Fax: (404)261-1578

Five Paces
3400 Peachtree Rd., Ste. 200
Atlanta, GA 30326
(404)439-8300
Fax: (404)439-8301
Website: http://www.fivepaces.com

Frontline Capital, Inc.
3475 Lenox Rd., Ste. 400
Atlanta, GA 30326
(404)240-7280
Fax: (404)240-7281

Fuqua Ventures LLC
1201 W. Peachtree St. NW, Ste. 5000
Atlanta, GA 30309
(404)815-4500
Fax: (404)815-4528
Website: http://www.fuquaventures.com

Noro-Moseley Partners
4200 Northside Pkwy., Bldg. 9
Atlanta, GA 30327
(404)233-1966
Fax: (404)239-9280
Website: http://www.noro-moseley.com

Renaissance Capital Corp.
34 Peachtree St. NW, Ste. 2230
Atlanta, GA 30303
(404)658-9061
Fax: (404)658-9064

River Capital, Inc.
Two Midtown Plaza
1360 Peachtree St. NE, Ste. 1430
Atlanta, GA 30309
(404)873-2166
Fax: (404)873-2158

State Street Bank & Trust Co.
3414 Peachtree Rd. NE, Ste. 1010
Atlanta, GA 30326
(404)364-9500
Fax: (404)261-4469

UPS Strategic Enterprise Fund
55 Glenlake Pkwy. NE
Atlanta, GA 30328
(404)828-8814
Fax: (404)828-8088
E-mail: jcacyce@ups.com
Website: http://www.ups.com/sef/
sef_home

Wachovia
191 Peachtree St. NE, 26th Fl.
Atlanta, GA 30303

(404)332-1000
Fax: (404)332-1392
Website: http://www.wachovia.com/wca

Brainworks Ventures
4243 Dunwoody Club Dr.
Chamblee, GA 30341
(770)239-7447

First Growth Capital Inc.
Best Western Plaza, Ste. 105
PO Box 815
Forsyth, GA 31029
(912)781-7131

Financial Capital Resources, Inc.
21 Eastbrook Bend, Ste. 116
Peachtree City, GA 30269
(404)487-6650

Hawaii

HMS Hawaii Management Partners
Davies Pacific Center
841 Bishop St., Ste. 860
Honolulu, HI 96813
(808)545-3755
Fax: (808)531-2611

Idaho

Sun Valley Ventures
160 Second St.
Ketchum, ID 83340
(208)726-5005
Fax: (208)726-5094

Illinois

Open Prairie Ventures
115 N. Neil St., Ste. 209
Champaign, IL 61820
(217)351-7000
Fax: (217)351-7051
E-mail: inquire@openprairie.com
Website: http://www.openprairie.com

ABN AMRO Private Equity
208 S. La Salle St., 10th Fl.
Chicago, IL 60604
(312)855-7079
Fax: (312)553-6648
Website: http://www.abnequity.com

Alpha Capital Partners, Ltd.
122 S. Michigan Ave., Ste. 1700
Chicago, IL 60603
(312)322-9800
Fax: (312)322-9808
E-mail: acp@alphacapital.com

Ameritech Development Corp.
30 S. Wacker Dr., 37th Fl.
Chicago, IL 60606
(312)750-5083
Fax: (312)609-0244

Apex Investment Partners
225 W. Washington, Ste. 1450
Chicago, IL 60606
(312)857-2800
Fax: (312)857-1800
E-mail: apex@apexvc.com
Website: http://www.apexvc.com

Arch Venture Partners
8725 W. Higgins Rd., Ste. 290
Chicago, IL 60631
(773)380-6600
Fax: (773)380-6606
Website: http://www.archventure.com

The Bank Funds
208 South LaSalle St., Ste. 1680
Chicago, IL 60604
(312)855-6020
Fax: (312)855-8910

Batterson Venture Partners
303 W. Madison St., Ste. 1110
Chicago, IL 60606-3309
(312)269-0300
Fax: (312)269-0021
Website: http://www.battersonvp.com

William Blair Capital Partners, L.L.C.
222 W. Adams St., Ste. 1300
Chicago, IL 60606
(312)364-8250
Fax: (312)236-1042
E-mail: privateequity@wmblair.com
Website: http://www.wmblair.com

Bluestar Ventures
208 South LaSalle St., Ste. 1020
Chicago, IL 60604
(312)384-5000
Fax: (312)384-5005
Website: http://www.bluestarventures.com

The Capital Strategy Management Co.
233 S. Wacker Dr.
Box 06334
Chicago, IL 60606
(312)444-1170

DN Partners
77 West Wacker Dr., Ste. 4550
Chicago, IL 60601
(312)332-7960
Fax: (312)332-7979

Dresner Capital Inc.
29 South LaSalle St., Ste. 310
Chicago, IL 60603
(312)726-3600
Fax: (312)726-7448

Eblast Ventures LLC
11 South LaSalle St., 5th Fl.
Chicago, IL 60603
(312)372-2600
Fax: (312)372-5621
Website: http://www.eblastventures.com

Essex Woodlands Health Ventures, L.P.
190 S. LaSalle St., Ste. 2800
Chicago, IL 60603
(312)444-6040
Fax: (312)444-6034
Website: http://www.essexwoodlands.com

First Analysis Venture Capital
233 S. Wacker Dr., Ste. 9500
Chicago, IL 60606
(312)258-1400
Fax: (312)258-0334
Website: http://www.firstanalysis.com

Frontenac Co.
135 S. LaSalle St., Ste.3800
Chicago, IL 60603
(312)368-0044
Fax: (312)368-9520
Website: http://www.frontenac.com

GTCR Golder Rauner, LLC
6100 Sears Tower
Chicago, IL 60606
(312)382-2200
Fax: (312)382-2201
Website: http://www.gtcr.com

High Street Capital LLC
311 South Wacker Dr., Ste. 4550
Chicago, IL 60606
(312)697-4990
Fax: (312)697-4994
Website: http://www.highstr.com

IEG Venture Management, Inc.
70 West Madison
Chicago, IL 60602
(312)644-0890
Fax: (312)454-0369
Website: http://www.iegventure.com

JK&B Capital
180 North Stetson, Ste. 4500
Chicago, IL 60601
(312)946 1200
Fax: (312)946-1103

E-mail: gspencer@jkbcapital.com
Website: http://www.jkbcapital.com

Kettle Partners L.P.
350 W. Hubbard, Ste. 350
Chicago, IL 60610
(312)329-9300
Fax: (312)527-4519
Website: http://www.kettlevc.com

Lake Shore Capital Partners
20 N. Wacker Dr., Ste. 2807
Chicago, IL 60606
(312)803-3536
Fax: (312)803-3534

LaSalle Capital Group Inc.
70 W. Madison St., Ste. 5710
Chicago, IL 60602
(312)236-7041
Fax: (312)236-0720

Linc Capital, Inc.
303 E. Wacker Pkwy., Ste. 1000
Chicago, IL 60601
(312)946-2670
Fax: (312)938-4290
E-mail: bdemars@linccap.com

Madison Dearborn Partners, Inc.
3 First National Plz., Ste. 3800
Chicago, IL 60602
(312)895-1000
Fax: (312)895-1001
E-mail: invest@mdcp.com
Website: http://www.mdcp.com

Mesirow Private Equity Investments Inc.
350 N. Clark St.
Chicago, IL 60610
(312)595-6950
Fax: (312)595-6211
Website: http://www.meisrowfinancial.com

Mosaix Ventures LLC
1822 North Mohawk
Chicago, IL 60614
(312)274-0988
Fax: (312)274-0989
Website: http://www.mosaixventures.com

Nesbitt Burns
111 West Monroe St.
Chicago, IL 60603
(312)416-3855
Fax: (312)765-8000
Website: http://www.harrisbank.com

Polestar Capital, Inc.
180 N. Michigan Ave., Ste. 1905
Chicago, IL 60601
(312)984-9090
Fax: (312)984-9877
E-mail: wl@polestarvc.com
Website: http://www.polestarvc.com

Prince Ventures (Chicago)
10 S. Wacker Dr., Ste. 2575
Chicago, IL 60606-7407
(312)454-1408
Fax: (312)454-9125

Prism Capital
444 N. Michigan Ave.
Chicago, IL 60611
(312)464-7900
Fax: (312)464-7915
Website: http://www.prismfund.com

Third Coast Capital
900 N. Franklin St., Ste. 700
Chicago, IL 60610
(312)337-3303
Fax: (312)337-2567
E-mail: manic@earthlink.com
Website: http://www.third
coastcapital.com

Thoma Cressey Equity Partners
4460 Sears Tower, 92nd Fl.
233 S. Wacker Dr.
Chicago, IL 60606
(312)777-4444
Fax: (312)777-4445
Website: http://www.thomacressey.com

Tribune Ventures
435 N. Michigan Ave., Ste. 600
Chicago, IL 60611
(312)527-8797
Fax: (312)222-5993
Website: http://www.tribuneventures.com

Wind Point Partners (Chicago)
676 N. Michigan Ave., Ste. 330
Chicago, IL 60611
(312)649-4000
Website: http://www.wppartners.com

Marquette Venture Partners
520 Lake Cook Rd., Ste. 450
Deerfield, IL 60015
(847)940-1700
Fax: (847)940-1724
Website: http://www.marquette
ventures.com

Duchossois Investments Limited, LLC
845 Larch Ave.
Elmhurst, IL 60126

(630)530-6105
Fax: (630)993-8644
Website: http://www.duchtec.com

Evanston Business Investment Corp.
1840 Oak Ave.
Evanston, IL 60201
(847)866-1840
Fax: (847)866-1808
E-mail: t-parkinson@nwu.com
Website: http://www.ebic.com

Inroads Capital Partners L.P.
1603 Orrington Ave., Ste. 2050
Evanston, IL 60201-3841
(847)864-2000
Fax: (847)864-9692

The Cerulean Fund/WGC Enterprises
1701 E. Lake Ave., Ste. 170
Glenview, IL 60025
(847)657-8002
Fax: (847)657-8168

Ventana Financial Resources, Inc.
249 Market Sq.
Lake Forest, IL 60045
(847)234-3434

Beecken, Petty & Co.
901 Warrenville Rd., Ste. 205
Lisle, IL 60532
(630)435-0300
Fax: (630)435-0370
E-mail: hep@bpcompany.com
Website: http://www.bpcompany.com

Allstate Private Equity
3075 Sanders Rd., Ste. G5D
Northbrook, IL 60062-7127
(847)402-8247
Fax: (847)402-0880

KB Partners
1101 Skokie Blvd., Ste. 260
Northbrook, IL 60062-2856
(847)714-0444
Fax: (847)714-0445
E-mail: keith@kbpartners.com
Website: http://www.kbpartners.com

Transcap Associates Inc.
900 Skokie Blvd., Ste. 210
Northbrook, IL 60062
(847)753-9600
Fax: (847)753-9090

Graystone Venture Partners, L.L.C. / Portage Venture Partners
One Northfield Plaza, Ste. 530
Northfield, IL 60093

(847)446-9460
Fax: (847)446-9470
Website: http://www.portage
ventures.com

Motorola Inc.
1303 E. Algonquin Rd.
Schaumburg, IL 60196-1065
(847)576-4929
Fax: (847)538-2250
Website: http://www.mot.com/mne

Indiana

Irwin Ventures LLC
500 Washington St.
Columbus, IN 47202
(812)373-1434
Fax: (812)376-1709
Website: http://www.irwinventures.com

Cambridge Venture Partners
4181 East 96th St., Ste. 200
Indianapolis, IN 46240
(317)814-6192
Fax: (317)944-9815

CID Equity Partners
One American Square, Ste. 2850
Box 82074
Indianapolis, IN 46282
(317)269-2350
Fax: (317)269-2355
Website: http://www.cidequity.com

Gazelle Techventures
6325 Digital Way, Ste. 460
Indianapolis, IN 46278
(317)275-6800
Fax: (317)275-1101
Website: http://www.gazellevc.com

Monument Advisors Inc.
Bank One Center/Circle
111 Monument Circle, Ste. 600
Indianapolis, IN 46204-5172
(317)656-5065
Fax: (317)656-5060
Website: http://www.monumentadv.com

MWV Capital Partners
201 N. Illinois St., Ste. 300
Indianapolis, IN 46204
(317)237-2323
Fax: (317)237-2325
Website: http://www.mwvcapital.com

First Source Capital Corp.
100 North Michigan St.
PO Box 1602
South Bend, IN 46601

(219)235-2180
Fax: (219)235-2227

Iowa

Allsop Venture Partners
118 Third Ave. SE, Ste. 837
Cedar Rapids, IA 52401
(319)368-6675
Fax: (319)363-9515

InvestAmerica Investment Advisors, Inc.
101 2nd St. SE, Ste. 800
Cedar Rapids, IA 52401
(319)363-8249
Fax: (319)363-9683

Pappajohn Capital Resources
2116 Financial Center
Des Moines, IA 50309
(515)244-5746
Fax: (515)244-2346
Website: http://www.pappajohn.com

Berthel Fisher & Company Planning Inc.
701 Tama St.
PO Box 609
Marion, IA 52302
(319)497-5700
Fax: (319)497-4244

Kansas

Enterprise Merchant Bank
7400 West 110th St., Ste. 560
Overland Park, KS 66210
(913)327-8500
Fax: (913)327-8505

Kansas Venture Capital, Inc. (Overland Park)
6700 Antioch Plz., Ste. 460
Overland Park, KS 66204
(913)262-7117
Fax: (913)262-3509
E-mail: jdalton@kvci.com

Child Health Investment Corp.
6803 W. 64th St., Ste. 208
Shawnee Mission, KS 66202
(913)262-1436
Fax: (913)262-1575
Website: http://www.chca.com

Kansas Technology Enterprise Corp.
214 SW 6th, 1st Fl.
Topeka, KS 66603-3719
(785)296-5272
Fax: (785)296-1160

E-mail: ktec@ktec.com
Website: http://www.ktec.com

Kentucky

Kentucky Highlands Investment Corp.
362 Old Whitley Rd.
London, KY 40741
(606)864-5175
Fax: (606)864-5194
Website: http://www.khic.org

Chrysalis Ventures, L.L.C.
1850 National City Tower
Louisville, KY 40202
(502)583-7644
Fax: (502)583-7648
E-mail: bobsany@chrysalisventures.com
Website: http://www.chrysalis
ventures.com

Humana Venture Capital
500 West Main St.
Louisville, KY 40202
(502)580-3922
Fax: (502)580-2051
E-mail: gemont@humana.com
George Emont, Director

Summit Capital Group, Inc.
6510 Glenridge Park Pl., Ste. 8
Louisville, KY 40222
(502)332-2700

Louisiana

Bank One Equity Investors, Inc.
451 Florida St.
Baton Rouge, LA 70801
(504)332-4421
Fax: (504)332-7377

Advantage Capital Partners
LLE Tower
909 Poydras St., Ste. 2230
New Orleans, LA 70112
(504)522-4850
Fax: (504)522-4950
Website: http://www.advantagecap.com

Maine

CEI Ventures / Coastal Ventures LP
2 Portland Fish Pier, Ste. 201
Portland, ME 04101
(207)772-5356
Fax: (207)772-5503
Website: http://www.ceiventures.com

Commwealth Bioventures, Inc.
4 Milk St.
Portland, ME 04101

(207)780 0904
Fax: (207)780-0913

Maryland

Annapolis Ventures LLC
151 West St., Ste. 302
Annapolis, MD 21401
(443)482-9555
Fax: (443)482-9565
Website: http://www.annapolis
ventures.com

Delmag Ventures
220 Wardour Dr.
Annapolis, MD 21401
(410)267-8196
Fax: (410)267-8017
Website: http://www.delmag
ventures.com

Abell Venture Fund
111 S. Calvert St., Ste. 2300
Baltimore, MD 21202
(410)547-1300
Fax: (410)539-6579
Website: http://www.abell.org

ABS Ventures (Baltimore)
1 South St., Ste. 2150
Baltimore, MD 21202
(410)895-3895
Fax: (410)895-3899
Website: http://www.absventures.com

Anthem Capital, L.P.
16 S. Calvert St., Ste. 800
Baltimore, MD 21202-1305
(410)625-1510
Fax: (410)625-1735
Website: http://www.anthemcapital.com

Catalyst Ventures
1119 St. Paul St.
Baltimore, MD 21202
(410)244-0123
Fax: (410)752-7721

Maryland Venture Capital Trust
217 E. Redwood St., Ste. 2200
Baltimore, MD 21202
(410)767-6361
Fax: (410)333-6931

New Enterprise Associates (Baltimore)
1119 St. Paul St.
Baltimore, MD 21202
(410)244-0115
Fax: (410)752-7721
Website: http://www.nea.com

T. Rowe Price Threshold Partnerships
100 E. Pratt St., 8th Fl.
Baltimore, MD 21202
(410)345-2000
Fax: (410)345-2800

Spring Capital Partners
16 W. Madison St.
Baltimore, MD 21201
(410)685-8000
Fax: (410)727-1436
E-mail: mailbox@springcap.com

Arete Corporation
3 Bethesda Metro Ctr., Ste. 770
Bethesda, MD 20814
(301)657-6268
Fax: (301)657-6254
Website: http://www.arete-microgen.com

Embryon Capital
7903 Sleaford Place
Bethesda, MD 20814
(301)656-6837
Fax: (301)656-8056

Potomac Ventures
7920 Norfolk Ave., Ste. 1100
Bethesda, MD 20814
(301)215-9240
Website: http://www.potomac
ventures.com

Toucan Capital Corp.
3 Bethesda Metro Center, Ste. 700
Bethesda, MD 20814
(301)961-1970
Fax: (301)961-1969
Website: http://www.toucancapital.com

Kinetic Ventures LLC
2 Wisconsin Cir., Ste. 620
Chevy Chase, MD 20815
(301)652-8066
Fax: (301)652-8310
Website: http://www.kineticventures.com

Boulder Ventures Ltd.
4750 Owings Mills Blvd.
Owings Mills, MD 21117
(410)998-3114
Fax: (410)356-5492
Website: http://www.boulderventures.com

Grotech Capital Group
9690 Deereco Rd., Ste. 800
Timonium, MD 21093
(410)560-2000
Fax: (410)560-1910
Website: http://www.grotech.com

Massachusetts

Adams, Harkness & Hill, Inc.
60 State St.
Boston, MA 02109
(617)371-3900

Advent International
75 State St., 29th Fl.
Boston, MA 02109
(617)951-9400
Fax: (617)951-0566
Website: http://www.adventiner
national.com

American Research and Development
30 Federal St.
Boston, MA 02110-2508
(617)423-7500
Fax: (617)423-9655

Ascent Venture Partners
255 State St., 5th Fl.
Boston, MA 02109
(617)270-9400
Fax: (617)270-9401
E-mail: info@ascentvp.com
Website: http://www.ascentvp.com

Atlas Venture
222 Berkeley St.
Boston, MA 02116
(617)488-2200
Fax: (617)859-9292
Website: http://www.atlasventure.com

Axxon Capital
28 State St., 37th Fl.
Boston, MA 02109
(617)722-0980
Fax: (617)557-6014
Website: http://www.axxoncapital.com

BancBoston Capital/BancBoston Ventures
175 Federal St., 10th Fl.
Boston, MA 02110
(617)434-2509
Fax: (617)434-6175
Website: http://
www.bancbostoncapital.com

Boston Capital Ventures
Old City Hall
45 School St.
Boston, MA 02108
(617)227-6550
Fax: (617)227-3847
E-mail: info@bcv.com
Website: http://www.bcv.com

Boston Financial & Equity Corp.
20 Overland St.
PO Box 15071
Boston, MA 02215
(617)267-2900
Fax: (617)437-7601
E-mail: debbie@bfec.com

Boston Millennia Partners
30 Rowes Wharf
Boston, MA 02110
(617)428-5150
Fax: (617)428-5160
Website: http://www.millennia
partners.com

Bristol Investment Trust
842A Beacon St.
Boston, MA 02215-3199
(617)566-5212
Fax: (617)267-0932

Brook Venture Management LLC
50 Federal St., 5th Fl.
Boston, MA 02110
(617)451-8989
Fax: (617)451-2369
Website: http://www.brookventure.com

Burr, Egan, Deleage, and Co. (Boston)
200 Clarendon St., Ste. 3800
Boston, MA 02116
(617)262-7770
Fax: (617)262-9779

Cambridge/Samsung Partners
One Exeter Plaza
Ninth Fl.
Boston, MA 02116
(617)262-4440
Fax: (617)262-5562

Chestnut Street Partners, Inc.
75 State St., Ste. 2500
Boston, MA 02109
(617)345-7220
Fax: (617)345-7201
E-mail: chestnut@chestnutp.com

Claflin Capital Management, Inc.
10 Liberty Sq., Ste. 300
Boston, MA 02109
(617)426-6505
Fax: (617)482-0016
Website: http://www.claflincapital.com

Copley Venture Partners
99 Summer St., Ste. 1720
Boston, MA 02110
(617)737-1253
Fax: (617)439-0699

Corning Capital / Corning Technology Ventures
121 High Street, Ste. 400
Boston, MA 02110
(617)338-2656
Fax: (617)261-3864
Website: http://www.corningventures.com

Downer & Co.
211 Congress St.
Boston, MA 02110
(617)482-6200
Fax: (617)482-6201
E-mail: cdowner@downer.com
Website: http://www.downer.com

Fidelity Ventures
82 Devonshire St.
Boston, MA 02109
(617)563-6370
Fax: (617)476-9023
Website: http://www.fidelityventures.com

Greylock Management Corp. (Boston)
1 Federal St.
Boston, MA 02110-2065
(617)423-5525
Fax: (617)482-0059

Gryphon Ventures
222 Berkeley St., Ste.1600
Boston, MA 02116
(617)267-9191
Fax: (617)267-4293
E-mail: all@gryphoninc.com

Halpern, Denny & Co.
500 Boylston St.
Boston, MA 02116
(617)536-6602
Fax: (617)536-8535

Harbourvest Partners, LLC
1 Financial Center, 44th Fl.
Boston, MA 02111
(617)348-3707
Fax: (617)350-0305
Website: http://www.hvpllc.com

Highland Capital Partners
2 International Pl.
Boston, MA 02110
(617)981-1500
Fax: (617)531-1550
E-mail: info@hcp.com
Website: http://www.hcp.com

Lee Munder Venture Partners
John Hancock Tower T-53
200 Clarendon St.
Boston, MA 02103

(617)380-5600
Fax: (617)380-5601
Website: http://www.leemunder.com

M/C Venture Partners
75 State St., Ste. 2500
Boston, MA 02109
(617)345-7200
Fax: (617)345-7201
Website: http://www.mcventure
partners.com

Massachusetts Capital Resources Co.
420 Boylston St.
Boston, MA 02116
(617)536-3900
Fax: (617)536-7930

Massachusetts Technology Development Corp. (MTDC)
148 State St.
Boston, MA 02109
(617)723-4920
Fax: (617)723-5983
E-mail: jhodgman@mtdc.com
Website: http://www.mtdc.com

New England Partners
One Boston Place, Ste. 2100
Boston, MA 02108
(617)624-8400
Fax: (617)624-8999
Website: http://www.nepartners.com

North Hill Ventures
Ten Post Office Square
11th Fl.
Boston, MA 02109
(617)788-2112
Fax: (617)788-2152
Website: http://www.northhill
ventures.com

OneLiberty Ventures
150 Cambridge Park Dr.
Boston, MA 02140
(617)492-7280
Fax: (617)492-7290
Website: http://www.oneliberty.com

Schroder Ventures
Life Sciences
60 State St., Ste. 3650
Boston, MA 02109
(617)367-8100
Fax: (617)367-1590
Website: http://www.shroderventures.com

Shawmut Capital Partners
75 Federal St., 18th Fl.
Boston, MA 02110

(617)368-4900
Fax: (617)368-4910
Website: http://www.shawmutcapital.com

Solstice Capital LLC
15 Broad St., 3rd Fl.
Boston, MA 02109
(617)523-7733
Fax: (617)523-5827
E-mail: solticecapital@solcap.com

Spectrum Equity Investors
One International Pl., 29th Fl.
Boston, MA 02110
(617)464-4600
Fax: (617)464-4601
Website: http://www.spectrumequity.com

Spray Venture Partners
One Walnut St.
Boston, MA 02108
(617)305-4140
Fax: (617)305-4144
Website: http://www.sprayventure.com

The Still River Fund
100 Federal St., 29th Fl.
Boston, MA 02110
(617)348-2327
Fax: (617)348-2371
Website: http://www.stillriverfund.com

Summit Partners
600 Atlantic Ave., Ste. 2800
Boston, MA 02210-2227
(617)824-1000
Fax: (617)824-1159
Website: http://www.summitpartners.com

TA Associates, Inc. (Boston)
High Street Tower
125 High St., Ste. 2500
Boston, MA 02110
(617)574-6700
Fax: (617)574-6728
Website: http://www.ta.com

TVM Techno Venture Management
101 Arch St., Ste. 1950
Boston, MA 02110
(617)345-9320
Fax: (617)345-9377
E-mail: info@tvmvc.com
Website: http://www.tvmvc.com

UNC Ventures
64 Burough St.
Boston, MA 02130-4017
(617)482-7070
Fax: (617)522-2176

Venture Investment Management Company (VIMAC)
177 Milk St.
Boston, MA 02190-3410
(617)292-3300
Fax: (617)292-7979
E-mail: bzeisig@vimac.com
Website: http://www.vimac.com

MDT Advisers, Inc.
125 Cambridge Park Dr.
Cambridge, MA 02140-2314
(617)234-2200
Fax: (617)234-2210
Website: http://www.mdtai.com

TTC Ventures
One Main St., 6th Fl.
Cambridge, MA 02142
(617)528-3137
Fax: (617)577-1715
E-mail: info@ttcventures.com

Zero Stage Capital Co. Inc.
101 Main St., 17th Fl.
Cambridge, MA 02142
(617)876-5355
Fax: (617)876-1248
Website: http://www.zerostage.com

Atlantic Capital
164 Cushing Hwy.
Cohasset, MA 02025
(617)383-9449
Fax: (617)383-6040
E-mail: info@atlanticcap.com
Website: http://www.atlanticcap.com

Seacoast Capital Partners
55 Ferncroft Rd.
Danvers, MA 01923
(978)750-1300
Fax: (978)750-1301
E-mail: gdeli@seacoastcapital.com
Website: http://www.seacoast
capital.com

Sage Management Group
44 South Street
PO Box 2026
East Dennis, MA 02641
(508)385-7172
Fax: (508)385-7272
E-mail: sagemgt@capecod.net

Applied Technology
1 Cranberry Hill
Lexington, MA 02421-7397
(617)862-8622
Fax: (617)862-8367

Royalty Capital Management
5 Downing Rd.
Lexington, MA 02421-6918
(781)861-8490

Argo Global Capital
210 Broadway, Ste. 101
Lynnfield, MA 01940
(781)592-5250
Fax: (781)592-5230
Website: http://www.gsmcapital.com

Industry Ventures
6 Bayne Lane
Newburyport, MA 01950
(978)499-7606
Fax: (978)499-0686
Website: http://
www.industryventures.com

Softbank Capital Partners
10 Langley Rd., Ste. 202
Newton Center, MA 02459
(617)928-9300
Fax: (617)928-9305
E-mail: clax@bvc.com

Advanced Technology Ventures (Boston)
281 Winter St., Ste. 350
Waltham, MA 02451
(781)290-0707
Fax: (781)684-0045
E-mail: info@atvcapital.com
Website: http://www.atvcapital.com

Castile Ventures
890 Winter St., Ste. 140
Waltham, MA 02451
(781)890-0060
Fax: (781)890-0065
Website: http://www.castileventures.com

Charles River Ventures
1000 Winter St., Ste. 3300
Waltham, MA 02451
(781)487-7060
Fax: (781)487-7065
Website: http://www.crv.com

Comdisco Venture Group (Waltham)
Totton Pond Office Center
400-1 Totten Pond Rd.
Waltham, MA 02451
(617)672-0250
Fax: (617)398-8099

Marconi Ventures
890 Winter St., Ste. 310
Waltham, MA 02451
(781)839-7177

Fax: (781)522-7477
Website: http://www.marconi.com

Matrix Partners
Bay Colony Corporate Center
1000 Winter St., Ste.4500
Waltham, MA 02451
(781)890-2244
Fax: (781)890-2288
Website: http://www.matrix
partners.com

North Bridge Venture Partners
950 Winter St. Ste. 4600
Waltham, MA 02451
(781)290-0004
Fax: (781)290-0999
E-mail: eta@nbvp.com

Polaris Venture Partners
Bay Colony Corporate Ctr.
1000 Winter St., Ste. 3500
Waltham, MA 02451
(781)290-0770
Fax: (781)290-0880
E-mail: partners@polarisventures.com
Website: http://www.polar
isventures.com

Seaflower Ventures
Bay Colony Corporate Ctr.
1000 Winter St. Ste. 1000
Waltham, MA 02451
(781)466-9552
Fax: (781)466-9553
E-mail: moot@seaflower.com
Website: http://www.seaflower.com

Ampersand Ventures
55 William St., Ste. 240
Wellesley, MA 02481
(617)239-0700
Fax: (617)239-0824
E-mail: info@ampersandventures.com
Website: http://www.ampersand
ventures.com

Battery Ventures (Boston)
20 William St., Ste. 200
Wellesley, MA 02481
(781)577-1000
Fax: (781)577-1001
Website: http://www.battery.com

Commonwealth Capital Ventures, L.P.
20 William St., Ste.225
Wellesley, MA 02481
(781)237-7373
Fax: (781)235-8627
Website: http://www.ccvlp.com

Fowler, Anthony & Company
20 Walnut St.
Wellesley, MA 02481
(781)237-4201
Fax: (781)237-7718

Gemini Investors
20 William St.
Wellesley, MA 02481
(781)237-7001
Fax: (781)237-7233

Grove Street Advisors Inc.
20 William St., Ste. 230
Wellesley, MA 02481
(781)263-6100
Fax: (781)263-6101
Website: http://www.groves
treetadvisors.com

Mees Pierson Investeringsmaat B.V.
20 William St., Ste. 210
Wellesley, MA 02482
(781)239-7600
Fax: (781)239-0377

Norwest Equity Partners
40 William St., Ste. 305
Wellesley, MA 02481-3902
(781)237-5870
Fax: (781)237-6270
Website: http://www.norwestvp.com

Bessemer Venture Partners (Wellesley Hills)
83 Walnut St.
Wellesley Hills, MA 02481
(781)237-6050
Fax: (781)235-7576
E-mail: travis@bvpny.com
Website: http://www.bvp.com

Venture Capital Fund of New England
20 Walnut St., Ste. 120
Wellesley Hills, MA 02481-2175
(781)239-8262
Fax: (781)239-8263

Prism Venture Partners
100 Lowder Brook Dr., Ste. 2500
Westwood, MA 02090
(781)302-4000
Fax: (781)302-4040
E-mail: dwbaum@prismventure.com

Palmer Partners LP
200 Unicorn Park Dr.
Woburn, MA 01801
(781)933-5445
Fax: (781)933-0698

Michigan

Arbor Partners, L.L.C.
130 South First St.
Ann Arbor, MI 48104
(734)668-9000
Fax: (734)669-4195
Website: http://www.arborpartners.com

EDF Ventures
425 N. Main St.
Ann Arbor, MI 48104
(734)663-3213
Fax: (734)663-7358
E-mail: edf@edfvc.com
Website: http://www.edfvc.com

White Pines Management, L.L.C.
2401 Plymouth Rd., Ste. B
Ann Arbor, MI 48105
(734)747-9401
Fax: (734)747-9704
E-mail: ibund@whitepines.com
Website: http://www.whitepines.com

Wellmax, Inc.
3541 Bendway Blvd., Ste. 100
Bloomfield Hills, MI 48301
(248)646-3554
Fax: (248)646-6220

Venture Funding, Ltd.
Fisher Bldg.
3011 West Grand Blvd., Ste. 321
Detroit, MI 48202
(313)871-3606
Fax: (313)873-4935

Investcare Partners L.P. / GMA Capital LLC
32330 W. Twelve Mile Rd.
Farmington Hills, MI 48334
(248)489-9000
Fax: (248)489-8819
E-mail: gma@gmacapital.com
Website: http://www.gmacapital.com

Liberty Bidco Investment Corp.
30833 Northwestern Highway, Ste. 211
Farmington Hills, MI 48334
(248)626-6070
Fax: (248)626-6072

Seaflower Ventures
5170 Nicholson Rd.
PO Box 474
Fowlerville, MI 48836
(517)223-3335
Fax: (517)223-3337
E-mail: gibbons@seaflower.com
Website: http://www.seaflower.com

Ralph Wilson Equity Fund LLC
15400 E. Jefferson Ave.
Gross Pointe Park, MI 48230
(313)821-9122
Fax: (313)821-9101
Website: http://www.Ralph
WilsonEquityFund.com
J. Skip Simms, President

Minnesota

Development Corp. of Austin
1900 Eighth Ave., NW
Austin, MN 55912
(507)433-0346
Fax: (507)433-0361
E-mail: dca@smig.net
Website: http://www.spamtownusa.com

Northeast Ventures Corp.
802 Alworth Bldg.
Duluth, MN 55802
(218)722-9915
Fax: (218)722-9871

Medical Innovation Partners, Inc.
6450 City West Pkwy.
Eden Prairie, MN 55344-3245
(612)828-9616
Fax: (612)828-9596

St. Paul Venture Capital, Inc.
10400 Vicking Dr., Ste. 550
Eden Prairie, MN 55344
(612)995-7474
Fax: (612)995-7475
Website: http://www.stpaulvc.com

Cherry Tree Investments, Inc.
7601 France Ave. S, Ste. 150
Edina, MN 55435
(612)893-9012
Fax: (612)893-9036
Website: http://www.cherrytree.com

Shared Ventures, Inc.
6550 York Ave. S
Edina, MN 55435
(612)925-3411

Sherpa Partners LLC
5050 Lincoln Dr., Ste. 490
Edina, MN 55436
(952)942-1070
Fax: (952)942-1071
Website: http://www.sherpapartners.com

Affinity Capital Management
901 Marquette Ave., Ste. 1810
Minneapolis, MN 55402
(612)252-9900

Fax: (612)252-9911
Website: http://www.affinitycapital.com

Artesian Capital
1700 Foshay Tower
821 Marquette Ave.
Minneapolis, MN 55402
(612)334-5600
Fax: (612)334-5601
E-mail: artesian@artesian.com

Coral Ventures
60 S. 6th St., Ste. 3510
Minneapolis, MN 55402
(612)335-8666
Fax: (612)335-8668
Website: http://www.coralventures.com

Crescendo Venture Management, L.L.C.
800 LaSalle Ave., Ste. 2250
Minneapolis, MN 55402
(612)607-2800
Fax: (612)607-2801
Website: http://www.crescendo
ventures.com

Gideon Hixon Venture
1900 Foshay Tower
821 Marquette Ave.
Minneapolis, MN 55402
(612)904-2314
Fax: (612)204-0913

Norwest Equity Partners
3600 IDS Center
80 S. 8th St.
Minneapolis, MN 55402
(612)215-1600
Fax: (612)215-1601
Website: http://www.norwestvp.com

Oak Investment Partners (Minneapolis)
4550 Norwest Center
90 S. 7th St.
Minneapolis, MN 55402
(612)339-9322
Fax: (612)337-8017
Website: http://www.oakinv.com

Pathfinder Venture Capital Funds (Minneapolis)
7300 Metro Blvd., Ste. 585
Minneapolis, MN 55439
(612)835-1121
Fax: (612)835-8389
E-mail: jahrens620@aol.com

U.S. Bancorp Piper Jaffray Ventures, Inc.
800 Nicollet Mall, Ste. 800
Minneapolis, MN 55402

(612)303-5686
Fax: (612)303-1350
Website: http://www.paperjaffrey
ventures.com

The Food Fund, Ltd. Partnership
5720 Smatana Dr., Ste. 300
Minnetonka, MN 55343
(612)939-3950
Fax: (612)939-8106

Mayo Medical Ventures
200 First St. SW
Rochester, MN 55905
(507)266-4586
Fax: (507)284-5410
Website: http://www.mayo.edu

Missouri

Bankers Capital Corp.
3100 Gillham Rd.
Kansas City, MO 64109
(816)531-1600
Fax: (816)531-1334

Capital for Business, Inc. (Kansas City)
1000 Walnut St., 18th Fl.
Kansas City, MO 64106
(816)234-2357
Fax: (816)234-2952
Website: http://
www.capitalforbusiness.com

De Vries & Co. Inc.
800 West 47th St.
Kansas City, MO 64112
(816)756-0055
Fax: (816)756-0061

InvestAmerica Venture Group Inc. (Kansas City)
Commerce Tower
911 Main St., Ste. 2424
Kansas City, MO 64105
(816)842-0114
Fax: (816)471-7339

Kansas City Equity Partners
233 W. 47th St.
Kansas City, MO 64112
(816)960-1771
Fax: (816)960-1777
Website: http://www.kcep.com

Bome Investors, Inc.
8000 Maryland Ave., Ste. 1190
St. Louis, MO 63105
(314)721-5707
Fax: (314)721-5135

Website: http://www.gateway
ventures.com

Capital for Business, Inc. (St. Louis)
11 S. Meramac St., Ste. 1430
St. Louis, MO 63105
(314)746-7427
Fax: (314)746-8739
Website: http://www.capitalfor
business.com

Crown Capital Corp.
540 Maryville Centre Dr., Ste. 120
Saint Louis, MO 63141
(314)576-1201
Fax: (314)576-1525
Website: http://www.crown-
cap.com

Gateway Associates L.P.
8000 Maryland Ave., Ste. 1190
St. Louis, MO 63105
(314)721-5707
Fax: (314)721-5135

Harbison Corp.
8112 Maryland Ave., Ste. 250
Saint Louis, MO 63105
(314)727-8200
Fax: (314)727-0249

Heartland Capital Fund, Ltd.
PO Box 642117
Omaha, NE 68154
(402)778-5124
Fax: (402)445-2370
Website: http://www.heartland
capitalfund.com

Odin Capital Group
1625 Farnam St., Ste. 700
Omaha, NE 68102
(402)346-6200
Fax: (402)342-9311
Website: http://www.odincapital.com

Nevada

Edge Capital Investment Co. LLC
1350 E. Flamingo Rd., Ste. 3000
Las Vegas, NV 89119
(702)438-3343
E-mail: info@edgecapital.net
Website: http://www.edgecapital.net

The Benefit Capital Companies Inc.
PO Box 542
Logandale, NV 89021
(702)398-3222
Fax: (702)398-3700

Millennium Three Venture Group LLC
6880 South McCarran Blvd., Ste. A-11
Reno, NV 89509
(775)954-2020
Fax: (775)954-2023
Website: http://www.m3vg.com

New Jersey

Alan I. Goldman & Associates
497 Ridgewood Ave.
Glen Ridge, NJ 07028
(973)857-5680
Fax: (973)509-8856

CS Capital Partners LLC
328 Second St., Ste. 200
Lakewood, NJ 08701
(732)901-1111
Fax: (212)202-5071
Website: http://www.cs-capital.com

Edison Venture Fund
1009 Lenox Dr., Ste. 4
Lawrenceville, NJ 08648
(609)896-1900
Fax: (609)896-0066
E-mail: info@edisonventure.com
Website: http://www.edisonventure.com

Tappan Zee Capital Corp. (New Jersey)
201 Lower Notch Rd.
PO Box 416
Little Falls, NJ 07424
(973)256-8280
Fax: (973)256-2841

The CIT Group/Venture Capital, Inc.
650 CIT Dr.
Livingston, NJ 07039
(973)740-5429
Fax: (973)740-5555
Website: http://www.cit.com

Capital Express, L.L.C.
1100 Valleybrook Ave.
Lyndhurst, NJ 07071
(201)438-8228
Fax: (201)438-5131
E-mail: niles@capitalexpress.com
Website: http://www.capitalexpress.com

Westford Technology Ventures, L.P.
17 Academy St.
Newark, NJ 07102
(973)624-2131
Fax: (973)624-2008

Accel Partners
1 Palmer Sq.
Princeton, NJ 08542

(609)683-4500
Fax: (609)683-4880
Website: http://www.accel.com

Cardinal Partners
221 Nassau St.
Princeton, NJ 08542
(609)924-6452
Fax: (609)683-0174
Website: http://www.cardinal
healthpartners.com

Domain Associates L.L.C.
One Palmer Sq., Ste. 515
Princeton, NJ 08542
(609)683-5656
Fax: (609)683-9789
Website: http://www.domainvc.com

Johnston Associates, Inc.
181 Cherry Valley Rd.
Princeton, NJ 08540
(609)924-3131
Fax: (609)683-7524
E-mail: jaincorp@aol.com

Kemper Ventures
Princeton Forrestal Village
155 Village Blvd.
Princeton, NJ 08540
(609)936-3035
Fax: (609)936-3051

Penny Lane Parnters
One Palmer Sq., Ste. 309
Princeton, NJ 08542
(609)497-4646
Fax: (609)497-0611

Early Stage Enterprises L.P.
995 Route 518
Skillman, NJ 08558
(609)921-8896
Fax: (609)921-8703
Website: http://www.esevc.com

MBW Management Inc.
1 Springfield Ave.
Summit, NJ 07901
(908)273-4060
Fax: (908)273-4430

BCI Advisors, Inc.
Glenpointe Center W.
Teaneck, NJ 07666
(201)836-3900
Fax: (201)836-6368
E-mail: info@bciadvisors.com
Website: http://www.bci
partners.com

Demuth, Folger & Wetherill / DFW Capital Partners
Glenpointe Center E., 5th Fl.
300 Frank W. Burr Blvd.
Teaneck, NJ 07666
(201)836-2233
Fax: (201)836-5666
Website: http://www.dfwcapital.com

First Princeton Capital Corp.
189 Berdan Ave., No. 131
Wayne, NJ 07470-3233
(973)278-3233
Fax: (973)278-4290
Website: http://www.lytellcatt.net

Edelson Technology Partners
300 Tice Blvd.
Woodcliff Lake, NJ 07675
(201)930-9898
Fax: (201)930-8899
Website: http://www.edelsontech.com

New Mexico

Bruce F. Glaspell & Associates
10400 Academy Rd. NE, Ste. 313
Albuquerque, NM 87111
(505)292-4505
Fax: (505)292-4258

High Desert Ventures, Inc.
6101 Imparata St. NE, Ste. 1721
Albuquerque, NM 87111
(505)797-3330
Fax: (505)338-5147

New Business Capital Fund, Ltd.
5805 Torreon NE
Albuquerque, NM 87109
(505)822-8445

SBC Ventures
10400 Academy Rd. NE, Ste. 313
Albuquerque, NM 87111
(505)292-4505
Fax: (505)292-4528

Technology Ventures Corp.
1155 University Blvd. SE
Albuquerque, NM 87106
(505)246-2882
Fax: (505)246-2891

New York

New York State Science & Technology Foundation
Small Business Technology Investment Fund
99 Washington Ave., Ste. 1731
Albany, NY 12210

(518)473-9741
Fax: (518)473-6876

Rand Capital Corp.
2200 Rand Bldg.
Buffalo, NY 14203
(716)853-0802
Fax: (716)854-8480
Website: http://www.randcapital.com

Seed Capital Partners
620 Main St.
Buffalo, NY 14202
(716)845-7520
Fax: (716)845-7539
Website: http://www.seedcp.com

Coleman Venture Group
5909 Northern Blvd.
PO Box 224
East Norwich, NY 11732
(516)626-3642
Fax: (516)626-9722

Vega Capital Corp.
45 Knollwood Rd.
Elmsford, NY 10523
(914)345-9500
Fax: (914)345-9505

Herbert Young Securities, Inc.
98 Cuttermill Rd.
Great Neck, NY 11021
(516)487-8300
Fax: (516)487-8319

Sterling/Carl Marks Capital, Inc.
175 Great Neck Rd., Ste. 408
Great Neck, NY 11021
(516)482-7374
Fax: (516)487-0781
E-mail: stercrlmar@aol.com
Website: http://www.serling
carlmarks.com

Impex Venture Management Co.
PO Box 1570
Green Island, NY 12183
(518)271-8008
Fax: (518)271-9101

Corporate Venture Partners L.P.
200 Sunset Park
Ithaca, NY 14850
(607)257-6323
Fax: (607)257-6128

Arthur P. Gould & Co.
One Wilshire Dr.
Lake Success, NY 11020
(516)773-3000
Fax: (516)773-3289

Dauphin Capital Partners
108 Forest Ave.
Locust Valley, NY 11560
(516)759-3339
Fax: (516)759-3322
Website: http://www.dauphincapital.com

550 Digital Media Ventures
555 Madison Ave., 10th Fl.
New York, NY 10022
Website: http://www.550dmv.com

Aberlyn Capital Management Co., Inc.
500 Fifth Ave.
New York, NY 10110
(212)391-7750
Fax: (212)391-7762

Adler & Company
342 Madison Ave., Ste. 807
New York, NY 10173
(212)599-2535
Fax: (212)599-2526

Alimansky Capital Group, Inc.
605 Madison Ave., Ste. 300
New York, NY 10022-1901
(212)832-7300
Fax: (212)832-7338

Allegra Partners
515 Madison Ave., 29th Fl.
New York, NY 10022
(212)826-9080
Fax: (212)759-2561

The Argentum Group
The Chyrsler Bldg.
405 Lexington Ave.
New York, NY 10174
(212)949-6262
Fax: (212)949-8294
Website: http://www.argentum
group.com

Axavision Inc.
14 Wall St., 26th Fl.
New York, NY 10005
(212)619-4000
Fax: (212)619-7202

Bedford Capital Corp.
18 East 48th St., Ste. 1800
New York, NY 10017
(212)688-5700
Fax: (212)754-4699
E-mail: info@bedfordnyc.com
Website: http://www.bedfordnyc.com

Bloom & Co.
950 Third Ave.

New York, NY 10022
(212)838-1858
Fax: (212)838-1843

Bristol Capital Management
300 Park Ave., 17th Fl.
New York, NY 10022
(212)572-6306
Fax: (212)705-4292

**Citicorp Venture Capital Ltd.
(New York City)**
399 Park Ave., 14th Fl.
Zone 4
New York, NY 10043
(212)559-1127
Fax: (212)888-2940

CM Equity Partners
135 E. 57th St.
New York, NY 10022
(212)909-8428
Fax: (212)980-2630

Cohen & Co., L.L.C.
800 Third Ave.
New York, NY 10022
(212)317-2250
Fax: (212)317-2255
E-mail: nlcohen@aol.com

Cornerstone Equity Investors, L.L.C.
717 5th Ave., Ste. 1100
New York, NY 10022
(212)753-0901
Fax: (212)826-6798
Website: http://www.cornerstone-
equity.com

CW Group, Inc.
1041 3rd Ave., 2nd fl.
New York, NY 10021
(212)308-5266
Fax: (212)644-0354
Website: http://www.cwventures.com

DH Blair Investment Banking Corp.
44 Wall St., 2nd Fl.
New York, NY 10005
(212)495-5000
Fax: (212)269-1438

Dresdner Kleinwort Capital
75 Wall St.
New York, NY 10005
(212)429-3131
Fax: (212)429-3139
Website: http://www.dresdnerkb.com

East River Ventures, L.P.
645 Madison Ave., 22nd Fl.

New York, NY 10022
(212)644-2322
Fax: (212)644-5498

Easton Hunt Capital Partners
641 Lexington Ave., 21st Fl.
New York, NY 10017
(212)702-0950
Fax: (212)702-0952
Website: http://www.eastoncapital.com

Elk Associates Funding Corp.
747 3rd Ave., Ste. 4C
New York, NY 10017
(212)355-2449
Fax: (212)759-3338

EOS Partners, L.P.
320 Park Ave., 22nd Fl.
New York, NY 10022
(212)832-5800
Fax: (212)832-5815
E-mail: mfirst@eospartners.com
Website: http://www.eospartners.com

Euclid Partners
45 Rockefeller Plaza, Ste. 3240
New York, NY 10111
(212)218-6880
Fax: (212)218-6877
E-mail: graham@euclidpartners.com
Website: http://www.euclidpartners.com

Evergreen Capital Partners, Inc.
150 East 58th St.
New York, NY 10155
(212)813-0758
Fax: (212)813-0754

Exeter Capital L.P.
10 E. 53rd St.
New York, NY 10022
(212)872-1172
Fax: (212)872-1198
E-mail: exeter@usa.net

Financial Technology Research Corp.
518 Broadway
Penthouse
New York, NY 10012
(212)625-9100
Fax: (212)431-0300
E-mail: fintek@financier.com

4C Ventures
237 Park Ave., Ste. 801
New York, NY 10017
(212)692-3680
Fax: (212)692-3685
Website: http://www.4cventures.com

Fusient Ventures
99 Park Ave., 20th Fl.
New York, NY 10016
(212)972-8999
Fax: (212)972-9876
E-mail: info@fusient.com
Website: http://www.fusient.com

Generation Capital Partners
551 Fifth Ave., Ste. 3100
New York, NY 10176
(212)450-8507
Fax: (212)450-8550
Website: http://www.genpartners.com

Golub Associates, Inc.
555 Madison Ave.
New York, NY 10022
(212)750-6060
Fax: (212)750-5505

Hambro America Biosciences Inc.
650 Madison Ave., 21st Floor
New York, NY 10022
(212)223-7400
Fax: (212)223-0305

Hanover Capital Corp.
505 Park Ave., 15th Fl.
New York, NY 10022
(212)755-1222
Fax: (212)935-1787

Harvest Partners, Inc.
280 Park Ave, 33rd Fl.
New York, NY 10017
(212)559-6300
Fax: (212)812-0100
Website: http://www.harvpart.com

Holding Capital Group, Inc.
10 E. 53rd St., 30th Fl.
New York, NY 10022
(212)486-6670
Fax: (212)486-0843

Hudson Venture Partners
660 Madison Ave., 14th Fl.
New York, NY 10021-8405
(212)644-9797
Fax: (212)644-7430
Website: http://www.hudsonptr.com

IBJS Capital Corp.
1 State St., 9th Fl.
New York, NY 10004
(212)858-2018
Fax: (212)858-2768

InterEquity Capital Partners, L.P.
220 5th Ave.
New York, NY 10001

(212)779-2022
Fax: (212)779-2103
Website: http://www.interequity-capital.com

The Jordan Edmiston Group Inc.
150 East 52nd St., 18th Fl.
New York, NY 10022
(212)754-0710
Fax: (212)754-0337

Josephberg, Grosz and Co., Inc.
633 3rd Ave., 13th Fl.
New York, NY 10017
(212)974-9926
Fax: (212)397-5832

J.P. Morgan Capital Corp.
60 Wall St.
New York, NY 10260-0060
(212)648-9000
Fax: (212)648-5002
Website: http://www.jpmorgan.com

The Lambda Funds
380 Lexington Ave., 54th Fl.
New York, NY 10168
(212)682-3454
Fax: (212)682-9231

Lepercq Capital Management Inc.
1675 Broadway
New York, NY 10019
(212)698-0795
Fax: (212)262-0155

Loeb Partners Corp.
61 Broadway, Ste. 2400
New York, NY 10006
(212)483-7000
Fax: (212)574-2001

Madison Investment Partners
660 Madison Ave.
New York, NY 10021
(212)223-2600
Fax: (212)223-8208

MC Capital Inc.
520 Madison Ave., 16th Fl.
New York, NY 10022
(212)644-0841
Fax: (212)644-2926

McCown, De Leeuw and Co. (New York)
65 E. 55th St., 36th Fl.
New York, NY 10022
(212)355-5500
Fax: (212)355-6283
Website: http://www.mdcpartners.com

Morgan Stanley Venture Partners
1221 Avenue of the Americas, 33rd Fl.
New York, NY 10020
(212)762-7900
Fax: (212)762-8424
E-mail: msventures@ms.com
Website: http://www.msvp.com

Nazem and Co.
645 Madison Ave., 12th Fl.
New York, NY 10022
(212)371-7900
Fax: (212)371-2150

Needham Capital Management, L.L.C.
445 Park Ave.
New York, NY 10022
(212)371-8300
Fax: (212)705-0299
Website: http://www.needhamco.com

Norwood Venture Corp.
1430 Broadway, Ste. 1607
New York, NY 10018
(212)869-5075
Fax: (212)869-5331
E-mail: nvc@mail.idt.net
Website: http://www.norven.com

Noveltek Venture Corp.
521 Fifth Ave., Ste. 1700
New York, NY 10175
(212)286-1963

Paribas Principal, Inc.
787 7th Ave.
New York, NY 10019
(212)841-2005
Fax: (212)841-3558

Patricof & Co. Ventures, Inc. (New York)
445 Park Ave.
New York, NY 10022
(212)753-6300
Fax: (212)319-6155
Website: http://www.patricof.com

The Platinum Group, Inc.
350 Fifth Ave, Ste. 7113
New York, NY 10118
(212)736-4300
Fax: (212)736-6086
Website: http://www.platinumgroup.com

Pomona Capital
780 Third Ave., 28th Fl.
New York, NY 10017
(212)593-3639
Fax: (212)593-3987
Website: http://www.pomonacapital.com

Prospect Street Ventures
10 East 40th St., 44th Fl.
New York, NY 10016
(212)448-0702
Fax: (212)448-9652
E-mail: wkohler@prospectstreet.com
Website: http://www.prospectstreet.com

Regent Capital Management
505 Park Ave., Ste. 1700
New York, NY 10022
(212)735-9900
Fax: (212)735-9908

Rothschild Ventures, Inc.
1251 Avenue of the Americas, 51st Fl.
New York, NY 10020
(212)403-3500
Fax: (212)403-3652
Website: http://www.nmrothschild.com

Sandler Capital Management
767 Fifth Ave., 45th Fl.
New York, NY 10153
(212)754-8100
Fax: (212)826-0280

Siguler Guff & Company
630 Fifth Ave., 16th Fl.
New York, NY 10111
(212)332-5100
Fax: (212)332-5120

Spencer Trask Ventures Inc.
535 Madison Ave.
New York, NY 10022
(212)355-5565
Fax: (212)751-3362
Website: http://www.spencertrask.com

Sprout Group (New York City)
277 Park Ave.
New York, NY 10172
(212)892-3600
Fax: (212)892-3444
E-mail: info@sproutgroup.com
Website: http://www.sproutgroup.com

US Trust Private Equity
114 W.47th St.
New York, NY 10036
(212)852-3949
Fax: (212)852-3759
Website: http://www.ustrust.com/
privateequity

Vencon Management Inc.
301 West 53rd St., Ste. 10F
New York, NY 10019
(212)581-8787
Fax: (212)397-4126
Website: http://www.venconinc.com

Venrock Associates
30 Rockefeller Plaza, Ste. 5508
New York, NY 10112
(212)649-5600
Fax: (212)649-5788
Website: http://www.venrock.com

Venture Capital Fund of America, Inc.
509 Madison Ave., Ste. 812
New York, NY 10022
(212)838-5577
Fax: (212)838-7614
E-mail: mail@vcfa.com
Website: http://www.vcfa.com

Venture Opportunities Corp.
150 E. 58th St.
New York, NY 10155
(212)832-3737
Fax: (212)980-6603

Warburg Pincus Ventures, Inc.
466 Lexington Ave., 11th Fl.
New York, NY 10017
(212)878-9309
Fax: (212)878-9200
Website: http://www.warburgpincus.com

Wasserstein, Perella & Co. Inc.
31 W. 52nd St., 27th Fl.
New York, NY 10019
(212)702-5691
Fax: (212)969-7879

Welsh, Carson, Anderson, & Stowe
320 Park Ave., Ste. 2500
New York, NY 10022-6815
(212)893-9500
Fax: (212)893-9575

Whitney and Co. (New York)
630 Fifth Ave. Ste. 3225
New York, NY 10111
(212)332-2400
Fax: (212)332-2422
Website: http://www.jhwitney.com

Winthrop Ventures
74 Trinity Place, Ste. 600
New York, NY 10006
(212)422-0100

The Pittsford Group
8 Lodge Pole Rd.
Pittsford, NY 14534
(716)223-3523

Genesee Funding
70 Linden Oaks, 3rd Fl.
Rochester, NY 14625
(716)383-5550
Fax: (716)383-5305

Gabelli Multimedia Partners
One Corporate Center
Rye, NY 10580
(914)921-5395
Fax: (914)921-5031

Stamford Financial
108 Main St.
Stamford, NY 12167
(607)652-3311
Fax: (607)652-6301
Website: http://www.stamford
financial.com

Northwood Ventures LLC
485 Underhill Blvd., Ste. 205
Syosset, NY 11791
(516)364-5544
Fax: (516)364-0879
E-mail: northwood@northwood.com
Website: http://www.north
woodventures.com

Exponential Business Development Co.
216 Walton St.
Syracuse, NY 13202-1227
(315)474-4500
Fax: (315)474-4682
E-mail: dirksonn@aol.com
Website: http://www.exponential-ny.com

Onondaga Venture Capital Fund Inc.
714 State Tower Bldg.
Syracuse, NY 13202
(315)478-0157
Fax: (315)478-0158

Bessemer Venture Partners (Westbury)
1400 Old Country Rd., Ste. 109
Westbury, NY 11590
(516)997-2300
Fax: (516)997-2371
E-mail: bob@bvpny.com
Website: http://www.bvp.com

Ovation Capital Partners
120 Bloomingdale Rd., 4th Fl.
White Plains, NY 10605
(914)258-0011
Fax: (914)684-0848
Website: http://www.ovation
capital.com

North Carolina

Carolinas Capital Investment Corp.
1408 Biltmore Dr.
Charlotte, NC 28207
(704)375-3888
Fax: (704)375-6226

First Union Capital Partners
1st Union Center, 12th Fl.
301 S. College St.
Charlotte, NC 28288-0732
(704)383-0000
Fax: (704)374-6711
Website: http://www.fucp.com

Frontier Capital LLC
525 North Tryon St., Ste. 1700
Charlotte, NC 28202
(704)414-2880
Fax: (704)414-2881
Website: http://www.frontierfunds.com

Kitty Hawk Capital
2700 Coltsgate Rd., Ste. 202
Charlotte, NC 28211
(704)362-3909
Fax: (704)362-2774
Website: http://www.kittyhawk
capital.com

Piedmont Venture Partners
One Morrocroft Centre
6805 Morisson Blvd., Ste. 380
Charlotte, NC 28211
(704)731-5200
Fax: (704)365-9733
Website: http://www.piedmontvp.com

Ruddick Investment Co.
1800 Two First Union Center
Charlotte, NC 28282
(704)372-5404
Fax: (704)372-6409

The Shelton Companies Inc.
3600 One First Union Center
301 S. College St.
Charlotte, NC 28202
(704)348-2200
Fax: (704)348-2260

Wakefield Group
1110 E. Morehead St.
PO Box 36329
Charlotte, NC 28236
(704)372-0355
Fax: (704)372-8216
Website: http://www.wakefiel
dgroup.com

Aurora Funds, Inc.
2525 Meridian Pkwy., Ste. 220
Durham, NC 27713
(919)484-0400
Fax: (919)484-0444
Website: http://www.aurora
funds.com

Intersouth Partners
3211 Shannon Rd., Ste. 610
Durham, NC 27707
(919)493-6640
Fax: (919)493-6649
E-mail: info@intersouth.com
Website: http://www.intersouth.com

Geneva Merchant Banking Partners
PO Box 21962
Greensboro, NC 27420
(336)275-7002
Fax: (336)275-9155
Website: http://www.geneva
merchantbank.com

The North Carolina Enterprise Fund, L.P.
3600 Glenwood Ave., Ste. 107
Raleigh, NC 27612
(919)781-2691
Fax: (919)783-9195
Website: http://www.ncef.com

Ohio

Senmend Medical Ventures
4445 Lake Forest Dr., Ste. 600
Cincinnati, OH 45242
(513)563-3264
Fax: (513)563-3261

The Walnut Group
312 Walnut St., Ste. 1151
Cincinnati, OH 45202
(513)651-3300
Fax: (513)929-4441
Website: http://www.thewal
nutgroup.com

Brantley Venture Partners
20600 Chagrin Blvd., Ste. 1150
Cleveland, OH 44122
(216)283-4800
Fax: (216)283-5324

Clarion Capital Corp.
1801 E. 9th St., Ste. 1120
Cleveland, OH 44114
(216)687-1096
Fax: (216)694-3545

Crystal Internet Venture Fund, L.P.
1120 Chester Ave., Ste. 418
Cleveland, OH 44114
(216)263-5515
Fax: (216)263-5518
E-mail: jf@crystalventure.com
Website: http://www.crystal
venture.com

Key Equity Capital Corp.
127 Public Sq., 28th Fl.
Cleveland, OH 44114
(216)689-3000
Fax: (216)689-3204
Website: http://www.keybank.com

Morgenthaler Ventures
Terminal Tower
50 Public Square, Ste. 2700
Cleveland, OH 44113
(216)416-7500
Fax: (216)416-7501
Website: http://www.morgenthaler.com

National City Equity Partners Inc.
1965 E. 6th St.
Cleveland, OH 44114
(216)575-2491
Fax: (216)575-9965
E-mail: nccap@aol.com
Website: http://www.nccapital.com

Primus Venture Partners, Inc.
5900 LanderBrook Dr., Ste. 2000
Cleveland, OH 44124-4020
(440)684-7300
Fax: (440)684-7342
E-mail: info@primusventure.com
Website: http://www.primusventure.com

Banc One Capital Partners (Columbus)
150 East Gay St., 24th Fl.
Columbus, OH 43215
(614)217-1100
Fax: (614)217-1217

Battelle Venture Partners
505 King Ave.
Columbus, OH 43201
(614)424-7005
Fax: (614)424-4874

Ohio Partners
62 E. Board St., 3rd Fl.
Columbus, OH 43215
(614)621-1210
Fax: (614)621-1240

Capital Technology Group, L.L.C.
400 Metro Place North, Ste. 300
Dublin, OH 43017
(614)792-6066
Fax: (614)792-6036
E-mail: info@capitaltech.com
Website: http://www.capitaltech.com

Northwest Ohio Venture Fund
4159 Holland-Sylvania R., Ste. 202
Toledo, OH 43623
(419)824-8144

Fax: (419)882-2035
E-mail: bwalsh@novf.com

Oklahoma

Moore & Associates
1000 W. Wilshire Blvd., Ste. 370
Oklahoma City, OK 73116
(405)842-3660
Fax: (405)842-3763

Chisholm Private Capital Partners
100 West 5th St., Ste. 805
Tulsa, OK 74103
(918)584-0440
Fax: (918)584-0441
Website: http://www.chisholmvc.com

Davis, Tuttle Venture Partners (Tulsa)
320 S. Boston, Ste. 1000
Tulsa, OK 74103-3703
(918)584-7272
Fax: (918)582-3404
Website: http://www.davistuttle.com

RBC Ventures
2627 E. 21st St.
Tulsa, OK 74114
(918)744-5607
Fax: (918)743-8630

Oregon

Utah Ventures II LP
10700 SW Beaverton-Hillsdale Hwy.,
Ste. 548
Beaverton, OR 97005
(503)574-4125
E-mail: adishlip@uven.com
Website: http://www.uven.com

Orien Ventures
14523 SW Westlake Dr.
Lake Oswego, OR 97035
(503)699-1680
Fax: (503)699-1681

OVP Venture Partners (Lake Oswego)
340 Oswego Pointe Dr., Ste. 200
Lake Oswego, OR 97034
(503)697-8766
Fax: (503)697-8863
E-mail: info@ovp.com
Website: http://www.ovp.com

Oregon Resource and Technology Development Fund
4370 NE Halsey St., Ste. 233
Portland, OR 97213-1566
(503)282-4462
Fax: (503)282-2976

Shaw Venture Partners
400 SW 6th Ave., Ste. 1100
Portland, OR 97204-1636
(503)228-4884
Fax: (503)227-2471
Website: http://www.shawventures.com

Pennsylvania

Mid-Atlantic Venture Funds
125 Goodman Dr.
Bethlehem, PA 18015
(610)865-6550
Fax: (610)865-6427
Website: http://www.mavf.com

Newspring Ventures
100 W. Elm St., Ste. 101
Conshohocken, PA 19428
(610)567-2380
Fax: (610)567-2388
Website: http://www.news
printventures.com

Patricof & Co. Ventures, Inc.
455 S. Gulph Rd., Ste. 410
King of Prussia, PA 19406
(610)265-0286
Fax: (610)265-4959
Website: http://www.patricof.com

Loyalhanna Venture Fund
527 Cedar Way, Ste. 104
Oakmont, PA 15139
(412)820-7035
Fax: (412)820-7036

Innovest Group Inc.
2000 Market St., Ste. 1400
Philadelphia, PA 19103
(215)564-3960
Fax: (215)569-3272

Keystone Venture Capital Management Co.
1601 Market St., Ste. 2500
Philadelphia, PA 19103
(215)241-1200
Fax: (215)241-1211
Website: http://www.keystonevc.com

Liberty Venture Partners
2005 Market St., Ste. 200
Philadelphia, PA 19103
(215)282-4484
Fax: (215)282-4485
E-mail: info@libertyvp.com
Website: http://www.libertyvp.com

Penn Janney Fund, Inc.
1801 Market St., 11th Fl.
Philadelphia, PA 19103

(215)665-4447
Fax: (215)557-0820

Philadelphia Ventures, Inc.
The Bellevue
200 S. Broad St.
Philadelphia, PA 19102
(215)732-4445
Fax: (215)732-4644

Birchmere Ventures Inc.
2000 Technology Dr.
Pittsburgh, PA 15219-3109
(412)803-8000
Fax: (412)687-8139
Website: http://www.birchmerevc.com

CEO Venture Fund
2000 Technology Dr., Ste. 160
Pittsburgh, PA 15219-3109
(412)687-3451
Fax: (412)687-8139
E-mail: ceofund@aol.com
Website: http://www.ceoventure
fund.com

Innovation Works Inc.
2000 Technology Dr., Ste. 250
Pittsburgh, PA 15219
(412)681-1520
Fax: (412)681-2625
Website: http://www.innovation
works.org

Keystone Minority Capital Fund L.P.
1801 Centre Ave., Ste. 201
Williams Sq.
Pittsburgh, PA 15219
(412)338-2230
Fax: (412)338-2224

Mellon Ventures, Inc.
One Mellon Bank Ctr., Rm. 3500
Pittsburgh, PA 15258
(412)236-3594
Fax: (412)236-3593
Website: http://www.mellon
ventures.com

Pennsylvania Growth Fund
5850 Ellsworth Ave., Ste. 303
Pittsburgh, PA 15232
(412)661-1000
Fax: (412)361-0676

Point Venture Partners
The Century Bldg.
130 Seventh St., 7th Fl.
Pittsburgh, PA 15222
(412)261-1966
Fax: (412)261-1718

Cross Atlantic Capital Partners
5 Radnor Corporate Center, Ste. 555
Radnor, PA 19087
(610)995-2650
Fax: (610)971-2062
Website: http://www.xacp.com

Meridian Venture Partners (Radnor)
The Radnor Court Bldg., Ste. 140
259 Radnor-Chester Rd.
Radnor, PA 19087
(610)254-2999
Fax: (610)254-2996
E-mail: mvpart@ix.netcom.com

TDH
919 Conestoga Rd., Bldg. 1, Ste. 301
Rosemont, PA 19010
(610)526-9970
Fax: (610)526-9971

Adams Capital Management
500 Blackburn Ave.
Sewickley, PA 15143
(412)749-9454
Fax: (412)749-9459
Website: http://www.acm.com

S.R. One, Ltd.
Four Tower Bridge
200 Barr Harbor Dr., Ste. 250
W. Conshohocken, PA 19428
(610)567-1000
Fax: (610)567-1039

Greater Philadelphia Venture Capital Corp.
351 East Conestoga Rd.
Wayne, PA 19087
(610)688-6829
Fax: (610)254-8958

PA Early Stage
435 Devon Park Dr., Bldg. 500, Ste. 510
Wayne, PA 19087
(610)293-4075
Fax: (610)254-4240
Website: http://www.paearlystage.com

The Sandhurst Venture Fund, L.P.
351 E. Constoga Rd.
Wayne, PA 19087
(610)254-8900
Fax: (610)254-8958

TL Ventures
700 Bldg.
435 Devon Park Dr.
Wayne, PA 19087-1990
(610)975-3765
Fax: (610)254-4210
Website: http://www.tlventures.com

Rockhill Ventures, Inc.
100 Front St., Ste. 1350
West Conshohocken, PA 19428
(610)940-0300
Fax: (610)940-0301

Puerto Rico

Advent-Morro Equity Partners
Banco Popular Bldg.
206 Tetuan St., Ste. 903
San Juan, PR 00902
(787)725-5285
Fax: (787)721-1735

North America Investment Corp.
Mercantil Plaza, Ste. 813
PO Box 191831
San Juan, PR 00919
(787)754-6178
Fax: (787)754-6181

Rhode Island

Manchester Humphreys, Inc.
40 Westminster St., Ste. 900
Providence, RI 02903
(401)454-0400
Fax: (401)454-0403

Navis Partners
50 Kennedy Plaza, 12th Fl.
Providence, RI 02903
(401)278-6770
Fax: (401)278-6387
Website: http://www.navis
partners.com

South Carolina

Capital Insights, L.L.C.
PO Box 27162
Greenville, SC 29616-2162
(864)242-6832
Fax: (864)242-6755
E-mail: jwarner@capitalinsights.com
Website: http://www.capitalin
sights.com

Transamerica Mezzanine Financing
7 N. Laurens St., Ste. 603
Greenville, SC 29601
(864)232-6198
Fax: (864)241-4444

Tennessee

Valley Capital Corp.
Krystal Bldg.
100 W. Martin Luther King Blvd.,
Ste. 212

Organizations, Agencies, & Consultants

Chattanooga, TN 37402
(423)265-1557
Fax: (423)265-1588

Coleman Swenson Booth Inc.
237 2nd Ave. S
Franklin, TN 37064-2649
(615)791-9462
Fax: (615)791-9636
Website: http://
www.colemanswenson.com

Capital Services & Resources, Inc.
5159 Wheelis Dr., Ste. 106
Memphis, TN 38117
(901)761-2156
Fax: (907)767-0060

Paradigm Capital Partners LLC
6410 Poplar Ave., Ste. 395
Memphis, TN 38119
(901)682-6060
Fax: (901)328-3061

SSM Ventures
845 Crossover Ln., Ste. 140
Memphis, TN 38117
(901)767-1131
Fax: (901)767-1135
Website: http://www.ssm
ventures.com

Capital Across America L.P.
501 Union St., Ste. 201
Nashville, TN 37219
(615)254-1414
Fax: (615)254-1856
Website: http://
www.capitalacrossamerica.com

Equitas L.P.
2000 Glen Echo Rd., Ste. 101
PO Box 158838
Nashville, TN 37215-8838
(615)383-8673
Fax: (615)383-8693

Massey Burch Capital Corp.
One Burton Hills Blvd., Ste. 350
Nashville, TN 37215
(615)665-3221
Fax: (615)665-3240
E-mail: tcalton@masseyburch.com
Website: http://www.masseyburch.com

Nelson Capital Corp.
3401 West End Ave., Ste. 300
Nashville, TN 37203
(615)292-8787
Fax: (615)385-3150

Texas

Phillips-Smith Specialty Retail Group
5080 Spectrum Dr., Ste. 805 W
Addison, TX 75001
(972)387-0725
Fax: (972)458-2560
E-mail: pssrg@aol.com
Website: http://www.phillips-smith.com

Austin Ventures, L.P.
701 Brazos St., Ste. 1400
Austin, TX 78701
(512)485-1900
Fax: (512)476-3952
E-mail: info@ausven.com
Website: http://www.austinventures.com

The Capital Network
3925 West Braker Lane, Ste. 406
Austin, TX 78759-5321
(512)305-0826
Fax: (512)305-0836

Techxas Ventures LLC
5000 Plaza on the Lake
Austin, TX 78746
(512)343-0118
Fax: (512)343-1879
E-mail: bruce@techxas.com
Website: http://www.techxas.com

Alliance Financial of Houston
218 Heather Ln.
Conroe, TX 77385-9013
(936)447-3300
Fax: (936)447-4222

Amerimark Capital Corp.
1111 W. Mockingbird, Ste. 1111
Dallas, TX 75247
(214)638-7878
Fax: (214)638-7612
E-mail: amerimark@amcapital.com
Website: http://www.amcapital.com

AMT Venture Partners / AMT Capital Ltd.
5220 Spring Valley Rd., Ste. 600
Dallas, TX 75240
(214)905-9757
Fax: (214)905-9761
Website: http://www.amtcapital.com

Arkoma Venture Partners
5950 Berkshire Lane, Ste. 1400
Dallas, TX 75225
(214)739-3515
Fax: (214)739-3572
E-mail: joelf@arkomavp.com

Capital Southwest Corp.
12900 Preston Rd., Ste. 700
Dallas, TX 75230
(972)233-8242
Fax: (972)233-7362
Website: http://
www.capitalsouthwest.com

Dali, Hook Partners
One Lincoln Center, Ste. 1550
5400 LBJ Freeway
Dallas, TX 75240
(972)991-5457
Fax: (972)991-5458
E-mail: dhook@hookpartners.com
Website: http://www.hookpartners.com

HO2 Partners
Two Galleria Tower
13455 Noel Rd., Ste. 1670
Dallas, TX 75240
(972)702-1144
Fax: (972)702-8234
Website: http://www.ho2.com

Interwest Partners (Dallas)
2 Galleria Tower
13455 Noel Rd., Ste. 1670
Dallas, TX 75240
(972)392-7279
Fax: (972)490-6348
Website: http://www.interwest.com

Kahala Investments, Inc.
8214 Westchester Dr., Ste. 715
Dallas, TX 75225
(214)987-0077
Fax: (214)987-2332

MESBIC Ventures Holding Co.
2435 North Central Expressway, Ste. 200
Dallas, TX 75080
(972)991-1597
Fax: (972)991-4770
Website: http://www.mvhc.com

North Texas MESBIC, Inc.
9500 Forest Lane, Ste. 430
Dallas, TX 75243
(214)221-3565
Fax: (214)221-3566

Richard Jaffe & Company, Inc,
7318 Royal Cir.
Dallas, TX 75230
(214)265-9397
Fax: (214)739-1845

Sevin Rosen Management Co.
13455 Noel Rd., Ste. 1670
Dallas, TX 75240

(972)702-1100
Fax: (972)702-1103
E-mail: info@srfunds.com
Website: http://www.srfunds.com

Stratford Capital Partners, L.P.
300 Crescent Ct., Ste. 500
Dallas, TX 75201
(214)740-7377
Fax: (214)720-7393
E-mail: stratcap@hmtf.com

Sunwestern Investment Group
12221 Merit Dr., Ste. 935
Dallas, TX 75251
(972)239-5650
Fax: (972)701-0024

Wingate Partners
750 N. St. Paul St., Ste. 1200
Dallas, TX 75201
(214)720-1313
Fax: (214)871-8799

Buena Venture Associates
201 Main St., 32nd Fl.
Fort Worth, TX 76102
(817)339-7400
Fax: (817)390-8408
Website: http://www.buenaventure.com

The Catalyst Group
3 Riverway, Ste. 770
Houston, TX 77056
(713)623-8133
Fax: (713)623-0473
E-mail: herman@thecatalystgroup.net
Website: http://www.thecatalyst
group.net

Cureton & Co., Inc.
1100 Louisiana, Ste. 3250
Houston, TX 77002
(713)658-9806
Fax: (713)658-0476

Davis, Tuttle Venture Partners (Dallas)
8 Greenway Plaza, Ste. 1020
Houston, TX 77046
(713)993-0440
Fax: (713)621-2297
Website: http://www.davistuttle.com

Houston Partners
401 Louisiana, 8th Fl.
Houston, TX 77002
(713)222-8600
Fax: (713)222-8932

Southwest Venture Group
10878 Westheimer, Ste. 178

Houston, TX 77042
(713)827-8947
(713)461-1470

AM Fund
4600 Post Oak Place, Ste. 100
Houston, TX 77027
(713)627-9111
Fax: (713)627-9119

Ventex Management, Inc.
3417 Milam St.
Houston, TX 77002-9531
(713)659-7870
Fax: (713)659-7855

MBA Venture Group
1004 Olde Town Rd., Ste. 102
Irving, TX 75061
(972)986-6703

First Capital Group Management Co.
750 East Mulberry St., Ste. 305
PO Box 15616
San Antonio, TX 78212
(210)736-4233
Fax: (210)736-5449

The Southwest Venture Partnerships
16414 San Pedro, Ste. 345
San Antonio, TX 78232
(210)402-1200
Fax: (210)402-1221
E-mail: swvp@aol.com

Medtech International Inc.
1742 Carriageway
Sugarland, TX 77478
(713)980-8474
Fax: (713)980 6343

Utah

First Security Business Investment Corp.
15 East 100 South, Ste. 100
Salt Lake City, UT 84111
(801)246-5737
Fax: (801)246-5740

Utah Ventures II, L.P.
423 Wakara Way, Ste. 206
Salt Lake City, UT 84108
(801)583-5922
Fax: (801)583-4105
Website: http://www.uven.com

Wasatch Venture Corp.
1 S. Main St., Ste. 1400
Salt Lake City, UT 84133
(801)524-8939

Fax: (801)524-8941
E-mail: mail@wasatchvc.com

Vermont

North Atlantic Capital Corp.
76 Saint Paul St., Ste. 600
Burlington, VT 05401
(802)658-7820
Fax: (802)658-5757
Website: http://www.north
atlanticcapital.com

Green Mountain Advisors Inc.
PO Box 1230
Quechee, VT 05059
(802)296-7800
Fax: (802)296-6012
Website: http://www.gmtcap.com

Virginia

Oxford Financial Services Corp.
Alexandria, VA 22314
(703)519-4900
Fax: (703)519-4910
E-mail: oxford133@aol.com

Continental SBIC
4141 N. Henderson Rd.
Arlington, VA 22203
(703)527-5200
Fax: (703)527-3700

Novak Biddle Venture Partners
1750 Tysons Blvd., Ste. 1190
McLean, VA 22102
(703)847-3770
Fax: (703)847-3771
E-mail: roger@novakbiddle.com
Website: http://www.novakbiddle.com

Spacevest
11911 Freedom Dr., Ste. 500
Reston, VA 20190
(703)904-9800
Fax: (703)904-0571
E-mail: spacevest@spacevest.com
Website: http://www.spacevest.com

Virginia Capital
1801 Libbie Ave., Ste. 201
Richmond, VA 23226
(804)648-4802
Fax: (804)648-4809
E-mail: webmaster@vacapital.com
Website: http://www.vacapital.com

Calvert Social Venture Partners
402 Maple Ave. W
Vienna, VA 22180

(703)255-4930
Fax: (703)255-4931
E-mail: calven2000@aol.com

Fairfax Partners
8000 Towers Crescent Dr., Ste. 940
Vienna, VA 22182
(703)847-9486
Fax: (703)847-0911

Global Internet Ventures
8150 Leesburg Pike, Ste. 1210
Vienna, VA 22182
(703)442-3300
Fax: (703)442-3388
Website: http://www.givinc.com

Walnut Capital Corp. (Vienna)
8000 Towers Crescent Dr., Ste. 1070
Vienna, VA 22182
(703)448-3771
Fax: (703)448-7751

Washington

Encompass Ventures
777 108th Ave. NE, Ste. 2300
Bellevue, WA 98004
(425)486-3900
Fax: (425)486-3901
E-mail: info@evpartners.com
Website: http://www.encom
passventures.com

Fluke Venture Partners
11400 SE Sixth St., Ste. 230
Bellevue, WA 98004
(425)453-4590
Fax: (425)453-4675
E-mail: gabelein@flukeventures.com
Website: http://www.flukeventures.com

Pacific Northwest Partners SBIC, L.P.
15352 SE 53rd St.
Bellevue, WA 98006
(425)455-9967
Fax: (425)455-9404

Materia Venture Associates, L.P.
3435 Carillon Pointe
Kirkland, WA 98033-7354
(425)822-4100
Fax: (425)827-4086

OVP Venture Partners (Kirkland)
2420 Carillon Pt.
Kirkland, WA 98033
(425)889-9192
Fax: (425)889-0152
E-mail: info@ovp.com
Website: http://www.ovp.com

Digital Partners
999 3rd Ave., Ste. 1610
Seattle, WA 98104
(206)405-3607
Fax: (206)405-3617
Website: http://www.digitalpartners.com

Frazier & Company
601 Union St., Ste. 3300
Seattle, WA 98101
(206)621-7200
Fax: (206)621-1848
E-mail: jon@frazierco.com

Kirlan Venture Capital, Inc.
221 First Ave. W, Ste. 108
Seattle, WA 98119-4223
(206)281-8610
Fax: (206)285-3451
Website: http://www.kirlanventure.com

Phoenix Partners
1000 2nd Ave., Ste. 3600
Seattle, WA 98104
(206)624-8968
Fax: (206)624-1907

Voyager Capital
800 5th St., Ste. 4100
Seattle, WA 98103
(206)470-1180
Fax: (206)470-1185
E-mail: info@voyagercap.com
Website: http://www.voyagercap.com

Northwest Venture Associates
221 N. Wall St., Ste. 628
Spokane, WA 99201
(509)747-0728
Fax: (509)747-0758
Website: http://www.nwva.com

Wisconsin

Venture Investors Management, L.L.C.
University Research Park
505 S. Rosa Rd.
Madison, WI 53719
(608)441-2700
Fax: (608)441-2727
E-mail: roger@ventureinvestors.com
Website: http://www.venture
investers.com

Capital Investments, Inc.
1009 West Glen Oaks Lane, Ste. 103
Mequon, WI 53092
(414)241-0303
Fax: (414)241-8451
Website: http://
www.capitalinvestmentsinc.com

Future Value Venture, Inc.
2745 N. Martin Luther King
Dr., Ste. 204
Milwaukee, WI 53212-2300
(414)264-2252
Fax: (414)264-2253
E-mail: fvventures@aol.com
William Beckett, President

Lubar and Co., Inc.
700 N. Water St., Ste. 1200
Milwaukee, WI 53202
(414)291-9000
Fax: (414)291-9061

GCI
20875 Crossroads Cir., Ste. 100
Waukesha, WI 53186
(262)798-5080
Fax: (262)798-5087

Glossary of Small Business Terms

Absolute liability
Liability that is incurred due to product defects or negligent actions. Manufacturers or retail establishments are held responsible, even though the defect or action may not have been intentional or negligent.

ACE
See Active Corps of Executives

Accident and health benefits
Benefits offered to employees and their families in order to offset the costs associated with accidental death, accidental injury, or sickness.

Account statement
A record of transactions, including payments, new debt, and deposits, incurred during a defined period of time.

Accounting system
System capturing the costs of all employees and/or machinery included in business expenses.

Accounts payable
See Trade credit

Accounts receivable
Unpaid accounts which arise from unsettled claims and transactions from the sale of a company's products or services to its customers.

Active Corps of Executives (ACE)
A group of volunteers for a management assistance program of the U.S. Small Business Administration; volunteers provide one-on-one counseling and teach workshops and seminars for small firms.

ADA
See Americans with Disabilities Act

Adaptation
The process whereby an invention is modified to meet the needs of users.

Adaptive engineering
The process whereby an invention is modified to meet the manufacturing and commercial requirements of a targeted market.

Adverse selection
The tendency for higher-risk individuals to purchase health care and more comprehensive plans, resulting in increased costs.

Advertising
A marketing tool used to capture public attention and influence purchasing decisions for a product or service. Utilizes various forms of media to generate consumer response, such as flyers, magazines, newspapers, radio, and television.

Age discrimination
The denial of the rights and privileges of employment based solely on the age of an individual.

Agency costs
Costs incurred to insure that the lender or investor maintains control over assets while allowing the borrower or entrepreneur to use them. Monitoring and information costs are the two major types of agency costs.

Agribusiness
The production and sale of commodities and products from the commercial farming industry.

America Online
An online service which is accessible by computer modem. The service features Internet access, bulletin boards, online periodicals, electronic mail, and other services for subscribers.

Americans with Disabilities Act (ADA)
Law designed to ensure equal access and opportunity to handicapped persons.

Annual report
Yearly financial report prepared by a business that adheres to the requirements set forth by the Securities and Exchange Commission (SEC).

Antitrust immunity
Exemption from prosecution under antitrust laws. In the transportation industry, firms with antitrust immunity are permitted under certain conditions to set schedules and sometimes prices for the public benefit.

Applied research
Scientific study targeted for use in a product or process.

Asians
A minority category used by the U.S. Bureau of the Census to represent a diverse group that includes Aleuts, Eskimos, American Indians, Asian Indians, Chinese, Japanese, Koreans, Vietnamese, Filipinos, Hawaiians, and other Pacific Islanders.

Assets
Anything of value owned by a company.

Audit
The verification of accounting records and business procedures conducted by an outside accounting service.

Average cost
Total production costs divided by the quantity produced.

Balance Sheet
A financial statement listing the total assets and liabilities of a company at a given time.

Bankruptcy
The condition in which a business cannot meet its debt obligations and petitions a federal district court either for reorganization of its debts (Chapter 11) or for liquidation of its assets (Chapter 7).

Basic research
Theoretical scientific exploration not targeted to application.

Basket clause
A provision specifying the amount of public pension funds that may be placed in investments not included on a state's legal list (see separate citation).

BBS
See Bulletin Board Service

BDC
See Business development corporation

Benefit
Various services, such as health care, flextime, day care, insurance, and vacation, offered to employees as part of a hiring package. Typically subsidized in whole or in part by the business.

BIDCO
See Business and industrial development company

Billing cycle
A system designed to evenly distribute customer billing throughout the month, preventing clerical backlogs.

Birth
See Business birth

Blue chip security
A low-risk, low-yield security representing an interest in a very stable company.

Blue sky laws
A general term that denotes various states' laws regulating securities.

Bond
A written instrument executed by a bidder or contractor (the principal) and a second party (the surety or sureties) to assure fulfillment of the principal's obligations to a third party (the obligee or government) identified in the bond. If the principal's obligations are not met, the bond assures payment to the extent stipulated of any loss sustained by the obligee.

Bonding requirements
Terms contained in a bond (see separate citation).

Bonus
An amount of money paid to an employee as a reward for achieving certain business goals or objectives.

Brainstorming
A group session where employees contribute their ideas for solving a problem or meeting a company objective without fear of retribution or ridicule.

Brand name

The part of a brand, trademark, or service mark that can be spoken. It can be a word, letter, or group of words or letters.

Bridge financing

A short-term loan made in expectation of intermediateterm or long-term financing. Can be used when a company plans to go public in the near future.

Broker

One who matches resources available for innovation with those who need them.

Budget

An estimate of the spending necessary to complete a project or offer a service in comparison to cash-on-hand and expected earnings for the coming year, with an emphasis on cost control.

Bulletin Board Service (BBS)

An online service enabling users to communicate with each other about specific topics.

Business and industrial development company (BIDCO)

A private, for-profit financing corporation chartered by the state to provide both equity and long-term debt capital to small business owners (see separate citations for equity and debt capital).

Business birth

The formation of a new establishment or enterprise. The appearance of a new establishment or enterprise in the Small Business Data Base (see separate citation).

Business conditions

Outside factors that can affect the financial performance of a business.

Business contractions

The number of establishments that have decreased in employment during a specified time.

Business cycle

A period of economic recession and recovery. These cycles vary in duration.

Business death

The voluntary or involuntary closure of a firm or establishment. The disappearance of an establishment or enterprise from the Small Business Data Base (see separate citation).

Business development corporation (BDC)

A business financing agency, usually composed of the financial institutions in an area or state, organized to assist in financing businesses unable to obtain assistance through normal channels; the risk is spread among various members of the business development corporation, and interest rates may vary somewhat from those charged by member institutions. A venture capital firm in which shares of ownership are publicly held and to which the Investment Act of 1940 applies.

Business dissolution

For enumeration purposes, the absence of a business that was present in the prior time period from any current record.

Business entry

See Business birth

Business ethics

Moral values and principles espoused by members of the business community as a guide to fair and honest business practices.

Business exit

See Business death

Business expansions

The number of establishments that added employees during a specified time.

Business failure

Closure of a business causing a loss to at least one creditor.

Business format franchising

The purchase of the name, trademark, and an ongoing business plan of the parent corporation or franchisor by the franchisee.

Business license

A legal authorization issued by municipal and state governments and required for business operations.

Business name

Enterprises must register their business names with local governments usually on a "doing business as" (DBA) form. (This name is sometimes referred to as a "fictional name.") The procedure is part of the business licensing process and prevents any other business from using that same name for a similar business in the same locality.

Business norms
See Financial ratios

Business permit
See Business license

Business plan
A document that spells out a company's expected course of action for a specified period, usually including a detailed listing and analysis of risks and uncertainties. For the small business, it should examine the proposed products, the market, the industry, the management policies, the marketing policies, production needs, and financial needs. Frequently, it is used as a prospectus for potential investors and lenders.

Business proposal
See Business plan

Business service firm
An establishment primarily engaged in rendering services to other business organizations on a fee or contract basis.

Business start
For enumeration purposes, a business with a name or similar designation that did not exist in a prior time period.

Cafeteria plan
See Flexible benefit plan

Capacity
Level of a firm's, industry's, or nation's output corresponding to full practical utilization of available resources.

Capital
Assets less liabilities, representing the ownership interest in a business. A stock of accumulated goods, especially at a specified time and in contrast to income received during a specified time period. Accumulated goods devoted to production. Accumulated possessions calculated to bring income.

Capital expenditure
Expenses incurred by a business for improvements that will depreciate over time.

Capital gain
The monetary difference between the purchase price and the selling price of capital. Capital gains are taxed at a rate of 28% by the federal government.

Capital intensity
The relative importance of capital in the production process, usually expressed as the ratio of capital to labor but also sometimes as the ratio of capital to output.

Capital resource
The equipment, facilities and labor used to create products and services.

Caribbean Basin Initiative
An interdisciplinary program to support commerce among the businesses in the nations of the Caribbean Basin and the United States. Agencies involved include: the Agency for International Development, the U.S. Small Business Administration, the International Trade Administration of the U.S. Department of Commerce, and various private sector groups.

Catastrophic care
Medical and other services for acute and long-term illnesses that cost more than insurance coverage limits or that cost the amount most families may be expected to pay with their own resources.

CDC
See Certified development corporation

CD-ROM
Compact disc with read-only memory used to store large amounts of digitized data.

Certified development corporation (CDC)
A local area or statewide corporation or authority (for profit or nonprofit) that packages U.S. Small Business Administration (SBA), bank, state, and/or private money into financial assistance for existing business capital improvements. The SBA holds the second lien on its maximum share of 40 percent involvement. Each state has at least one certified development

corporation. This program is called the SBA 504 Program.

Certified lenders
Banks that participate in the SBA guaranteed loan program (see separate citation). Such banks must have a good track record with the U.S. Small Business Administration (SBA) and must agree to certain conditions set forth by the agency. In return, the SBA agrees to process any guaranteed loan application within three business days.

Champion
An advocate for the development of an innovation.

Channel of distribution
The means used to transport merchandise from the manufacturer to the consumer.

Chapter 7 of the 1978 Bankruptcy Act
Provides for a court-appointed trustee who is responsible for liquidating a company's assets in order to settle outstanding debts.

Chapter 11 of the 1978 Bankruptcy Act
Allows the business owners to retain control of the company while working with their creditors to reorganize their finances and establish better business practices to prevent liquidation of assets.

Closely held corporation
A corporation in which the shares are held by a few persons, usually officers, employees, or others close to the management; these shares are rarely offered to the public.

Code of Federal Regulations
Codification of general and permanent rules of the federal government published in the Federal Register.

Code sharing
See Computer code sharing

Coinsurance
Upon meeting the deductible payment, health insurance participants may be required to make additional health care cost-sharing payments. Coinsurance is a payment of a fixed percentage of the cost of each service; copayment is usually a fixed amount to be paid with each service.

Collateral
Securities, evidence of deposit, or other property pledged by a borrower to secure repayment of a loan.

Collective ratemaking
The establishment of uniform charges for services by a group of businesses in the same industry.

Commercial insurance plan
See Underwriting

Commercial loans
Short-term renewable loans used to finance specific capital needs of a business.

Commercialization
The final stage of the innovation process, including production and distribution.

Common stock
The most frequently used instrument for purchasing ownership in private or public companies. Common stock generally carries the right to vote on certain corporate actions and may pay dividends, although it rarely does in venture investments. In liquidation, common stockholders are the last to share in the proceeds from the sale of a corporation's assets; bondholders and preferred shareholders have priority. Common stock is often used in firstround start-up financing.

Community development corporation
A corporation established to develop economic programs for a community and, in most cases, to provide financial support for such development.

Competitor
A business whose product or service is marketed for the same purpose/use and to the same consumer group as the product or service of another.

Computer code sharing
An arrangement whereby flights of a regional airline are identified by the two-letter code of a major carrier in the computer reservation system to help direct passengers to new regional carriers.

Consignment
A merchandising agreement, usually referring to secondhand shops, where the dealer pays the owner of an item a percentage of the profit when the item is sold.

Consortium
A coalition of organizations such as banks and corporations for ventures requiring large capital resources.

Consultant
An individual that is paid by a business to provide advice and expertise in a particular area.

Consumer price index
A measure of the fluctuation in prices between two points in time.

Consumer research
Research conducted by a business to obtain information about existing or potential consumer markets.

Continuation coverage
Health coverage offered for a specified period of time to employees who leave their jobs and to their widows, divorced spouses, or dependents.

Contractions
See Business contractions

Convertible preferred stock
A class of stock that pays a reasonable dividend and is convertible into common stock (see separate citation). Generally the convertible feature may only be exercised after being held for a stated period of time. This arrangement is usually considered second-round financing when a company needs equity to maintain its cash flow.

Convertible securities
A feature of certain bonds, debentures, or preferred stocks that allows them to be exchanged by the owner for another class of securities at a future date and in accordance with any other terms of the issue.

Copayment
See Coinsurance

Copyright
A legal form of protection available to creators and authors to safeguard their works from unlawful use or claim of ownership by others. Copyrights may be acquired for works of art, sculpture, music, and published or unpublished manuscripts. All copyrights should be registered at the Copyright Office of the Library of Congress.

Corporate financial ratios
The relationship between key figures found in a company's financial statement expressed as a numeric value. Used to evaluate risk and company performance. Also known as Financial averages, Operating ratios, and Business ratios.

Corporation
A legal entity, chartered by a state or the federal government, recognized as a separate entity having its own rights, privileges, and liabilities distinct from those of its members.

Cost containment
Actions taken by employers and insurers to curtail rising health care costs; for example, increasing employee cost sharing (see separate citation), requiring second opinions, or preadmission screening.

Cost sharing
The requirement that health care consumers contribute to their own medical care costs through deductibles and coinsurance (see separate citations). Cost sharing does not include the amounts paid in premiums. It is used to control utilization of services; for example, requiring a fixed amount to be paid with each health care service.

Cottage industry
Businesses based in the home in which the family members are the labor force and family-owned equipment is used to process the goods.

Credit Rating
A letter or number calculated by an organization (such as Dun & Bradstreet) to represent the ability and disposition of a business to meet its financial obligations.

Customer service
Various techniques used to ensure the satisfaction of a customer.

Cyclical peak
The upper turning point in a business cycle.

Cyclical trough
The lower turning point in a business cycle.

DBA
See Business name

Death
See Business death

Debenture
A certificate given as acknowledgment of a debt (see separate citation) secured by the general credit of the issuing corporation. A bond, usually without security, issued by a corporation and sometimes convertible to common stock.

Debt
Something owed by one person to another. Financing in which a company receives capital that must be repaid; no ownership is transferred.

Debt capital
Business financing that normally requires periodic interest payments and repayment of the principal within a specified time.

Debt financing
See Debt capital

Debt securities
Loans such as bonds and notes that provide a specified rate of return for a specified period of time.

Deductible
A set amount that an individual must pay before any benefits are received.

Demand shock absorbers
A term used to describe the role that some small firms play by expanding their output levels to accommodate a transient surge in demand.

Demographics
Statistics on various markets, including age, income, and education, used to target specific products or services to appropriate consumer groups.

Demonstration
Showing that a product or process has been modified sufficiently to meet the needs of users.

Deregulation
The lifting of government restrictions; for example, the lifting of government restrictions on the entry of new businesses, the expansion of services, and the setting of prices in particular industries.

Desktop Publishing
Using personal computers and specialized software to produce camera-ready copy for publications.

Disaster loans
Various types of physical and economic assistance available to individuals and businesses through the U.S. Small Business Administration (SBA). This is the only SBA loan program available for residential purposes.

Discrimination
The denial of the rights and privileges of employment based on factors such as age, race, religion, or gender.

Diseconomies of scale
The condition in which the costs of production increase faster than the volume of production.

Dissolution
See Business dissolution

Distribution
Delivering a product or process to the user.

Distributor
One who delivers merchandise to the user.

Diversified company
A company whose products and services are used by several different markets.

Doing business as (DBA)
See Business name

Dow Jones
An information services company that publishes the Wall Street Journal and other sources of financial information.

Dow Jones Industrial Average
An indicator of stock market performance.

Earned income
A tax term that refers to wages and salaries earned by the recipient, as opposed to monies earned through interest and dividends.

Economic efficiency
The use of productive resources to the fullest practical extent in the provision of the set of goods and services that is most preferred by purchasers in the economy.

Economic indicators
Statistics used to express the state of the economy. These include the length of the average work week, the rate of unemployment, and stock prices.

Economically disadvantaged
See Socially and economically disadvantaged

Economies of scale
See Scale economies

EEOC
See Equal Employment Opportunity Commission

8(a) Program
A program authorized by the Small Business Act that directs federal contracts to small businesses owned and operated by socially and economically disadvantaged individuals.

Electronic mail (e-mail)
The electronic transmission of mail via phone lines.

E-mail
See Electronic mail

Employee leasing
A contract by which employers arrange to have their workers hired by a leasing company and then leased back to them for a management fee. The leasing company typically assumes the administrative burden of payroll and provides a benefit package to the workers.

Employee tenure
The length of time an employee works for a particular employer.

Employer identification number
The business equivalent of a social security number. Assigned by the U.S. Internal Revenue Service.

Enterprise
An aggregation of all establishments owned by a parent company. An enterprise may consist of a single, independent establishment or include subsidiaries and other branches under the same ownership and control.

Enterprise zone
A designated area, usually found in inner cities and other areas with significant unemployment, where businesses receive tax credits and other incentives to entice them to establish operations there.

Entrepreneur
A person who takes the risk of organizing and operating a new business venture.

Entry
See Business entry

Equal Employment Opportunity Commission (EEOC)
A federal agency that ensures nondiscrimination in the hiring and firing practices of a business.

Equal opportunity employer
An employer who adheres to the standards set by the Equal Employment Opportunity Commission (see separate citation).

Equity
The ownership interest. Financing in which partial or total ownership of a company is surrendered in exchange for capital. An investor's financial return comes from dividend payments and from growth in the net worth of the business.

Equity capital
See Equity; Equity midrisk venture capital

Equity financing
See Equity; Equity midrisk venture capital

Equity midrisk venture capital
An unsecured investment in a company. Usually a purchase of ownership interest in a company that occurs in the later stages of a company's development.

Equity partnership
A limited partnership arrangement for providing start-up and seed capital to businesses.

Equity securities
See Equity

Equity-type
Debt financing subordinated to conventional debt.

Establishment
A single-location business unit that may be independent (a single-establishment enterprise) or owned by a parent enterprise.

Establishment and Enterprise Microdata File
See U.S. Establishment and Enterprise Microdata File

Establishment birth
See Business birth

Establishment Longitudinal Microdata File
See U.S. Establishment Longitudinal Microdata File

Ethics
See Business ethics

Evaluation
Determining the potential success of translating an invention into a product or process.

Exit
See Business exit

Experience rating
See Underwriting

Export
A product sold outside of the country.

Export license
A general or specific license granted by the U.S. Department of Commerce required of anyone wishing to export goods. Some restricted articles need approval from the U.S. Departments of State, Defense, or Energy.

Failure
See Business failure

Fair share agreement
An agreement reached between a franchisor and a minority business organization to extend business ownership to minorities by either reducing the amount of capital required or by setting aside certain marketing areas for minority business owners.

Feasibility study
A study to determine the likelihood that a proposed product or development will fulfill the objectives of a particular investor.

Federal Trade Commission (FTC)
Federal agency that promotes free enterprise and competition within the U.S.

Federal Trade Mark Act of 1946
See Lanham Act

Fictional name
See Business name

Fiduciary
An individual or group that hold assets in trust for a beneficiary.

Financial analysis
The techniques used to determine money needs in a business. Techniques include ratio analysis, calculation of return on investment, guides for measuring profitability, and break-even analysis to determine ultimate success.

Financial intermediary
A financial institution that acts as the intermediary between borrowers and lenders. Banks, savings and loan associations, finance companies, and venture capital companies are major financial intermediaries in the United States.

Financial ratios
See Corporate financial ratios; Industry financial ratios

Financial statement
A written record of business finances, including balance sheets and profit and loss statements.

Financing
See First-stage financing; Second-stage financing; Thirdstage financing

First-stage financing
Financing provided to companies that have expended their initial capital, and require funds to start full-scale manufacturing and sales. Also known as First-round financing.

Fiscal year
Any twelve-month period used by businesses for accounting purposes.

504 Program
See Certified development corporation

Flexible benefit plan
A plan that offers a choice among cash and/or qualified benefits such as group term life insurance, accident and health insurance, group legal services, dependent care assistance, and vacations.

FOB
See Free on board

Format franchising
See Business format franchising; Franchising

401(k) plan
A financial plan where employees contribute a percentage of their earnings to a fund that is invested in stocks, bonds, or money markets for the purpose of saving money for retirement.

Four Ps
Marketing terms referring to Product, Price, Place, and Promotion.

Franchising
A form of licensing by which the owner-the franchisor- distributes or markets a product, method, or service through affiliated dealers called franchisees. The product, method, or service being marketed is identified by a brand name, and the franchisor maintains control over the marketing methods employed. The franchisee is often given exclusive access to a defined geographic area.

Free on board (FOB)
A pricing term indicating that the quoted price includes the cost of loading goods into transport vessels at a specified place.

Frictional unemployment
See Unemployment

FTC
See Federal Trade Commission

Fulfillment
The systems necessary for accurate delivery of an ordered item, including subscriptions and direct marketing.

Full-time workers
Generally, those who work a regular schedule of more than 35 hours per week.

Garment registration number
A number that must appear on every garment sold in the U.S. to indicate the manufacturer of the garment, which may or may not be the same as the label under which the garment is sold. The U.S. Federal Trade Commission assigns and regulates garment registration numbers.

Gatekeeper
A key contact point for entry into a network.

GDP
See Gross domestic product

General obligation bond
A municipal bond secured by the taxing power of the municipality. The Tax Reform Act of 1986 limits the purposes for which such bonds may be issued and establishes volume limits on the extent of their issuance.

GNP
See Gross national product

Good Housekeeping Seal
Seal appearing on products that signifies the fulfillment of the standards set by the Good Housekeeping Institute to protect consumer interests.

Goods sector
All businesses producing tangible goods, including agriculture, mining, construction, and manufacturing businesses.

GPO
See Gross product originating

Gross domestic product (GDP)
The part of the nation's gross national product (see separate citation) generated by private business using resources from within the country.

Gross national product (GNP)
The most comprehensive single measure of aggregate economic output. Represents the market value of the total output of goods and services produced by a nation's economy.

Gross product originating (GPO)
A measure of business output estimated from the income or production side using employee compensation, profit income, net interest, capital consumption, and indirect business taxes.

HAL
See Handicapped assistance loan program

Handicapped assistance loan program (HAL)
Low-interest direct loan program through the U.S. Small Business Administration (SBA) for handicapped persons. The SBA requires that these persons demonstrate that their disability is such that it is

impossible for them to secure employment, thus making it necessary to go into their own business to make a living.

Health maintenance organization (HMO)
Organization of physicians and other health care professionals that provides health services to subscribers and their dependents on a prepaid basis.

Health provider
An individual or institution that gives medical care. Under Medicare, an institutional provider is a hospital, skilled nursing facility, home health agency, or provider of certain physical therapy services.

Hispanic
A person of Cuban, Mexican, Puerto Rican, Latin American (Central or South American), European Spanish, or other Spanish-speaking origin or ancestry.

HMO
See Health maintenance organization

Home-based business
A business with an operating address that is also a residential address (usually the residential address of the proprietor).

Hub-and-spoke system
A system in which flights of an airline from many different cities (the spokes) converge at a single airport (the hub). After allowing passengers sufficient time to make connections, planes then depart for different cities.

Human Resources Management
A business program designed to oversee recruiting, pay, benefits, and other issues related to the company's work force, including planning to determine the optimal use of labor to increase production, thereby increasing profit.

Idea
An original concept for a new product or process.

Import
Products produced outside the country in which they are consumed.

Income
Money or its equivalent, earned or accrued, resulting from the sale of goods and services.

Income statement
A financial statement that lists the profits and losses of a company at a given time.

Incorporation
The filing of a certificate of incorporation with a state's secretary of state, thereby limiting the business owner's liability.

Incubator
A facility designed to encourage entrepreneurship and minimize obstacles to new business formation and growth, particularly for high-technology firms, by housing a number of fledgling enterprises that share an array of services, such as meeting areas, secretarial services, accounting, research library, on-site financial and management counseling, and word processing facilities.

Independent contractor
An individual considered self-employed (see separate citation) and responsible for paying Social Security taxes and income taxes on earnings.

Indirect health coverage
Health insurance obtained through another individual's health care plan; for example, a spouse's employersponsored plan.

Industrial development authority
The financial arm of a state or other political subdivision established for the purpose of financing economic development in an area, usually through loans to nonprofit organizations, which in turn provide facilities for manufacturing and other industrial operations.

Industry financial ratios
Corporate financial ratios averaged for a specified industry. These are used for comparison purposes and reveal industry trends and identify differences between the performance of a specific company and the performance of its industry. Also known as Industrial averages, Industry ratios, Financial averages, and Business or Industrial norms.

Inflation
Increases in volume of currency and credit, generally resulting in a sharp and continuing rise in price levels.

Informal capital
Financing from informal, unorganized sources; includes informal debt capital such as trade credit or loans from friends and relatives and equity capital from informal investors.

Initial public offering (IPO)
A corporation's first offering of stock to the public.

Innovation
The introduction of a new idea into the marketplace in the form of a new product or service or an improvement in organization or process.

Intellectual property
Any idea or work that can be considered proprietary in nature and is thus protected from infringement by others.

Internal capital
Debt or equity financing obtained from the owner or through retained business earnings.

Internet
A government-designed computer network that contains large amounts of information and is accessible through various vendors for a fee.

Intrapreneurship
The state of employing entrepreneurial principles to nonentrepreneurial situations.

Invention
The tangible form of a technological idea, which could include a laboratory prototype, drawings, formulas, etc.

IPO
See Initial public offering

Job description
The duties and responsibilities required in a particular position.

Job tenure
A period of time during which an individual is continuously employed in the same job.

Joint marketing agreements
Agreements between regional and major airlines, often involving the coordination of flight schedules, fares, and baggage transfer. These agreements help regional carriers operate at lower cost.

Joint venture
Venture in which two or more people combine efforts in a particular business enterprise, usually a single transaction or a limited activity, and agree to share the profits and losses jointly or in proportion to their contributions.

Keogh plan
Designed for self-employed persons and unincorporated businesses as a tax-deferred pension account.

Labor force
Civilians considered eligible for employment who are also willing and able to work.

Labor force participation rate
The civilian labor force as a percentage of the civilian population.

Labor intensity
The relative importance of labor in the production process, usually measured as the capital-labor ratio; i.e., the ratio of units of capital (typically, dollars of tangible assets) to the number of employees. The higher the capital-labor ratio exhibited by a firm or industry, the lower the capital intensity of that firm or industry is said to be.

Labor surplus area
An area in which there exists a high unemployment rate. In procurement (see separate citation), extra points are given to firms in counties that are designated a labor surplus area; this information is requested on procurement bid sheets.

Labor union
An organization of similarly-skilled workers who collectively bargain with management over the conditions of employment.

Laboratory prototype
See Prototype

LAN
See Local Area Network

Lanham Act
Refers to the Federal Trade Mark Act of 1946. Protects registered trademarks, trade names, and other service marks used in commerce.

Large business-dominated industry
Industry in which a minimum of 60 percent of employment or sales is in firms with more than 500 workers.

LBO
See Leveraged buy-out

Leader pricing
A reduction in the price of a good or service in order to generate more sales of that good or service.

Legal list
A list of securities selected by a state in which certain institutions and fiduciaries (such as pension funds, insurance companies, and banks) may invest. Securities not on the list are not eligible for investment. Legal lists typically restrict investments to high quality securities meeting certain specifications. Generally, investment is limited to U.S. securities and investment-grade blue chip securities (see separate citation).

Leveraged buy-out (LBO)
The purchase of a business or a division of a corporation through a highly leveraged financing package.

Liability
An obligation or duty to perform a service or an act. Also defined as money owed.

License
A legal agreement granting to another the right to use a technological innovation.

Limited partnerships
See Venture capital limited partnerships

Liquidity
The ability to convert a security into cash promptly.

Loans
See Commercial loans; Disaster loans; SBA direct loans; SBA guaranteed loans; SBA special lending institution categories Local Area Network (LAN) Computer networks contained within a single building or small area; used to facilitate the sharing of information.

Local development corporation
An organization, usually made up of local citizens of a community, designed to improve the economy of the area by inducing business and industry to locate and expand there. A local development corporation establishes a capability to finance local growth.

Long-haul rates
Rates charged by a transporter in which the distance traveled is more than 800 miles.

Long-term debt
An obligation that matures in a period that exceeds five years.

Low-grade bond
A corporate bond that is rated below investment grade by the major rating agencies (Standard and Poor's, Moody's).

Macro-efficiency
Efficiency as it pertains to the operation of markets and market systems.

Managed care
A cost-effective health care program initiated by employers whereby low-cost health care is made available to the employees in return for exclusive patronage to program doctors.

Management Assistance Programs
See SBA Management Assistance Programs

Management and technical assistance
A term used by many programs to mean business (as opposed to technological) assistance.

Mandated benefits
Specific treatments, providers, or individuals required by law to be included in commercial health plans.

Market evaluation
The use of market information to determine the sales potential of a specific product or process.

Market failure
The situation in which the workings of a competitive market do not produce the best results from the point of view of the entire society.

Market information
Data of any type that can be used for market evaluation, which could include demographic data, technology forecasting, regulatory changes, etc.

Market research
A systematic collection, analysis, and reporting of data about the market and its preferences, opinions, trends, and plans; used for corporate decision-making.

Market share
In a particular market, the percentage of sales of a specific product.

Marketing
Promotion of goods or services through various media.

Master Establishment List (MEL)
A list of firms in the United States developed by the U.S. Small Business Administration; firms can be selected by industry, region, state, standard metropolitan statistical area (see separate citation), county, and zip code.

Maturity
The date upon which the principal or stated value of a bond or other indebtedness becomes due and payable.

Medicaid (Title XIX)
A federally aided, state-operated and administered program that provides medical benefits for certain low income persons in need of health and medical care who are eligible for one of the government's welfare cash payment programs, including the aged, the blind, the disabled, and members of families with dependent children where one parent is absent, incapacitated, or unemployed.

Medicare (Title XVIII)
A nationwide health insurance program for disabled and aged persons. Health insurance is available to insured persons without regard to income. Monies from payroll taxes cover hospital insurance and monies from general revenues and beneficiary premiums pay for supplementary medical insurance.

MEL
See Master Establishment List

MESBIC
See Minority enterprise small business investment corporation

MET
See Multiple employer trust

Metropolitan statistical area (MSA)
A means used by the government to define large population centers that may transverse different governmental jurisdictions. For example, the Washington, D.C. MSA includes the District of Columbia and contiguous parts of Maryland and Virginia because all of these geopolitical areas comprise one population and economic operating unit.

Mezzanine financing
See Third-stage financing

Micro-efficiency
Efficiency as it pertains to the operation of individual firms.

Microdata
Information on the characteristics of an individual business firm.

Mid-term debt
An obligation that matures within one to five years.

Midrisk venture capital
See Equity midrisk venture capital

Minimum premium plan
A combination approach to funding an insurance plan aimed primarily at premium tax savings. The employer self-funds a fixed percentage of estimated monthly claims and the insurance company insures the excess.

Minimum wage
The lowest hourly wage allowed by the federal government.

Minority Business Development Agency
Contracts with private firms throughout the nation to sponsor Minority Business Development Centers which provide minority firms with advice and technical assistance on a fee basis.

Minority Enterprise Small Business Investment Corporation (MESBIC)
A federally funded private venture capital firm licensed by the U.S. Small Business Administration to provide capital to minority-owned businesses (see separate citation).

Minority-owned business
Businesses owned by those who are socially or economically disadvantaged (see separate citation).

Mom and Pop business
A small store or enterprise having limited capital, principally employing family members.

Moonlighter
A wage-and-salary worker with a side business.

MSA
See Metropolitan statistical area

Multi-employer plan
A health plan to which more than one employer is required to contribute and that may be maintained through a collective bargaining agreement and required to meet standards prescribed by the U.S. Department of Labor.

Multi-level marketing
A system of selling in which you sign up other people to assist you and they, in turn, recruit others to help them. Some entrepreneurs have built successful companies on this concept because the main focus of their activities is their product and product sales.

Multimedia
The use of several types of media to promote a product or service. Also, refers to the use of several different types of media (sight, sound, pictures, text) in a CD-ROM (see separate citation) product.

Multiple employer trust (MET)
A self-funded benefit plan generally geared toward small employers sharing a common interest.

NAFTA
See North American Free Trade Agreement

NASDAQ
See National Association of Securities Dealers Automated Quotations

National Association of Securities Dealers Automated Quotations
Provides price quotes on over-the-counter securities as well as securities listed on the New York Stock Exchange.

National income
Aggregate earnings of labor and property arising from the production of goods and services in a nation's economy.

Net assets
See Net worth

Net income
The amount remaining from earnings and profits after all expenses and costs have been met or deducted. Also known as Net earnings.

Net profit
Money earned after production and overhead expenses (see separate citations) have been deducted.

Net worth
The difference between a company's total assets and its total liabilities.

Network
A chain of interconnected individuals or organizations sharing information and/or services.

New York Stock Exchange (NYSE)
The oldest stock exchange in the U.S. Allows for trading in stocks, bonds, warrants, options, and rights that meet listing requirements.

Niche
A career or business for which a person is well-suited. Also, a product which fulfills one need of a particular market segment, often with little or no competition.

Nodes
One workstation in a network, either local area or wide area (see separate citations).

Nonbank bank
A bank that either accepts deposits or makes loans, but not both. Used to create many new branch banks.

Noncompetitive awards
A method of contracting whereby the federal government negotiates with only one contractor to supply a product or service.

Nonmember bank
A state-regulated bank that does not belong to the federal bank system.

Nonprofit
An organization that has no shareholders, does not distribute profits, and is without federal and state tax liabilities.

Norms
See Financial ratios

North American Free Trade Agreement (NAFTA)
Passed in 1993, NAFTA eliminates trade barriers among businesses in the U.S., Canada, and Mexico.

NYSE
See New York Stock Exchange

Occupational Safety & Health Administration (OSHA)
Federal agency that regulates health and safety standards within the workplace.

Optimal firm size
The business size at which the production cost per unit of output (average cost) is, in the long run, at its minimum.

Organizational chart
A hierarchical chart tracking the chain of command within an organization.

OSHA
See Occupational Safety & Health Administration

Overhead
Expenses, such as employee benefits and building utilities, incurred by a business that are unrelated to the actual product or service sold.

Owner's capital
Debt or equity funds provided by the owner(s) of a business; sources of owner's capital are personal savings, sales of assets, or loans from financial institutions.

P & L
See Profit and loss statement

Part-time workers
Normally, those who work less than 35 hours per week. The Tax Reform Act indicated that part-time workers who work less than 17.5 hours per week may be excluded from health plans for purposes of complying with federal nondiscrimination rules.

Part-year workers
Those who work less than 50 weeks per year.

Partnership
Two or more parties who enter into a legal relationship to conduct business for profit. Defined by the U.S. Internal Revenue Code as joint ventures, syndicates, groups, pools, and other associations of two or more persons organized for profit that are not specifically classified in the IRS code as corporations or proprietorships.

Patent
A grant made by the government assuring an inventor the sole right to make, use, and sell an invention for a period of 17 years.

PC
See Professional corporation

Peak
See Cyclical peak

Pension
A series of payments made monthly, semiannually, annually, or at other specified intervals during the lifetime of the pensioner for distribution upon retirement. The term is sometimes used to denote the portion of the retirement allowance financed by the employer's contributions.

Pension fund
A fund established to provide for the payment of pension benefits; the collective contributions made by all of the parties to the pension plan.

Performance appraisal
An established set of objective criteria, based on job description and requirements, that is used to evaluate the performance of an employee in a specific job.

Permit
See Business license

Plan
See Business plan

Pooling
An arrangement for employers to achieve efficiencies and lower health costs by joining together to purchase group health insurance or self-insurance.

PPO
See Preferred provider organization

Preferred lenders program
See SBA special lending institution categories

Preferred provider organization (PPO)
A contractual arrangement with a health care services organization that agrees to discount its health care rates in return for faster payment and/or a patient base.

Premiums
The amount of money paid to an insurer for health insurance under a policy. The premium is generally paid periodically (e.g., monthly), and often is split between the employer and the employee. Unlike deductibles and coinsurance or copayments, premiums are paid for coverage whether or not benefits are actually used.

Prime-age workers
Employees 25 to 54 years of age.

Prime contract
A contract awarded directly by the U.S. Federal Government.

Private company
See Closely held corporation

Private placement
A method of raising capital by offering for sale an investment or business to a small group of investors (generally avoiding registration with the Securities and Exchange Commission or state securities registration agencies). Also known as Private financing or Private offering.

Pro forma
The use of hypothetical figures in financial statements to represent future expenditures, debts, and other potential financial expenses.

Proactive
Taking the initiative to solve problems and anticipate future events before they happen, instead of reacting to an already existing problem or waiting for a difficult situation to occur.

Procurement
A contract from an agency of the federal government for goods or services from a small business.

Prodigy
An online service which is accessible by computer modem. The service features Internet access, bulletin boards, online periodicals, electronic mail, and other services for subscribers.

Product development
The stage of the innovation process where research is translated into a product or process through evaluation, adaptation, and demonstration.

Product franchising
An arrangement for a franchisee to use the name and to produce the product line of the franchisor or parent corporation.

Production
The manufacture of a product.

Production prototype
See Prototype

Productivity
A measurement of the number of goods produced during a specific amount of time.

Professional corporation (PC)
Organized by members of a profession such as medicine, dentistry, or law for the purpose of conducting their professional activities as a corporation. Liability of a member or shareholder is limited in the same manner as in a business corporation.

Profit and loss statement (P & L)
The summary of the incomes (total revenues) and costs of a company's operation during a specific period of time. Also known as Income and expense statement.

Proposal
See Business plan

Proprietorship
The most common legal form of business ownership; about 85 percent of all small businesses are proprietorships. The liability of the owner is unlimited in this form of ownership.

Prospective payment system
A cost-containment measure included in the Social Security Amendments of 1983 whereby Medicare

payments to hospitals are based on established prices, rather than on cost reimbursement.

Prototype
A model that demonstrates the validity of the concept of an invention (laboratory prototype); a model that meets the needs of the manufacturing process and the user (production prototype).

Prudent investor rule or standard
A legal doctrine that requires fiduciaries to make investments using the prudence, diligence, and intelligence that would be used by a prudent person in making similar investments. Because fiduciaries make investments on behalf of third-party beneficiaries, the standard results in very conservative investments. Until recently, most state regulations required the fiduciary to apply this standard to each investment. Newer, more progressive regulations permit fiduciaries to apply this standard to the portfolio taken as a whole, thereby allowing a fiduciary to balance a portfolio with higher-yield, higher-risk investments. In states with more progressive regulations, practically every type of security is eligible for inclusion in the portfolio of investments made by a fiduciary, provided that the portfolio investments, in their totality, are those of a prudent person.

Public equity markets
Organized markets for trading in equity shares such as common stocks, preferred stocks, and warrants. Includes markets for both regularly traded and nonregularly traded securities.

Public offering
General solicitation for participation in an investment opportunity. Interstate public offerings are supervised by the U.S. Securities and Exchange Commission (see separate citation).

Quality control
The process by which a product is checked and tested to ensure consistent standards of high quality.

Rate of return
The yield obtained on a security or other investment based on its purchase price or its current market price. The total rate of return is current income plus or minus capital appreciation or depreciation.

Real property
Includes the land and all that is contained on it.

Realignment
See Resource realignment

Recession
Contraction of economic activity occurring between the peak and trough (see separate citations) of a business cycle.

Regulated market
A market in which the government controls the forces of supply and demand, such as who may enter and what price may be charged.

Regulation D
A vehicle by which small businesses make small offerings and private placements of securities with limited disclosure requirements. It was designed to ease the burdens imposed on small businesses utilizing this method of capital formation.

Regulatory Flexibility Act
An act requiring federal agencies to evaluate the impact of their regulations on small businesses before the regulations are issued and to consider less burdensome alternatives.

Research
The initial stage of the innovation process, which includes idea generation and invention.

Research and development financing
A tax-advantaged partnership set up to finance product development for start-ups as well as more mature companies.

Resource mobility
The ease with which labor and capital move from firm to firm or from industry to industry.

Resource realignment
The adjustment of productive resources to interindustry changes in demand.

Resources
The sources of support or help in the innovation process, including sources of financing, technical evaluation, market evaluation, management and business assistance, etc.

Retained business earnings
Business profits that are retained by the business rather than being distributed to the shareholders as dividends.

Revolving credit
An agreement with a lending institution for an amount of money, which cannot exceed a set maximum, over a specified period of time. Each time the borrower repays a portion of the loan, the amount of the repayment may be borrowed yet again.

Risk capital
See Venture capital

Risk management
The act of identifying potential sources of financial loss and taking action to minimize their negative impact.

Routing
The sequence of steps necessary to complete a product during production.

S corporations
See Sub chapter S corporations

SBA
See Small Business Administration

SBA direct loans
Loans made directly by the U.S. Small Business Administration (SBA); monies come from funds appropriated specifically for this purpose. In general, SBA direct loans carry interest rates slightly lower than those in the private financial markets and are available only to applicants unable to secure private financing or an SBA guaranteed loan.

SBA 504 Program
See Certified development corporation

SBA guaranteed loans
Loans made by lending institutions in which the U.S. Small Business Administration (SBA) will pay a prior agreed-upon percentage of the outstanding principal in the event the borrower of the loan defaults. The terms of the loan and the interest rate are negotiated between theborrower and the lending institution, within set parameters.

SBA loans
See Disaster loans; SBA direct loans; SBA guaranteed loans; SBA special lending institution categories

SBA Management Assistance Programs
Classes, workshops, counseling, and publications offered by the U.S. Small Business Administration.

SBA special lending institution categories
U.S. Small Business Administration (SBA) loan program in which the SBA promises certified banks a 72-hour turnaround period in giving its approval for a loan, and in which preferred lenders in a pilot program are allowed to write SBA loans without seeking prior SBA approval.

SBDB
See Small Business Data Base

SBDC
See Small business development centers

SBI
See Small business institutes program

SBIC
See Small business investment corporation

SBIR Program
See Small Business Innovation Development Act of 1982

Scale economies
The decline of the production cost per unit of output (average cost) as the volume of output increases.

Scale efficiency
The reduction in unit cost available to a firm when producing at a higher output volume.

SCORE
See Service Corps of Retired Executives

SEC
See Securities and Exchange Commission

SECA
See Self-Employment Contributions Act

Second-stage financing
Working capital for the initial expansion of a company that is producing, shipping, and has growing accounts receivable and inventories. Also known as Second-round financing.

Glossary

Secondary market
A market established for the purchase and sale of outstanding securities following their initial distribution.

Secondary worker
Any worker in a family other than the person who is the primary source of income for the family.

Secondhand capital
Previously used and subsequently resold capital equipment (e.g., buildings and machinery).

Securities and Exchange Commission (SEC)
Federal agency charged with regulating the trade of securities to prevent unethical practices in the investor market.

Securitized debt
A marketing technique that converts long-term loans to marketable securities.

Seed capital
Venture financing provided in the early stages of the innovation process, usually during product development.

Self-employed person
One who works for a profit or fees in his or her own business, profession, or trade, or who operates a farm.

Self-Employment Contributions Act (SECA)
Federal law that governs the self-employment tax (see separate citation).

Self-employment income
Income covered by Social Security if a business earns a net income of at least $400.00 during the year. Taxes are paid on earnings that exceed $400.00.

Self-employment retirement plan
See Keogh plan

Self-employment tax
Required tax imposed on self-employed individuals for the provision of Social Security and Medicare. The tax must be paid quarterly with estimated income tax statements.

Self-funding
A health benefit plan in which a firm uses its own funds to pay claims, rather than transferring the financial risks of paying claims to an outside insurer in exchange for premium payments.

Service Corps of Retired Executives (SCORE)
Volunteers for the SBA Management Assistance Program who provide one-on-one counseling and teach workshops and seminars for small firms.

Service firm
See Business service firm

Service sector
Broadly defined, all U.S. industries that produce intangibles, including the five major industry divisions of transportation, communications, and utilities; wholesale trade; retail trade; finance, insurance, and real estate; and services.

Set asides
See Small business set asides

Short-haul service
A type of transportation service in which the transporter supplies service between cities where the maximum distance is no more than 200 miles.

Short-term debt
An obligation that matures in one year.

SIC codes
See Standard Industrial Classification codes

Single-establishment enterprise
See Establishment

Small business
An enterprise that is independently owned and operated, is not dominant in its field, and employs fewer than 500 people. For SBA purposes, the U.S. Small Business Administration (SBA) considers various other factors (such as gross annual sales) in determining size of a business.

Small Business Administration (SBA)
An independent federal agency that provides assistance with loans, management, and advocating interests before other federal agencies.

Small Business Data Base
A collection of microdata (see separate citation) files on individual firms developed and maintained by the U.S. Small Business Administration.

Small business development centers (SBDC)
Centers that provide support services to small businesses, such as individual counseling, SBA advice, seminars and conferences, and other learning center activities. Most services are free of charge, or available at minimal cost.

Small business development corporation
See Certified development corporation

Small business-dominated industry
Industry in which a minimum of 60 percent of employment or sales is in firms with fewer than 500 employees.

Small Business Innovation Development Act of 1982
Federal statute requiring federal agencies with large extramural research and development budgets to allocate a certain percentage of these funds to small research and development firms. The program, called the Small Business Innovation Research (SBIR) Program, is designed to stimulate technological innovation and make greater use of small businesses in meeting national innovation needs.

Small business institutes (SBI) program
Cooperative arrangements made by U.S. Small Business Administration district offices and local colleges and universities to provide small business firms with graduate students to counsel them without charge.

Small business investment corporation (SBIC)
A privately owned company licensed and funded through the U.S. Small Business Administration and private sector sources to provide equity or debt capital to small businesses.

Small business set asides
Procurement (see separate citation) opportunities required by law to be on all contracts under $10,000 or a certain percentage of an agency's total procurement expenditure.

Smaller firms
For U.S. Department of Commerce purposes, those firms not included in the Fortune 1000.

SMSA
See Metropolitan statistical area

Socially and economically disadvantaged
Individuals who have been subjected to racial or ethnic prejudice or cultural bias without regard to their qualities as individuals, and whose abilities to compete are impaired because of diminished opportunities to obtain capital and credit.

Sole proprietorship
An unincorporated, one-owner business, farm, or professional practice.

Special lending institution categories
See SBA special lending institution categories

Standard Industrial Classification (SIC) codes
Four-digit codes established by the U.S. Federal Government to categorize businesses by type of economic activity; the first two digits correspond to major groups such as construction and manufacturing, while the last two digits correspond to subgroups such as home construction or highway construction.

Standard metropolitan statistical area (SMSA)
See Metropolitan statistical area

Start-up
A new business, at the earliest stages of development and financing.

Start-up costs
Costs incurred before a business can commence operations.

Start-up financing
Financing provided to companies that have either completed product development and initial marketing or have been in business for less than one year but have not yet sold their product commercially.

Stock
A certificate of equity ownership in a business.

Stop-loss coverage
Insurance for a self-insured plan that reimburses the company for any losses it might incur in its health claims beyond a specified amount.

Strategic planning
Projected growth and development of a business to establish a guiding direction for the future. Also used

to determine which market segments to explore for optimal sales of products or services.

Structural unemployment
See Unemployment

Sub chapter S corporations
Corporations that are considered noncorporate for tax purposes but legally remain corporations.

Subcontract
A contract between a prime contractor and a subcontractor, or between subcontractors, to furnish supplies or services for performance of a prime contract (see separate citation) or a subcontract.

Surety bonds
Bonds providing reimbursement to an individual, company, or the government if a firm fails to complete a contract. The U.S. Small Business Administration guarantees surety bonds in a program much like the SBA guaranteed loan program (see separate citation).

Swing loan
See Bridge financing

Target market
The clients or customers sought for a business' product or service.

Targeted Jobs Tax Credit
Federal legislation enacted in 1978 that provides a tax credit to an employer who hires structurally unemployed individuals.

Tax number
A number assigned to a business by a state revenue department that enables the business to buy goods without paying sales tax.

Taxable bonds
An interest-bearing certificate of public or private indebtedness. Bonds are issued by public agencies to finance economic development.

Technical assistance
See Management and technical assistance

Technical evaluation
Assessment of technological feasibility.

Technology
The method in which a firm combines and utilizes labor and capital resources to produce goods or services; the application of science for commercial or industrial purposes.

Technology transfer
The movement of information about a technology or intellectual property from one party to another for use.

Tenure
See Employee tenure

Term
The length of time for which a loan is made.

Terms of a note
The conditions or limits of a note; includes the interest rate per annum, the due date, and transferability and convertibility features, if any.

Third-party administrator
An outside company responsible for handling claims and performing administrative tasks associated with health insurance plan maintenance.

Third-stage financing
Financing provided for the major expansion of a company whose sales volume is increasing and that is breaking even or profitable. These funds are used for further plant expansion, marketing, working capital, or development of an improved product. Also known as Third-round or Mezzanine financing.

Time deposit
A bank deposit that cannot be withdrawn before a specified future time.

Time management
Skills and scheduling techniques used to maximize productivity.

Trade credit
Credit extended by suppliers of raw materials or finished products. In an accounting statement, trade credit is referred to as "accounts payable."

Trade name
The name under which a company conducts business, or by which its business, goods, or services are identified. It may or may not be registered as a trademark.

Trade periodical
A publication with a specific focus on one or more aspects of business and industry.

Trade secret
Competitive advantage gained by a business through the use of a unique manufacturing process or formula.

Trade show
An exhibition of goods or services used in a particular industry. Typically held in exhibition centers where exhibitors rent space to display their merchandise.

Trademark
A graphic symbol, device, or slogan that identifies a business. A business has property rights to its trademark from the inception of its use, but it is still prudent to register all trademarks with the Trademark Office of the U.S. Department of Commerce.

Translation
See Product development

Treasury bills
Investment tender issued by the Federal Reserve Bank in amounts of $10,000 that mature in 91 to 182 days.

Treasury bonds
Long-term notes with maturity dates of not less than seven and not more than twenty-five years.

Treasury notes
Short-term notes maturing in less than seven years.

Trend
A statistical measurement used to track changes that occur over time.

Trough
See Cyclical trough

UCC
See Uniform Commercial Code

UL
See Underwriters Laboratories

Underwriters Laboratories (UL)
One of several private firms that tests products and processes to determine their safety. Although various firms can provide this kind of testing service, many local and insurance codes specify UL certification.

Underwriting
A process by which an insurer determines whether or not and on what basis it will accept an application for insurance. In an experience-rated plan, premiums are based on a firm's or group's past claims; factors other than prior claims are used for community-rated or manually rated plans.

Unfair competition
Refers to business practices, usually unethical, such as using unlicensed products, pirating merchandise, or misleading the public through false advertising, which give the offending business an unequitable advantage over others.

Unfunded accrued liability
The excess of total liabilities, both present and prospective, over present and prospective assets.

Unemployment
The joblessness of individuals who are willing to work, who are legally and physically able to work, and who are seeking work. Unemployment may represent the temporary joblessness of a worker between jobs (frictional unemployment) or the joblessness of a worker whose skills are not suitable for jobs available in the labor market (structural unemployment).

Uniform Commercial Code (UCC)
A code of laws governing commercial transactions across the U.S., except Louisiana. Their purpose is to bring uniformity to financial transactions.

Uniform product code (UPC symbol)
A computer-readable label comprised of ten digits and stripes that encodes what a product is and how much it costs. The first five digits are assigned by the Uniform Product Code Council, and the last five digits by the individual manufacturer.

Unit cost
See Average cost

UPC symbol
See Uniform product code

U.S. Establishment and Enterprise Microdata (USEEM) File
A cross-sectional database containing information on employment, sales, and location for individual

enterprises and establishments with employees that have a Dun & Bradstreet credit rating.

U.S. Establishment Longitudinal Microdata (USELM) File

A database containing longitudinally linked sample microdata on establishments drawn from the U.S. Establishment and Enterprise Microdata file (see separate citation).

U.S. Small Business Administration 504 Program

See Certified development corporation

USEEM

See U.S. Establishment and Enterprise Microdata File

USELM

See U.S. Establishment Longitudinal Microdata File

VCN

See Venture capital network

Venture capital

Money used to support new or unusual business ventures that exhibit above-average growth rates, significant potential for market expansion, and are in need of additional financing to sustain growth or further research and development; equity or equity-type financing traditionally provided at the commercialization stage, increasingly available prior to commercialization.

Venture capital company

A company organized to provide seed capital to a business in its formation stage, or in its first or second stage of expansion. Funding is obtained through public or private pension funds, commercial banks and bank holding companies, small business investment corporations licensed by the U.S. Small Business Administration, private venture capital firms, insurance companies, investment management companies, bank trust departments, industrial companies seeking to diversify their investment, and investment bankers acting as intermediaries for other investors or directly investing on their own behalf.

Venture capital limited partnerships

Designed for business development, these partnerships are an institutional mechanism for providing capital for young, technology-oriented businesses. The investors' money is pooled and invested in money market assets until venture investments have been selected. The general partners are experienced investment managers who select and invest the equity and debt securities of firms with high growth potential and the ability to go public in the near future.

Venture capital network (VCN)

A computer database that matches investors with entrepreneurs.

WAN

See Wide Area Network

Wide Area Network (WAN)

Computer networks linking systems throughout a state or around the world in order to facilitate the sharing of information.

Withholding

Federal, state, social security, and unemployment taxes withheld by the employer from employees' wages; employers are liable for these taxes and the corporate umbrella and bankruptcy will not exonerate an employer from paying back payroll withholding. Employers should escrow these funds in a separate account and disperse them quarterly to withholding authorities.

Workers' compensation

A state-mandated form of insurance covering workers injured in job-related accidents. In some states, the state is the insurer; in other states, insurance must be acquired from commercial insurance firms. Insurance rates are based on a number of factors, including salaries, firm history, and risk of occupation.

Working capital

Refers to a firm's short-term investment of current assets, including cash, short-term securities, accounts receivable, and inventories.

Yield

The rate of income returned on an investment, expressed as a percentage. Income yield is obtained by dividing the current dollar income by the current market price of the security. Net yield or yield to maturity is the current income yield minus any premium above par or plus any discount from par in purchase price, with the adjustment spread over the period from the date of purchase to the date of maturity.

Index

Listings in this index are arranged alphabetically by business plan type, then alphabetically by business plan name. Users are provided with the volume number in which the plan appears.

Index

Index

Index